DWIGHT GOLANN

MEDIATING
Legal Disputes

Effective Strategies for Neutrals and Advocates

ABA Section of
Dispute Resolution

**Defending Liberty
Pursuing Justice**

Cover design by ABA Publishing.

The materials contained herein represent the opinions and views of the authors and/or the editors, and should not be construed to be the views or opinions of the law firms or companies with whom such persons are in partnership with, associated with, or employed by, nor of the American Bar Association or the Section of Dispute Resolution, unless adopted pursuant to the bylaws of the Association.

Nothing contained in this book is to be considered as the rendering of legal advice, either generally or in connection with any specific issue or case; nor do these materials purport to explain or interpret any specific bond or policy, or any provisions thereof, issued by any particular franchise company, or to render franchise or other professional advice. Readers are responsible for obtaining advice from their own lawyers or other professionals. This book and any forms and agreements herein are intended for educational and informational purposes only.

© 2009 American Bar Association. All rights reserved.

No part of this publication may be reproduced, stored in a retrieval system, or transmitted in any form or by any means, electronic, mechanical, photocopying, recording, or otherwise, without the prior written permission of the publisher. For permission, contact the ABA Copyrights & Contracts Department at copyright@americanbar.org or via fax at 312-988-6030.

Printed in the United States of America.

20 19 18   8 7 6

Library of Congress Cataloging-in-Publication Data

Golann, Dwight.
  Mediating commercial disputes / By Dwight Golann. — 1st ed.
    p. cm.
  Includes index.
  ISBN 978-1-60442-303-7 (alk. paper)
  1. Arbitration and award—United States. 2. Mediation—United States.
3. Commercial law—United States. I. Title.

  KF9085.G63 2008
  347.73'9—dc22

                                                    2008048212

Discounts are available for books ordered in bulk. Special consideration is given to state bars, CLE programs, and other bar-related organizations. Inquire at Book Publishing, ABA Publishing, American Bar Association, 321 North Clark Street, Chicago, Illinois 60654-7598.
www.ShopABA.org

To my wife Helaine—my primary editor, co-author, and most loyal supporter—and to my children, David and Aspen, who have taught me a great deal about negotiation.

Contents

Chapter 5

Process Obstacles: Interest-Based Negotiation and Other Issues   69

Chapter 6

Psychological Issues: Strong Emotions and Cognitive Forces   93

Helaine Scarlett Golann

Chapter 7

Merits Barriers: Information Exchange and Analysis   123

Part III
Representing Clients in Mediation: Advice for Lawyers

Chapter 11
How to Borrow a Mediator's Powers

Chapter 12
Advocacy at Specific Stages

Part IV

The Skills of a Mediator DVD

Table of Contents

About the Contributors

Principal Author

Dwight Golann

Dwight Golann is Professor of Law at Suffolk University in Boston, where he teaches mediation and negotiation. Professor Golann has trained lawyers and judges in mediation skills for the American Bar Association, the U.S. Department of Justice, the European Union, the JAMS national panel, the leading arbitration center of China, and state and federal courts. He has been appointed as visiting professor at several law schools and taught mediation at the Program of Instruction for Lawyers at Harvard Law School. Professor Golann has mediated cases in a wide variety of subject areas, and is a member of the Panel of Distinguished Neutrals of the International Institute for Conflict Prevention and Resolution, the ADR Center of Rome, and the U.S.–China Business Mediation Center in Beijing.

In recognition of his work in dispute resolution, Professor Golann has been named an Honorary Member of the American College of Civil Trial Mediators, recipient of the ABA Legal Educators Award, and chair of ADR programs for the ABA's Sections of Litigation and Business Law. He is the author of several books and numerous articles, and has twice won the CPR Institute's Annual Award for best book and best article in the field of dispute resolution.

Professor Golann was formerly a civil litigator with a private law firm. He also served as Chief of the Government Bureau and Trial Division of the Attorney General of Massachusetts, where he directed the defense of cases in a wide variety of subject areas, implemented programs to mediate public disputes, and tried and argued cases at every level of the court system. He is a graduate of Amherst College and Harvard Law School.

Contributing Authors

Marjorie Corman Aaron

Marjorie Aaron is Professor of Clinical Law and Director of The Center for Practice at the University of Cincinnati College of Law. A mediator of legal disputes for more than twenty years, she is a member the Panel of Distinguished Neutrals of the CPR Institute and other neutral panels. Professor Aaron designs and teaches workshops on mediation, negotiation, and client counseling for law firms and corporations, and is the author of articles, book chapters, simulation cases, and guides in the field of dispute resolution.

Professor Aaron is the former Executive Director of the Program on Negotiation at Harvard Law School and a former Vice President and Senior Mediator at Endispute, Inc. A graduate of Princeton University and Harvard Law School, she formerly served as a criminal prosecutor and practiced civil litigation at the Boston firm of Goodwin Procter.

Helaine Scarlett Golann

Helaine Golann is a practicing clinical psychologist who treats and lectures on emotional barriers to dispute resolution. Dr. Golann has held appointments as an Associate Professor in the graduate program of the Massachusetts School of Professional Psychology, and has served on the faculty of the Harvard Medical School and Tufts-New England Medical Center. She has spoken on psychological issues in mediation under the auspices of the CPR Institute and has participated in training for JAMS.

Dr. Golann has more than thirty years' experience as a therapist working with individuals and families, and holds a Ph.D. from Clark University, where she published research on social development and gender differences in communication.

Eric D. Green

Eric Green is co-founder and a principal of Resolutions LLC, in Boston. He was co-founder of JAMS/Endispute and a member of the CPR Institute at its inception. He has written books and articles on dispute resolution and evidence and was formerly Professor of Law at Boston University.

Professor Green maintains an active ADR practice for complex disputes and has settled thousands of cases. He was the mediator of *United States v. Microsoft* and other major cases, as well as the co-inventor of the mini-trial. Professor Green is the recipient of the Lifetime Achievement Award from the American College of Civil Trial Mediators. He is a graduate of Harvard Law School and Brown University.

J. Anderson Little

Andy Little is a mediator and mediation trainer in North Carolina. He chaired the North Carolina Dispute Resolution Commission and also chaired legislative and rule drafting projects for mediation programs in state trial and family courts.

Mr. Little is a graduate of Davidson College, Union Theological Seminary, and UNC School of Law. He practiced law in North Carolina for seventeen years as a civil litigator before becoming a full-time mediator. He has mediated over 4,000 cases, mainly in the context of civil litigation. His book, *Making Money Talk: How to Mediate Insured Claims and Other Monetary Disputes*, was published by the American Bar Association in 2008.

Susan T. Mackenzie

Susan Mackenzie is a full-time neutral with over thirty years of experience as a mediator and arbitrator of employment, commercial, and labor-management disputes. Ms. Mackenzie served as a court-designated Dalkon Shield Referee, a court-appointed facilitator in the multiparty Breast Implant Litigation, and an adjunct professor at Cardozo School of Law.

Ms. Mackenzie frequently lectures and conducts training at the Cornell University ILR School and under the auspices of the ABA and other professional associations. She is a graduate of Smith College (B.A.), Cornell University (M.S.), and Columbia University Law School (J.D.).

David W. Plant

David Plant has practiced as a neutral and teacher since 1999. From 1957 through 1998, Mr. Plant practiced law in New York City with the firm of Fish & Neave. For more than twenty-five years Mr. Plant has served as an arbitrator and mediator in U.S. and international disputes for the ICC, Stockholm, UNCITRAL, AAA, ICDR, CPR, and WIPO, and in court-annexed and ad hoc proceedings in more than 350 matters.

Mr. Plant is a Fellow of the Chartered Institute of Arbitrators (Arbitration and Mediation) and is an accredited CEDR mediator. In 2006 Mr. Plant received the American Bar Association Section of Dispute Resolution's Lawyer as Problem Solver Award. His most recent book, *We Must Talk Because We Can*, was published by the ICC in 2008.

Carmin C. Reiss

Carmin Reiss is a principal of Resolutions LLC in Boston and was formerly a Senior Mediator with JAMS/Endispute. Since 1990 she has had an active mediation practice focusing on environmental, construction, commercial, insurance, employment, professional liability, and personal injury disputes, often in the form of complex multiparty controversies.

Prior to becoming a mediator, Ms. Reiss was a trial lawyer at Bingham McCutchen and a member of that firm's Environmental Practice Group. She is a graduate of Brandeis College and Boston University Law School.

Margaret L. Shaw

Margaret Shaw is a mediator with JAMS in New York City. A former civil litigator, Ms. Shaw has maintained an active ADR practice for more than twenty-five years. She was a co-founder of ADR Associates, which merged with JAMS in 2004. She has participated in the resolution of well over a thousand disputes nationwide.

Ms. Shaw is a Fellow of the College of Labor and Employment Lawyers, an adjunct professor of Law at NYU Law School, where she teaches ADR and negotiation, and the author of numerous articles on a variety of subjects in the ADR field.

Carol A. Wittenberg

Carol Wittenberg is a panelist with JAMS in New York City. Ms. Wittenberg has mediated hundreds of employment disputes involving claims of discrimination. She also serves as a labor-management arbitrator and is listed on more than thirty permanent arbitration panels.

Ms. Wittenberg served on the Extension Faculty of Cornell University's School of Industrial and Labor Relations for twenty years, where she developed training programs in dispute resolution for a variety of corporations, government agencies, and labor unions. Ms. Wittenberg is a graduate of Cornell University and Hunter College.

Introduction

This book explains how to mediate commercial disputes—controversies with legal issues serious enough for parties to hire lawyers and file lawsuits. It is intended to provide beginning mediators, experienced neutrals, and advocates with the techniques they need to resolve difficult cases.

In recent years, commercial mediation has exploded in popularity. Disputes over business contracts, patent rights, commercial ventures, personal injuries, employment, construction, and other issues go to mediation today as a matter of course. When peoples' strong hopes and disappointments combine with legal warfare conducted by professional combatants, the result is often a toxic brew. To settle such disputes, parties often need the assistance of a professional neutral.

What Makes This Book Unique?

Most books about mediation focus on teaching how to promote communication and understanding and how to help parties develop creative solutions. Such methods can be very helpful, especially when parties have a strong incentive to repair a troubled relationship.

This approach is not well suited, however, to resolving serious legal disputes. Parties in such cases hire lawyers, make serious allegations against each other, and often endure years of bitter and expensive litigation before they think seriously about settling their dispute. By this time, whatever interest the litigants may have had in relating with each other is usually gone, and many would prefer not even to talk with the other. In this kind of dispute, the ability to facilitate dialogue is still important, but to achieve settlement, a neutral must use a broad range of techniques.

This book explains how to apply both traditional mediation techniques and other methods to overcome the special barriers that make settlements of legal disputes so difficult. It teaches, for example, how to:

○ Mediate effectively between parties who want to communicate only through lawyers.

○ Deal with hard-money bargaining strategies such as "insulting" first offers, "backward steps," and other adversarial tactics.

○ Change parties' assessments of the likelihood they will win in court, using methods such as evaluation and decision analysis.

○ Overcome stubborn impasses with "confidential listener," "range" bargaining, the "mediator's proposal," and other specialized techniques.

This book is also unique in that it includes many examples of actual mediated cases to illustrate teaching points. You will see how specific methods have been applied in mediations of failed business ventures, complex construction disputes, allegations of employment discrimination, and a variety of other issues.

DVD: The Skills of a Legal Mediator

This book is unique in one other respect. It is the first mediation book that includes a DVD in which experts demonstrate techniques described in the text. You be able to see professionals execute the tactics you read about in the context of an international business case.

Organization of This Book

This book is four volumes in one. It contains sections addressed to novice mediators, experienced neutrals, advocates, and persons interested in specific subject areas.

○ *Part One* is intended for readers new to the process. It gives an overview of basic mediation strategy and what occurs at each stage of the process.

○ *Part Two* is the core of this book. It describes cutting-edge techniques to resolve difficult cases and deal with process obstacles, psychological issues, merits-based barriers, and stubborn impasses.

○ *Part Three* focuses on the role of advocates in mediation, explaining how a lawyer can use the special powers of mediators and the qualities of the process to achieve better outcomes for clients.

○ *Part Four* describes special issues that arise in mediations of disputes in five specific areas: employment, personal injury, intellectual property, environmental, and "mega-cases." Each chapter is written by an expert in the field.

A Note about Writing Style

Almost all of the examples in this book are drawn from my own practice, with details changed to protect confidentiality. I do not usually use the first person, however, instead referring to "the mediator." I have done this so that readers can more easily place themselves in the neutral's position and think about how they would use each technique.

I also refer to "court" or "trial" as the likely alternative to settling, although in practice, parties who don't agree may opt for arbitration or litigate and settle later. By using these words, I mean to include all legal alternatives to settlement.

And I have written as if all disputes consist of only two parties, a plaintiff and a defendant. In real life, of course, controversies may include many parties and combinations of players. Each of these conventions is used in the interest of simplicity. Readers may want to substitute other contexts and participants as they read about various examples and techniques.

You will find it extraordinarily rewarding, at the end of a difficult day, to bring litigants to a peaceful resolution of a difficult conflict. But it is a complex and challenging task. This book is meant to give you the tools you need to perform it well.

PART **I**

· ·

An Overview of the Process: Advice for Novices

Part I gives people new to commercial mediation an overview of the process. Chapter One provides a basic strategy for conducting a mediation, and Chapter Two explains what to do at different stages of the process.

Experienced neutrals may wish to skip ahead to Part II, which examines the mediation process in more depth. Some experienced mediators find, however, that the first two chapters provide a useful framework, helping them identify and organize the techniques they apply instinctively in their practices.

A Basic Strategy

To be effective, a mediator needs to have a strategy. Some mediators develop their approach as they go along, relying on their experience to suggest the right tactic as issues arise. If you are new to the field, however, you will find it nearly impossible to think through your strategy in real time, while the parties are talking to you and arguing with each other. Even experienced neutrals prefer not to rely entirely on their reflexes and plan in advance as much as possible.

Your understanding of what is keeping the parties apart will deepen over the course of a mediation, and the obstacles themselves may change as the process goes forward. Ideally, you would have a unique strategy for each case. In practice, however, this may not be possible. Many mediators use a similar sequence of techniques designed to overcome common barriers, customizing their approach as they go along.

This chapter sets forth a six-step strategy that works effectively in many situations and that you can apply as a default framework. Suggestions for dealing with more complex issues follow in Chapters Three through Nine.

1. Build a Foundation for Success

The Challenge: Missing elements—people, data, interactions. Negotiations often fail because some essential element is missing. One side may have the wrong people—for example, a key decision maker may be missing, or one of the bargainers may be so emotional he cannot make good decisions. At other times, parties do not have the data they need to settle: defense counsel may not, for instance, know how the claimed damages were computed, and without this information cannot get authority to settle. Such problems are difficult to fix once mediation begins and the clock begins to run.

The Response: Identify issues and address them in advance. To identify and resolve such problems, it is best to start work before the parties meet to mediate. The first step is to ask the lawyers for mediation statements and set up telephone conversations with each of them. Ask each lawyer who he plans to bring and who needs to attend from the other party. If a decision maker is absent, work to bring her to the table. If key information is missing, suggest a party provide it. You will find you can elicit information and persuade people to attend in circumstances where the same request would be rejected if made by a party.

Example: A company bought a shipping line, and later sued an accounting firm for allegedly overstating the enterprise's profitability and misleading the buyer into overpaying for it. The buyer's lawyer called the mediator ahead of time to warn her that it was crucial his client, the buyer's chief executive officer (CEO), attend the mediation. However, he said, the CEO would not come unless the managing partner of the defendant accounting firm did as well, and he would not commit to attend first for fear of seeming overeager to settle. The mediator called the defense lawyer, who agreed that it would be very helpful if the principals attended, but said his client also did not want to be the first to agree to come.

The neutral decided to ask each side to tell her privately whether it would bring its principal if the other did so. They both answered positively. She then announced that both decision makers would attend.

Alternatively, you may learn that one of the participants is in the grip of strong emotions or, for other reasons needs to talk with you. With the assent of the parties you can meet privately with a disputant ahead of time, allowing the person to work through difficult emotions and arrive at mediation ready to make decisions. Or a lawyer may have a convincing reason to use an unconventional format for the process itself; if so, you can arrange it.

In summary, before the parties meet to mediate:

○ Ask for statements and talk with lawyers to identify potential obstacles.

○ Address issues such as inadequate information or missing participants.

○ If necessary, meet with individuals to work through an especially difficult issue.

For examples of a mediator conducting a pre-mediation meeting, see Chapters 1 and 2 of "The Skills of a Mediator" DVD.

2. Allow Participants to Argue and Express Feelings

The Challenge: Unresolved process and emotional needs. If parties do not settle, it is often because one or more of them want something more than the right settlement terms. A litigant may be looking for a process: the opportunity to appear before a neutral person, state her grievances, and know she has been heard. Or a party may have a need to express strong feelings directly to an adversary or a neutral.

People may enter litigation expecting to have this opportunity, only to learn that emotions are relevant to the legal process only when they serve a strategic purpose. As a result, disputants can remain trapped in feelings of anger and grief for years, never having a chance to speak freely. Until they feel heard out, however, parties are often not ready to settle.

The Response: An opportunity to speak and feel heard. This aspect of the strategy has three elements:

○ Give disputants a "day in court."

○ Allow them to express feelings to a mediator or adversary.

○ Help them hear what others are saying.

Mediation is not a court session and mediators are not judges, but the process can give parties the experience of having received a hearing. They see their lawyer argue their case or present it themselves, and listen to their opponent's arguments. The mediator will not decide the dispute and may never express an opinion about the merits, but she can demonstrate she has heard the disputants. The experience of telling one's story and feeling heard out by a neutral person can have a surprising impact on a person's willingness to settle. Arguing the merits also focuses participants on the facts and legal principles relevant to the controversy. Knowing a neutral person will be listening encourages the parties to think through arguments and avoid extremes, helping them later to find acceptable compromises.

This aspect of the process often has an emotional component as well. The need to express strong feelings to one's adversary is a very human one, felt by executives and mailroom clerks alike. In the opening session and later caucuses, parties can express some of their feelings about the dispute and each other.

Example: A state trooper began a high-speed chase of a drunk driver in a small New England town. The driver ran a stop sign; straining to keep up, the policeman hit a third car that was crossing the intersection. The trooper was unhurt, but the driver of the third vehicle died instantly. He was a 17-year-old boy, only weeks away from his high school graduation.

The driver's family sued the state, arguing the trooper had been negligent in ignoring the stop sign. It was a typical tort case in which a jury would have to decide whether the officer had acted carelessly. Defense counsel investigated, looking for facts to show the victim had been drinking or careless. It seemed, however, that the boy was a model student—in fact, the valedictorian of his class—and left behind a loving family. On the other hand, the trooper was showing initiative in giving chase to a dangerous driver. It was a difficult case, but one the defense thought could be won, and counsel began the usual process of discovery.

Two years later, as trial approached, the defense decided to make a settlement offer. It was rejected. Defense counsel waited a few weeks and then made a more substantial offer. The word came back from the plaintiffs' lawyer that his clients would not settle. Why, the defense counsel asked: didn't the family understand that juries in the area had been very hard on claimants lately, and the trooper had a reasonable defense? The plaintiffs' lawyer was apologetic, but said the family was adamant and refused even to make a counteroffer. Instead, he suggested they mediate, and emphasized that the family wanted to begin with a meeting with the trooper.

Defense counsel agreed to mediate but resisted the idea of a joint meeting: what was the point of having angry people rehash the facts, given that the evidence was largely undisputed and the state, not the trooper, would pay for any settlement? Eventually, however, they agreed to the process.

The opening session was an extraordinary event. The victim's mother, father, and sisters came; they talked not about the case, but about their lost son and brother. The mother read a poem to the trooper describing the hopes she had had for her dead son, and the life she knew they would never be able to share.

The officer surprised everyone as well. Although he maintained he had not been negligent, he said he felt awful about what had happened.

He had three sons, and had thought over and over about how he would feel if one of them were killed. He had asked to be assigned to desk work, he told the family, because he could no longer do high-speed chases.

The parties did not reach an agreement that day, but as the family walked out, one of the children turned to the trooper. "It's been three years since my brother died," she said, "and now I feel he's finally had a funeral." Two weeks later the defense settlement offer was accepted.

Emotional discussions are often uncomfortable for the participants and make people temporarily feel angrier, but over the course of the process they can help disputants let go of feelings and consider settlement. In the preceding example, for instance, the fact that no legal issue was resolved at the meeting and the trooper denied being negligent did not matter. The key was that the family felt they had finally been able to express their feelings to the person responsible and knew he had heard them. You can achieve a great deal simply by allowing the parties to talk about their feelings and disagreements in a controlled setting. Chapter Six describes techniques for managing such discussions successfully. To facilitate expression of feelings and arguments:

○ Give the parties an opportunity to argue the merits directly to each other.

○ Allow participants to express emotions, even unpleasant ones, intervening only as needed to maintain order.

○ Don't focus on weaknesses in a party's arguments in front of an opponent. Wait instead for a private meeting to follow up on controversial issues or difficult feelings.

For examples of facilitating arguments and emotional exchanges, see Chapters 3 and 4 of the DVD.

3. Moderate the Bargaining

The Challenge: Positional tactics leading to impasse. Negotiators often have trouble reaching settlement because they use a "positional" approach to bargaining, each making a monetary offer and then trading concessions until they reach agreement. Positional bargaining can be successful, but it often makes negotiators frustrated and angry. One party, for example, will open with an extreme position in the hope of setting up a favorable compromise. This will lead its opponent to complain the offer is "insulting" and refuse to counter, or make a very small concession. The result often is impasse.

The Response: Become the moderator of the process. Ideally a mediator would avoid adversarial bargaining over money entirely, by convincing parties to look for a settlement based on fair principles or their underlying interests. In commercial mediation, however, parties usually arrive suspicious of each other and determined to engage in money bargaining. A mediator's only practical option in such cases is to facilitate the process the parties want, while looking for an opportunity to move to a more effective approach.

One way to facilitate money negotiations is to act as a coach to each side. You can, for example:

○ Ask a bargainer to support its number with an explanation. ("I'll communicate it, but if they ask how you got there what should I tell them?)

○ Help a disputant assess how its planned tactic will affect its opponent. ("What do you think their response will be if you start at $10,000?")

If coaching is not enough, you can become a moderator, giving bargainers advice about what they need to do to keep the process moving. ("If you want them to get to $100,000 with the next round, I think your offer to them needs to be in the range of 700 to 800K . . .")

Chapter Four gives suggestions for facilitating money bargaining. By using these steps in combination with a continuing discussion of the legal case, you can often orchestrate a "dance" of concessions to move the parties toward settlement. In sum:

○ Parties in commercial disputes usually arrive determined to negotiate over money. When this occurs, help the disputants conduct the bargaining effectively.

○ Coach each side, helping them to see how their tactics will be received and encouraging them to provide explanations as well as numbers.

○ If necessary moderate the bargaining, advising parties how to move toward settlement.

For examples of moderating bargaining, see Chapters 6 and 8 of the DVD.

4. Seek Out and Address Hidden Issues

The Challenge: Disregard of hidden issues and missed opportunities. Negotiations in legal cases are often blocked by hidden psychological obstacles. They may include the following:

○ *Strong feelings.* I have talked about the usefulness of drawing out feelings in pre-mediation discussions or the opening session, but this is often not possible. Participants in commercial mediation typically arrive with "game faces on," presenting a businesslike demeanor even as feelings boil beneath the surface. When this occurs, simply giving a disputant the chance to express emotions is often not enough.

○ *Unexploited opportunities for gain.* Negotiators can often create more valuable outcomes by including nonmoney terms in settlement agreements. The key is for each side to offer the other things that carry a low cost for the giver but provide high value to the recipient. A discharged employee, for instance, might value a change to his personnel file to indicate a voluntary quit or outplacement assistance, while his employer would value the employee's agreement to keep the settlement confidential. Even "pure-money" settlements can be enhanced by terms that meet the parties' underlying interests, such as provisions for payment over time.

The Response: Probe for and deal with hidden issues. Even as you are carrying out other tasks, look for clues to hidden emotions and overly narrow approaches to settlement. Chapter Five describes ways to promote valuable settlements, while Chapter Six gives suggestions about how to identify and deal with emotional issues. In general,

○ Look for clues that hidden issues are present. Ask about them in private discussions.

○ Don't be discouraged by initial brush-offs, and raise the issue again later.

○ If you sense an issue exists, encourage disputants to talk about it. If necessary, advocate a solution yourself.

For examples of exploring non-legal issues, see Chapters 5 and 9 of the DVD.

5. Test the Parties' Alternatives; If Necessary, Evaluate the Adjudication Option

The Challenge: Lack of realism about the outcome in adjudication. Participants in legal disputes often justify hard bargaining positions in terms of the merits of the dispute. They are asking for a great deal or offering little, they say, because they have a strong legal case. The problem, of course, is that both parties usually argue they will win in court.

To some degree, parties bluff about their litigation options to justify aggressive bargaining positions and do not expect to be taken literally. However, to a surprising degree disputants actually believe in their clashing predictions. Even when parties are told, for example, that their predictions of success in court add up to more than 100 percent (one believes that it has a 70 percent chance of winning, for instance, while the other thinks it has a 60 percent chance of prevailing) and this is impossible, their confidence in their own prediction remains unshaken. It is the other side, they say, that is being unrealistic. The problem is illustrated by the following experiment:

Example: Students at Harvard Law School are preparing to negotiate the settlement of a personal injury case. Before they begin, the students are asked to make a private prediction of their chances of winning based on their confidential instructions. What the students don't know is that there is nothing confidential about the instructions: both sides have received exactly the same data, with different labels. Because both sides have the same information, they should come out with the same answers—but this is not what occurs.

In fact, hundreds of law and business students told to negotiate for the plaintiff assess her chances of winning as being nearly 20 percent higher than students who are assigned to the defense. The two sides' predictions total nearly 120 percent.

Asked to estimate what damages a jury will award if the plaintiff does win, there is a similar disparity: plaintiff bargainers estimate her damages at an average of $264,000, while defense negotiators looking at the same data estimate a verdict of only $188,000.

What caused these distortions? It was not due to disparities in information, because both sides had the same facts. Nor was it due to lack of experience. When I asked seasoned litigators training to be mediators to take on roles in the same problem, their predictions were similarly distorted. Disagreements like these are a serious barrier to settlement, because parties understandably resist accepting an outcome worse than their honest (but inflated) estimate of the value of their case.

As we will see in Chapter Seven, there are two basic causes for disputants' distorted thinking about their legal alternatives. One is lack of information. The other is their inability to interpret the data they do have accurately.

First Response: Foster an information exchange. Your first response to a disagreement over the legal merits should be to help parties exchange information. Modern discovery rules are intended to require parties to disclose key evidence, but it is often surprising how little one side knows about the other's case, even after years of litigation.

You can be an effective facilitator of an information exchange. If, for example, a plaintiff has explained its theory of liability in detail but has given no explanation for its damage claim, you can suggest it flesh out damages. Parties will often respond cooperatively to your request, although they would have refused the same inquiry coming from their opponent. Suggestions about how to foster information exchanges appear in Chapter Seven.

Second Response: Reality test. As the Harvard study showed, even when parties have the relevant information they often do not interpret it accurately. Another way to help to solve merits-based problems is, therefore, to help disputants analyze their legal case.

The least intrusive way to accomplish this is through questions that help parties focus on evidence and issues they have missed. It is important both that you ask questions pointed enough to prompt someone to confront a problem and avoid comments so tough the disputant concludes you have taken sides against her.

Questions. Begin with open-ended questions asked in a spirit of curiosity; in this mode, you are simply trying to understand the dispute and the parties' arguments. ("Tell me what you think are the key facts here?" or "Can you give me your take on the defendant's contract argument?") Your questions can progress gradually from open-ended queries ("Have you thought about . . . ?") to more pointed requests ("They are resisting making a higher offer because they believe you won't be able to prove causation . . . What should I tell them?")

Analysis. You may also want to take a party through an analysis of each element in a case, applying a systematic framework to prevent disputants from skipping over an embarrassing weakness.

Discussing the merits can help to narrow litigants' disagreement about the likely outcome in adjudication for several reasons. For one thing, it helps counteract disputants' tendency to be overly optimistic. Doing so also assists lawyers who are dealing with an unrealistic client but are reluctant to disagree with the party for fear of damaging the client's confidence in them. Talking over the merits can also give a disputant a face-saving excuse for a compromise it secretly knows is necessary.

Evaluative feedback. In some cases questioning and analysis is not enough; a disputant may be wedded to an unrealistic viewpoint or require support to justify a settlement to a supervisor. In such situations you have the option to go further, by offering an opinion about how a court is likely to decide a key issue or even the entire case. Evaluations can be structured in a wide variety of ways; for example, "My experience with Judge Jones is that she usually denies summary judgment in this kind of situation" or "If the plaintiff prevails on liability, what I know of Houston juries suggests they would value damages at somewhere between $125,000 and $150,000."

One key point to note about these examples is that the mediator is not saying how she *personally* would decide the case, but rather is predicting the attitude of an *outside decision maker*. Expressing your personal opinion about what is "right" or "fair" in a dispute is almost always a bad idea because it is likely to leave a listener feeling you have taken sides against him. Properly performed, a neutral evaluation can be helpful in producing an agreement. However, a poorly done or badly timed opinion can derail the settlement process. More advice about how to use evaluation effectively appears in Chapter Eight.

To deal with disagreements about the merits:

○ Ask each party open-ended questions about the case.

○ Ask them to respond to specific points.

○ Lead each side through a systematic analysis.

○ If necessary, offer a prediction of how a court would decide a specific issue or the entire case. Delay any evaluation as long and keep it as general as possible.

For examples of facilitating analysis see Chapters 10 and 13, and for an evaluation see Chapter 16, of the DVD.

6. Break Bargaining Impasses

The Challenge: Closing the final gap. Often the barriers to agreement are too high, causing bargaining to stall and provoking an impasse.

The Responses: You have several options to deal with a stalled bargaining process.

Persevere and project optimism. The first bit of advice may seem overly simple, but it embodies a basic truth about mediation: when in doubt, persevere. Even experienced mediators find, more often than not, that parties get stuck at some point. It often happens during the late afternoon or early evening, when energy levels decline and each side has made all the compromises it feels it ought to and more. The key thing to remember at this point is that this mediation probably *will* succeed. If you can keep the parties talking and avoid a freeze-up, they will find a solution.

The disputants will be looking for signals from you about whether it is worth continuing, and it is important to send positive signs, as long as you remain within the bounds of reality. You can say that you believe a deal is possible, but don't suggest you are ignoring the very real gap that must be bridged.

Return to a prior tactic. Another option at impasse is to return to an earlier stage or tactic. You may wonder why, if an approach has not worked once, it would be successful the second time around. Surprisingly often, however, something that was rejected earlier will evoke a positive response later in the process. Peoples' emotional states shift over the course of a mediation, they learn new facts, and they realize their original strategy is not working. As this occurs they often become more open to compromise.

Invite the disputants to take the initiative. A simple tactic is to ask the disputants to take the initiative. You could, for instance, say, "What do you think we should do?" and then wait quietly. If disputants realize they cannot simply sit back intransigently and demand you produce results, they will sometimes offer surprising ideas. If you do this, however, be prepared to wait a couple of minutes.

Test flexibility privately. Another option is to test the disputants' flexibility in private. Parties may refuse to offer anything more to an opponent whom they think is being unreasonable, but still be willing to give private hints to you. You can, for example, ask "What if?" questions ("What if I could get them down to $50,000; would that be acceptable?") or use techniques such as a *confidential listener* or a *mediator's proposal* described in Chapter Nine.

Adjourn and follow up. If the disputants are psychologically spent or have run out of authority, the best response may be to adjourn temporarily. You can follow up with shuttle diplomacy by telephone, propose a second mediation session, or set a deadline to prompt the parties to make difficult decisions.

In summary, to deal with bargaining impasses:

○ Persevere and remain optimistic. Even parties in apparent impasse will usually find a path to settlement.

○ Return to a prior tactic, such as analyzing the legal case or exploring nonlegal concerns.

○ Ask the disputants to take the initiative.

○ Probe the parties' flexibility in private.

○ Adjourn and follow up with telephone diplomacy, another session, or a deadline.

For examples of impasse-breaking techniques, see Chapters 12, 14 and 18 through 21 of the DVD.

Conclusion

This six-step strategy will produce success in many situations, particularly when a case is relatively straightforward and the parties have a strong incentive to settle. It is a solid foundation on which to premise your mediative efforts. No single set of strategies, however, can overcome all obstacles. Relying on these tactics alone is like playing a musical instrument with only one octave or being a pitcher with only two pitches: you may accomplish less than you are capable of, and will sometimes fail where a more comprehensive approach would bring success.

Experienced mediators use this basic strategy as a foundation, modifying their approach to deal with the specific obstacles they encounter in each dispute. In Part II we will go deeper into the process, exploring a variety of barriers, and approaches to overcome them.

7. A Strategy Chart

Challenges	Responses
1. Missing elements: people, data, emotions	• Contact counsel ahead of time to learn about the dispute. • Arrange for information to be exchanged and decision makers to attend. • If necessary, meet with participants ahead of time to begin working through emotional issues.
2. Lack of opportunity to present arguments and express feelings	• Provide disputants with a "day in court" to argue their case. • Provide a setting in which they can express their feelings to you and the other party. • Encourage participants to listen to each other's views.
3. Positional tactics leading to impasse	• Encourage principled and interest-based approaches, but support pure-money bargaining if the parties want to use it. • Advise bargainers about the likely impact of their tactics. • If necessary, coach or moderate the bargaining.
4. Hidden issues	• Probe for hidden emotional obstacles. • Identify personal and business interests. • Treat emotional and cognitive problems. Encourage the parties to consider imaginative terms.
5. Lack of realism about the outcome in adjudication	• Foster an exchange of information. • Ask questions about legal and factual issues. • Point out neglected issues, and lead an analysis of the merits. • If necessary, predict the likely court outcome on one or more issues.
6. Inability to reach agreement	• Persevere and remain optimistic. • Repeat earlier tactics. • Invite the disputants to take the initiative. • Adjourn and follow up.

The Stages of Mediation

Commercial mediation usually moves through several stages: pre-mediation, the opening session, and private caucuses, often accompanied by follow-up. This chapter focuses on the time the parties and the mediator spend together in the opening session, and caucusing, discussing what occurs at each stage.

1. The Opening Session

The opening session is the first time in most mediations that the disputants meet as a group. It is often referred to as the "joint" session, but I use "opening" to avoid implying that this is the only time disputants will meet together. Lawyers and (usually) the parties are present during the opening session, and the mediator moderates it.

Should you hold an opening session at all?

In some areas, commercial mediation is now conducted almost exclusively through caucuses and participants do not meet together at all. Even when opening sessions are customary, lawyers often suggest skipping them. Among the less persuasive reasons given for avoiding an opening session are:

- We've heard it all before. (Who is "we"?)
- They'll blow up. (Not likely, in commercial cases)
- They'll get angry and refuse to settle. (For how long?)
- We don't have time. (What's more important?)

Example: A condominium association sued a developer over major defects in construction. The developer in turn sued its architect, contractors, and insurers. The parties agreed to mediate for two days and more than 40 people convened for the event.

The lawyers had strongly advised the mediator not to hold an opening session. Just hearing from 15 parties, they said, would chew up most of the first day, leaving little time for private discussions and bargaining, and in any case they all knew each other's arguments. The better strategy, they said, would be to caucus immediately. The mediator agreed and went directly into caucusing.

The discussions were difficult, but by the end of the second day the parties had narrowed an initial gap of $5 million to $400,000. At that point, however, the condo association directors refused to move any further. When the mediator asked why, one of them complained of years of frustration with the development company's predecessor. He insisted on explaining this to the current developer's CEO who, he said, didn't know what the unit owners had gone through.

The mediator adjourned the process, and a week later convened the plaintiffs and the developer for a special two-hour meeting. Reading from binders full of documents, the board members traced their past frustrations while the developer's CEO listened. The discussion deteriorated into thinly veiled threats, and the meeting broke up without apparent progress. Two weeks later, however, the board agreed to an additional compromise, and the case settled.

Be very reluctant to eliminate an opening session because of lawyers' claims that "we've heard it all before," for example. Even if this is true for the lawyers, it usually is not for the parties. And, as long as basic ground rules are enforced, even angry parties can talk with each other without provoking a damaging confrontation.

There are a few circumstances in which there is little risk in skipping an opening session—for instance, if each of the following factors is present:

○ All of the participants are dispute professionals: lawyers, adjusters, etc.

○ The professionals are the real decision makers in the case.

○ Each side has received full discovery about the other's case.

○ No one is too angry—the case is largely, if not entirely, about money.

Example: A large manufacturer sued two insurers to recover the cost of remediating a large plume of pollution that had been spilled from one it its plants and entered the water table hundreds of feet below the ground. The estimated cost was more than $20 million.

Despite the large amount of money involved, none of the people at the mediation seemed emotional about the case. The spill had occurred in the late 1960s and no one now involved with the company felt responsible for it. The adjusters representing the insurers viewed the case as a typical problem of trying to allocate risk under uncertainty: the underlying facts were buried in the past, relevant insurance policies had been lost, and so on. In addition, a nationally known venture capitalist who controlled the defendant insurance company was, by coincidence, that very day making a takeover bid for the manufacturer. As a result, both sides' negotiators knew the dispute might soon be "all in the family."

At the participants' request, I agreed to dispense with an opening session and go directly into caucusing. My role turned out to be a small one. The disputants had gone to mediation primarily to create a settlement event and did not need much outside help. They quickly traded concessions of $1 million or more, and within a few hours had a deal.

a. Goals

Your overall goal for the opening session is to create a foundation for productive bargaining. You should structure it as a serious meeting rather than an adjudicatory proceeding. You will want to:

○ Begin to build good working relationships.

○ Explain the process.

○ Give lawyers an opportunity to argue and the parties to listen.

○ Give disputants a chance to express viewpoints and feelings.

○ Help parties exchange information.

Begin to build good working relationships

Your primary goal from your first contact with the disputants is to build their trust and confidence so that they will accept your guidance. You need to give each party the feeling you are genuinely interested in their viewpoint and want to help them achieve a good result. The opening session is usually the first time the parties, and perhaps also the lawyers, have met you, apart perhaps from a brief chat in the waiting room. Particularly if you have a goal-oriented, "get it done" personality, this may seem like pointless schmoozing, but as noted earlier, surveys of clients of commercial mediators show that it is crucial to success. Don't let your interest in moving the process along get in the way of trying to make a personal connection with each disputant.

Explain the process

The opening session is also your best opportunity to explain mediation to the disputants. Often the parties are first-time participants. By describing the process, you can clear away misconceptions and make them feel on more of a level playing field with experienced participants. Even lawyers who are familiar with mediation often welcome a brief explanation, both for the benefit of their clients and to confirm that key ground rules are understood by everyone.

Before reaching mediation, the parties will often have been involved in bitter litigation and failed negotiations, so you also want to set a positive tone for the process, suggesting that it will be different from what has gone on before.

Give lawyers an opportunity to argue and the parties to listen

We have seen that opening sessions can play a significant psychological function for both lawyers and clients—the opportunity to have a "day in court." Lawyers sometimes also need to demonstrate the strength of their arguments and their commitment to their clients. And the opening session allows a client to hear, often in blunt terms, what his opponent will say if the case goes to trial.

Allow the disputants to express views and feelings

The opening session allows participants, directly or through their lawyer, to express feelings such as anger or grief directly to the other party. Indeed, mediation is often the first and only chance a party has to talk directly with its opponent during the entire litigation process. Parties are free to talk about business and personal issues, but commercial litigants usually focus on their legal case.

Help parties exchange information

The opening session is an opportunity for disputants to exchange information. This is particularly valuable when mediation takes place at the outset of a dispute, at a point when the parties have not conducted formal discovery.

b. Techniques

Overall format

The format of an opening session is flexible, but typically follows this structure:

- ⭘ The parties meet and introduce themselves.
- ⭘ The mediator welcomes the participants and explains the process.
- ⭘ The lawyers, and perhaps also the parties, make statements.
- ⭘ Disputants exchange questions and comments, and the mediator may pose clarifying questions.
- ⭘ The mediator concludes the session and transitions to caucusing.

Opening moments

Greet people as they arrive and make small talk as you would at the start of a business meeting, but don't put yourself in a position one side may interpret as bias toward the other. For example, unless it has been cleared in advance, a party should not arrive to find you talking with its opponent behind a closed door.

Follow the cues of the disputants concerning formality. If they already are on a first-name basis or doff their suit coats, you can do so. If, however, you sense a participant is uncomfortable with this, err on the side of formality at the outset. Disputants from other cultures in particular may interpret American casualness as lack of respect.

Mediator's comments

Mediators almost always make opening comments. Experienced mediators tend to keep these relatively short, especially if the parties are professionals who have probably been briefed by their lawyers. They also know that most people cannot remember more than a few minutes of oral comments when they are tense, as is true of disputants. A transcript of suggested opening comments appears in the Appendix.

Parties' statements

After opening comments, the mediator gives each side the opportunity to speak. What a party says is in its discretion, but typically lawyers make statements, sometimes supplemented by comments from a party or an expert. As the mediator you will want to:

○ *Set the agenda and encourage participants to listen.* The plaintiff usually speaks first as a matter of convention. Occasionally, if the plaintiff's position has been explained in advance and the defendant's views are not known, it may make sense to start with the defense. Notify the lawyers in advance if you decide to do so.

Participants often listen with a focus on rebuttal, rather than taking in what they hear. Encourage the parties to listen carefully to what their adversary says, noting that it may well be a preview of what they will hear in court if the case is not resolved.

○ *Listen carefully, and show you are doing so.* Remain quiet but engaged. As each person speaks, turn to look at him or her. Demonstrate that you are listening by nodding or taking notes. Intervene as moderator only if necessary: this is the disputants' chance to speak freely.

You may want to pose a clarifying question or make a comment occasionally to show you are listening or that you have "done your homework." If you sense your comments may be misinterpreted, explain your intent. ("My questions are meant only to clarify what I'm hearing; I don't mean to express any view about the merits of the case, and I expect to be asking the same kinds of questions when the other side speaks.")

○ Encourage the parties as well as the lawyers to talk. Lawyers' instinct is often to keep clients under wraps, and parties themselves may be reluctant to talk. Encourage them to speak but make it clear that there is no pressure to do so.

Example: A retired executive bought an antiques company, only to conclude a few months later that the seller had deceived him about its condition. He filed suit but then agreed to mediate. The mediator called each lawyer before the mediation and mentioned that he would invite their clients to talk. The executive's lawyer said that he thought his client would welcome the chance. The attorney for the seller, however, warned that her client was an "engineer-type" who would not want to say much.

The purchaser showed up with a four-page single-spaced text and described how he'd entered the deal in good faith, only to find himself betrayed by deceptions ranging from inflated inventory to a clientele outraged at the prior owner's failure to meet shipping dates.

After 30 minutes the purchaser finished and the seller began to talk. Belying his counsel's prediction, he spoke articulately and at length. There was a back-and-forth discussion in which the lawyers participated but which was dominated by the principals. When the discussion became heated and repetitive, the mediator deferred to the lawyers' request they move into caucusing. Still, the opening session went on for 2 1/2 hours and later that day the case settled.

○ *Promote discussion but maintain order.* The opening session is often the first time the principals have met since the dispute began. Parties are sometimes hostile and lawyers sometimes feel the need to play aggressive roles. Your goal when this happens should ordinarily be to manage a "controlled confrontation." This includes confrontation—allowing participants to express conflict and emotions—and control—not permitting the process to degenerate into bitter accusations. You might think of your role as similar to a chef preparing pasta: to cook it well, the water should boil vigorously, but not overflow the pot. Success in mediation also lies in having enough heat to produce change, without making a mess.

Outbursts are rare in commercial cases, probably because disputants feel they would lose face if they were chided by a mediator in front of an opponent. (This is also a reason to be very polite when intervening, so that you are not perceived to be "slapping the disputant's hand.") If a discussion starts to spin into a confrontation, a cautionary comment will restore order quickly. ("The plaintiff has the floor at the moment, Mr. Smith. I'll ask you to take careful notes, and once the plaintiff is finished, I want to hear how you see this.")

Information exchange

Opening sessions are an excellent opportunity for parties to exchange information. Parties can also do this once they are in caucuses, of course, but at that stage questions and answers must be relayed through the mediator.

Once each side has made an opening statement and offered a rebuttal if it wishes, I encourage the parties to talk directly with each other. If lawyers want to head prematurely for their caucus rooms, I encourage them to stay. As a rule of thumb, I do not become concerned about moving out of joint session until one-third of the expected time for mediation has gone by.

Transition to caucuses

At some point in almost every session, one or both lawyers will suggest the parties go into caucuses. Or you may decide that the joint discussion has run its course or the participants are becoming too adversarial, and decide to move into caucusing.

Confidentiality rules in caucusing

One question is what rule of confidentiality to announce for the caucusing phase. Will everything a disputant says be confidential unless the disputant authorizes the mediator to disclose it, or will the mediator have discretion to transmit information unless a disputant affirmatively flags it as confidential? I prefer the second option, because I find that in the heat of mediating I often forget to ask for permission, and cannot always foresee what I will need to disclose in the other caucus room.

For examples of an opening session, see Chapters 3 and 4 of the DVD.

2. Private Caucuses

Almost all commercial mediations involve some private caucusing, with the mediator moving back and forth between parties sitting in separate rooms; in most cases, disputants spend most of their time in caucuses. The typical format of commercial mediation thus contrasts sharply with family and community mediation, where parties typically remain in joint session throughout.

Should parties caucus at all?

Most commercial mediators believe the advantages of having private conversations with disputants strongly outweigh the disadvantages of separating them. Occasionally, however, even commercial mediators do not caucus, usually because the parties prefer to talk directly.

Example: Two women built up a small graphic design firm. Then one of them decided to take an inside position with a large client of the firm, while her partner opted to continue the business on her own. The women remained friendly, but the situation created tension. The partner who planned to stay was anxious about becoming solely responsible for the business and felt somewhat abandoned. Her colleague, by contrast, tended to take an everything-will-work-out approach to life and found it hard to credit her partner's concerns.

The mediator ordinarily used a caucus-based format, but decided in this case to keep the two women together. He thought that, with assistance, they could negotiate directly and was concerned that if he held separate meetings it would be taken as a signal their disagreements were serious. Most important, the women expressed a preference for face-to-face discussions. The mediation went forward smoothly, although between sessions each partner would occasionally communicate concerns to the mediator over the telephone.

Patterns in caucusing

A mediator's goals and techniques will change as caucusing progresses. In the first round, your primary goal will usually be to allow disputants to explain their perspective, express feelings, and develop confidence in you. To do this, focus on listening and drawing people out and try not to challenge what you hear.

As the process goes on, you will want to become more active, posing pointed questions and offering advice about bargaining. During the last stages of the process, you will often feel it appropriate to make specific suggestions about what the parties need to do to achieve a settlement and perhaps give an opinion about the likely outcome if the case is litigated.

Mediators tend to progress from a restrained to a more active role for several reasons. First, as the process goes forward participants become increasingly convinced they have been heard and gain confidence in the mediator, making them more willing to listen to suggestions. At the same time the mediator learns more about the legal issues and the parties' concerns, making the neutral more confident about giving advice. Disputants are also likely to become increasingly frustrated with the results of traditional bargaining, making them more receptive to suggestions about other ways to approach the dispute.

a. Early Caucuses

(1) Goals

During the first round or two of caucusing, you will have the following goals:

- ○ Continue to build relationships.
- ○ Make the disputants feel fully heard.
- ○ Gather sensitive information.
- ○ Control negative communications.
- ○ Identify interests and probe for hidden obstacles.

Continue to build relationships

A primary goal continues to be to build a working relationship with each side. Good relationships will make you more effective later in the process as you deliver unwelcome news and suggest painful compromises. The first caucus is usually the first time you talk privately with either principal, making the interaction particularly important.

Make the disputants feel fully heard

It is important to create an atmosphere in which disputants feel free to express feelings, perspectives, and wishes that they may not have felt comfortable stating in the presence of their opponent. In the privacy of the caucus, parties can speak their minds without concern about being embarrassed. Your goal at this stage is to listen well and show you are listening; it is not to offer advice. I try to keep in mind that during the first caucus the parties and lawyers are entitled to "have it their way." There will be time later to point out the errors and inconsistencies in their case if I have to.

Gather sensitive information

Caucuses allow a mediator to gather sensitive information the parties want to hide from an adversary. Disputants may be guarded about disclosures at first, but will often become more open as the process goes on.

Control negative communications

The caucus format allows you to translate one side's angry or provocative language into words the other party can hear. If you cannot put a statement into acceptable language, you can withhold it until the recipient is able to listen or the speaker has become calmer.

Identify interests, and probe for obstacles

Because caucus discussions can be less guarded and more free-ranging than joint meetings, they are a good opportunity to look for hidden obstacles and encourage disputants to identify underlying interests.

(2) Techniques

During the first caucus meeting with each side try to follow these guidelines:

○ Ask open-ended questions.
○ Engage the principals.
○ Start slowly and listen carefully.
○ Show interest and empathy.
○ Perhaps start the bargaining process.
○ Keep rough track of time.

With whom to start?

The convention in mediation is to meet first with the plaintiff. You will occasionally want to start with the defense, however, particularly if it is the defendant's turn to make an offer. Even then I usually begin with the plaintiff, if only for a few minutes. Disputants sometimes read significance into where a mediator begins, so give a reason for your decision. ("It's traditional to begin with the plaintiff, so that's what I'm going to do . . ." or "Since the plaintiff made the last offer, I think I will start with the defense . . .")

Ask open-ended questions

Start with open-ended questions that invite disputants to talk freely. I often start with: "Is there anything you didn't feel comfortable mentioning in front of the other side, but you think I should know to understand the situation?" Alternatively, if a party seems to have been in a personally trying situation, you might begin by acknowledging this and inviting the person to elaborate. ("This sounds like it was an awful experience for you Ms. Smith . . .")

Focus your initial comments on the issues raised by the people with whom you are meeting, rather than the other side's comments. Most disputants want to know their own views have been considered before they will deal with an opponent's concerns.

Engage the principals

Focus some of your questions on the parties rather than the lawyers. To avoid making them uncomfortable, ask factual rather than legal questions. ("Mr. Yao, can you tell me where you feel the pain?" or "Ms. Green, I heard your counsel say you were seeking reinstatement. Do you know if your position has been filled?") Or you might ask a general question such as, "Jim, how do you feel about all this?"

Start slowly and listen carefully

Resist the temptation to "cut to the chase." Unless the process is operating under a tight time constraint, be wary of directing the agenda, making suggestions, or using confrontational tactics during the first round of caucusing. Even evaluative mediators rarely offer opinions during their first caucus meeting with each side.

Show interest and empathy

It is vital that the participants feel heard out. Listen in a way that shows the speaker she has been heard and understood. You can convey this by taking notes, maintaining eye contact, and checking your understanding. ("So if I understand you correctly, you feel the defendant never intended to comply with the contract?") Suggestions about good listening are set out in Chapter Six.

Perhaps start the bargaining process

You can wait until the second round to ask for offers, or suggest that a party make an offer at the end of the first caucus meeting. If there is no clear signal, you can offer the party whose turn it is a choice. ("You could make a first offer now, or treat this round of talks as focusing on information and wait for the next round to put out a number. We probably won't get an offer from the other side until you have made one, but we have time. It's really up to you.")

Keep rough track of time

Early caucus meetings are usually much longer than later ones because more information is being gathered and communicated. Disputants are sometimes frustrated at waiting while a mediator talks with the other side. If a session extends for much more than an hour, you may want to step out and "touch base" with the side that is waiting.

For examples of early caucuses, see Chapters 5 through 8 of the DVD.

b. Middle Caucuses

As the caucusing progresses, parties gradually move from exchanging data and arguments to analyzing the case and making offers. Mediators become more active participants in the discussions, for example, by pushing parties to consider the costs and uncertainties of litigation. Middle caucuses tend to mix case analysis with active bargaining and sometimes exploration of interests. During this stage you are likely to:

- ○ Moderate the bargaining process.
- ○ Encourage information exchange.
- ○ Ask about interests and probe priorities.
- ○ Reframe disputants' views.
- ○ Change disputants' assessments of the merits.

Moderate the bargaining process

Bargaining over money, coupled with arguments over the value of each side's litigation option, take up most caucus discussions in the typical commercial case. Facilitating hard money negotiations is a frustrating and difficult task. You can play a helpful role by advising disputants how to interpret offers, predicting an opponent's likely reactions to a party's planned offer, and suggesting tactics to move the process forward.

Bear in mind that parties often come to mediation with unreasonable expectations about what the other side will be willing to do, and even realistic parties often take extreme positions for tactical reasons. Disputants often realize only gradually how much they will have to compromise to get a settlement and need time to adjust to unwelcome news.

The first caucus is usually too soon to ask a party to make a real effort, but as the process progresses you will probably need to push and coach parties to compromise. Chapter Four gives suggestions on how to facilitate pure-money negotiations.

Encourage information exchange

We have seen that one of the main reasons people are unable to negotiate successfully is they do not have enough information, and a mediator can help negotiate exchanges of data. This process is likely to become more intense as it becomes clearer where the parties disagree.

You might, for instance, say to a plaintiff who has refused to disclose information: "I think the defendant is not coming up because he hasn't seen a detailed critique of his statute of limitations defense. To get the kind of movement you need here, I'd suggest you authorize me to explain how you plan to defeat it."

Ask about interests and develop options

At first, parties and their lawyers usually want to talk only about their legal case and money offers. As time goes on, however, disputants sometimes become more open to considering nonlegal issues and options. The middle caucuses are a good time to suggest that disputants focus on their business or personal interests and factors that might motivate their opponent to settle. You can also ask about the parties' relative priorities and give each side a signal about what is more or less acceptable to the other. Suggestions about how to do this appear in Chapter Five.

Reframe disputants' views

Mediators work to change disputants' views of the controversy and each other, by suggesting a different way, or "frame," in which to see a situation.

Example: A homeowner was bitterly opposing a neighboring business's expansion plans before a local licensing board. The company proposed a buyout of the homeowner's property. The homeowner reacted angrily, saying he could not understand why the company would try to "drive me out of my home."

The mediator responded, "From what they're telling me in the other room, the company is impressed by your tenacity. They're convinced you'll fight every effort they make to grow their business. In one sense it's not too surprising why they see it that way: you've filed protests to their expansion applications for the last ten years, and succeeded in delaying a lot of them.

"To them, paying you money to drop this particular objection looks like giving you a war chest to fight the next battle. I think that's what's motivating their request for a buyout. Is there anything we could tell them that would give them confidence that if they settle without it, they'll be able to live peacefully with you?"

Change disputants' assessments of the merits

Middle caucuses are also the time when a mediator can start to push parties to assess their best alternative to settlement, which is usually to continue in litigation. The court outcome may be the focus of your discussions, but you should seek to define "alternative" more broadly to include:

○ *The cost of litigation:* how much will the party have to pay to pursue its adjudication option?

○ *The intangible costs of remaining in conflict:* personal stress, business distraction, and other nonlegal factors.

○ *Whether the alternative is, in fact, adjudication:* Only a small percentage of cases are ever decided on the merits. Most parties who break off talks spend time and money litigating, only to find themselves back in negotiations in the future.

○ *The likely outcome if a court adjudicates the dispute.*

During this stage, you can help parties analyze each aspect of their alternative to reaching agreement, bringing each side's arguments and perspectives to the other and asking for help responding to them. ("They are challenging your claim for emotional distress because they say there aren't any medical records to back it up. Is there anything I can give them so they will make a better offer?")

As the process goes on, you can become increasingly active, explaining and emphasizing each side's key points to the other and probing assumptions about liability, damages, and the cost of litigation. Your goal will be to make each side confront, perhaps for the first time, the full costs of pursuing the dispute and the possibility that if they do so they will lose. Ideas on how to do this appear in Chapter Seven.

For examples of middle caucuses, see Chapters 9 through 13 of the DVD.

c. Later Caucuses

As the process moves toward closure, disputants focus less on the value of their case and more on pure bargaining. Indeed, toward the end, caucus sessions may last only a few minutes. Disputants are usually more willing to accept advice from the mediator at this stage, but at the same time are resistant to making additional concessions, feeling they have already given up more than they should. During the later caucuses a mediator can:

- ○ Maintain momentum.
- ○ Set up joint meetings.
- ○ Offer or initiate process options.
- ○ Commit agreements to writing.
- ○ If necessary, adjourn and try again.

Maintain momentum

Maintain the momentum of the process by keeping the mediation in session. Participants will look to you for cues about whether there is real hope of settling; to the extent possible, you should you should emphasize the positive.

Set up joint meetings

Many commercial mediators stay in caucus continuously after the opening session, bringing participants together only to sign a settlement agreement. It can be helpful, however, to convene the participants to talk or bargain directly with each other. Full teams can meet, but more often one or a few members of each side will gather for a private discussion. The participants may be CEOs, lawyers, or experts: what is appropriate depends on the situation. Chapter Nine gives suggestions about this.

Offer or initiate process options

If bargaining falters, you can suggest options to restart the process or apply them on your own initiative. They may include:

- ○ "Confidential listener" or a "mediator's proposal," discussed in Chapter Nine.
- ○ An evaluation of one or more issues, discussed in Chapter Eight.
- ○ Anything else that seems likely to be helpful.

For ideas about what a mediator can do to overcome impasse at the end of the process, see Chapter Nine.

Commit agreements to writing

If the parties reach agreement, the next step is to convene the lawyers to write up the terms. Usually disputants prepare a handwritten memorandum that sets out key terms and calls for the execution of formal documents and payment within a specified period of time. Lawyers may take over this process, but often you will be asked to serve as the moderator or scribe; if you do, be careful to avoid acting in a way one side may interpret as biased.

For examples of later caucuses, see Chapters 14 through 21 of the DVD.

3. Follow-up Efforts

If parties are not able to reach agreement, don't give up. Instead suggest they adjourn and think things over. Contact them a day or two later to take the temperature of each camp, and then either conduct shuttle diplomacy by telephone or e-mail, or schedule another mediation session. Suggestions about how to conduct a follow-up process appear in Chapter Nine.

Conclusion

Mediation is a flexible process. Don't hesitate to modify the usual structure to meet the needs of particular situations. That said, opening sessions and private caucuses, preceded and often followed up by telephone contacts and in-person meetings, are the settings in which most commercial mediators do their work.

4. Summary of Key Points

Opening Session
- Introduce the participants
- Explain the process
- Give the lawyers an opportunity to argue and parties to listen
  - Encourage listening
  - Show you are doing so
  - Encourage the parties to talk
- Promote discussion but maintain order
- Encourage discussion and pose clarifying questions
- Make a transition to caucuses

Private Caucuses
a. Early Caucuses
- Ask open-ended questions
- Engage the principals
- Start slowly and listen carefully

- Show interest and empathy
- Perhaps start the bargaining process
- Keep rough track of time

b. Middle Caucuses

- Moderate the bargaining process
- Encourage information exchange
- Ask about interests and probe priorities
- Reframe disputants' views
- Change disputants' assessments of the merits

c. Later Caucuses

- Maintain momentum
- Set up joint meetings
- Offer or initiate process options
- Commit agreements to writing
- If necessary, adjourn and try again

In the Process: Practical Strategies and More Complex Techniques

Part II is intended for more experienced mediators. It describes the wide range of obstacles that prevent legal disputes from settling and suggests strategies to overcome them. The problems include:

○ Process barriers, such as tough tactics and narrow perspectives.

○ Psychological issues such as strong emotions and cognitive forces.

○ Merits-based obstacles such as gaps in information and poor analysis.

A Reminder about the Importance of Rapport

Before focusing on specific issues, recall something mentioned in the Introduction: your success will depend more on how people feel toward you than any specific skill. If one thing separates busy neutrals from others, it is the ability of successful mediators to establish rapport with people. Don't let a focus on technique prevent you from making rapport-building a priority throughout your work.

> *Example:* One of the best-known mediators in the world—someone whose calendar is filled months in advance with complex cases—is, of course, skilled and intelligent. What separates this mediator from other neutrals, though, is his ability to make connections with people. When a lawyer or executive calls, he chats with them in a warm tone, seeming (in a metaphorical sense) to put his arm around them. His manner is not overly familiar, but it communicates strong personal interest in the disputants and their problem.

This mediator also makes a point of mentioning a personal connection to almost everyone. In my case, it is that we climbed together more than 20 years ago. When we talk, I'm often surprised to hear him mention a mountaineering event in the Himalayas; the effect is to make me feel a special connection with him. Not surprisingly, his rapport with lawyers and parties makes them listen to his advice and seek him out when they have a challenging case.

Before the Mediation Session

You can create the foundation for success through the work you do before the parties meet to mediate. This chapter describes how to handle the pre-mediation phase of the process.

1. First Contacts

Initial questions

In a commercial case, the person who contacts you will almost always be a lawyer, most often a single attorney, calling either by agreement with other counsel or on her own initiative. What should you ask in such a conversation? Specific questions will depend on the dispute, but the following inquiries are often useful.

What are the names of the parties? Who is opposing counsel? If you have a conflict of interest, the names of the parties should alert you to it. If you know one of the lawyers, you will have an indication of why you were selected and perhaps a lead on how to proceed.

Can you give me a thumbnail sketch of the case? Lawyers' answers to this question almost always focus on legal issues, and often give you more data than you want at this point, but be patient about listening.

I do not worry about being prejudiced by one side's advocacy (it is usually identical to what they will say in their mediation statement). If, however, I know the lawyer who is calling but not the lawyer on the other side, I may caution the first lawyer not to tell me too much. ("I'm a little concerned because I know you and I've never met Mr. Gonzales. I wouldn't want him to think we've teaming up against him, so maybe we should wait to get deeper into the merits until I've called him.")

Where is the case in the litigation process? The history of the case gives an indication of how much the parties have invested in it, whether they are influenced by fresh anger or battle weariness, and whether a court date is driving the process.

Lawyers may also have questions for you. At the outset they are likely to ask about:

○ Your availability on certain dates.
○ Whether you have a bio the lawyer can show to a client or opposing counsel. (Have one ready, preferably in a form that can be e-mailed.)
○ Whether you have a conflict of interest.
○ Your fee.

Conflicts of interest

This is the time to identify potential conflicts of interest. As a practical matter, conflicts are rarely an issue for mediators who do not also practice law. People who mix law practice with mediation are more likely to confront problems, especially if they practice in a large law firm. A conflict may exist, for example, if:

○ *You are active in an organization similar to a party.* (For example, you are on the board of a church and the dispute is between a religious and secular organization, or you are a leader in the Girls' Club and the case involves the Boy Scouts.)
○ *You have a connection with one of the lawyers.* (You left the firm representing the plaintiff a few years ago, but remain socially friendly with people there.)
○ *You are active in the same organization as a party.* (You both coach in the same children's soccer league.)

Lawyers are not usually concerned about conflicts in mediation because they know that mediators have no binding authority, and as a result waive objections to issues that would almost surely disqualify an arbitrator. Indeed, savvy lawyers sometimes want their opponent to feel a connection to a mediator, thinking that this will make the party more receptive to advice from the neutral.

If a disputant has any concerns about your impartiality, it is best to decline the case. Arbitrators can reject unjustified claims of bias and go on to decide a matter, but a mediator who does not have the disputants' trust will probably fail regardless of the true facts of the situation. The key to dealing with conflicts is thus to:

○ *Disclose any potential conflicts even if they seem insignificant.* (They will almost always be waived, and you'll get points for honesty.)

○ *Ask the lawyers if their clients would be concerned by the connection* (Again, what matters is perception, not reality.)

○ *If you see a possible conflict, make a record of disclosing it in an e-mail to counsel or a memo to the file.*

2. Administrative Issues

You may work in an organization that administers cases, leaving you free to focus on mediating. If you are in a solo or small-firm practice, however, you are likely to be responsible for dealing with administrative issues. My practice is as follows:

Initial e-mail

As soon as a lawyer confirms that I have been engaged to mediate a dispute, I ask him for the e-mail addresses of counsel and the formal names of the parties. I then send an introductory e-mail and transfer the party names into a form mediation agreement.

The e-mail covers these topics:

○ Date and start time of the mediation.
○ Location.
○ That I am attaching a mediation agreement for counsel to review.
○ My policy on deposits and cancellations.
○ A request that the lawyers let me know of any concerns about who will attend.
○ My preference as to pre-mediation briefing.
○ My wish to speak privately with each side prior to the mediation session.

A sample e-mail appears in the Appendix. It usually answers lawyers' questions, and I receive very few follow-up queries.

Mediation agreement

All participants must agree on the ground rules for the mediation, preferably in writing. In some states, rules are imposed by a statute or court; in private mediation, however, most rules are set out in a written mediation agreement. The agreement deals with topics such as confidentiality, mediator immunity, and responsibility for mediation costs. An example appears in the Appendix.

Conference calls

I usually do not hold conference calls as part of my preparation for mediation because I do not find them very useful. I find most issues can be resolved by e-mail, and some of those that cannot are impossible to resolve in a joint telephone call. Individual conversations, for example, are much more effective in smoking out hidden barriers.

In multiple-party cases, however, a joint call makes sense. Examples include construction, environmental contamination, mass tort, and similar disputes. My rule of thumb is to suggest a joint call in any case that involves more than a half-dozen different law firms. The number of formal parties and lawyers is unimportant, because one lawyer can represent several parties and multiple lawyers in a firm may appear for a single client. What matters for organizational purposes is the number of different interests in the case, and this is usually indicated by the number of law firms.

E-mails in multiple-lawyer situations can trigger strings of replies, which sometimes become adversarial, especially if attorneys are posturing for clients. When this happens I schedule a conference call in which I can moderate the conversation. Such a call might cover these points:

- How many days of mediation should be scheduled and likely dates.
- Where the mediation will be held.
- The overall timeframe for the process.
- Who will provide the mediator with common information, such as a copy of relevant documents.
- Whether a site visit or other special briefing is needed.
- Deadlines for filing mediation statements and rules about exchanging statements.
- A standstill order for pending litigation.

Location

You will need an appropriate facility for the process. A neutral setting is usually best, but meeting at a lawyer's office or a meeting room at a courthouse is usually acceptable. If you use disputants' offices, try to alternate between "home courts" and avoid sites that will be seen by one side as upsetting or unfair. An employment mediation, for example, should not ordinarily take place at the employer's offices. In some situations, an informal setting, such as a country inn, can be conducive to agreement.

The main meeting room should have a table and comfortable chairs, making participants feel they are in a safe and businesslike atmosphere. If possible, the negotiators should be close enough to talk informally, but not so near they can touch (although I have never seen commercial disputants physically confront each other).

Each party should have a room in which to confer. Codefendants and insurance representatives often need separate spaces in which to meet. The rooms should be soundproof or far enough away from each other to ensure privacy. The main room at least should contain a flip chart or whiteboard. Cell phones have made landlines largely superfluous, but a speakerphone is useful to allow participants to speak with an absent decision maker or advisor.

Provide, at a minimum, coffee, tea, and water. If the session will last more than a couple of hours, make snacks available to maintain participants' energy. If the process will continue into the afternoon, order food delivered to the site to keep the participants energized and focused on the case.

3. Dealing with Inadequate Authority and Missing Stakeholders

Mediation works in large part by changing the participants' perceptions of the dispute and each other, and people are much more likely to be influenced by a process if they actively participate in it and if the right people are at the bargaining table. Who are the key people in a dispute? Everyone with significant influence over whether an agreement will be reached, whether or not they are formally a party.

There are two kinds of missing-player problems: party representatives who are present but do not have adequate authority to agree to a deal, and people who are missing from the process entirely but have enough influence to frustrate a settlement.

Inadequate authority

Ideally, mediation would bring together all of the principals in a dispute. In commercial cases, however, at least one of the parties is usually an organization, and all but the smallest organizations must act through representatives. Problems arise when the representative does not have the ability to make the difficult compromises needed to settle.

Parties may withhold authority as a tactic. ("That's all the money I've got—take it or leave it.") Often, however, the problem arises from other causes. Outside litigators may not be able to persuade senior management to focus on a dispute, or an adjuster may not want to take the time to travel personally to a mediation. Even individual parties sometimes do not appear, for instance because their lawyer wants to use lack of authority as a negotiating ploy. When this occurs, you may go through a difficult process of bargaining, only to learn that the real decision maker is not available or understands little about the dynamics of the case.

It is hard to identify authority issues ahead of time, but it is worth making at least an effort to do so because if you do not learn about them until the parties have assembled, your options are much more limited (what to do in the midst of a mediation is discussed in Chapter Five). You can use the following steps to identify authority problems.

Ask about the client. Ask each lawyer who will attend for her side. It is usually not useful to ask a lawyer directly whether a client representative will have adequate authority; such inquiries usually elicit responses such as: "We'll have someone there who can make decisions" or "The inside counsel has complete authority," when in fact he does not. If you have a relationship with the lawyer, you may be able to pick up useful hints from her about authority issues. Lawyers also experience frustrations getting the attention of their clients, and as long as they need not embarrass a client, they can be an ally in identifying problems.

You may be able to identify an authority issue by the title of the person who will attend. You can ask about the person's role at the company and his involvement with the dispute. Hearing that a chief executive officer (CEO) or chief financial officer (CFO) will attend is usually good news, for example, while learning that a party will be represented by the manager whose conduct is at issue is a danger signal.

Ask about the other side. It is often more useful to ask each attorney: "Who needs be present from the *other party* for the process to succeed?" The parties know more about their adversaries than you and can often provide valuable information about authority issues. A lawyer may tell you, for example, that the other side's managing partner or insurance adjuster needs to be present. Even if a lawyer does not name someone, asking makes it less likely you will be blamed if a problem arises later.

Ask about insurers. Many claims are covered at least in part by insurance, and as a result insurance adjusters are often key decision makers. Adjusters are constantly asked to attend mediations, however, and often try to avoid this by promising to be available by telephone. ("We'll have the adjuster on call if we need him.") The problem is that if an adjuster is not present, he may never feel involved in the process and by the time a hard decision is needed, will be away from his desk or on his way home. To avoid this, ask if there is insurance involved and, if so, who will attend for the carrier. If no one is coming and the case is significant, ask the lawyer if there is a way to get the adjuster to the mediation, and consider alerting opposing counsel to the issue.

Once an authority problem is identified, what can you do to address it? Options include:

- ○ Invite the missing decision maker.
- ○ Arrange for partial participation.
- ○ Make participation conditional on an event.
- ○ Brief absent decision makers periodically.
- ○ Alert the other side to the problem.
- ○ Arrange for recommendation authority.

Invite the missing decision maker. People who ordinarily would refuse to attend will sometimes do so if the mediator invites them personally. Sometimes the key is who will participate for the other side. Recall, for instance, the case mentioned in Chapter One, in which a mediator brokered an agreement in which the CEO for one side and managing partner of the other would attend provided the other did so.

Arrange for partial participation. If it is not possible to persuade a decision maker to be present throughout the process, you may be able to convince him to participate for part of it. An executive might, for example, be willing to attend key events such as the opening session and the mediator's first caucus with his side, exposing him to his opponent's arguments and allowing you to establish some personal contact.

Another option is to have an absent person participate by telephone. This is much less effective than personal presence, because you cannot observe the absent person and she will not develop as much investment in the process. Indeed, the absentee may have so much difficulty following a discussion over the telephone that she effectively drops out of it. Still, telephones allow a person to listen and, with special attention by the mediator, participate in the process.

Example: A high-tech company sued a former employee who had resigned to join a competitor and then recruited her software team to join her. For technical reasons, the new employer was not a party to the litigation, but it was the de facto defendant because it had agreed to indemnify the employee for any liability she incurred in the case. The competitor's general counsel refused my request that she come to the mediation, however, stressing that her company was not a party and the mediation was being held on the East Coast while she was based in Seattle.

After I emphasized the importance of the case for her company, the general counsel agreed to listen in on the opening session beginning at 6:30 AM local time, and participate by phone in every meeting I held with her side. Her presence, although limited, proved crucial to securing a settlement.

Make participation conditional on an event. If a decision maker is not willing to commit to participate, try to convince him to join if you confirm that his involvement at a certain point could be decisive. Such an arrangement both assures busy people that the burden on them will be limited and plays to their sense of importance.

Brief absent decision makers periodically. You may be able to arrange for an absent decision maker to be available to be briefed at key points.

Alert the other side to the problem. If an authority problem cannot be resolved, you should alert the other side in advance to it. It is possible an opponent will pull out of the process, but this rarely happens. The more serious danger is that a party surprised by an authority problem will accuse its adversary of bad faith.

Arrange for recommendation authority. Sometimes negotiators cannot obtain complete authority. Insurers, for example, often require settlements above a certain level to be approved by a committee, and government agencies require high officials to sign off on significant settlements.

If this occurs, an alternative is to ask a party to commit to "recommendation" authority. Here, a representative agrees to make a good-faith effort to secure approval from her superiors or constituents. The arrangement includes a "no nibbling" rule: outside reviewers are entitled to vote "yes" or "no," but cannot send the agreement back with a demand for changes.

Missing stakeholders

At times, a participant has the power to make a decision but, as a practical matter, is subject to the influence of an outsider—a so-called missing stakeholder. Dealing with a missing stakeholder is very much like addressing an authority issue, except it is even harder to identify in advance. Once the issue is identified, you can attempt to convince the missing player to participate. If that cannot be arranged, other options include setting up periodic consultations or agreeing on a process for reviewing a tentative agreement.

Example: Two siblings, David and Barbara, were fighting over the business empire of their deceased uncle. They spent five years and more than $2 million apiece on litigation, leaving Barbara bitter and David, who had been thrown out of the company when the conflict erupted, impoverished. After the first phase of the trial ended inconclusively, the two agreed to mediate. We went through a difficult first day, however, because I encountered ambivalence from David. He would make an offer, but then withdraw it after I left the room.

Barbara's lawyer became angry at this, and I hinted to him what was happening. He told me David couldn't decide anything without first talking to his wife. Unfortunately, the wife was not at the mediation; to earn money for the family she had taken a job as a bookkeeper at a local store. "Why don't you go talk to her before we meet tomorrow?" the lawyer suggested. With the assent of David's attorney, I agreed.

Early the next morning, I drove out to the auto parts store where she worked as an accountant, walked down to the basement, and, amid boxes of parts, sat down to talk with David's wife. After listening to a tearful story of family betrayal and sacrifice, I suggested that she accompany me to the mediation: it was her family's future we were discussing after all. In the ensuing hours, the wife proved to be much more decisive than her husband, and also better with numbers. The dispute eventually settled.

As this example illustrates, counsel is often helpful in identifying missing stakeholder or advisor problems, and such issues can be resolved even if they only become apparent after mediation has begun. It is much better, however, to address authority and missing-player problems in advance.

4. Information Gathering and Private Meetings

It can be useful to facilitate exchanges of information, gather data, or hold a private meeting with a disputant, before the parties meet to mediate.

Conversation with attorneys

After reading the parties' mediation statements, my practice is to have a private conversation with each lawyer. Occasionally clients will join the call, but I do not push for this because it often is impractical or makes lawyers uncomfortable. In some ways, it would be desirable to hold such a conversation immediately after being retained, but I find if I talk with lawyers weeks before a mediation, they often have not thought carefully about the process. This conversation includes questions such as:

○ *What can you tell me about the bargaining dynamics and personalities in the case? What nonlegal issues should be on my radar screen for me to be helpful to you at mediation?* These questions are meant to encourage counsel to talk about nonlegal issues.

○ *Do you need additional information from the other side to mediate effectively?* This sometimes identifies gaps in information that can be remedied before the process begins.

○ *Who is going to be present for you? Who needs to be there from the other side? Will you bring your adjuster?* Again, if there is an issue of getting the right people to the table, you need to know this.

○ *What is the bargaining history of the case? What offers have been made?* The answers may indicate obstacles to agreement. They will also give you warning about disagreements over whose turn it is to make a concession or attempts to withdraw or renege on an offer.

○ *How did this case get to mediation?* You may learn that only one side wants to mediate and has forced the other party into the process by invoking a contract clause or by getting a court order. This does not mean the process will fail, but the presence of an "unhappy camper" is important to know. It is also a reason to require deposits, because reluctant parties have a tendency to cancel on short notice.

○ *If you and opposing counsel were negotiating without any involvement by the clients, do you think you could settle without the need for mediation?* This is a nice way to ask whether negotiations are being hampered by client problems.

Information to provide

In this second conversation I state my practice about:

○ *The opening session.* I note my preference to hold a joint session. Lawyers may object to this, stimulating a discussion of whether and how to have one.

○ *Party participation.* I say that it's my custom to invite the parties to speak after their lawyer if they haven't done so already, but I don't put pressure on anyone to talk. This gives lawyers a "heads up" to prepare their clients and prevents anyone from being embarrassed by an unexpected request.

○ *Duration of the process.* I note that it's my expectation the mediation process will go as long as necessary to reach agreement; lawyers will usually warn me if someone has to leave at a specific time.

Exchanging information

The earlier in a dispute parties agree to mediate, the less likely it is they will have all the information they need to make settlement decisions. If you sense that a party is lacking a piece of data, work to ensure that they get it.

Example: A town sued a company for negligently designing a solid-waste treatment plant. It complained that the sludge produced by the plant, which it had expected to be able to market as fertilizer, was not solid enough; not only did farmers refuse the sludge but it could not be stored effectively, imposing unexpected disposal costs.

As the mediator received the parties' pre-mediation statements, he realized the town had described the alleged errors in great detail, but had given no explanation of how it calculated its $3 million demand for damages. The mediator checked with defense counsel, who confirmed that his insurer had been unable to value the claim for purposes of authorizing an offer.

The mediator explained the problem to the town's lawyer and recommended that he provide a damage calculation to the defense. A day later it arrived, totaling slightly more than $1.7 million. Counsel reviewed the document and passed it along to the insurer, who arrived at mediation with the authority to close a deal.

Techniques for fostering an information exchange are discussed in Chapter Seven.

Private meetings

People are sometimes so upset that they cannot make difficult compromises within the typical one-day time frame of commercial mediation. This is particularly true in employment, close corporation, and other disputes involving important relationships or allegations of intentional wrongdoing. In high-emotion cases, it can be helpful to meet with a party in advance, letting her begin to tell her story, form a relationship with you, and start to come to terms with her feelings before the "formal" mediation process begins.

Example: A faculty member at a Midwestern college sued her employer for sexual harassment that, she said, had cost her tenure. According to the allegations, the department chair had an "Indiana Jones" complex that included bush hats and other accoutrements. Older male faculty passed it off as "Jim's little affectation," but it made life hellish for female colleagues who did not relish his attentions.

As the mediator talked with the complainant's lawyer, it became clear the mediation would have to include discussion of how the college could support her quest for a job at another institution, and this would require the plaintiff's participation. She was not willing, however, to talk to college officials. The mediator asked the college's lawyers if they would object to him talking ahead of time with the complainant. The lawyers said they would welcome it—they didn't want to sit there while he held a long session with her.

The mediator met with the complainant for more than two hours and listened to her story. Nothing was resolved, but she seemed to begin the painful process of adjusting to her lost hopes. He talked with her about what she could say to the college president and how the session could be structured to make her as comfortable as possible. She expressed a wish to speak, but not in the presence of the professor she had accused. The president agreed to a private session and listened carefully to what the plaintiff said. She seemed calmer afterward, and the mediation went forward to a settlement.

For examples of a pre-mediation meeting, see Chapters 1 and 2 of the DVD.

Site Visits

Particularly in construction and architectural malpractice cases, parties sometimes suggest that mediators make a site visit. I do not usually find visits very helpful—photographs and drawings are generally enough to understand the situation—and they add to the cost of the process. However, if both parties want a site visit I agree if possible.

Example: A school district was litigating with a contractor over allegedly poor construction at a new elementary school. Before the mediation, the contractor's lawyer proposed a site visit. The reason, he said, was that the chairman of the school committee was complaining about issues, such as mismatched wood grain on pairs of cabinet doors, that the defendant felt had no impact on functionality and probably would not even be noticed by the teachers and children.

The school's lawyer agreed to the visit, and I toured the facility in their company. Seeing the workmanship turned out, in fact, to be helpful when I had to help the parties separate major from minor issues, allowing me to avoid "If you had only seen it" objections.

5. Early Bargaining Problems: Preconditions and Backward Steps

Preconditions

Attendance. Parties sometimes agree to mediate but then impose preconditions on the process. A typical example is attendance: a party may say that if a certain person does not attend, or occasionally if someone from the other side does appear, the process will fail. Demands that someone attend usually do not offend the other side, although they may be rejected as impractical. A request that people stay away, however, is much more likely to cause offense, because such demands are seen as insulting to the person involved and as "dictating" whom a party can select as its representative or advisor.

> *Example:* A manufacturer and general contractor were at odds over the installation of a complex heating, ventilation, and air-conditioning system in a factory. The manufacturer claimed the system was defective, while the contractor and its subcontractors countersued over the manufacturer's refusal to pay them.
>
> In a pre-mediation phone call, the lawyer for the contractor warned that the manufacturer's director of facilities could not attend the mediation. "If he's calling the shots," she said, "it's not worth mediating at all. He's an opinionated s.o.b., abrasive, and very defensive about this project. He was impossible in earlier negotiations and his lawyer couldn't control him. If he's in the mediation, my client is just not going to move."
>
> The mediator checked with the manufacturer's lawyer, who said the facilities director was going to come and the contractor had no right to tell them otherwise. After two weeks of angry telephone calls and e-mails, the contractor side reluctantly agreed to participate despite his presence.
>
> The challenged official turned out to be the soul of reason, suggesting how misunderstandings had arisen and proposing imaginative fixes. The mediator's take on the transformation was that the contractor's complaints had indirectly accomplished its goal: the director was now bending over backward to demonstrate his reasonableness to the other members of his team.

Bargaining. Disputants sometimes place preconditions on the bargaining process itself. A party may, for instance, refuse to mediate unless the other side first makes a concession. ("We won't come unless they drop to $500,000 to show their good faith.") Bargaining preconditions create problems for two reasons. First, they typically infuriate opposing parties, who see them as power plays. Second, resolving preconditions requires a mediator to begin mediating with disputants over the telephone and by e-mail, usually without the advantage of having met them first.

The fact that preconditions cause disruption makes it a good idea to check with each side ahead of time about the bargaining history of the case, asking the amount of each side's most recent offer and who bid last. If there is a disagreement, you can work to resolve it before the mediation, using the following tactics:

- ○ If a party imposes a precondition, ask for a justification.
- ○ Point out the risk of the tactic to achieving the party's larger goal, settlement.
- ○ Suggest that the party could achieve the same result by starting at its original offer and making smaller concessions.
- ○ Offer to tell other side that the party intended to impose a precondition, but agreed not to do so at your request.
- ○ Point out that the precondition will force you to start mediating without the benefit of having met the other side, reducing the chances for success.

Backward steps

A party may also take a "backward step" by retracting a prior offer. A defendant who put $100,000 on the table in negotiations six months earlier, for example, may announce in a pre-mediation conversation that there have been significant developments in the case and it is therefore cutting its offer back to $50,000. (It is also possible you will not learn about a backward step until the mediation itself.)

Opposing negotiators typically react angrily to a backward step, and they are even more likely to see it as a bad-faith tactic than a precondition. They may react by refusing to bargain until the retractor returns to its earlier position, threatening to walk out, or retracting a concession of their own.

The possibility of a backward step is another reason to ask each side ahead of time for a history of prior bargaining. If one side says it is retracting an offer, you have early notice of the problem. Even if it does not, checking the parties' histories against each other can reveal it.

Because backward steps are a form of hard positional bargaining and often do not appear until a mediation is under way, methods to deal with them are covered in Chapter Four.

6. A Pre-Mediation Checklist

Before the mediation

- ○ Have all parties agreed to mediate, and confirmed their availability on a specific date and time?
- ○ Do you have a conflict of interest? Has any potential issue been disclosed and waived?
- ○ Will all necessary persons be present, or at least available by telephone?
- ○ Have all participants paid deposits?
- ○ Have rooms been reserved and food and beverages ordered?
- ○ Have pre-mediation statements been requested? Received?
- ○ If a conference call or private conversation is appropriate, has it been scheduled?

At the start of the session

- ○ Have all parties signed the mediation agreement?
- ○ Have any nonparty participants, such as experts, signed a confidentiality agreement?

After the mediation

- ○ Has the mediation fee been paid?
- ○ Have you destroyed your private notes and confidential documents?

7. Summary of Key Points

Initial Questions

Questions you might ask lawyers:
- • What are the names of the parties? Who is opposing counsel?
- • Can you give me a thumbnail sketch of the case?
- • Where is the case in the litigation process?

Questions lawyers may ask you:
- • What dates are you available?
- • Do you have a bio to distribute?
- • Do you have a conflict of interest?
- • What is your fee structure?

Conflicts of Interest
- Disclose potential conflicts.
- Ask lawyers if their clients might be concerned by them.
- Make a record of disclosing any potential conflict.

Inadequate Authority
To identify problems:
- Ask each lawyer who will attend for her side.
- Ask who should attend for the other side.
- Ask about insurers.

To Deal with Problems:
- Invite the missing decision maker.
- Arrange for partial participation.
- Make participation conditional on an event.
- Alert the other side to the problem.
- Arrange for recommendation authority.

Preconditions
- Ask for justification.
- Point out the risk in imposing it.
- Suggest the party start at its original offer but make smaller concessions.
- Offer to tell the other side they intended to impose a precondition, but did not do so at your request.
- Point out that preconditions require you to pre-mediate by telephone.

Process Obstacles: Positional Bargaining

Process is the essence of mediation. Rather than impose a particular outcome, a mediator helps disputants communicate, bargain, analyze options, and make settlement decisions. This chapter and the next focus on the process of bargaining.

In legal disputes, parties typically arrive at mediation expecting to exchange money offers in a gradual "dance" toward agreement—so-called positional bargaining. If bargainers are experienced, have a good working relationship, or have strong reasons to reach a deal, they can usually accomplish this dance successfully. Often, however, positional negotiations degenerate into impasse. Because such bargaining so often dominates the mediation process in legal disputes, this chapter focuses on techniques to manage it.

Why not focus instead on principles or interests?

If a mediator could decide what kind of bargaining parties would use, she would probably advise disputants to avoid a simple exchange of money offers in favor of focusing on principles or satisfying parties' underlying interests. In practice, however, commercial disputants usually want to negotiate only over dollars. When this happens a mediator's practical choice is between facilitating the negotiation tactics the disputants want to use or giving up. I prefer to support positional bargaining, because I believe a money settlement is better than continued conflict and find that as the mediation process continues, disputants are sometimes willing to move into other forms of negotiation.

This does not mean you should not ask parties about principles or suggest that they consider interests. Even when disputants insist on engaging in positional bargaining, being asked to think seriously about what will happen if they do not settle makes them more realistic about their offers. If, for example, a discussion suggests that the likely damages in a case cannot exceed $500,000, a plaintiff is less likely to open with a demand of $3 million "to give us room to move." For similar reasons it makes sense to ask disputants about their underlying needs. Such inquiries are usually rebuffed, however, and in practice most commercial bargaining focuses on exchanges of money offers. When this happens what can a mediator do?

1. Give Parties the Initiative

The first suggestion may seem obvious, but it is often forgotten in the heat of the moment: until parties need your help, it is usually best to let them go forward on their own. Disputants arrive at mediation knowing that they will have to compromise, and may be able to make substantial progress. As long as the process is moving forward, you can step back and let disputants do the work. There is usually little risk in providing information, helping parties analyze data, and perhaps clearing up misperceptions, but giving advice can create problems, especially if you don't know the parties well enough to gauge their reactions. Be tentative about interventions, and if you make a suggestion keep it limited—especially early on.

You might think of your role in mediating the bargaining process as similar to a driving instructor. Your students may not handle the wheel as well as you would, and there are likely to be nervous moments. But you are usually better off letting them find their way. Even when someone is swerving off the road, a brief touch on the wheel is usually enough to put them back on the pavement. Grabbing the steering wheel can annoy everyone, so don't do it unless it is necessary.

2. Coach Participants in Effective Tactics

When positional bargainers get into difficulty, your first option is to offer advice and coaching. This can take several forms:

○ Ask about their thinking.

○ Ask about the underlying message and the other side's likely response.

○ Ask for private information about their goals.

○ Offer advice.

○ Work to minimize feelings of loss.

○ Build up esteem, and accredit their opponent.

○ Ask to convey a better offer, with a message.

Ask about their thinking

A positional bargainer's first job is to decide on an opening offer. Negotiators can gain an advantage by starting at an extreme position—high for a plaintiff or low for a defendant. This is because people who are not sure about their opponent's bargaining intentions or the value of a legal case tend to be influenced by the first number they hear. A high opening demand sways an uncertain defendant toward believing the final settlement price will be high, while a low offer can have the same effect on a plaintiff. The less certain a listener is, the stronger this effect will be. Extreme numbers thus act as "anchors," in the sense that they tend to pull bargainers in their direction. For this reason, bargainers often open at unrealistic levels.

Sometimes, however, a party has not thought through its strategy or has adopted a poor one. If a party tells you it wants to open with an extreme offer, you can ask how it was formulated. ("Can you tell me how you got to that?") Your stance should be one of curiosity rather than disagreement—a belief they have a reason and a wish to understand it. Once you know what a bargainer intends to accomplish, you can discuss whether there are better ways to achieve it.

Ask about the underlying message and the other side's likely response

Numbers, like words, have meaning, and every monetary offer carries an implied message. Positional bargainers may, for example, make an extreme offer to express anger ("There—that's what I think of your case!") or frustration ("If the court system were fair, this is what we'd be paid!"), or to suggest that the other side has not made a realistic offer itself ("Until they get down into six figures, we're not going above $15,000"). When a money offer arrives without an explanation, the recipient must decide what it means, and disputants' tendency is to interpret ambiguous signals from an adversary in the worst light. You can help to avoid this by encouraging bargainers to state explicitly the message they intend to communicate by their offer.

Once you identify the message behind the number you may be able to suggest other ways to send it. A party may realize that it can convey its viewpoint through strong arguments rather than an extreme offer. Even when a party insists on presenting a "bad" number, you can suggest it provide reasoning for it. Even an unpersuasive explanation can reassure the recipient that the offeror is willing to compromise or is acting in good faith, and indicate what it needs to do to elicit a better offer.

> ○ "I'll take your number to them, but what is the message? That you see this as a nuisance case? Or is it that you see the plaintiff's demand as everything it could recover if it won at trial—and you are responding with an offer close to the result if you won, a zero verdict?"
>
> ○ "If you want me to tell them how angry you are with their behavior over the past few months, I can do that. Give me the details, and I will convey them as forcefully as I can. In terms of an offer that will tempt them to make serious concessions, though, I wonder if . . ."

The next step is to ask disputants to think about, or predict, the other side's response. There is risk to any extreme offer. Negotiators expect some exaggeration in an opponent's first position, but a "too unreasonable" offer makes recipients angry ("That's insulting!") or leads them to decide that further negotiation is fruitless. As a result, legal negotiations sometimes stall after the first offer.

Asking a negotiator how an opponent will react sometimes moderates his inclination to take an extreme stance. If a disputant is acting out of anger, thinking about his adversary's response can provide some of the satisfaction of taking an extreme position without actually doing so, much in the way rehearsing an angry comment privately can reduce the temptation to say it out loud.

> ○ "Let's try to game this out . . . If you drop to $1.675 million from 1.7 as a first move, what do you think they'll do?"
>
> ○ "Thinking back to what you told me about their anger over delays in the project, what would your making a first offer of $50,000 probably do? Will it get the reaction you want?"

If a disputant does not assess an opponent's likely reaction realistically, you can offer your own prediction.

> ○ "I'm concerned that if you come up only $15,000, we won't see the kind of movement you need . . ."

○ "If you start at $5 million, I think they'll assume you need a settlement well into the seven figures. You may get a response from that's in the $20,000 range."

Ask for private information about their goals

If a disputant is determined to put forward a tough proposal, you might ask for a private indication of the bargainer's ultimate goal for guidance. ("I understand you don't want to put any money on the table and I'll tell the other side that. But just for my information, where would you be willing to go if they did get reasonable? For example, if I could get them down to actual damages, what kind of offer could you make?")

By this approach, you are asking the disputant to ignore the other side's current stubbornness and share some of its strategy with you. The result can be a two-level negotiation: parties exchange extreme proposals and at the same time give more reasonable signals to you. At the right moment you can ask each side for permission to reveal what it has told you privately on the condition its opponent does so as well, creating a mutual "jump toward the center."

You can also ask a party for its assessment of the other side's goal in the negotiation. ("How far down the road do you think they are willing to go to get a deal today?") By asking this, you invite the disputant to step into an adversary's shoes. You are also asking subtly about the disputant's own goal in the case—how far a party says it thinks the other side will go to settle also suggests how much the disputant itself expects to compromise.

Offer advice

Positional bargainers often act as if they do not want an agreement at all, sometimes provoking an impasse. It can be tempting to offer advice to head off such problems, but be careful about how you do so, especially early in the process when you are still feeling your way.

If you offer advice it is usually better to start with a range than a specific number. ("I'm concerned that if it's not in the middle five figures, there's a real risk . . .") As the case goes along you can make your advice more pointed. ("I think if I go to them with that there's a good chance they'll pack their bags and go home. That will leave you back in court . . ." or "I'm pretty sure you need to get to $150,000 with this next move if you want to encourage them to stay in the game.")

Bear in mind that your tone of voice and phrasing are as important as the content of what you say. Advice given in a friendly, perhaps tentative tone will be accepted readily. The same words spoken in a directive way may be interpreted as interference or even condescension.

Work to minimize feelings of loss

We will see in Chapter Six that parties' bargaining decisions are heavily affected by whether they feel they are winning or losing. Feelings of loss are particularly acute in positional bargaining, because there is only a single measure of success—a monetary scale in which a dollar gained by one party is lost by the other. Often both sides in positional processes feel they are losing, because each is giving up more than it expected to concede going into the mediation. The feeling of losing is one of the strongest influences on decision making, and bargainers who think they are losing can become very upset.

As a mediator, you need to be alert to this feeling of loss and make special efforts to minimize it. The most effective approach is to reframe the situation, by suggesting the disputant measure success from a different point of reference. Disputants who use a more reasonable point for measurement are less likely to conclude they are losing by compromising.

> *Example:* It is 3 PM. Two parties are at $1.9 million and $700,000. The plaintiff, who has been making repeated drops of $200,000, has become frustrated by the defendant's responses, which were each only $50,000. He tells the mediator to warn the defendant that, "If they don't get into seven figures with the next move, we're done!" In response, the defendant makes a new offer of $900,000. The plaintiff is furious.
>
> The mediator responds: "It's true they didn't get to seven figures, but look what they did do. Their last two moves were $50,000 each; you've now pushed them to move *four times* as much as they had before. They are now equaling your moves, and they're not done compromising."
>
> By emphasizing how much better the defendant's latest move was than its earlier concessions and by comparing it to the party's last move rather than the plantiffs "line in the sand," the mediator can help the plaintiff to feel better about the situation, or at least to save face by accepting the mediator's frame on it.

Build up esteem, and accredit their opponent

Positional negotiators often fall into a contest of egos, focusing on how they are doing relative to each other—who is winning or losing—rather than on whether the outcome is objectively worthwhile. To mitigate this, a mediator can compliment negotiators over how well they are arguing or bargaining—building up bargainers' self-esteem and cushioning the frustration they feel about compromising.

It is even possible to make competitive bargainers feel better by telling them their adversary is also feeling frustrated. (Your comments should not, however, reveal confidential facts that would weaken the adversary's bargaining position.) It may seem odd that emphasizing the negative could make someone happier, but disputants sometimes feel better at hearing that their opponent is as miserable as they are. ("The other side is feeling very frustrated. I think they had set $800,000 as their limit going in, and to find themselves going south of that is very hard to take. I think they need some time to readjust.")

Given the suspicions disputants are prone to harbor about each other it can also be useful to accredit an opponent's intentions. ("I can't read their minds, of course, but the signals I'm getting suggest they are really trying to reach a resolution today . . ." or "I understand why you think their offer is much too low, but they seemed to honestly think they were sending a signal they were serious . . .")

It is worth stressing that in doing this, you should not certify that an offer is objectively reasonable (attesting to an offer's fairness is likely to offend rival bargainers, who usually see even reasonable concessions as inadequate). By saying you think the other side is acting in good faith, on the other hand, you are simply giving an assessment of its state of mind.

Ask to convey a better offer, with a message

Make a request. You might tell a party that if it makes a better offer, you will tell the other side that it was planning to make a tougher one and changed it only at your request. This allows a disputant to articulate a tough position and at the same time offer a number more likely to evoke a useful response, while placing partial responsibility on the mediator. ("I can tell the plaintiff your first reaction was to offer nothing at all, but I asked you to consider putting something on the table to get the process going, and you then agreed to offer $20,000.") This approach can also be used when a party has made an extreme demand, the other side has refused to counter, and the offeror needs a face-saving way to make a new offer at a more reasonable level.

Example: The plaintiff lawyer in a personal injury case made an opening demand of $1.2 million. The medical bills in the case totaled $6,000, making the reasonable settlement value of the case under local standards less than $50,000. The insurance adjuster refused to respond, saying she would not dignify this "wild" number.

Talking with the plaintiff and her lawyer, the mediator learned that the lawyer had started high not because he misevaluated the case, but because he was not familiar with the attitudes of local adjusters, who expected plaintiffs to make opening offers at three to five times their actual goal. The mediator suggested the plaintiff make a new offer at a more moderate level, offering to say he was doing so only to accommodate the neutral's request that both sides "cut to the chase" and expected the defendant to reply in a reasonable way. In response, the plaintiff dropped to $150,000 and the case settled three hours later for $27,500.

Certify a new offer. Another option is to say that if a party makes a better offer, you will tell the other side that you think it is a fair move. You might, for instance, tell a party that if it "stretches" into six figures, you will say you think the offer is a constructive step forward and encourage the other side to respond in kind. Again, however, be careful of putting your credibility on the line, and never do so if there is a risk that the recipient will think you have taken sides or been duped into losing your objectivity.

For examples of coaching and advising about money bargaining, see Chapters 6 and 8 of the DVD.

3. Moderate Money Bargaining

If advice is not enough, a mediator can go further, to become the moderator of the process. Moderating is similar to coaching, but it moves beyond providing advice to giving direction. You should usually wait to take on a moderator's role until the process has gone on long enough for you to gain a feeling for the bargaining dynamics. It may not be necessary to moderate—advice may be enough and if so that is all you should offer. Here, as in other aspects of mediation, "less is more." You can moderate positional processes in several ways:

- Rephrase or withhold adversarial comments.
- Ask for a specific step.
- Delay, or transmit, unhelpful offers.
- Suggest linked moves: simultaneous steps, range bargaining, "what if?," and parallel-track negotiations.
- Divert the disputants from their clash of wills.
- Ask disputants to take the initiative.

Rephrase or withhold adversarial comments

Rephrase. You can lower the abrasiveness that often infects positional bargaining by keeping disputants separated and acting as the sole channel of communication between them. This allows you to edit what parties tell you privately into more constructive language, for example, by transmitting the positive aspects of bargainers' statements and leaving out abrasive ones or by putting a hostile comment into more acceptable language.

○ "We'll come down to fifty, but tell them if they take this thing to trial, we'll fry the defendant on the stand!" becomes "They're dropping to $50,000" and "They seem pretty confident they can make good points on cross examination of your guy."

○ "That's our offer and if we don't see a lot of movement, we're out of here," can be rephrased as "They have dropped to $. . .I think it's important you make a significant move in response, or I have a real concern they'll become discouraged and the process will stall out."

Withhold. Another option is to withhold dysfunctional comments. If the comment is simply a characterization ("Tell them it's the most generous offer they're going to see, and they'd be crazy not to take it!"), you can often delete it without adverse impact.

If, however, the comment is about a party's intentions, then the decision is more difficult, because censoring a party's expression of intent can create practical and ethical issues. Suppose, for instance, a defendant says, "Tell them we'll offer $125,000, but that's our final offer—take it or leave it!" You need not transmit the "take it or leave it" characterization, but failing to tell the recipient an offer is "final" risks confusing the bargaining process. You could justifiably delay disclosing the characterization of an offer as final if you thought the bargainer was simply venting or might change her mind, or so you could prepare the recipient to deal with it. However, once it was clear the offer was, in fact, final and the recipient had been prepared as well as possible, you would have an obligation to inform him of this.

The key is to keep the process going, but not at the expense of misleading disputants about significant communications. Don't withhold information without a reason for doing so, and be careful to avoid creating prejudice or confusion as a result.

Ask for a specific step

You can go beyond questioning or general advice to ask or recommend a party take a specific step. ("In order to keep the process going, I think that you need to come down in your next move by at least $100,000. . .")

Another option is to make requests sequentially, asking one party and then the other to take the steps necessary to keep the process alive, adjusting your advice to one side in light of the reactions of the other.

For an example of asking for a specific step, see Chapter 6 of the DVD.

Suggest linked moves: simultaneous steps, range bargaining, "what if?," and parallel-track negotiations

Parties are often more willing to make monetary concessions if they know what they will get in return. Mediators can provide this information by proposing linked moves.

Simultaneous steps. One approach is to ask both sides to make concessions simultaneously. ("I'm going to ask you to drop $200,000, and at the same time I'll ask the defendant to go up $150,000.") This plays on the human wish for reciprocity: each party knows it will not have to move without getting something in return, and also what the reply will be. If parties agree to make a large mutual jump, it can reinvigorate the bargaining process by giving each side a signal that the other is seriously interested in a deal.

Range bargaining. A variant on this is range bargaining. Here, the mediator proposes that future bargaining will occur within a stated range of numbers. If parties are at, say, $80,000 and $200,000, a mediator might say, "Can we agree that we will bargain from this point on between $120,000 and $150,000?" This is the practical equivalent of parties making simultaneous jumps, but it is sometimes psychologically easier for litigants to accept, because each side can tell itself that it has agreed only to go as far as the specific number and most of the concessions from that point on will have to be made by the other.

"What if?" The simplest way to feel out parties about reciprocal concessions is to ask "What if?," as in: "What if I could get them to come down $200,000 . . . if I could get that much movement, could you make a deal at that point?" or "Let's say I could get them to drop that far—what do you think you could do in response?" The "what if" phrasing suggests that the other side is resisting the idea of conceding, reducing the listener's tendency to devalue the potential concession. It also suggests the adversary will have to make a concession first, satisfying a positional bargainer's wish to have its opponent "sweat for a deal."

Parallel-track negotiations. Parties are sometimes willing to indicate privately that they will compromise, but not to do so "publicly" to an opponent. The result can be a frustrating standoff, in which neither side is willing to be the first to make a serious concession. One way to deal with this is by conducting "hypothetical," or "parallel-track" bargaining.

Example: A plaintiff is at $3.5 million and a defendant at $500,000. The defendant admits privately to you it is willing to "go to the very low seven figures" to settle, but it won't do so until the plaintiff gets to a "reasonable" position, and, it says, $3.5 million is not it. You respond by asking, "What would you consider reasonable at this stage, given that you are at $500,000?" The defendant answers, "No more than $2 million." You then say "Assume for a moment the plaintiff is at $2 million. What offer would you be willing to make then?" The defendant answers "Then I'd go to $700,000."

Now you ask the plaintiff the same questions. "What would be a reasonable stance for the defendant to take at this point?" (Say the answer is, "$1 million.") "How much would you come down if the defendant got to $1 million?" ("$2.5 million") The result is that you now have the defendant at $700,000 and the plaintiff at $2.5 million (admittedly, based on different assumptions about the bargaining situation).

You can then repeat the process, asking the defendant, "What would you expect the plaintiff to do in response to your $700,000?" ("1.5 million") "What would you do if they did go there? ("850,000") You can then pose the same questions to the plaintiff. Gradually the parties will approach each other.

Lawyers may be wary of parallel bargaining because it calls for them to make a concession without having actually received one from the other side. But if they understand that the other party is working under the same ground rules, and if you seem confident about what you are doing, they will often cooperate. The effect is that parties can come quite close to each other without knowing it. At that point, you can ask each for permission to reveal its most recent offer and the assumption on which it was based, provided the other does so. Alternatively, you can use the information to support other approaches, such as a mediator's proposal.

For examples of "what if?" and range bargaining techniques, see Chapters 12 and 14 of the DVD.

Divert the disputants from their clash of wills

A mediator can sometimes help parties let go of the anger and frustration stirred up by positional bargaining by temporarily diverting them. A break can help a disputant let go of a position, reducing the feeling of loss at making an additional concession. Ideally, you would suggest disputants take a lengthy break, go to lunch, or even adjourn for the day and reconvene.

There are two obstacles to this. Disputants may bridle at the suggestion that they are too upset to make good decisions; a suggestion to "take a breather" should therefore be presented tactfully. One option is to say that it is you who needs the break, for instance to review complex data, and suggest the disputants take the opportunity to get a cup of coffee or walk outside. It is hard to arrange lengthy breaks even when participants want them because parties typically agree to meet for a single day and are reluctant to risk having to come back for another session. Even in a one-day process, however, one side can step away from the process for 30 to 60 minutes while you are caucusing with the other.

If a break is not feasible, you can sometimes provide a moment's distraction by changing the subject temporarily—for example, by telling a story or giving an example from another case. Another way to divert disputants is to ask them to consider nonmonetary issues and options, obscuring their benchmarks for measuring gain and loss.

4. Address Special Problems

a. "Insulting" First Offers

Disputants sometimes insist on making extreme first offers or offering inadequate concessions. When this happens, what should you do? The first question is whether to transmit an unproductive offer at all.

Disadvantages. Recipients of extreme offers and other hard positional tactics often become angry, or at least pretend to be upset. It is almost a cliché that bargainers respond to a tough first offer by exclaiming "That's insulting!"—often complaining that the other side is being unrealistic or acting in bad faith. Negotiators may also suggest that it's the mediator's job to make the other side "get reasonable," a demand often impossible to satisfy, at least in the short run. You may be concerned that the negotiation will break down completely if a bad offer is transmitted, creating a real temptation not to communicate extreme positions.

In my experience these concerns are overrated. Angry reactions are a staple of mediation, and the caucus structure is designed in part to allow disputants to blow off steam without irretrievably offending the other side. Most parties do not expect their mediator to be able to make the other side become reasonable quickly—after all, they came to mediation because of their inability to bargain directly with the same opponent. Walkouts also virtually never occur during the early stages of the process. Disputants go to considerable trouble and expense to set up a mediation and do not end the process at the first unreasonable move by an opponent. If a mediator expresses cautious optimism that progress can be made, parties will almost always give a neutral a few hours to produce results.

Advantages. Early in my practice I sometimes withheld unreasonable or "insulting" offers, but experience has convinced me to transmit almost all offers (although I may work to improve them first). I have learned that even objectively unreasonable offers rarely destroy the process, and sometimes even have a useful effect.

For one thing, people in mediation often feel the need to be in conflict—they often want to fight for a time. We have seen that tough proposals can be a form of communication, allowing litigants to express angry feelings ("I spit on your demand!") and enjoy the feeling of telling the other side what a just outcome would be ("If the system were fair, $1 million would be cheap for this case!"). Insulting offers and angry responses can be difficult to process, but making them often allows people to vent anger and become more open to accepting difficult compromises later in the day.

An extreme proposal can also help the bargaining process by reducing "buyer's remorse"—the nagging concern that a deal has been achieved too easily. A tough offer can deflate a party's unrealistic expectations ("You can tell them that opening at $15,000 means we just don't see this as a six-figure case"), making later moves look reasonable by comparison.

A mediator can also use extreme offers as a springboard to convey information ("Here's why I think they're at this level . . ."), gather data ("Until they see evidence about . . . , it's going to be hard to get them to . . ."), or discuss nonmonetary options ("Given where they are, maybe we should focus instead on . . ."). Finally, coming into a caucus room bearing an "insulting" offer can create sympathy for a mediator ("With people like that, you have your work cut out for you!"), reducing the risk you will be "shot" for delivering bad tidings later in the process.

If you don't transmit it. Despite all this, it does sometimes make sense not to transmit an offer. The most likely reason to delay communicating an offer temporarily is to allow you to persuade the offeror to become more reasonable, supply data to support the position, or prepare the recipient for bad news.

Keep in mind, however, that you have options between conveying a bad offer and saying nothing at all. You could, for instance, give the recipient a characterization of the offer. ("They have made an offer but it is quite low. I think they are still angry and we need to . . .") This delivers a negative message, but in a more general way and with enough explanation that the recipient is less likely to become angry or feel the need to act offended. Even if a party then demands to hear the offer, your characterization will help to cushion its impact.

If you decide not to transmit an offer, do you have to tell the offeror this? In almost all cases I advise offerors of my decision. ("Given their frame of mind, I decided not to transmit your offer for the time being . . .") There are, however, situations in which it is not necessary to say so—for instance, if the parties have turned to other issues and money is temporarily off the table. You should warn that an offer was not transmitted, however, whenever not doing so would prejudice the offeror. An example of this would be if the offeror thought the other side had received the offer and refused to respond to it, when in fact it had never been communicated.

For an example of conveying an "insulting" first offer, see Chapter 8 of the DVD.

b. Impatience

Occasionally a disputant does the opposite of haggling, by saying that he does not have the time to dance around, knows his bottom line, and simply wants to state it and see whether the other side will agree. If so they have a deal; if not, everyone can save a lot of wasted time.

At one level a "cut to the chase" attitude is good news, because such bargainers are usually prepared to make major concessions quickly. However, it can also lead to disaster. One problem is that opponents who receive a real "bottom-line" offer at the outset of a process rarely believe it because they expect the usual process of haggling. The other is that a bottom line set ahead of time may not be realistic. It often represents what a bargainer wishes would happen or thinks is fair, rather than what it will actually take to close a deal. And, once bargainers state a "final" number, they often feel obligated to stick with it.

Faced with a "cut to the chase" bargainer, I use either of two approaches. One is to suggest the disputant wait before making the offer. Delaying allows the negotiator to consider new information about the case and the other side's needs before committing himself. Or, if the bargainer insists on going forward, I will recommend he inflate his number to allow for the inevitable haggling.

> I'm afraid they simply won't believe your first number is your final one. Then they'll try to push you farther and if you've decided you won't go there, we'll have an impasse.
>
> I suggest you start out higher, maybe 30 to 50 percent more [to a plaintiff]/half to a third less [to a defendant] than your final target. That will give you room to see how they respond and move forward depending on what happens."

c. Backward Steps

When you learn a party has taken a "backward step," withdrawing a concession it made before the mediation process began or even in an earlier caucus session, what can you do about it?

○ Ask about the reasoning and analyze the motivation.

○ Probe the other side's reaction.

○ Use the steps suggested for positional bargaining generally.

Ask about the reasoning and analyze the motivation

Because backward steps violate a basic convention of positional bargaining—that parties will not withdraw a concession once it is put on the table—it is important to ask for an explanation for such a move. By assuming the retracting party is acting rationally, you may acquire useful information. At the same time, you convey the message that a bargainer cannot renege on a concession without justification.

The most common reason parties give for backward steps is that they made the earlier offer to avoid litigation costs, but the other side did not reciprocate and the case has continued, eliminating their hoped-for savings. While this is logical, unless the basis is very clear—a plaintiff, for instance, has spent $50,000 to hire an expert and had told the defendant it was making its earlier offer on the assumption that settlement would avoid this cost—the explanation is unlikely to be accepted. Opponents will point out that they, too, have incurred costs in the interim and could justify retracting their own last offer on the same logic.

The next most common reason retractors give is that their legal case has become stronger because of an intervening event. A bargainer may claim, for instance, to have discovered a "smoking gun" document or to have elicited an admission from an opposing witness. Even if the other side admits that something has changed, however, it almost always discounts the significance. ("That document is easily explainable . . .The witness gave both sides good stuff . . .") Even when the intervening event is a court ruling, parties typically disagree about its meaning. A plaintiff who has a claim dismissed, for instance, will shrug it off as peripheral, while the defendant will see the same ruling as crucial to the case. Intervening-event justifications usually involve assessments of the legal merits of a dispute and should be handled with the methods described in Chapter Eight.

Whatever the stated justification, the most common reason for a party to withdraw a prior concession or escalate a demand is emotional. Parties often retract an offer out of anger, for example because the other side never responded or its reply was seen as inadequate. This is a psychological issue and can be addressed with the techniques described in Chapter Six. Parties sometimes also retract positions to gain an advantage in bargaining. They know the backward step is likely to disrupt the process temporarily, but count on the mediator to put it back on track.

Example: A plaintiff lawyer made a demand of $500,000 in a wrongful death case six months before mediation. Just before mediation, however, she told the mediator her client was now demanding $700,000. Asked why, she said that any realistic plaintiff would have offered at least $100,000 in a death case, and they could then have negotiated to a reasonable number. The defense, however, offered the laughable sum of $20,000. Her purpose in going up was to send a signal that any settlement would have to be "well into the six figures."

Probe the other side's reaction

It is likely that the other side will be offended by a retraction, or at least pretend it is, but this is not always true. Occasionally, an opponent will say it knew its adversary was going to change its position and will be willing to work with the new offer.

If, as is much more likely, the opponent is offended, you can respond by commiserating. You might then argue that the change makes little practical difference because no one expects a first offer to be accepted in any event. Instead it's the *pattern* of offers by each side that matters. Rather than argue over the first offer, why not start the process by telling the retractor you object to its move but won't be affected by it, replying, and seeing where the process is really going?

If this is not successful, you might suggest the recipient make a smaller move than it would have if the offer had not changed. If necessary, the recipient can even say that it will not consider offering a substantial compromise until the other side moves back to its earlier position.

Use the steps suggested for positional bargaining generally

A backward step is an exaggerated positional move, which can be dealt with using the general techniques for managing positional bargaining. You could, for instance, ask about or predict the likely reaction or offer to communicate a message to the other side if the retractor returns to its earlier position. ("I'm prepared to tell the defense you were inclined to raise your last demand from $500,000 to $700,000 because of the new medical report, but I asked you to stay at the $500,000 level in the interest of exploring whether a deal is possible.")

I sometimes note that the usual effect of a backward step is to lead to lengthy bargaining simply to get back where the parties were at before the retraction. There may be reasons, I say, why the bargainer needs to do this, but I ask whether she is prepared to see a large part of the time available to mediate used in this way. This warning, coupled with having a mediator listen to their frustrations, sometimes convinces disputants that they have made their point and need not actually retract an offer.

Should you warn a party that a retraction has been announced before the mediation begins? My practice is to do so unless I am fairly confident the retractor will return to its previous position, in which case I temporarily delay telling the other side. By warning parties in advance, you give them time to adjust, lessening the danger they will retaliate in anger. I have never seen a retraction cause a disputant to walk out, but the tactic does make the process lengthier and more contentious.

Conclusion

Positional bargaining is common in commercial mediation, but these techniques can help you manage it successfully. Other methods of handling stubborn positional impasses are described in Chapter Nine. Such obstacles are only one kind of process barrier, however; others are explored in Chapter Five.

5. Summary of Key Points

Give Parties the Initiative

Coach Participants in Effective Positional Tactics
- Ask about their thinking
- Ask about the message they want to send, and the other side's likely response
- Ask for private information about their goals
- Offer advice
- Work to minimize feelings of loss
- Build up their esteem, and accredit their opponent
- Ask to convey a better offer, with a message

Moderate the Bargaining Process
- Rephrase or withhold adversarial comments
- Ask for a specific step
- Delay, or transmit, unhelpful offers
- Suggest linked moves: simultaneous steps, range bargaining, "what if?," and parallel-track negotiations
- Divert the disputants from their clash of wills
- Ask disputants to take the initiative

Address Special Problems

"Insulting" first offers:
- Suggest or coach the offeror to improve it.
- Transmit it, with a characterization or explanation.
- Disclose its existence but not the terms.
- If you do not transmit it, advise the offeror.

Impatience:
- Warn of the likely reaction.
- Suggest an alternative approach.

Backward steps:
- Ask about the reasoning and analyze the motivation.
- Probe the other side's reaction.
- Use the steps suggested for positional bargaining generally.

Chapter 5

Process Obstacles: Interest-Based Negotiation and Other Issues

Positional bargaining is not the only process issue that may block a settlement. Parties' inability to negotiate well over interests may be an equal obstacle, or at least a missed opportunity. This chapter discusses how to overcome barriers to interest-based negotiation and deal with other process barriers to bargaining.

1. Inability to Bargain over Interests

One of the most important advances in negotiation theory over the past generation is the recognition that people can gain value by finding terms that satisfy each other's underlying needs, going beyond pure-money terms to "win–win" solutions. At the same time, it is often extremely difficult to develop interest-based solutions in the context of legal disputes. The problem is exemplified by this story from a leading New York mediator:

> After I left my law firm I sought out training in a community-based mediation program. The strong orientation of the seminar was on interest-based bargaining, and I left determined to make win–win solutions a key aspect of my practice. I went into my first case, involving an employment discrimination claim, and met with the employer representatives. I probed their willingness to explore imaginative solutions and found them very open to the idea. They agreed to an array of terms, including changing the plaintiff's personnel file to show a voluntary resignation rather than a firing, a letter of reference and outplacement assistance. I took all this to the plaintiff's room and explained it to the plaintiff and his lawyer. She noted it all down, nodding as I spoke.
>
> When I finished I looked to the lawyer for a reaction. "That's all fine," she said, "but what's the offer?" That's when I realized I wasn't in Kansas anymore.

Fans of the *Wizard of Oz* will remember that Kansas was Dorothy's home, before she was whisked away to a strange land in which her verities were overturned. The reality of commercial mediation is that litigants usually resist mediators' efforts to focus on interests. How likely is it that a mediator will succeed in brokering an interest-based settlement, and what obstacles arise in doing so?

a. How Likely Are Interest-Based Settlements?

Despite the extensive discussion of interest-based techniques, there is very little data about how often commercial disputants reach win–win agreements in practice. I once investigated this issue by interviewing professional mediators around the United States about the outcomes they achieve in "relationship" cases (defined as legal disputes, other than divorce and collective bargaining matters, involving a claim of more than $50,000 and arising from a significant relationship). The results were as follows:

○ Mediators reported they were able to repair the relationship between commercial disputants in 15 to 20 percent of cases.

○ Almost all of the repairs occurred in what might be called "too expensive to get divorced" situations: the parties would have preferred to sever their connection completely, but it was not financially feasible. In one case, for instance, a landlord sued a commercial tenant who had not paid its rent. The landlord would have preferred to evict the tenant, but doing so would have driven the tenant into bankruptcy and made it impossible to recover the arrearage. The landlord therefore agreed to restructure the lease, allowing the tenant to stay at a higher rent and repay the arrearage over time.

○ Although money was primary in almost all the reported settlements, it is worth stressing that most included at least one significant interest-based term. The results were as follows:

Outcomes of Legal Mediation in "Relationship" Cases

Repair of relationship	Interest-based term and money, but no repair	Money terms only	Impasse
17%	29%	27%	27%

In employment cases, for example, plaintiffs obtained a letter of recommendation, a change in their file to show they had quit rather than been terminated, and/or an apology. Employers obtained a noncompetition agreement and/or agreement by the employee never to apply again for a job with the same employer.

Here are some additional business examples:

○ In a dispute over the performance of a commercial headhunter, the parties agreed to a clause governing how long the headhunter would refrain from recruiting employees it had previously placed with the plaintiff.

○ In a case involving a partial land taking, parties agreed to provide curb cuts and access to the plaintiff's remaining property.

○ In a breakup of a physician partnership, parties agreed that wages the junior partner had earned moonlighting and felt strongly were hers alone would not be counted as partnership revenues subject to division.

What are the implications of this survey? In most commercial cases arising from a prior relationship, it *is* possible to reach agreement on at least one term that addresses a disputant's underlying interests. At the same time, it is very unlikely that parties will repair their relationships, and when a repair does occur, it is usually because a break is not financially feasible. Finally, most of the process usually focuses on legal arguments and positional bargaining over money.

b. Obstacles to Interest-Based Bargaining

Why it so difficult to bring about settlements in legal disputes based on interests? The problem is not that disputants do not know the value of interest-based bargaining. Most commercial disputes arise from contracts, and most of these agreements contain terms intended to accommodate each side's needs. Litigants, in other words, arrive at mediation with a record of creating interest-based bargains, often in the very document that gave rise to the dispute. Once in a legal controversy, however, parties stop looking for creative options and focus on money solutions. There are three major reasons for this:

○ Mutual mistrust.

○ Limitations of the commercial mediation format.

○ Fixed-pie bias.

Mutual mistrust

The first obstacle is the air of suspicion that permeates most disputes. An interest-based solution typically requires litigants to work together, or for one side to provide the other with a product or service in the future, but for a party to accept a performance term requires that it trust the other side to carry it out.

Unfortunately, by the time parties are in legal dispute they are usually deeply suspicious of each other. One side often loses faith in the other's competence—to supply nondefective widgets, to complete a construction project, or to make payments under a revised schedule, for example. The more serious form of mistrust, however, involves suspicion of an opponent's intentions.

Attribution bias. Litigants tend to assume the worst about their opponent's motives. They view every ambiguous step taken by an adversary with suspicion, assuming it is motivated by bad intentions rather than mistakes ("They intended to mislead us") and that the other side's dubious acts are part of their basic character ("That is the kind of people they are"). By contrast, people tend to view their own doubtful conduct as unintentional or forced on them. ("I meant for the best," or "Under the circumstances, what choice did I have?") This phenomenon is known as "attribution bias."

In legal conflicts, parties' suspicions are likely to be magnified by the litigation process itself. Filing suit requires a plaintiff to accuse a defendant of a violation of law, and allegations are often exaggerated for pleading purposes. Having accused an opponent, or been accused themselves, of behavior unworthy of a decent professional, disputants are understandably reluctant to consider working with or relying on the same party in the future.

Example: A consulting firm sued a foreign software vendor whom it had hired to develop a website, alleging delays and inadequate performance. The vendor countersued for lack of payment, and the parties went to mediation. For several hours they exchanged money offers but eventually fell into impasse. From private conversations, it became apparent to the mediator that the vendor did not have the financial resources to pay the amount sought by the consulting firm. The mediator also concluded that vague specifications and excessive optimism, rather than incompetence, were at the heart of the parties' disagreement.

With the vendor's assent, the mediator revealed the financial problem to the plaintiff. He suggested it would make sense to consider restructuring the contract to provide clearer performance standards for the vendor, extended time for performance, and a payment discount to compensate the plaintiff for its past problems.

The plaintiff rejected the idea of any future relationship. "You've only known these people for a few hours," its CEO said. "When we first met them they seemed competent, too, so we're not surprised they look that way to you. It took a lot of bad experience for us to learn what they're really like. No way are we going back to them!" The vendor was equally suspicious, predicting the plaintiff would find a way to "jerk us around on milestones" and avoid paying for the work. Faced with a mutual refusal to consider a relationship, the mediator returned to facilitating money bargaining.

For an example of attribution bias, see Chapter 5 of the DVD.
The following responses can help alleviate distrust among disputants:

- ○ Confront the issue directly.
- ○ Promote confidence-building measures.
- ○ Provide certainty.
- ○ Reframe the risk as familiar.

Confront the issue directly. There is little point in pretending that feelings of anger or mistrust do not exist or in asking parties who have been in bitter conflict simply to let bygones be bygones. Indeed, you can earn credibility with the parties by acknowledging that each side has serious concerns about whether they can work together in the future.

Promote confidence-building measures. Having admitted a problem exists, you can begin to work on it. Most important is to change people's doubts about their adversary's intent. If parties trust an opponent, they may excuse or allow for perceived failures of performance, but as long as they doubt the other side's good faith, convincing them to resume a relationship is very difficult. Sometimes explaining how the problem arose is enough to uncover misunderstandings and restore trust.

Example: A franchisor and franchisee were in a dispute over the franchisor's alleged inability to deliver services and the franchisee's failure to pay a $60,000 quarterly fee. It became clear any settlement would require continuing the franchise relationship. The franchisor, however, would not consider this, arguing that the franchisee was a deadbeat who had made up her allegations simply to avoid paying the fee. Asked about this, the lawyer for the franchisee explained that his client had been planning to make the payment and had only withheld it because the lawyer told her to do so.

The mediator knew the opposing lawyers in the case respected each other, and asked the franchisee and her counsel if the lawyer would be willing to go into the franchisor's caucus room to explain why the payment had not been made. He suggested the lawyer go in alone, so there would be less suspicion that he was simply protecting his client.

The lawyer went into the other caucus, explained that the franchisee had acted on his instructions, and answered questions. After talking privately, the franchisor team told the mediator they thought the franchisee had gotten bad legal advice but were less concerned about her good faith and were willing to consider restructuring the contract.

Provide certainty. People strongly prefer certain outcomes over ones that involve even a small amount of risk—what psychologists call the "attraction to certainty" (described in Chapter Six). As a result, parties attach much less value to an offer if they see any chance that the other side will not perform it. Interest-based settlements suffer more from this effect than conventional deals, because it is typically easier to guarantee that a defendant will pay a flat sum of money than to ensure that someone will carry out sometimes-complex activities in the future.

It is usually not possible to eliminate risks of implementation entirely, but it may be feasible to convince a party that a risk is manageable. To do this you should analyze less-than-certain proposals with special care, so that parties understand that any risk is minor in objective terms. If possible go further, to arrange guarantees of compliance. For example:

○ "What you're asked to assume here is that the defendant will make payments under the new schedule. But the proposal gives you a judgment in escrow, a penalty for late payment, and a guarantee of lawyers' fees if you have to collect. Do they really have any incentive not to make a payment—and if they do miss one, can't you bring them into line pretty quickly?"

○ "It looks as if the contractor has been committing resources to this project for almost a year. That makes me concerned, if you now order it off the job you'll draw a huge damage claim. Is there a way to restructure the contract, maybe with an increased bond and milestones for performance? It might well be cheaper for you than a straight break."

Another option is to provide a reliable process to discourage the other side from cheating or provide assurance of rapid compensation if they do. "Summary arbitration" of disputes arising from a settlement, described in Chapter Nine, can accomplish this.

Reframe the risk as familiar. If people must take on a risk, they strongly prefer one that seems familiar. People are much more willing, for example, to accept a commonplace risk like jaywalking on a busy street than one they see as unusual, such as walking with a guide along a cliff. This is true even when the consequence is the same in either case (serious injury or death) and the familiar risk is actually more likely to occur than the novel one. Social scientists call this the "preference for familiar risks."

In the context of disputes, the preference for familiar risks means that parties worry much more about settlements that create risks unfamiliar to them than ones posing dangers that seem ordinary. To deal with parties' concern, try to reframe an unusual risk into familiar terms. You might say, for instance, "Taking responsibility for a new roof not leaking is just like giving a warranty. You give warranties on your work, don't you? What's the typical length of time they run?"

I sometimes analogize the risk posed by an imaginative option to the danger of using a mule to transport a load—something that is not exactly familiar to people, but seems relatively mundane and humorous. "In order to make use of a mule," I say, "you don't have to believe it will never kick, only that you won't get hurt as long as you don't stand in back of the mule. The issue is to find a way to restructure the deal so you get it to work for you, but not put yourself in a position to be kicked"—in other words, think of your opponent as a balky mule.

Other ways to deal with peoples' wish for certainty and familiarity are explored in Chapter Six.

Limitations of the commercial mediation format

A second obstacle to inventive bargaining is the structure of commercial mediation itself. Parties usually send, as their representatives, litigators and people with checkbook authority. Interest-based solutions, however, require bargainers who can think "outside the box." The more imaginative a proposal, the more likely it is that new people and information will have to be brought in to develop it.

This is difficult, however, because commercial mediations are usually scheduled for a single day. This confronts mediators with a difficult choice:

encourage parties to devote time and energy to exploring an imaginative option, or seek a simple deal based only on money? Adjourn and perhaps lose momentum so parties can gather data and consider options, or focus on hammering out a narrow agreement today? The following steps can reduce the problems posed by the commercial format:

○ Do advance work.

○ Adjourn temporarily.

○ Create parallel discussion tracks.

○ Suggest a time-limited discussion.

Do advance work. One step is to extend the process beyond a single day. This does not mean scheduling additional mediation sessions, but rather identifying underlying issues through pre-mediation conversations. Once an issue has been identified, you can ask the parties to assemble the information and bring in the people needed to address it.

Adjourn temporarily. Another option is to adjourn an ongoing mediation to permit an idea to be considered. There are obvious drawbacks to stopping, and doing so is a judgment call. The following is a case in which adjournment proved effective.

Example: A computer manufacturer brought a warranty claim against a chip maker that had inadvertently supplied it with defective chips. The manufacturer agreed that the chip maker was competent and the problem was caused by an adhesive compound supplied by a reputable outside company. It argued, however, that the chip maker was legally responsible for the problem under a warranty.

The chip maker said it did not have enough cash on hand to pay the tens of millions of dollars the manufacturer was demanding. It proposed making a low-seven-figure payment and providing additional compensation in the form of discounts on future chip orders. The manufacturer agreed to the concept, conceding privately to the mediator that it continued to need the chip maker's products. However, none of the lawyers or financial people at the mediation knew what products the manufacturer would require from the defendant over the next few years.

The parties agreed to adjourn for a month so their product teams could confer about a new chip the defendant had under development. Two months later, a deal was worked out that included cash and a discount on future orders.

Create parallel discussion tracks. You can also suggest that the parties bargain along parallel tracks, concurrently discussing monetary offers and interest-based proposals. I sometimes say, for example, "One of the advantages of mediation is that it can go forward on two levels at once. You can make offers back and forth, and at the same time authorize me to explore whether there is anything in addition to money that might help reach a settlement. To do this I need two things to take to the other side: a new money offer and the data you need to think about a restructured contract."

Suggest a time-limited discussion. If you are not sure whether an interest-based option is feasible, consider designating a limited time for discussion, leaving time for money bargaining if more imaginative options fail.

> *Example:* A condominium association sued several contractors over a leaking roof, demanding the roof be entirely replaced at a cost of $1.4 million. The case went to mediation. Six defendants argued vehemently that the roof could be repaired for no more than $300,000.
>
> Hearing this, the mediator said to the defendants: "I suggest we think about whether you as a group can agree to repair and guarantee the roof. From what you tell me, that might be a much lower-cost option. I'm aware, though, that Nancy has to leave for the airport at 4 PM, and she holds the largest checkbook. So I suggest we explore the repair option for the next hour and a half. If it doesn't work we can go back to putting together a money offer."
>
> The defendants talked cooperatively for 90 minutes, but the initiative foundered over their unwillingness to guarantee the repair for ten years. They then returned to talking about money—and within an hour the group raised their offer from $200,000 to $700,000. A month later the case settled at $1.1 million.

Fixed-pie bias

Even when they are not involved in a legal dispute, negotiators have great difficulty recognizing opportunities for interest-based bargains, because they assume the other side's interests are directly opposed to their own. Negotiators, in other words, view the "pie" of items over which they can negotiate as fixed, forcing them into win–lose bargaining. This phenomenon, known as "fixed-pie bias," inhibits bargainers from looking for mutually beneficial trade-offs. Fixed-pie bias is a special problem in legal mediation, because parties are typically represented by lawyers who naturally think in terms of the remedies a court could award, usually limited to money.

There is no single solution to narrow thinking. It helps to expand the participants to include executives and transactional lawyers, but even this will not change a team's thinking as long as it looks to its courtroom warrior for guidance. Usually, it is necessary to take other steps to stimulate broader thinking, a topic discussed in the next section.

c. Helping Parties Identify Interests

Apart from dealing with cognitive obstacles such as attribution bias and the preference for certainty, a mediator can encourage parties to think more broadly about interests in the following ways:

○ Ask specifically, and listen for clues.

○ Suggest needs, and give examples.

○ Ask each side to analyze the other's interests.

○ Be tactful but persistent.

Ask specifically, and listen for clues

It may seem obvious, but given the blinders with which disputants approach negotiations, you can often accomplish a good deal simply by inquiring actively about interests. Ask the parties directly about their needs and draw on their knowledge of their situation. Pose broad, open-ended questions and tolerate silence to encourage people to talk.

There is an issue of timing here. You can ask about nonlegal issues in pre-mediation conversations and refer to creative solutions in your opening comments. If the disputants do not respond, however, you should not pursue the issue in the opening session. It is usually better to save specific probing about interests for private meetings, because parties are often reluctant to mention nonlegal concerns in the presence of an opponent. Plaintiffs are especially sensitive about this, out of concern that if they show openness to other options, it will be taken as a signal they are not committed to their money demands. As the earlier *Wizard of Oz* example suggests, defendants tend to be more willing to discuss interest-based options because they see them as a substitute for money.

Even in private you will often have to wait to focus on interests. If you immediately push disputants about their needs, they may become annoyed that you are not paying enough attention to their legal arguments or are not being sufficiently "hardheaded." This is a particular risk if you are perceived as young or inexperienced.

When you do ask about interests, pursue them diplomatically. Don't press a lawyer or party hard about something she may not have thought through or may be reluctant to discuss. It may help to say that you are asking only as background information and will check back before mentioning the issue to the other side. Here are some other suggestions:

○ Whenever possible, mention reasons for looking beyond money, tying your suggestions to something you have seen in the case. ("Given that the parties had a good business relationship for more than ten years and no one is alleging intentional misconduct, I am wondering . . ." or "The defendant does not seem to have assets available you could collect if you won. Perhaps we should think about . . .")

○ When talking with plaintiffs, it is helpful to pose the issue as whether there are any items that could be included as *extra* items in a settlement, suggesting that the plaintiff will not have to sacrifice its money demands to achieve other goals. Once a party has articulated its interests, you can ask what priority to give to them.

○ Listen carefully for clues and references to nonlegal concerns. A gap or incongruity in a party's analysis can indicate that something lies beneath the surface. Sometimes one side will provide a lead to a problem in the other camp.

Example: A failed businessman sued a bank that had foreclosed on his property, claiming he had been misled by the bank's president when he took out his loan. As the mediator caucused with the defense, the lawyer asked in an irritated tone why the plaintiff was bothering to press the suit, since he had other creditors who would quickly seize any judgment he might obtain against the lender. The lender then threatened to buy up the other claims at a few cents on the dollar and use them as set-offs to cancel any judgment the plaintiff might obtain.

The mediator was intrigued by this and asked the plaintiff how he planned to deal with his other creditors. It turned out that the plaintiff was also attempting to buy up the debts but did not have enough money to do so. A settlement was eventually reached that included the bank's agreement to buy up the plaintiff's debts and then cancel them.

Suggest needs, and give examples

Suggest interests you think a party might have, and cite examples from other cases or your general experience in which litigants have achieved good deals by going beyond purely monetary solutions. ("I find that companies who sue for infringement are often willing to talk about a licensing deal, because of the risk their patent will be declared invalid. But they're concerned about distinguishing one deal from another to avoid having to give 'most favored nation' rights to other licensees. Is there something we can do to. . .?")

Ask each side to analyze the other's interests

Another option is to ask each side to think about what its opponent might value in a settlement. Such questions sometimes feel less threatening to litigants than inquiries about their own needs and produce interesting information. You can pose this question to a team as a "homework assignment" while you are meeting with their opponent.

Example: The president of an international disaster relief organization was abruptly removed from office just before a major conference at which she expected to be honored for her leadership. Members of the organization's board said they had acted out of concern that the president was authorizing large expenditures for the meeting and refusing to give them any information about finances. The ousted president sued for reinstatement, and after a year of legal maneuvering the case went to mediation.

The mediator quickly realized the plaintiff had a weak legal claim and, because the organization's officers served without pay, almost no out-of-pocket damages. She insisted, however, that the group pay her $100,000 to compensate her for her lost reputation. The organization representatives refused, ridiculing the damage claim and saying they would never waste members' contributions on a legal settlement.

The mediator remarked to the defense team that the plaintiff seemed to be motivated heavily by feelings of humiliation and lost honor. As he left the caucus room, he asked them to think about what could be done to satisfy her concerns. When he returned, the defense team suggested the organization could reinstate her as president-emeritus, with an appropriate statement of appreciation in the organization's newsletter and other gestures of respect.

Without indicating the source of the idea, the mediator floated it with the plaintiff, who responded positively. The discussion turned to how reinstatement would work and how any statement would be worded. The mediator said he would talk over the idea with the defendant group, and suggested that while he was gone the plaintiff begin to prepare a draft of an announcement.

Be tactful but persistent

When you ask about interests, don't be surprised or offended at being rebuffed, often with comments suggesting the whole topic is a waste of time. It's common for such questions to be dismissed initially. Persistence is required, and if an area seems fruitful, a good mediator will return to it periodically. Focusing on interests can be most effective late in the process, when disputants realize positional bargaining is not working or are seeking psychological "cover" for a concession they now realize is necessary.

> *Example:* In the computer chip case described earlier, the manufacturer's inside counsel had a difficult time convincing management to accept the cash component of the deal, which was much lower than the loss estimate the company had prepared for litigation. The clincher came when she was able to get the defendant to agree to give the company a 10 percent share of its recovery in any future lawsuit against the adhesive supplier. There was very little chance such a suit would succeed, but if it did the chip maker had estimated the recovery could total as much as $75 million, making the manufacturer's potential share a serious number. With that added to the mix, management approved the settlement.

For an example of exploring interests, see Chapters 1 and 9 of the DVD.

d. Assisting Parties to Develop Settlement Options

After identifying interests, the next task is to develop options to satisfy them. The following tactics are effective for doing this:

○ Change the format, and provide information.
○ Encourage direct communication.
○ Set up a brainstorming session.
○ Introduce new people.
○ Help the parties bargain over options.

Change the format, and provide information

The tension that accompanies most legal negotiations makes it hard for the participants to think creatively and exacerbates the problem of fixed-pie bias. Taking a short break can help spur inventiveness. Alternatively, you can change the physical configuration of the discussion—for instance, by inviting people to look together at a list of options sketched on a whiteboard. It can also help to suggest an exchange of information.

Encourage direct communication

There are obvious advantages to having parties talk directly rather than through a third party. Indeed if the goal is to find a way for parties to work together in the future, it is often essential for key personnel to talk directly.

Example: In the condominium roof dispute described earlier, the parties deadlocked at a demand of $1.1 million and an offer of $1.05 million. The gap was only $50,000, but neither side would move. The defendant's lawyer admitted privately to the mediator it made sense to settle even at the higher number, but he could not persuade his client to go any farther.

The mediator sensed that other factors were in play for both decision makers. The chairman appeared concerned about being attacked by militants on his board if he brought back a settlement below $1.1 million. The development company's lawyer indicated his client was worried that if he gave in on this point it would become a precedent in ongoing negotiations he was conducting with the board on other issues. Both lawyers said, however, that the chairman and the CEO got along well on a personal level.

The mediator suggested to the plaintiff's lawyer that his board chair ask the defendant's CEO to lunch. The two met, and the chair explained the pressures on him, asking if something could be worked out. A week later the CEO agreed to put in the extra $50,000, subject to the payment being spread over a three-year period. The condo board approved the terms and the case was resolved.

Set up a brainstorming session

There are advantages to having disputants meet together to explore interests; participants can exchange ideas quickly and get the feeling of working together. But disputants are often too angry or distrustful to speak candidly with each other, at least at first. Participants may also be afraid that if they talk directly, "cement will set" around an idea they later want to discard.

You can deal with these concerns by keeping the parties apart until they have developed confidence in their ideas. Another way to respond to cement-setting concerns is to set up a "brainstorming" session, in which parties talk together under a ground rule that participants are free to disavow any idea they later decide is unworkable. This sometimes makes people feel freer to throw out possibilities without first thoroughly vetting them.

Introduce new people

If the people involved in a mediation are not open to new ideas, consider bringing others into the process. Apart from having different expertise, people who have not been involved are less likely to feel locked into past proposals.

Help the parties bargain over options

Once an option has been developed, the next task is to negotiate terms to implement it. This stage can strongly resemble traditional bargaining, because the fact that parties have agreed to "bake a bigger pie" by focusing on interests does not mean that they have agreed how large a "slice" of the pie they each will receive. If, for example, two businesses agree to end a dispute by restructuring a contractual relationship, they must still work out how to allocate the risks and benefits of the new arrangement. The challenge at this stage is to help negotiators remain flexible enough to find the most valuable combination of terms, while at the same time bargaining for an appropriate share for themselves.

For an example of managing bargaining, see Chapter 17 of the DVD.

2. Clashes of Style and Tactics

So far the discussion has assumed that both negotiators are using the same bargaining approach, and the problem is that they are not able to carry out their strategy effectively. Parties are even more likely to run into difficulty, however, when each side uses a different style of bargaining. A negotiator who favors an interest-based approach, for example, may become frustrated when the other bargainer just demands a "number." Differences in how parties use language can also cause problems: words one negotiator sees simply as "the usual back and forth" of negotiating can anger another bargainer.

Clashes of tactics and style can be either innocent or intentional. A negotiator may fall into a problematic approach accidentally due to lack of experience or other causes, or may seek to place the other side at a disadvantage intentionally. To deal with clashes of style consider the following approaches:

○ Explain, reframe, or accredit the behavior.
○ Coach the offender.
○ Help disputants agree on process rules.
○ Act as a referee.
○ Separate the disputants.

Explain, reframe, or accredit the behavior

Explain. Sometimes the problem is less the behavior itself than how the other side interprets it. This is compounded by the tendency, mentioned earlier, of people in conflict to attribute the worst motives to each other's actions. A mediator can sometimes use her credibility to explain to an offended party that the other side sincerely believed certain behavior was appropriate. The explanation may convince the offended party to revise its interpretation of what occurred. Even if it does not, the party may pretend to accept the explanation as a face-saving reason to drop the issue and move on.

Example: Parties were meeting to resolve a dispute between a general contractor (General) and his electrical subcontractor (Sub) over work during the construction of an office building. The lawyer for the Sub arrived at mediation wearing jeans and a Mickey Mouse T-shirt. The General's representative was insulted, interpreting the shirt in particular as a disrespectful gesture.

During a bathroom break, the mediator chatted with the Sub's lawyer and said with a smile, "You know, if you wanted to drive Jim nuts with your shirt, I have a feeling you're succeeding. He thinks the message is that this whole negotiation is a joke." The lawyer replied that he'd worn the clothes to go out to look at the project, and that people in the construction trade often attended job meetings in work clothes. He admitted the mouse shirt might have been "a little over the top," but said he'd been in a rush and had just grabbed the first thing in his drawer.

The mediator said that he thought he could explain the informal clothes fairly easily, but the mouse emblem was really rubbing the other side the wrong way. The mediator then went to General's team and explained about the early-morning site visit. When the parties reconvened, the Sub's lawyer apologized for his clothes, the General's representative said he understood, and the process went forward more smoothly.

Reframe. Another option is to reframe the offending message. Reframing means suggesting either a different *meaning* for the behavior (for example, that the lawyer had picked the mouse shirt quickly out of his drawer and had not meant it as an insult) or a different *context* in which certain behavior is more acceptable (for instance, placing wearing jeans in the framework of a visit to a construction site). The following is another example of a mediator reframing an inflammatory remark.

Example: During a mediation of a case arising from a failed partnership, the defendant's lawyer argued vehemently that the plaintiff's lawyer had committed malpractice when drafting the partnership contract. This accusation inflamed the plaintiff side, requiring the mediation to be adjourned temporarily. A few days later the plaintiff lawyer produced a recently signed affidavit in which a key witness not only rebutted the defendant's version of events, but went on to say that the defense lawyer had told him he would be given free legal counsel if he changed his story, which the plaintiff lawyer said was intended to incentivize the witness to perjure himself.

When mediator shared this information with the defense, the attorney became angry and threatened to leave, saying he would not stand for being accused of misconduct. The mediator replied that he thought the abetting-perjury innuendo was simply a "high inside fastball," thrown by the other side in response to the defense lawyer's own "hardball" charge that the plaintiff lawyer had committed malpractice. The defense lawyer, who did not really want to walk out and didn't mind being characterized as a tough player in front of his client, sat down. Both the perjury and malpractice issues were tacitly dropped from the discussion.

Accredit. You can counteract some of disputants' tendency to attribute bad intentions to adversaries by lending your own credibility to the act at issue (for example, by suggesting to the offended side that its opponent did not really mean to insult it or that the conduct is otherwise explainable). In the T-shirt case, for instance, if the mediator went beyond reframing (repeating the plaintiff lawyer's explanation) to give his own take on the situation, by saying he personally did not think the lawyer meant any disrespect, he would be accrediting the lawyer's explanation.

Accreditation can sometimes be done for tactical reasons: a mediator may doubt the innocence of certain behavior, but think it is in both sides' interest to see it as acceptable. By suggesting that he believed the Sub lawyer's explanation, for instance, the mediator would make it easier for the other side to let the incident pass without losing face.

There is danger in accrediting, however, because it can put a mediator's credibility at issue. If the listener does not agree with the interpretation, or does not accept that the mediator, although wrong, is seeking to help both sides, she may decide the mediator has been taken in, impairing the neutral's future effectiveness.

Coach the offender

You may be able to coach an offender to use a less abrasive style, either by modeling good skills yourself or by alerting the person to the impact of her behavior. ("I think your referring to their conduct as 'fraud' is striking a raw nerve. Under the law it doesn't matter whether they made an inaccurate statement intentionally or carelessly—the damages are the same. I'd suggest referring to it simply as a 'misrepresentation' and not focusing on intent. You'll probably get more movement from them.") Even bargainers who are misbehaving intentionally will often stop or moderate their behavior if the mediator suggests it is harming the bargaining process.

Help disputants agree on process rules

Some behavior is irritating simply because it differs from the other negotiator's expectations. It would be considered insulting, for example, to appear an hour late for a business negotiation in America without a good explanation, but this may not be true in other cultures. Settings count as well: people become upset if they are kept on hold on the telephone for several minutes, but are less likely to be angry if an opposing team steps out of a meeting to confer for the same amount of time. If an explanation does not resolve a problem, you can treat it as an issue for negotiation.

> It is 9:50 am at a mediation scheduled to begin at 9:30. The plaintiff team and defense counsel are present, but the defendant has not appeared and cannot be contacted. The mediator asks, "Should we wait a while longer, or should I talk with plaintiff until the defendant gets here, and we'll then meet together for the joint session?"

Act as a referee

If parties cannot agree on how to handle an issue, you can impose ground rules to deal with it. Parties can decline to go forward under a mediator's proposed rule, but they are likely to accept it, both to avoid losing their investment in the process and because the neutral is seen as an honest broker.

> One side repeatedly arrives late at mediation sessions, annoying the other. The mediator responds by suggesting a ground rule: "We'll shoot for 9 AM but it's understood someone might be held up. If that happens, it's OK for me to start talking with whoever arrives first. Does that make sense?"

Separate the disputants

Most legal mediation occurs in a caucus format, allowing the mediator to control interactions. By keeping disputants separated, a neutral can edit abrasive comments. ("Tell them if they don't take it in the next 15 minutes we're out of here!" might become "They're feeling pretty frustrated. . .I think they need at least a preliminary signal soon to stay engaged. . .") You can also head off troublesome tactics before a party implements them. If nothing else works, use your power as translator to screen out counter-productive behavior.

A lawyer tells a mediator in caucus, "I don't see any point to my client sitting here any longer. She's going back to the office. I can phone her if there's any need to talk." The mediator fears the opponent will inter-pret this as the other side "blowing off" the process and not making an equal effort by staying at the mediation site, as he is doing.

In response, the mediator could explore the likely impact of the cli-ent leaving with his lawyer, perhaps mentioning that the other party is feeling equally frustrated. The mediator could ask the lawyer what she thinks can be done to deal with the problem. He might suggest that the party threatening to leave wait a bit longer so he can convey their frus-tration to the other side, or that the lawyer and client go out for a coffee break but keep their cell phones on so he can call them back.

For an example of a clash of styles, see Chapter 4 of the DVD.

3. Omission of Key Stakeholders or Decision Makers

Chapter Three described the problems that arise when parties do not send representatives to mediation with the authority needed to resolve a dispute. Ideally a mediator would identify an authority problem before a mediation began and deal with it (for instance, by negotiating for the right person to participate). Often, however, you will only learn about the problem when the process is under way. When this happens you have these additional options:

○ Look for indications of authority issues.

○ Make an ally of informal advisors.

○ Use limits on authority as an inducement to settle.

○ Neutralize a missing party.

Look for indications of authority issues

If a party appears to be having unusual difficulty making decisions or raises illogical objections, ask yourself whether they have an author-ity problem. If you suspect one exists, ask the representative or the law-yer about it. You might cushion the question by noting that there are inevitable limits to anyone's authority and ask whether the negotiator needs an OK from someone outside the room.

Make an ally of informal advisors

Sometimes the principal is present, but will not make decisions because he is relying on an absent advisor. This is particularly true of individual disputants, who often ask relatives or friends for advice. Such advisors may not be familiar with the facts of the case and may not have expertise in the subject matter; a plaintiff, for instance, may ask a brother who is a real estate lawyer for advice about an employment dispute.

It is important to identify such advisors and make sure they have an accurate picture of the situation. You can often convert absent advisors from obstacles into allies. An informal advisor, in particular, is often concerned primarily to ensure that the friend gets a reasonable result and that she is not criticized for it. If you can convince the advisor you are genuinely seeking to assist the party she will often become an ally, using her credibility to convince the disputant to accept your recommendations.

> *Example:* Recall the example in Chapter Three of two siblings fighting over the business empire of their deceased uncle. One of them repeatedly reneged on tentative offers. The mediator learned that the indecisive brother was consulting his wife, who was not present because she was working as a bookkeeper at a local store. The next morning the mediator went out to talk with her at her worksite, convinced her to participate, and drove her into the mediation. With his wife present, the husband became much more decisive and the case settled.

Use limits on authority as a lever to induce agreement

If you are persuaded a negotiator's authority is truly limited, ask for permission to reveal the problem to the other side. Doing so lessens the risk that the opponent will become angry over the seeming obstinacy of the party. In the right circumstances you can even use lack of authority as an inducement to settle, by pointing out that agreeing to terms within the other bargainer's authority will avoid the delay and unpredictability of consulting outsiders who are not familiar with what happened at mediation.

Neutralize a missing stakeholder

A related problem exists when a key stakeholder is not a party to the process at all. Most of the tactics described to deal with lack of authority also apply to situations in which stakeholders are missing entirely. If a missing stakeholder cannot be brought into the process, it is sometimes possible to neutralize the person's ability to interfere with a settlement.

Example: A real estate developer filed a petition for a zoning change in order to convert a building on the edge of a residential neighborhood into a nursing home. The court papers described the parties as the developer and several objecting abutters. The neutral later learned, however, that the moving force in the case was a neighborhood preservation group using the abutters to gain standing to sue. And, as later became apparent, the preservation group's legal bills were being paid by a rival nursing home owner who wanted to prevent the project from going forward at all.

If the mediator had dealt solely with the named parties to the zoning case, the dispute might never have been resolved. Working with the developer and the neighborhood group, however, the mediator arranged modifications of the project to meet the citizens' concerns. In return they assisted the developer to neutralize the behind-the-scenes attacks by the nursing home owner.

4. Inconsistent Interests

Even when the parties to a dispute would benefit from a settlement, their bargaining agents (for example, managers or lawyers) sometimes frustrate a resolution to protect themselves. Lawyers, for example, are sometimes accused of churning cases to increase their fee, and executives may resist outcomes that cast doubt on a prior decision. Because people do not disclose inconsistent motives and opponents tend to be overly suspicious of them, it is hard to know how often such problems actually arise. When confronted with a participant who seems to be motivated by interests inconsistent with settlement, you can take the following steps:

○ Satisfy or align interests.

○ Arrange settlement terms to accommodate the inconsistency.

○ Bring in new players whose interests are not in conflict.

○ Confront the player.

Satisfy or align interests

You may be able to align a disputant's personal interests with those of his principal, making the person more amenable to an agreement. If, for example, a bargainer is concerned a settlement will harm her reputation, you might make a point of complimenting her in front of her client for her toughness.

Arrange settlement terms to accommodate the inconsistency

Even when the client's best interests would call for a particular outcome, it may be necessary to build in additional terms to satisfy the special needs of a participant.

Example: Recall the case, described earlier, in which the president of a charitable organization was abruptly dismissed by her board. The board suggested an imaginative solution that would temporarily reinstate the president and extend appreciation for her service. There was a problem, however: the ousted president's lawyer had accumulated $20,000 in unpaid legal fees which he had planned to recover through a cash verdict or settlement. The board refused, however, to consider paying out hard-earned contributions to someone who they felt had harassed them.

The mediator talked with the organization's insurer, pointing out how much it would cost to defend the case and asking it to put in money to cover the plaintiff lawyer's fee. The insurer eventually agreed to pay $10,000 toward unspecified damages, with the check made out to the plaintiff's law firm, and the case settled.

Bring in new players whose interests are not in conflict

Mediation's flexible format provides opportunities for a neutral to bring in new participants, as well as to speak directly with the principals. You can, for example, avoid concerns that an lawyer is distorting the situation by explaining directly to a corporate executive, in the presence of his lawyer, why a settlement would serve the company's interests. If the obstacle is an individual party representative, you can work to involve someone else from the same side whose interests are more consistent with the party's.

Indeed, savvy lawyers sometimes go to mediation primarily to bypass an obstructive lawyer on the other side. You can sometimes accomplish the same result by asking both sides to bring in different personnel (for instance, CFOs or CEOs) to replace lower-level representatives who are not able to agree.

Confront the player

If players with inconsistent interests cannot be aligned or avoided, they can sometimes be confronted. You can, for example, note in a private conversation with a lawyer that you are aware of the lawyer's need to cover his fee and ask how a settlement might be structured to meet it. By raising such issues directly, you give the person an opportunity to suggest solutions, and at the same time make it clear you understand his agenda. Professionals sometimes back off from pursuing inconsistent personal goals when they realize their strategy is apparent to others.

5. Summary of Key Points

Inability to Take Advantage of Interests
a. Address Obstacles
- Mutual mistrust
- Limitations of the commercial format
- Fixed-pie bias

b. Help Parties Identify Interests
- Ask specifically about them, and listen carefully for clues
- Suggest needs and give examples
- Ask each side to analyze the other's interests
- Be tactful but persistent

c. Help Parties Develop Responsive Options
- Provide time, space, or information
- Encourage direct communication
- Encourage brainstorming
- Introduce new people
- Help the parties bargain over options

Clashes of Style and Tactics
- Explain, reframe, or accredit the behavior
- Coach the offender
- Help the disputants agree on process rules
- Act as a referee
- Separate the disputants

Omission of Key Stakeholders or Decision Makers
- Look for indications of authority issues
- Make an ally of informal advisors
- Use limits on authority as an inducement to settle
- Neutralize a missing party

Inconsistent Interests
- Satisfy or align interests
- Arrange settlement terms to accommodate the inconsistency
- Bring in new players whose interests are not in conflict
- Confront the player with the inconsistency

Chapter **6**

Psychological Issues: Strong Emotions and Cognitive Forces

Helaine Scarlett Golann

Lawyers and executives are tempted to treat conflicts as contests of logic or tactics. The problem, they say, is that the other side is not analyzing the case well or is not bargaining fairly, and the solution is for them, or the mediator, to do so. But feelings are at least as important as facts in creating and sustaining conflict, and legal negotiations are often derailed because of them.

Humans swim in a "sea of emotions." Like fish we may not perceive we are operating in an environment of feelings, but it exists all around us. The judgment of participants in legal cases is often affected, and sometimes overwhelmed, by strong feelings, ranging from guilt and sadness to jealousy, frustration, and anger. Emotions are usually triggered by the events that gave rise to the dispute—the belief the other side was deceitful or reckless in its allegations, for instance. Even when the substance of a dispute is not inflammatory, people often become angry and frustrated over the way it is litigated or negotiated. The family of an accident victim

93

or a party to a sexual harassment claim, for instance, is likely to experience intense emotions if they believe they are being forced to agree to an unfair compromise in their case.

Negative emotions are even more intense when a conflict affects someone's core identity. A person who loses his job, for example, often forfeits not only income but also important aspects of his personal identity and self-respect as a professional or breadwinner. An attack on a person's identity is like striking a raw nerve in a tooth—emotions are magnified, further disrupting the settlement process.

Example: A 60-year-old software engineer, James Evans, was terminated by his company. He filed suit, claiming he had been fired simply because his manager did not believe an older employee could do cutting-edge work. Evans asked for more than $2 million in damages. After more than a year of litigation, the employer moved to dismiss Evans's claim, arguing that he had failed to file his charge with his state antidiscrimination agency. As the parties awaited a court hearing on the motion, the company proposed mediation and Evans agreed.

During the parties' initial session, Evans and his lawyer argued strongly that there could be no reason for his firing other than age. The employer, however, maintained it had terminated Evans based on his performance, presenting mediocre reviews he had received from his manager. The company also argued that Evans's failure to file charges with the state agency would require the court to dismiss his lawsuit, regardless of merit. The mediator's private view was that the company's failure-to-file defense was very likely to prevail. However the employer knew the court might well delay ruling until trial, and thus had an incentive to settle. She began to work with the parties and made progress.

In the late afternoon, as the negotiations reached the point at which the disputants had to confront painful concessions, Evans began to act oddly. He had voiced anger all along at what he saw as his employer's duplicity and ingratitude, but now he began to act erratically. He would discuss legal risks rationally at one point, then a short time later refuse to talk about the case at all, exclaiming that he could not believe this was happening to him. At one point, Evans authorized the mediator to make a substantial concession, but when she returned with a counteroffer he became nearly hysterical, insisting that he had been "crazy" to make any move at all. At still other times he seemed deeply withdrawn, barely responding to the mediator or his counsel's suggestions.

Difficult feelings produce irrational decision making and abrasive behavior that often make it impossible for disputants to settle. In this chapter, we look more deeply into these psychological forces—and what a mediator can do to deal with them.

1. Strong Emotions

As a mediator you can contribute greatly to the settlement process by identifying and addressing emotional obstacles. To do so, you do not have to become a therapist or take on inappropriate roles. You must, however, be able to deal with strong displays of feeling without becoming flustered or feeling the need to squelch them. You may also have to contain or redirect feelings that are preventing parties from bargaining effectively. The following responses can help alleviate emotional issues:

- ○ Identify the issue.
- ○ Allow venting: listen, acknowledge, empathize.
- ○ Arrange a dialogue between the disputants.
- ○ Trace the issue back to its source.
- ○ Address its causes.
- ○ Circumvent or separate dysfunctional disputants.

Identify the issue

Identifying emotional issues in legal disputes can be difficult. Strong feelings are often present, but parties rarely acknowledge them. Most often, especially in business disputes, parties and lawyers present what I call "game faces," displaying only emotions consistent with their legal position, such as a claimant's emotional distress in an employment dispute or a litigant's anger over the other side's bargaining tactics.

Your first task in dealing with emotional issues is to identify what is churning underneath the surface of the discussion. Sometimes this is obvious from the expressions on disputants' faces, the tone of their voices, or the way they relate to each other, but you will often have to ask specific questions to overcome disputants' reluctance to discuss their feelings. Options include the following:

- ○ *Open-ended questions.* ("Are there any issues I should know about that weren't mentioned in the joint session?")
- ○ *Mildly prompting inquiries.* ("This must have been very difficult for you, Mr. Smith . . ." or "If that happened to me, I'd be very upset. How are you handling it?")

○ *Leading questions.* ("If I felt I'd been fired because of my age, I'd be angry—are you?")

○ *References to similar events or personal experiences.* Mentioning that you or someone you know has had a similar experience and describing how it felt can make it clear the feeling is a valid one. ("I have a friend who thought his mother had died because of a mistake at the hospital, and I remember how it ate away at him. . .") Sometimes it is easier for disputants if you mention a situation in a general way ("It's been my experience that when people have had things like this happen to them, they often feel. . . ."), allowing them to deny the emotion without seeming to disagree with you.

○ *Suggestions of a range of possible responses.* Suggesting that a disputant may be experiencing one of a variety of feelings implies that the same events can affect people differently. This can be less threatening to listeners, allowing them to explore possibilities and adopt the one that feels most true, or capable of being admitted. ("Well, I wasn't exactly angry, but I guess I felt misunderstood. . .and maybe even cheated!")

○ *Inquiries to lawyers.* If a party is not willing to talk about an emotional issue you may be able to gather valuable information by questioning lawyers about it privately.

Caucuses are usually the best setting in which to explore emotional barriers. There is a risk people will feel inhibited or humiliated at discussing difficult feelings in a joint meeting. Even in a private setting, an emotional issue may be too difficult for a person to discuss at first, or a lawyer may cut off an inquiry. Accept such brush-offs, at least at the outset; questions turned aside in the first round of caucusing will often be accepted later. The best approach is to be both diplomatic and persistent.

Example: A mediator was attempting to settle a claim by an auto dealer that a banker had unfairly foreclosed on his loan and driven him into bankruptcy, then sold his property at a bargain price to a business associate. During the first caucus, the neutral remarked to the dealer how crushing the experience must have been, but his lawyer interrupted, saying, "Never mind that—I want to know what they'll offer to settle this thing!" The mediator dropped the issue. The process later stalled, with the dealer insisting on a sum the mediator thought unrealistic in the circumstances.

The mediator reconvened the process a week later and again raised the emotional issue. The auto dealer hesitated and looked at his lawyer.

Gesturing expansively, the lawyer said, "Joe, tell her how you felt when the bank foreclosed on you. . ." A torrent of feelings about scheming lenders, the unfair way the public views car dealers, and other angry emotions poured out.

After talking for 45 minutes, the dealer calmed down. The mediator began to talk through the legal issues with the lawyer, the dealer listening quietly. After some time, the lawyer asked for a few minutes to talk with his client and, when the mediator came back in the room, said they were ready to talk about what could be done in a settlement.

In summary, to uncover emotional issues:

- ○ Look for nonverbal evidence of hidden feelings.
- ○ Ask explicitly about such issues.
- ○ If a participant is reticent, consider asking another team member.
- ○ Be diplomatic but persistent. Don't be discouraged by initial brush-offs.

Allow venting: listen, acknowledge, empathize

Once an emotional issue has been identified, you must decide how to deal with it. You have several options, including simple listening; "active" listening, in which you acknowledge what you have heard; or offering an empathetic response.

Listening. In some situations simply allowing the disputants to vent their feelings to you, and perhaps to each other, is enough to clear the way.

Example: A professor at a California university was stalked for years by a disturbed female student. He asked his university for assistance but felt that the deans ignored his plight, eventually forcing him to move to a secret location. He complained to the media about the university's perceived lack of response and later sued, demanding compensation and the right to teach from a remote location by videoconferencing. It was clear to the mediator that the professor was extremely distraught by the ordeal.

With the assent of the university's counsel, the mediator arranged to meet with the professor and his lawyer privately before the mediation began. He listened to the professor describe his feelings of anger and betrayal. Several days later, the parties met to mediate. The professor was less upset but still too angry to accept a compromise, and the university remained suspicious that the professor would continue to criticize it in the media after the case was settled.

Three weeks of telephone diplomacy ensued between the mediator and the lawyers. The parties then met again, this time on campus rather than at the mediator's office. The mediator went to the professor's office and again listened to his fears about what the stalker might do. He then arranged for the professor and the university president to talk privately. Each expressed anger—the professor over the university's response to the stalking and the president over the professor's attacks in the media.

A settlement was eventually reached that included a rearranged teaching load, a sensitization program for staff about stalking, special monitoring of the stalker, a nondisparagement clause, and a monetary payment.

Active listening. Usually an upset person will want someone to respond to what she says. You can do so by periodically noting or acknowledging what you have heard. ("That must have been very hard" or "I'm hearing that losing the contract cut at the foundation of your effort to build your company and upset you deeply. . .") What is appropriate will vary depending on the nature of the issue. A lawyer's anger over an opponent's tactics, for example, is very different from the feelings of a victim of sexual abuse.

Empathy. When you empathize with another person, you attmept to articulate (but not judge) what they are or were feeling. You might say, for instance: "I'm sensing the deposition was a very painful experience that you felt misunderstood and sometimes even manipulated or attacked...." If you interpret feelings correctly the person will feel "known." Even if you are wrong, the person will often appreciate that you tried.

Be careful, however, to distinguish between *empathy* and *sympathy*—the difference between naming what someone else is feeling and saying how you feel yourself. To acknowledge what someone else feels is empathy and is almost always appropriate. Saying how *you* personally feel ("I feel awful for what you went through.") is sympathy, a different response. Showing sympathy can be useful, but it can also ally you with one side's view of the case, impairing your neutrality.

You do not need to agree with a party's view of the facts in order to empathize with their emotional reaction to it. It is, however, important to keep the issue of what actually happened separate from how a disputant feels. Empathy with a feeling is quite appropriate, but agreeing with one side's interpretation of the merits is usually not. You can avoid appearing to endorse one side's viewpoint by using the word "if." For example, "If I felt I'd been cheated by a business partner I'd probably feel the same way. . ." or "I appreciate your frustration, given your feeling the company never tried to respond to your complaints. . ."

What makes dealing with feelings so difficult? Listening may sound easy to persons with legal experience: after all, gathering data is much of what lawyers do. But lawyers' instinctive response is often to focus on facts rather than feelings. We're skilled at collecting and analyzing data, but feelings may seem to "just get in the way." Pure analysis is often ineffective, however, because the problem is often not a lack of data or arguments. It's the feelings involved, which block a resolution until they are vented and acknowledged. Mediator Dana Curtis articulates some of the challenges lawyers face:

> Lawyers. . .in empathy training often shy away from empathizing with the speaker's feelings. One self-disclosing student—a litigator of 15 years—joked that he did not have problems identifying parties' feelings, as he had a broad range of them himself: hungry, sleepy, and angry. The obvious antidote is to start monitoring our own feelings and to attach words to them.
>
> One reason students shy away from feelings is that feelings often must be inferred, and they are afraid of making a mistake. Sometimes they do get it wrong. Either way, getting it wrong is not a problem. The speaker merely corrects the perception and moves on. What matters is that the mediator is listening attentively and trying to understand. . .

It is worth stressing that acknowledging or empathizing with a person's feelings does *not* require you become a therapist or have a solution for the problem. You can often accomplish a great deal simply by listening to the aggrieved party and showing you have heard and understood their feelings. You might think of your role as similar to that of a mourner at a funeral or a person responding to a colleague's serious illness: you cannot reverse the loss or cure the patient, and you are not expected to. Simply your presence and understanding helps them deal with difficult feelings.

> William Webster, a former federal judge who also served as Director of the CIA and FBI, later became a mediator. He was once asked what book he'd found most useful in his work as a neutral in complex corporate disputes. Webster's response: "When my wife and I had kids, I found Dr. Haim Ginnott's book, *Between Parent and Child*, very helpful. . . and I find it equally useful now."
>
> Dr. Ginnott emphasizes how important it is for parents to listen to children empathically, without expressing judgment on what they say.

This, Judge Webster was suggesting, is one of the most important skills a mediator can bring to a dispute—apparently as useful with angry CEOs as with upset children.

In summary,

○ Listening is valuable; showing you have heard and understood is even more effective.

○ Express empathy if appropriate, but distinguish between empathy and committing to a view of disputed facts.

○ You need not have a solution to be helpful with feelings.

For examples of listening to angry litigants see Chapters 1, 6 and 8, and for examples of empathizing see Chapters 5 and 8, of the DVD.

Arrange a dialogue between the disputants

Listening. Even more can be accomplished with emotional issues when you can bring an adversary into the process. You may, for example, be able to persuade a party to listen to an opponent express feelings.

Example: To a defense team in caucus: "She is distraught over her husband's death and blames the company for it. She wants to hear her lawyer say you were negligent, even reckless. I'm going to ask you to sit there and listen—please don't react except to acknowledge what you've heard. I don't think you can ever convince her it was an accident, and at this point it's not about arguing the legal case. She needs to state her feelings before she can move on to consider a settlement."

Responding. Sometimes disputants are able to go further and respond to what is said.

Example: A mediator was seeking to resolve an age discrimination claim filed by an employee against a small restaurant supply company. The legal claim was for a seven-figure sum. The defense lawyer warned the neutral that the company simply could not pay that kind of money. It appeared that a deal could be struck only if the employee returned to work. The emotional issues arising from the lawsuit itself, however, made this impossible for the company's CEO to swallow. In a hallway conversation, the defendant's lawyer told the mediator his client was adamant that the employee was a "gold digger" who deserved little more than nuisance money.

Delving into this, the mediator learned that both the employee and the CEO wanted an apology—from each other. Their demands appeared contradictory, but the mediator did not give up. She suggested to the employee that what he might be seeking was an "acknowledgment" of the impact on him and his family of being fired, a reframing the employee seemed to accept. She similarly recast the employer's demand for an apology as a need for him to tell the employee how much it had hurt him to be unfairly accused and how much the turmoil had harmed the company.

After hours of discussion, the mediator brought the two principals together without counsel and helped them explain the ways each had felt harmed by the other's conduct. She then adjourned the mediation to allow them to rest and absorb what had been said. A second session produced an agreement that included the employee's reinstatement into a different job.

Apologizing. In unusual situations, with parties communicating directly in a confidential setting, one disputant may even offer an apology to another.

Example: A well-known actress wanted to refurbish a mansion she had just purchased. She decided to draw her vision of what she wanted, hire a contractor who specialized in restorations, and have the contractor execute it. The contractor gave her a price of $650,000 for the job. She agreed and work began. The project, however, rapidly spun out of control. Changes were made, expenses mushroomed, and the eventual cost was more than double the estimate. The actress refused to pay the final bill and the contractor sued. The parties agreed to mediate.

Each side sat stiffly at a conference table while the mediator made his opening comments. After the actress's lawyer had summarized her legal arguments, the mediator asked the actress if she would like to say anything. Looking directly at the contractor, she said she realized she bore some of the responsibility for what had happened: she had wanted to realize a personal vision for her new home, but made the mistake of not using an architect. She felt that while the contractor should have done a better job of explaining the cost of the changes, part of the fault was hers.

As the actress spoke, the contractor visibly relaxed. He responded that he had tried to do his best but was willing to work to find a fair solution. After a day of hard bargaining, the case settled.

When arranging for expressions of empathy, regret, or apology between disputants, consider the following questions.

- ○ *Who should speak and who needs to hear?* A statement by a lawyer will not have nearly the emotional impact of something said directly by one party to another. In some situations, however, a lawyer-to-lawyer format may be the only option.

- ○ *What form should the communication take?* If the goal is personal reconciliation, a direct exchange is usually necessary. If, on the other hand, the listener's interest is in feeling vindicated, then a written statement may be necessary.

- ○ *What needs to be said?* To encourage a party to express regret, it is important to emphasize that doing so does not require admitting blame. Parties can be coached to acknowledge and even sympathize with the other side's situation without taking responsibility for having caused it.

Example: Chapter One described a tort claim brought by relatives of a teenage driver who was accidentally killed by a state trooper as he chased a drunk motorist. The victim's family demanded a private meeting with the trooper in which they talked about the impact of the boy's death. The trooper responded by saying he did not think he had been careless, but he had young children, was devastated by the accident, and had stopped driving patrols as a result. The exchange helped both sides work through their feelings, making possible a settlement of the legal case.

In summary, to arrange responses to emotional issues:

- ○ Set up a dialogue between the disputants.
- ○ If possible arrange for an acknowledgement, expression of regret, or apology.
- ○ Promote direct party-to-party discussion whenever feasible.

Trace the issue back to its source

Sometimes acknowledging or empathizing with the emotion is not enough: the person remains "stuck" in the feeling. When this occurs it may help to trace the emotion back to the events that stimulated it. You can encourage the disputant to tell you the story of how the situation developed and how his feelings changed over time. A simple request to tell one's story often has a calming effect, reducing the rigidity disputants adopt as a defensive posture.

By retracing the history of a dispute from a participant's perspective, you can explore the reasons for her feelings at a time when she does not feel under pressure to defend or justify them. You can also identify areas where emotion may be distorting people's reasoning and give them an opportunity to reexamine their assumptions. Also, by suggesting that the person once had different feelings about the situation, you open the possibility that his current state is not how he will feel in the future.

Distinguish the prior situation. Disputants may react negatively to a situation because of feelings carried over from a past experience. A plaintiff, for example, may be suspicious of a defense lawyer because of a bad experience in another case. When feelings generated by past events become obstacles to resolving the dispute at hand, you can draw attention to the issue in a diplomatic way, identify the source of the emotion, and help disputants distinguish past events from the present situation.

If, for example, the problem is a disputant's bad experience with a prior lawyer, you might ask about it. ("It sounds as if you've had bad experiences with lawyers in the past. . .") Once the past has been processed, you may be able to suggest there are differences between the two situations, or point to facts that support the credibility of the present lawyer.

Address its causes

All this assumes the events causing difficult feelings occurred in the past, but this may not be true. As noted in the last chapter, one side may be upset over an opponent's current bargaining tactics. Or the cause may be external: the parties may have to continue to work together on a project, for instance, causing repeated clashes. In either situation the approach is the same:

○ Probe diplomatically for the root cause of the problem.

○ Explore ways to ameliorate it.

○ Work to remove lingering traces that continue to affect the negotiation.

Example: A mediator was moderating discussions between a man and a woman who were dissolving a business partnership. The mediator pushed to wrap up the case because he knew the man was anxious to start a new job and the woman was pregnant. The woman partner, however, canceled out of a session at the last minute. The mediator learned she had been told of a potentially serious condition affecting her unborn child and was agonizing over the situation.

Exploring this issue gingerly with both partners, the mediator decided it would make sense to delay the process. The adjournment created an additional issue, however, because the woman was upset that her partner was making efforts to collect their outstanding bills. The partner had meant this as a gesture of assistance, but the woman interpreted it as a maneuver to change the value of their remaining receivables and thus the sale price of the business.

The mediator helped the male partner explain his motives. The partners then worked out an agreement under which the man would collect receivables under agreed criteria and the mediation was adjourned until the following week.

Circumvent or separate dysfunctional participants

The disputant whose feelings are blocking effective bargaining may not be a party but instead a lawyer, manager, or other participant. In one sense, this is an issue of inconsistent interests between a party and its negotiator, which can be handled using the strategies discussed in Chapter Five. When the cause is emotional, however, the player is likely to respond less rationally. A negotiator who is procrastinating in order to reap a personal gain, for instance, can be confronted about it and may give in, but an angry disputant is often unable to process issues or make good decisions.

When it is impossible to calm or defuse a dysfunctional participant, the most effective approach may be to circumvent or even replace him.

Example: It was the tenth hour of mediation in a case in which parents claimed their infant daughter's death had been caused by a defective baby carriage manufactured by the defendant. Plaintiffs had been slowly moving toward what the mediator saw as a reasonable settlement range. The defendant's decision maker, however, was its inside counsel, who refused to offer anything beyond $50,000 "nuisance value," despite his outside litigator's admission that it would cost at least $100,000 more to defend the case through trial. At 6 PM, the mediator brought a $500,000 demand to the defense, which it refused to counter.

As the neutral left to give the news to the plaintiffs, the litigator caught him in the hallway. She said the inside counsel deeply disliked the plaintiff lawyer and this was distorting his judgment. It was the defense firm's first case with this client, she said, and she didn't have the clout to control him. The lawyer suggested the mediator ask to speak with senior management by speakerphone, predicting the company's CFO would take a rational approach to the case.

The mediator returned to the caucus room and asked to talk with the CFO. She quickly assessed the situation and authorized offering the cost of defense. As the neutral left the room, the CFO and the lawyers continued to talk. Two hours later the case settled at $235,000.

Sometimes the dysfunctional party or negotiator cannot be circumvented or replaced. If so, you may be able to control the situation by keeping the combatants in caucus and editing comments that would disrupt the bargaining.

2. Cognitive Forces

We have seen that cognitive forces often distort bargaining decisions, for example, by leading disputants to suspect adversaries' motives and react negatively even to reasonable offers. The problems go beyond any particular form of bargaining, however. This section offers ideas about how to deal with some common cognitive distortions.

a. Reactive Devaluation

Reactive devaluation is the tendency to devalue any offer made by an opponent, simply because the opponent made it. Probably your single greatest advantage as a mediator is that you will not be subject to reactive devaluation. Potential ways to use your status to advantage include:

- ○ Offer a proposal as your own.
- ○ Discuss the merits of an idea in the abstract.
- ○ Offer a disputant a choice of packages.
- ○ Accredit an adversary's proposal.

Offer a proposal as your own

If you float a proposal—for instance, that a contractual relationship be restructured or parties agree to an expert appraisal of a disputed piece of property—the disputants are likely to listen politely. They will not devalue your proposal automatically, as they would if it came from the other side.

There are two dangers in doing so, however. First, if the listener thinks you are simply communicating an idea generated by an adversary, devaluation will apply with full force. Second, if the listener sees the proposal as skewed in favor of his opponent, he may decide that you have taken sides against him. It is, therefore, important to think through not just whether an idea makes sense in the abstract, but also how a partisan listener will interpret it. Citing objective criteria or principles to support your ideas is also useful; even if the listener is not convinced by them, it will help to reassure him that although mistaken, you are acting in good faith.

Discuss the merits of an idea in the abstract

The flip side of disputants' tendency to devalue ideas because opponents favor them is that if an opponent has not yet agreed to an option, devaluation is less likely to occur. Put another way, a hypothetical offer is not yet cursed by the fact the other side is actually willing to make it. If the party agrees that an offer not yet on the table might be acceptable, it is at least partially "inoculated" against being devalued if the other side later signs on.

Presenting an offer as out of reach also takes advantage of the so-called scarcity principle—the fact that people instinctively want things that are not available. To take advantage of this effect, test out proposals as uncertain possibilities even if you are fairly sure you can persuade the other side to agree to them. ("You know, I think if we could ever get them up to $100,000, it would be worth serious consideration. . .What do you think?")

Indeed, it sometimes seems that disputants are subject to another force I call "reactive *valuation*." Ironically, the very fact that their adversary *dis*likes an idea sometimes makes them willing to consider it. So if one side is resistant to an idea you are presenting, you might consider mentioning this to an opponent, who may react by becoming more open to it.

For examples of a mediator suggesting disputants focus on interests, see Chapter 9 of the DVD.

Offer a disputant a choice

If you present two or three settlement options and indicate that an opponent has not decided in favor of any of them, it is less likely they will be devalued. ("I think I may be able to convince the defendant either to pay the money within 60 days or over a year at a reasonable rate of interest. Which would you prefer?")

More generally, people like the feeling of having a choice, even if none of the proposals are very attractive. (Think of a child who is inveigled into going to bed by being asked whether he would prefer red or blue pajamas.)

A warning however: psychologists have found that having too many choices can be a problem. Subjects in experiments who are given several options, for example, tend to become confused and indecisive. To avoid paralyzing people, offer them only a couple of the most likely choices.

Accredit an adversary's proposal

If you genuinely believe an adversary's proposal is constructive, you can say so, using your credibility to persuade the listener it is worth considering. In doing so, you may want to note that the proposal certainly has flaws from the perspective of the listener—it almost certainly will—but may be worth considering despite this. Be careful, however, not to sacrifice your relationship with a party by advocating a solution it will see as seriously biased.

b. Attraction to Certainty and Familiarity

We saw in Chapter Five that parties will pay a significant premium to achieve certainty, placing less value on options that are equivalent from an objective standpoint, but do not eliminate all risk. Thus, for example, people will pay something to reduce a risk of an adverse event from, say, 20 to 10 percent, but they will usually pay significantly more to reduce the same risk from 10 percent to zero, although a statistician would say the two choices are identical because each one reduces the likelihood of an event by 10 percent. Thus, certainty has extra value to human beings.

This means that when the outcome of a negotiation is not certain, parties will give up much less to obtain it, even if the actual risk appears minor in objective terms. If bargainers are not sure the other side intends or is capable of carrying out a deal, for instance, they often discount the result severely. By contrast, a settlement with certainty has special value to disputants.

Mediators must also deal with people's preference for familiar risks over ones that appear unusual. We have seen that parties prefer taking on risks that are within their past experience and therefore seem familiar to them over risks they have never encountered. Chapter Five suggested the following steps to deal with uncertain and with unfamiliar risks arising from interest-based settlements:

○ Analyze less-than-certain proposals and unfamiliar risks with special care.
○ Analogize unfamiliar risks to more common ones.
○ Provide a mechanism to reduce the level of uncertainty.

One additional option is available, particularly when settlement terms center on money:

○ Stress the certainty inherent in settling.

Most settlements do provide the parties with certainty, by eliminating the risks invloved in litigation. Thus a typical agreement in a commercial dispute will provide that the plaintiff will be paid a sum certain and in return the defendant will receive a dismissal of the case "with prejudice" and a complete release of "all claims. . .from the beginning of time. . ." If this is the situation, you can use the "certainty effect" to advantage, as a lever to persuade parties to compromise. Usually the certainty is about the result—sure terms of settlement—but you can also sometimes offer disputants certainty about how far they will be asked to go in the process.

> *Certainty of outcome*: "If you can just take one more step and go to $150,000, you will have a final deal. The plaintiff will dismiss all its claims with prejudice, and this litigation will disappear. You will never have to talk to these people again. I know it's much more than you see as fair, but what would it be worth to put this all behind you once and for all?"
>
> *Certainty about bargaining*: "If you can agree to drop to $275,000 that will be it. I'll present it to them as your last and final offer—a take-it-or-leave-it. It'll be the end of the process, one way or another. I guarantee I won't come back and ask for more."

For an example of offering certainty to obtain a better offer, see Chapter 20 of the DVD.

c. Loss Aversion

We have seen that people in conflict feel intense emotions, and many of these feelings are negative. Of all the emotions that appear in legal conflicts, the one most often responsible for the failure of settlement efforts, in my judgment, is the feeling of loss. How do these feelings arise?

The origin of feelings of loss. Disputants often develop an opinion about the "right" outcome in a case early in the process. They form these opinions based on statements by friends about what is "right" in their dispute, chance comments by lawyers, stories they see in the media about superficially similar cases, and other sources. Their opinion then becomes an internal benchmark for the correct result.

> *Example:* A tort plaintiff hears on television about a $500,000 verdict in a case that seems similar to his. The plaintiff then begins to think of $500,000 as the "right" amount at which to settle his own claim. Two years later a mediator suggests that information produced in discovery

has lowered the plaintiff's chances of winning and that verdicts in this kind of case rarely exceed $100,000. The plaintiff, however, clings to his $500,000 benchmark and feels a strong sense of loss at being asked to settle for less.

Parties also invest large resources in their cases, in terms of out-of-pocket costs for legal fees, time, and aggravation. Each party is then likely to factor the cost of litigation into its benchmark for a fair outcome: plaintiffs feel that they must recover enough both to cover their legal costs and to pay them a fair amount, while defendants are likely to deduct their defense costs from what they believe is a fair outcome. As a matter of law, parties can rarely recover their legal costs in court regardless of the outcome, so what a party has spent on a case should be irrelevant to decisions about settlement. As a matter of psychology, however, litigation costs become part of what must not be "lost" in settlement.

To settle a dispute, however, each side must ordinarily accept an outcome that falls well short of its initial goals. In an employment case, for instance, a typical settlement will require the employee to accept a money payment much lower than his claimed damages and the employer to pay a sum inconsistent with its prior claims of innocence. In a contract dispute, a plaintiff will typically accept a sum lower than its anticipated profit from the contract, and the defendant will forfeit much of its expected payment and lose a client to boot. Moreover, most settlements do not compensate either side for its litigation costs. In short, mediated settlements almost inevitably create serious feelings of loss for both sides.

The impact of feelings of loss on decision making. Feelings of loss are extremely painful. Economic studies have shown, for instance, that people who lose $1.00 in a manner that seems "unfair" to them feel as if they have in fact "lost" the equivalent of $2.50 to $2.75.

Example: Students at Stanford University who had expected to attend a seminar without charge are told after they arrive they will each have to pay $20 when they leave the room to cover unexpected expenses. They can, however, spin a roulette wheel with three chances in four of paying nothing and one chance of having to pay $100. The odds thus discourage gambling—since the average cost of spinning the wheel is 100/4, or $25, the smart choice is simply to pay the $20. However, 70% of the students tested choose to spin the wheel. Having expected to pay nothing, they apparently experience the demand for $20 as an unwelcome loss and are willing to take objectively unreasonable risks to avoid it.

People involved in legal disputes behave much like the Stanford students. They often develop expectations about the "right" outcome for their case, cling to it even when presented with contrary evidence, and experience strong feelings of loss if asked to settle for less. And, like the students, people involved in disputes will take unreasonably high risks to avoid what they see as a "loss" (Arrow, 1995). The phenomenon of loss aversion frustrates settlements in mediation more than any other single factor.

Mediator responses to loss aversion. To deal with feelings of loss, consider the following:

○ Identify loss benchmarks.
○ Recharacterize the situation.
○ Distance current circumstances from prior ones.
○ Use humor to reframe a situation.
○ Suggest new terms to distract a party.
○ Play on parties' fear of losing an outstanding offer.

Identify loss benchmarks

The first task is to identify the benchmarks by which disputants are measuring losses or gains. You can do so, for example, by asking parties what they think would be a fair outcome and how they arrived at their opinion. Remember not to argue with a party—your goal at this point is to identify the issue, not to resolve it.

As you do so, be alert for selective perception. The problem of "selective perception," which exists in most disputes, and is described in Chapter Seven, is exacerbated by feelings of impending loss. People automatically disregard or downplay information they sense will lead them toward a loss. To deal with this, use the tactics suggested in Chapter Seven.

Recharacterize the situation

Because loss calculations are inherently subjective, you can reduce or eliminate feelings of loss by persuading a disputant to use a more realistic benchmark.

Example: A discharged employee brought an age discrimination claim against his employer and became convinced his claim would bring $200,000 or more. Over two years of litigation, however, he got no settlement offers at all and became increasingly frustrated with his ex-employer's bad faith.

The case eventually went to court-ordered mediation. After five hours of discussion, the employer put $40,000 on the table. From the perspective of the employee's initial goal, this was extremely disappointing, and he complained about this to the mediator. In response the mediator said, "For two years now, you've seen nothing at all. The defendant has ignored you! But now we've got his attention and there's $40,000 on the table. The challenge at this point is to find out just how far you can push him—then decide if you want to take it."

The employee listened, seeming to take satisfaction at having finally forced the employer to pay attention to his claim. His focus shifted to how to "push" his former employer to its limit, measuring progress from the employer's last offer rather than the prior benchmark.

Example: A company sued its former accounting firm for mis-valuing a corporate acquisition. The plaintiff's CFO was angry that his company was being offered only $60,000, an amount far less than the company's initial damages estimate of $500,000 or even the $120,000 it had spent in legal fees. The problem, the mediator thought, was that discovery had turned up documents in the company's files that contradicted portions of its damage claims and indicated that errors by its own staff contributed to the mis-valuation. Still, the executive remained focused on his legal expenses and early damages estimate and refused to consider lowering the company's demand.

Rather than telling the executive that his focus on the initial assessment or past expenses was illogical, the mediator listened to the CFO's reasons for setting a $500,000 value on the case. The neutral went on to ask about the history of the litigation and how the problems with it had appeared. It became evident the executive had personally advocated spending money to litigate and was now embarrassed that the claim appeared to be deeply flawed.

The mediator commiserated with the executive's situation. He suggested there was no reasonable way he could have known the company's records would contradict what he had been told by staff, and went on to tell of having gotten into a similar situation when he was a litigator. The mediator then characterized the issue as one of making a tough business decision: should the CFO put additional money into an investment that had proven disappointing, or close out the venture and cut the company's losses? The neutral also said he would be willing to brief the company's top management about why it made sense to settle.

> As the discussion went on, the executive became less tense and defensive, gradually admitting the claim had problems and focusing on how to get the best possible deal now.

Distance current circumstances from prior ones

We have seen that people affected by feelings of loss are usually using an inaccurate or obsolete frame of reference. As a result, you can often make progress by distancing the prior (inaccurate) benchmark from the one you are suggesting be used.

The feeling of losing is aggravated if a settlement suggests that a disputant made a bad decision by pursuing the case as far as she has. If so, you can lower the person's feeling of loss by accrediting her initial decisions in the case. You might suggest, for instance, that her initial assessment was reasonable based on what she knew at the time, implying the person could agree to a compromise without conceding that her earlier judgment was poor. You might highlight the difference between a former viewpoint and present reality by placing lists of prior assumptions and currently known facts side-by-side or in different colors.

Use humor to reframe a situation

A disputant can sometimes see a situation differently through humor. You might, for example, tell a story that illustrates the illogic of life, helping the listener let go of the feeling that an apparent loss has great meaning. An irreverent joke can serve as a mini-break, helping a disputant to relax and shake loose from a rigid position.

> *Example:* A mediator was attempting to convince a real estate investor to contribute to a settlement of a lender-liability case in which a bank had allegedly swindled a borrower out of a piece of land. The investor had bought the property through a private deal with the president of the defendant bank at what he indignantly insisted was a fair-market price. He protested that it was totally unfair to be asked to give up a profit he had fairly earned.
>
> The mediator felt that the investor was probably more aware of the problems with the transaction than he was now admitting, but saw no point in highlighting this. Instead he told a story about a recent case involving the trustees of a church who became concerned about reports their minister was appearing nude in his office. The trustees asked his psychiatrist about this and were told the minister had a "problem with

self-exposure." The minister then sued his doctor for violating patient confidentiality and also the board for "inducing" the violation. A court ruled the trustees could be held liable, despite their innocent intent in asking the questions. The implication was that one could find oneself legally liable despite the best of intentions.

The investor shook his head, laughing at the irrationality of it all, and 20 minutes later agreed to throw in the $50,000 needed to close the settlement.

Suggest new terms to distract a party

Feelings of loss are more painful when there is only a single benchmark or issue in play, making each party's loss easily measurable. This, for instance, is why loss aversion is such a problem when parties engage in positional bargaining over money. By contrast, when there are multiple issues and parties are considering new settlement structures, losses are harder to measure and easier to ignore. If a new issue is introduced into the mix, disputants often have no benchmark for measuring what they ought to get or seeing the outcome on that issue as a loss.

It is said, perhaps apocryphally, that former Secretary of State Henry Kissinger ascribed his success in mediating agreements between Arabs and Israelis to the tactic of "making the deal so complicated no one could tell who was winning." In essence, he used complex proposals attuned to the parties' sensitivities to distract the parties from measuring agreements against their prior benchmarks.

Play on parties' fear of losing an outstanding offer

Once there is a significant offer on the table, it is possible to use loss aversion to persuade parties to settle. The trick lies in framing the situation so the offer is already "in the pocket" of a party, and the party's choice is whether to risk "losing" the offer by pursuing the dispute. It is most effective with plaintiffs who have been offered a substantial sum of money, but it can apply to an offer by a plaintiff that would protect the defendant from exposure at trial.

To a plaintiff: "The defendant has put a $200,000 offer on the table. The check won't bounce and the money will be paid to you within a couple of weeks. This gives you a choice: should you keep this guaranteed

> $200,000, or take the money out of your bank account and buy a ticket in the litigation lottery?
>
> "If you take out the money and buy a ticket, you might win a half million dollars or more at trial. But you could also lose every dollar you've gained. It's up to you. . ."

For an example of using loss aversion to persuade a disputant to compromise, see Chapter 17 of the DVD.

d. Delayed Loss Reactions

"It's hard…There's a finality about it…When we sign, then it's done. He's really gone."

> —The widow of a victim of the 9/11 disaster, describing her delay in applying for compensation to which she was clearly entitled

The mediation of the age discrimination case described at the start of the chapter was unusual. The typical money negotiation resembles an uphill slog, but in this case the process was more like a ride on a roller coaster. The employee's emotions were striking not merely because of their variation, but also because they followed a distinct pattern. Indeed, he seemed to go through phases similar to those observed in people mourning the loss of a close relative. In this case, however, the loss was of something other than a human being. This phenomenon, which might be called a "delayed loss reaction," poses special problems for legal mediators.

The psychology of grieving

To understand how people deal with feelings of loss during settlement negotiations, it is helpful to think about how they respond to very personal losses such as the end of a close relationship. Sigmund Freud, Elizabeth Kubler-Ross, and other theorists have developed models of human response to such traumas.

Freud (1917) gave the classic analysis of how people respond to the loss of a loved one. Such a victim, he observed, typically goes through an initial period of shock and withdrawal and often clings to the fiction that the object of his affection—the lost person—continues to exist. Gradually, however, most victims begin to reconcile with reality and realize the departed person is truly lost. Freud saw the process of grieving as an internal negotiation, in which the mind of the bereaved reluctantly works out a compromise between its wish the relationship continue and the realization it cannot.

Other clinicians have developed different models of reaction to loss. Perhaps the best known is that of Elizabeth Kubler-Ross (1969), who described patients' response to being told they are terminally ill. She reported that such patients typically go through five distinct stages: numbness/denial, anger, bargaining, depression, and acceptance. This series of emotions might be called a "loss reaction."

When a person in a legal dispute suffers the loss of a claim or a defense important to his self-image, he often reacts in the same way as someone grieving over the loss of a personal relationship. Indeed litigants like Mr. Evans, the employment discrimination claimant, go through reactions that resemble those of Kubler-Ross's victims of terminal disease (Golann, 2004).

Delayed responses to loss

This still does not explain, though, why these emotions sometimes arise for the first time in mediation. The age discrimination claimant, for instance, displayed symptoms more than a year after he lost his job. Why is this? The answer lies in the psychology of abnormal reactions to loss.

Freud found that while most mourners gradually work through their loss, some do not. This latter group remains "stuck," unable to deal with feelings of deprivation and disabled from moving on. Psychiatrists have described patients who maintain themselves in denial over a loss by "the substitution of. . .a fantasy or an action, or something of that sort. . .the defensive use of action in order to do away with something painful and unpleasant" (Sandler and A. Freud, 1985).

Some civil litigants fall into this trap. They avoid feeling the loss caused by a dispute by taking action to do away with the feeling, investing their lawsuit with their lost hopes. A terminated employee, for example, may escape some of the pain of losing his job by convincing himself that a court will fully compensate and perhaps reinstate him. A defendant may also cling to the belief that she will be vindicated by the judicial system.

In mediation, however, disputants are required to make serious compromises that are not compatible with illusions of victory. A litigant who has been pretending for years that a court will vindicate her suddenly confronts the reality that it will not, and experiences the feelings she has been avoiding. She may respond emotionally, sometimes with the reactions of someone who has just lost a loved one. This is exemplified by the poignant words of the wife in the 9/11 disaster who would not claim compensation for her husband's loss: "When we sign, it's done. He's really gone."

Implications for bargaining

What are the implications of delayed loss reactions for a mediator? A delayed reaction is hard to recognize because disputants suffering from one behave very much like adversarial bargainers, presenting their arguments in a distorted way, clinging stubbornly to a viewpoint, and/or agreeing to terms and then reneging. In the age discrimination mediation, for example, the plaintiff authorized the mediator to make an offer, but then later denounced the same proposal as "crazy." An opposing party who encounters someone in the throes of a loss reaction often interprets the behavior as unethical bargaining, when in fact the disputant's actions are driven purely by strong feelings.

A second problem arises from the fact that loss reactions are likely to occur unexpectedly. They arise not at the outset of a negotiation but later, when disputants must confront painful compromises. As a result, they can catch a mediator by surprise, forcing her suddenly to confront strong emotions and irrational behavior when she is focused on other issues. At that point, the opposing party is often frustrated and anxious to wind up the process. Even the mediator may feel the "listening to feelings" stage is, or should be, over. As a result, both mediators and opposing parties may either ignore the reaction or become angry at it.

Potential responses

How should a mediator deal with a disputant who is acting out because of a delayed loss reaction? The most useful lesson is to be ready for such reactions and recognize them when they occur. If you realize a loss reaction is happening, you will be able to better understand why a disputant is suddenly behaving in an inconsistent, even offensive, manner and will be less likely to become annoyed with him. You can also warn opposing negotiators, who are likely to interpret irrational behavior as bad faith, that something different is causing the problem. ("Mr. Evans seems pretty emotional at the moment; I think we have to wait a little while to pursue that issue. . .")

You can treat loss reactions with techniques similar to those applied to emotional issues generally—for example, inviting a person to take time to examine his feelings, noting inconsistencies in behavior, and patiently exploring the reasons for the underlying feelings. You might also seek to reframe how the person views the situation.

Bear in mind, however, that the process of working through a reaction may take longer than a single day. Be ready, if necessary, to adjourn the process. Delayed loss reactions are one of the many factors that make resolving disputes a less-than-fully-rational experience.

3. Moral and Symbolic Issues

Litigants sometimes resist settlement because they believe their case involves a moral or symbolic principle too important to compromise or that requires a public decision. These issues arise most often in controversies involving public policy, such as disputes over environmental issues or drug testing, but they can also appear in private claims. It is also possible for one side to consider an issue routine, while the other party sees it as involving bedrock values.

Mediators also encounter illusory symbolic issues, in which claims of principle are a smokescreen for other agendas. Parties may raise a fake symbolic issue as leverage or because the person involved genuinely confuses a personal issue with a larger concern. In business disputes, for example, people sometimes characterize a controversy as "a matter of principle." Months or years later, however, they come to see the same issue as an annoyance and just want it resolved quickly. Recognizing this, one federal judge developed a custom of asking litigants, "Is this case about 'princi*ple*' or 'princi*pal*'"?

In response to moral or symbolic barriers, a mediator can:

○ Lower the surrounding pressure.
○ Reframe the issue.
○ Emphasize another principle that can be achieved through settlement.
○ Emphasize the risk to the principle if negotiations fail.
○ Point out inconsistencies with the person's past views.
○ Introduce a third party with special moral authority.

Lower the surrounding pressure

Feelings of pressure caused by litigation and business deadlines, personal friction, and simple fatigue make people cling more strongly to principles than one might predict from the facts of a situation and turn what otherwise would be minor matters into deal-breakers. The following steps, recommended for emotional issues, can also be helpful here:

○ Inject humor or tell a story (it need not be entirely relevant to the case).
○ Redirect the participants' attention (for example, by asking them to list their settlement priorities).
○ Adjourn the process temporarily to allow people to rest and regroup.

Reframe the issue

Not all issues of principle have to be decided; a settlement can sometimes be structured to avoid deciding the principle. If, for instance, the issue is one of several alternative theories raised by a party, it may be possible to fashion an agreement that does not mention or decide the controversial issue.

Example: A mediator was drawn into a federal investigation of political corruption by a government official. In the course of the probe, the prosecutors had issued a subpoena to a state court demanding copies of the politician's divorce records, which they thought might disclose illicit income. These records were confidential under state law.

The state court judge was determined to preserve the principle of confidentiality and state sovereignty. Could the mediator find some way, he asked, to induce the federal prosecutors to appear in state court and ask for access to the records, which he was confident would be granted? The federal officials spurned this proposal and demanded that any hearing occur before a federal judge. There appeared to be an unresolvable clash between federal and state interests.

The mediator, however, asked more questions: What was the politician's viewpoint? How seriously did he care about the confidentiality of the records? Contrary to everyone's assumptions, the politician had no concern at all about confidentiality; his only wish was to avoid the publicity that would result from a court hearing on the issue.

The mediator suggested the politician turn over the records directly to the federal authorities, with the mediator available to vouch for their accuracy. On hearing the politician was willing to produce the records, the prosecutors lost their interest in them (another example of reactive devaluation) and withdrew the subpoena. The clash between state and federal authority evaporated.

Emphasize another principle that can be achieved through settlement

If a mediator cannot diminish the importance of a principle in the mind of a party, he may be able to suggest another important goal that can be achieved through agreement, then argue that a settlement would free the disputant from the distractions of the present case and free her to pursue that other goal.

Example: A lender in the southeastern United States was pursuing homeowners behind on their mortgage payments. The lender was willing to negotiate payment plans that would keep the borrowers in their homes, but was frustrated by the refusal of borrowers to agree to any plan that did not include tithing to their church.

The lender tried without success to induce the borrowers to be flexible by citing the Biblical principle that one should pay one's just debts. The company then engaged a mediator, who made some progress by citing the Biblical obligation to provide a stable home for one's children, a duty they could not fulfill if they lost their houses. This helped, but the final step in settling the case involved a different tactic, described below.

Emphasize the risk to the principle if negotiations fail

It can sometimes be helpful to point out the worst-case scenario: if the dispute goes to judgment, the principle will be publicly repudiated. You may be able to convince a party that while the issue is important, this is the wrong ground on which to fight.

Point out inconsistencies with the person's past views

If a person's commitment to an issue seems to be newly found, you can gently confront him or her with the inconsistency. Did this issue seem as important six months ago as it does now? Can the person say that if the dispute were resolved he would feel as strongly about the issue a year hence? Such questions may provoke resentment, but if posed in the right way, they can sometimes help a party put a symbolic issue into perspective or expose a symbolic smoke screen, opening the way to a compromise.

Introduce a third party with special moral authority

Sometimes it is effective to bring in a third party who can help the disputant reframe a moral issue.

Example: In the tithing homeowner case, the mediator clinched a settlement by arranging for the debtors to talk with their minister, a person of special stature who advised them that the debtors' obligation to provide a home for their families was more important than their obligation to tithe to his church.

Example: Retired General Colin Powell, acting as a presidential envoy in the 1994 Haitian crisis, was able to avert a war by convincing the ruling junta that the honorable role of a general in the face of America's overwhelming force was not to fight to the bitter end, as one Haitian general had argued, but rather to protect his troops from unnecessary death. Powell's status as a professional soldier of Caribbean descent made it possible for him to influence the moral reasoning of the Haitian generals in ways his skilled colleague, former President Jimmy Carter, could not.

Conclusion

Participants in legal disputes are tempted to think of all impasses as stemming from disagreements about the merits. In fact, peoples' susceptibility to emotion and psychological distortions is the major factor blocking agreement in many disputes. By focusing on emotional issues, you will often find keys to settlement that are missing from purely logical analyses.

4. Summary of Key Points

Strong Emotions
- Identify the issue
- Allow venting: listen, acknowledge, empathize
- Arrange a dialogue between the disputants
- Trace the issue back to its source
- Address its causes
- Circumvent or separate dysfunctional disputants

Cognitive Forces
- Reactive devaluation
  - Offer a proposal as your own
  - Discuss the merits of an idea in the abstract
  - Offer a disputant a choice of packages
  - Accredit an adversary's proposal
- Attraction to certainty and familiarity
  - Analyze less-than-certain proposals and unfamiliar risks with special care
  - Analogize unfamiliar risks to more common ones
  - Provide a mechanism to reduce the level of uncertainty
  - Stress certainty to persuade parties to settle
- Loss aversion
  - Identify loss benchmarks
  - Recharacterize the situation
  - Distance current circumstances from prior ones
  - Use humor to reframe a situation
  - Suggest new terms to distract a party
  - Play on parties' fear of losing an outstanding offer

- Delayed loss reactions
  - Be aware loss reactions can occur
  - Apply the techniques used for other emotional reactions
  - If necessary, adjourn

Moral and Symbolic Issues

- Lower the surrounding pressure
- Reframe the issue
- Emphasize another principle that can be achieved through settlement
- Emphasize the risk to the principle if negotiations fail
- Point out inconsistencies with the person's past views
- Introduce a third party with special moral authority

Chapter 7

Merits Barriers: Information Exchange and Analysis

Most lawyers and parties frame their bargaining positions in terms of the value of their legal case. A plaintiff is demanding X, it will say, because that is what its case is worth in court, while a defendant will only offer Y because, again, that is the realistic value of the case at trial. The early discussion in commercial mediation is therefore typically focused on legal issues—who has the better argument and the value of the case in court.

To a degree, this approach is entirely logical. Negotiation theory teaches bargainers to measure any agreement against the value of their best alternative away from the table, and in legal disputes the most likely alternative is to go to court. The problem, however, is that disputants rarely agree about their prospects in litigation. To a degree, these disagreements are feigned—parties bluff about their chances of winning to justify extreme bargaining positions. But disputes about case value are often all too real.

> *Example:* Recall the experiment in Chapter One in which Harvard students were assigned to bargain for a party in a legal case and asked to make a private estimate of their client's chances of winning. Unbeknownst to them, both sides had the same data, but they nevertheless disagreed about the likely outcome. Both thought their side was more

likely to win, and the students' combined percentage chances of success totaled almost 120 percent—an impossible number.

The students' estimates of the likely damage verdict if the plaintiff did win diverged even more. Business students representing the plaintiff estimated the verdict at an average of $286,000, while students representing the defendant estimated it at $189,000—a difference of nearly $100,000!

The Harvard experiment was merely a classroom exercise, without any of the passions that distort the judgment of real-life disputants. Actual litigants disagree about case value even more strongly, and these differences create serious obstacles to settlement. After all, if each side expects to win in court, how can they agree about what would be a fair outcome? A plaintiff who believes, for example, that he has a 60 percent chance of winning a $500,000 verdict will think that any settlement should pay him at least $300,000. The defendant in the same case may think, however, that the plaintiff has only a 40 percent chance of winning and that the likely verdict if he does will be only $250,000, leading her to believe that $100,000 would a fair settlement number. Each side may be willing to compromise somewhat, but as long as they value their alternatives to settlement so differently, it will be hard for them to agree.

What causes parties to disagree so strongly about the value of legal cases? Disputes can arise from several sources.

○ *Lack of information.* Often parties do not have the same information. Their data may conflict, or they may be making inconsistent assumptions about unknown facts.

○ *Poor analysis of the litigation alternative.* Even when disputants have identical evidence, they usually disagree about its meaning.

○ *Concerns about precedent and reputation.* Even when parties agree about the value of a case, they sometimes refuse to settle out of fear of setting a bad precedent or hurting their reputation.

This chapter and the next focus on merits-based barriers to agreement and strategies to overcome them.

1. Lack of Information

The simplest reason for litigants to disagree about the likely court outcome is a lack of information. It is often surprising how little parties know about each other's cases, even after years of litigation. Discovery rules are intended to give each side near-complete disclosure of the facts, but often this does not happen—in part because litigants conceal evidence as much as possible.

> *Example:* A sales manager who had been fired by a computer software company sued his former employer for violating his contract. The company maintained that the termination was lawful. The case remained in discovery for years and then went to mediation. As the neutral caucused with the parties, it quickly became apparent that a major component of the manager's claims was lost stock options in the company. The plaintiff, however, had never been able to obtain the internal financial reports needed to value the options. He assumed that the company was concealing its wealth and intended to go public in the near future, an event that would make his options very valuable.
>
> Questioned about this in caucus, the company CEO said that he had ordered the data withheld from the plaintiff because "It's none of his business!" In fact, the company was only marginally profitable and everyone's options were "under water"—essentially worthless.
>
> The mediator suggested to the CEO that if there really was no pot of gold in the case, he could help settle it by letting the plaintiff know this. The CEO agreed and the parties reviewed the financial data together. Within an hour, the plaintiff was persuaded that his potential damages were much lower than he had thought, and a settlement was worked out that included verification of the company's financial representations and termination of the options.

To deal with disagreements caused by lack of information:

○ Promote an exchange of data.

○ Suggest reliance on representations, with a right to verification.

○ Take advantage of confidentiality.

○ Suggest a neutral analysis.

Promote an exchange of data

The simplest response to information problems is to arrange for parties to give each other the missing data. Parties will often volunteer information without a quid pro quo, as in the stock options case, because in the context of mediation they hope to get something in return—a settlement—and trust the mediator to ensure that their openness will not be exploited. If lawyers do object to providing "free discovery" for the other side, emphasize that it may be in the party's own interest to provide it. ("You know that any significant settlement will be paid by the insurance company. My experience is that to get enough authority the adjuster will need as much specificity as you can provide. We can label the documents confidential so you won't be boxed in if the case doesn't settle, but I think it's in your interest to give them that data. Without it they won't be able to get the money you'll need to settle the case.")

Information problems arise most often between adverse parties, but this is not always true. Lawyers sometimes have difficulty getting data from their own client, for example because someone in the organization feels defensive or does not see the case as a priority. Codefendants sometimes hide data from each other in an effort to minimize their share of responsibility for a problem. You may have to persuade a client to provide data to her own lawyer, or one defendant to share information with another. At times you will need to facilitate a negotiation over data. A defendant, for example, may agree to disclose information about his defenses in return for the plaintiff providing backup for a damage claim.

For an example of promoting an exchange of data see Chapter 5, and for an example of conveying data see Chapter 7, of the DVD.

Suggest reliance on representations, with a right to verification

Ideally, parties would exchange data before mediation begins. Often, however, a problem does not become apparent until the process is under way. At that point, a document needed to verify a key representation is not available—it may be in a filing cabinet or database back at the client's offices. Retrieving the document may require a long delay, disrupting the flow of the mediation. To avoid delays and at the same time assure parties that they will not be "sandbagged" by misleading representations, my practice is to suggest the following:

○ Parties will rely on oral representations from each other for purposes of bargaining. If a defendant says, for example, "We only have $75,000 in the bank," the plaintiff will take that as true.

○ If there is a settlement, however, then a party is entitled to reasonable verification of any representation on which it relied in making a settlement decision.

Parties typically respond positively to this and move forward with the process based on representations. Interestingly, litigants rarely ask for verification once a deal has been struck.

Take advantage of confidentiality

In a typical negotiation, a lawyer cannot use a document without exposing it to discovery, and as a result lawyers often withhold information that could help settle a case. The special confidentiality rules that apply to mediation, however, allow lawyers to disclose information with less concern that they will be disadvantaged if the case does not settle. For example, you can:

○ Offer to write "Confidential Mediation Document"—and perhaps also place your initials or signature and the date on the document—before it is disclosed to the other side. Doing so may trigger a mediation confidentiality rule, but even if it does not, having the mediator label a document as "confidential" may make a lawyer more confident he will be able to prevent the item from being admitted into evidence if the case does not settle.

○ Suggest a "no copies allowed" or "all copies returned" rule. Again, such rules make participants more confident that they will not be burned in litigation with a document that they disclose for purposes of settlement.

Example: A French consultant sued an American software company for failing to pay for services it provided. The company refused to offer a substantial cash settlement payment, claiming that it had almost no cash available. The plaintiff was skeptical of this but did not want to throw the defendant into bankruptcy because, as an unsecured creditor, it would recover almost nothing.

Defense counsel told the mediator that the defendant's CFO, who was at the mediation, had the startup company's most recent financials on his laptop, in the same form as presented to the company's investors only two weeks before. Hearing this, the mediator suggested that the defense allow a member of the plaintiff team to come in and examine the data. Defense counsel agreed, on the condition that the visitor could ask questions but not take notes on what he saw. The plaintiff lawyer came into the defense caucus room, reviewed and asked questions about the data, and returned to her caucus room. A half hour later the plaintiff side indicated it was willing to accept a payout over time, secured by the company's stock.

In this example, the conditions of disclosure helped persuade the plaintiff lawyer, and in turn her client, that the CFO's document was an honest summary of the defendant's financial status. She was willing to rely on the data because she knew that the defendant was unlikely to have created a false financial statement for mediation and that in any case she would be entitled to verification if the case settled. The defense, for its part, was willing to give the plaintiff a "peek" at its financials because the mediator had certified that it was sensible, and because the plaintiff would not receive the document itself.

○ Evaluate information and provide your conclusion, but not the evidence itself, to the other side.

This last option provides the most protection to the discloser because the other side never sees the actual document, but it may be less persuasive to adversaries because they will tend to discount evidence they have not personally examined.

As these examples show, the confidentiality guarantees common in mediation can allow parties to communicate information with less fear of giving an adversary an advantage if negotiations do not succeed. If, however, a document is not protected by a privilege, then identifying it allows the opponent to make a discovery request for it if the litigation continues. For more on mediation confidentiality, see Chapter Ten.

Suggest a neutral analysis

Some cases involve complex data that cannot be analyzed by laypersons. A securities class action, for example, may require assessment of complicated financial statements and an environmental dispute an analysis of future contamination. In such situations, parties typically hire partisan experts—who disagree with each other.

One option is for the parties to agree to hire a neutral expert within the context of mediation. Conclusions of an expert engaged by a mediator are not ordinarily admissible in court. Engaging an expert requires time, however, and—unless arranged in advance—requires adjourning the mediation. It may also involve added expense, and the lawyers may be instinctively fearful of an expert they do not control. As a result, neutral experts are rarely hired except in the very largest cases. I sometimes suggest engaging one, however, to test parties' belief in their arguments.

Example: A couple signed an offer to buy a home in a Miami suburb. The deal fell through, and the buyers sued the seller for breach of contract. The two sides argued strongly about liability, but the mediator soon realized that their disagreement over damages posed a much more serious obstacle. The buyers claimed that the sale price was more than $250,000 below the fair market value of the house, giving them a large "benefit of the bargain" claim. The seller said that the sale occurred at most $25,000 below market value, so the plaintiffs had no significant damage claim.

Narrowing the parties' disagreement over liability seemed useless as long as they disagreed so strongly about damages. I also thought that the dispute over fair market value would be much simpler to resolve than the disagreement about liability, which turned on witnesses' credibility.

Therefore, I suggested that the parties authorize me to hire an independent appraiser, who would provide a confidential report, not usable in court. The defendants agreed immediately, but the plaintiffs rejected the idea, saying that they preferred to get their own appraiser. By doing so they tacitly admitted that the claim that the house was a great bargain was a bluff, although they might be able to find a partisan appraiser to support their argument. The discussion then turned to the risk and cost to both sides of going to trial. A month later the case settled.

2. Poor Analysis of the Litigation Alternative

a. Responses to Cognitive Distortions

We have seen that providing information is rarely enough to resolve disputes over legal issues, because disputants consistently disagree about the likely outcome even when the evidence is essentially uncontested. This is because cognitive forces make people consistently fail to perceive data accurately and often to misevaluate the significance of what they do see. It is very difficult to eliminate the effect of cognitive forces completely, but there are steps that you can take to minimize their impact. This section describes some of the key cognitive forces that distort disputants' analysis of legal cases and suggests techniques to deal with them.

Selective perception

Humans instinctively form a viewpoint or image of any new situation—in mediation terms, they create a "frame" in which they view a dispute. People then process any new information they receive about the situation through their existing frame. When a person receives data that conflict with his frame, it creates clashing images in his mind—"cognitive dissonance." The human brain tries to eliminate this dissonance by unconsciously filtering out data that conflict with the existing frame.

This tendency to disregard data is known as "selective perception." Selective perception most likely explains, for example, the results of the Harvard experiment mentioned at the start of this chapter: students assigned to the plaintiff instinctively formed an image of the case that favored their client and then unconsciously filtered out data in the instructions that contradicted their image, while students assigned to the defendant did the opposite.

Selective perception poses a serious problem in mediation. A typical litigant will quickly form an opinion about who is right in a controversy. Most people instinctively prefer to see themselves as in the right, because viewing oneself as at fault provokes feelings of shame and perhaps the duty to make amends. Once litigants adopt a view that they are in the right, however, they are subject to selective perception. Each side unconsciously filters out data that conflict with its "take" on the case and, at the same time, give full weight to information that reaffirms it, becoming even more convinced that its initial view was correct. Mediators often encounter cases in which the facts are largely undisputed but parties disagree vehemently about who will win in court. Each litigant's perspective seems plausible to itself, because selective perception has caused it to disregard the evidence that contradicts it.

The effects of selective perception are aggravated by the task of advocacy itself. When lawyers and parties become involved in litigating a case, a key challenge is to present a favorable view of their position. They do so by stressing facts and arguments that support their viewpoint and denigrating ones that undermine it. A lawyer's job, in other words, often requires acting as if she has selective perception. Ideally, people would separate the task of building a case from the responsibility of analyzing it. Many disputants find it impossible, however, to separate advocacy from assessment and become convinced by their own arguments. To deal with the problem of selective perception, consider these options:

- ○ Encourage the parties to speak.
- ○ Use charts and other visual aids.
- ○ Explicitly question gaps.
- ○ If you repeat, use different words and tone.
- ○ Ask disputants to summarize the other side's key points.

Encourage the parties to speak. One excellent option is to encourage parties to speak for themselves, either during an opening session or in ad hoc tête-à-têtes with a counterpart on the other side. The reason is that a party is much more likely to listen to an opponent than to a lawyer. Fairly or not, disputants tend to view the lawyer on the other side as a hired gun and to disregard what he says. Listeners are usually also suspicious of what opponents say, but are likely to listen more carefully to them—if only to see whether the speaker makes an admission or misrepresentation about what happened. As a result, both lawyers and parties pay better attention to statements made by an opposing party.

Use charts and other visual aids. Lawyers are accustomed to dealing with printed documents, especially the proverbial "fine print." Nonlawyers, by contrast, may absorb information more effectively when it is presented in other formats. A disputant who misses information in a memo, for example, may be able to absorb it if presented or reinforced with a chart or graph. Similarly, data that are skipped over in black-and-white type may be remembered if highlighted in color, and information that fades out on a printed page can become much clearer if projected in bullet points or enlarged on a foamcore board.

Explicitly question gaps. As a mediator discusses issues with disputants, it often becomes apparent that they are slighting, or missing, certain data. The most straightforward way to deal with such gaps is to ask about them, in effect shining a spotlight on the omitted item. Questions can be asked in a wide variety of ways; how to do this is discussed in the next section.

If you repeat, use different words and tone. It may be useful to repeat something that someone else has said, especially if the first speaker is someone your listener might tend to ignore. You may even want to repeat yourself if a listener does not "get it." Repeating something in the same words and tone, however, is often ineffective and irritating. If you have to repeat a statement, vary your tone or wording (for example, by turning a question into a declarative sentence).

Ask disputants to summarize the other side's key points. It can be useful to ask someone to summarize points made by an opponent; gaps will stand out, and the tone of voice may tell you something about the speaker's attitude. Asking disputants to summarize an argument may also push them to confront its strength or focus attention on an issue they have slighted.

I do not ask parties to summarize arguments in their opponent's presence, however, because they are likely to resent being asked to "parrot" an adversary's "bogus" argument and often do not do it justice, stimulating an adversarial exchange. I prefer to do this in the privacy of the caucus. I may:

○ Express doubt about what the other side is saying and ask for help. ("I'm not sure which is their main argument on the contract issue. . .what do you understand them to be saying?")

○ Note that the disputant has been living with the case much longer and so probably better appreciates the opponent's position.

○ If, as often occurs, a summary seems erroneous or incomplete, point this out diplomatically. ("Hmm. . .what I thought I heard was that. . .")

Over-optimism

Humans are always overly optimistic about the future. People in surveys, for example, consistently predict that they will be healthier and earn more than the general population. Humans also tend to believe that more good things, and fewer bad ones, will happen to them than to people as a whole.

Disputants are also overly optimistic about the likely outcome of their cases. One reason is that they adopt biased points of comparison. A plaintiff, for example, may "latch on" to a particular case reported in the news in which a party recovered a very large judgment, while a defendant is more likely to remember a case in which the defense prevailed. Both sides may admit that the current case is somewhat different from their comparison case, but they overemphasize the degree of similarity. A plaintiff may agree, for instance, that its claim is not the same as the one in which a claimant recovered $5 million, but will argue that its case must be worth at least $1 million, when to an outside observer the two cases seem entirely different.

A second reason for unrealistic assessments is not that disputants see their cases as similar to others, but rather as exceptions. Parties will sometimes concede, for instance, that a particular jurisdiction is not friendly to their kind of case, but argue nevertheless that their case is "special" in some respect and that therefore the general run of poor results does not apply to them.

The "endowment effect." The root of disputants' tendency to think that their own case is worth more than the general run of claims may lie in what psychologists call the "endowment effect." It is illustrated by the following experiment:

> *Example:* People are assigned to negotiate over the sale of a typical coffee mug. Before bargaining, each side is told to make a confidential estimate of the true value of the mug. A control group of observers is asked to make the same assessment. The results are as follows:
>
> | | |
> |---|---|
> | Persons given a mug and told to sell it: | $7.12 |
> | Persons told to buy the same mug: | $2.87 |
> | Observers told to appraise the mug: | $3.12 |

This experiment demonstrates that sellers of items consistently tend to "endow" what they own with special value. Buyers tend to undervalue the same items, but as the results of the control group show, the major distortion occurs in the minds of sellers. In the context of settlement, it is plaintiffs who are "selling" a claim to defendants, who pay money to "buy" and extinguish it. Because of the endowment effect, plaintiffs in particular have difficulty assigning a realistic value to their claims.

The effect of these forces is that parties in mediation are consistently overly optimistic about their chances of prevailing in court. If a plaintiff has what an objective observer would see as a slightly-better-than-even chance, it tends to see its prospects as excellent, a case that an outsider would view as weak is 50–50, and so on. Defendants also err, but on the downside—for example, seeing a case that is realistically a toss-up as a clear winner. Again, when both sides in a dispute—or even just one of them—is overly optimistic, they are likely to disagree about what would be a fair settlement.

The two primary causes of over-optimism, unrealistic points of reference, and the tendency to see one's case as special, call for different responses.

- ○ Discuss case outcomes generally.
- ○ Question the special characteristics of the case.

Discuss case outcomes generally. If the problem is a false point of reference—if, for example, a plaintiff is comparing her case to the equivalent of the "megabucks winner" in the state lottery—you might first acknowledge the existence of the megabucks result and then introduce other, more modest outcomes. Ask the lawyer how many comparable cases have been decided in the jurisdiction recently and then ask how many of these have won a large verdict, a small verdict, or nothing at all.

If the lawyer is realistic, he may use your question as "cover" to offer a less optimistic viewpoint. If, however, the lawyer's numbers seem skewed, you may be able to provide anecdotes from your own knowledge. As a Boston-based mediator, for instance, I sometimes mention to unrealistic plaintiffs that although we may be known as the "socialist republic of Massachusetts," local court verdicts reflect Yankee stinginess and consistently lag national averages (plaintiff lawyers often nod knowingly at this point). Through comments like this, my hope is to get a disputant, without abandoning her original unrealistic reference, to start to compare her case to more common outcomes.

Question the special characteristics of the case. If the reason for over-optimism is that the litigant thinks his case is special and therefore immune from the general run of mediocre results, you can respond in two ways. You could draw out important characteristics of comparison cases, demonstrating that the disputant's case is not, in fact, as unique as he thinks. Or you can probe why the disputant thinks that the cited characteristics, although concededly unique, will have a significant impact on the outcome.

Example: An American company was in a contract dispute with a Saudi supplier. The mediator pointed out the mediocre verdicts in the local court system, but the plaintiff lawyer argued that these results were irrelevant because his client's situation was special: the defendant was a Middle Eastern company, and jurors would instinctively dislike it.

In response, the mediator drew out the lack of evidence supporting the plaintiff's liability theory, suggesting that this kind of evidence was more likely to drive the court outcome than general animosity toward Arabs. Alternatively, the mediator could have asked why the party thought that attitudes about Middle Eastern terrorists would carry over to executives from a country known to be allied with the United States.

Judgmental overconfidence

Consider this question: "What is the diameter of the sun?" To make the task easier, you can answer in terms of a range: pick a high and low number that are far enough apart that you have a 90 percent chance of being right. (Stop now and ask yourself: what is your high and low estimate of the sun's diameter?)

One would think that almost no one would fail to answer such a question correctly, because they are free to select as wide a range as necessary to account for their lack of certainty. But when I have asked a series of such questions to a variety of audiences, every group has answered most questions wrong. The problem is that people tend to answer with ranges that are too narrow. For example, someone who has no idea whether the sun's diameter 10,000 or 10 million miles will nevertheless answer in relatively narrow terms: "400,000 to 500,000 miles." (The actual diameter of the sun is 861,400 miles.)

What this example demonstrates is that in addition to being over-optimistic, human beings are overconfident about their ability to judge unknown facts. Peoples' tendency to be overconfident appears to spring from placing too much weight on aspects of a situation that they know about, while undervaluing facts about which they are ignorant. Stated in another way, people do not discount adequately for what they don't know.

In litigation, of course, parties and lawyers are required to estimate something that is hard to gauge—their chance of winning. Judgmental overconfidence suggests that litigants will consistently be overconfident about their ability to predict court outcomes. A party, for instance, might put its chances for success in a case at 60 to 70 percent. An objective observer, however, would build in a larger margin for error, perhaps estimating the chances at 40 to 70 percent—a 30 percent spread in the possible outcome rather than 10 percent. Overconfidence—especially about judgments that are also likely to be too optimistic—can be quite dangerous to litigants.

To counteract litigants' tendency to be both over-optimistic and overconfident about their predictions:

○ Discuss best and worst-case scenarios.

○ Focus on the most likely outcome: a mediocre result.

Discuss best- and worst-case scenarios. If a disputant has misevaluated a case because she is using a false point of comparison, it is helpful to present other examples, making the risk of loss more concrete in the litigant's mind. Parties are more likely to listen to warnings about bad outcomes if you first acknowledge the possibility of a good one. I often begin, therefore, by admitting that a big win is possible for the party and discussing it for a little while. This allows the party to "have it their way" for a time.

Having covered the best possibility, you can move on to other, less attractive outcomes. Ask the lawyer, for example, if he has seen bad results in this kind of case and what they have been. If counsel says that a loss is inconceivable, you might ask if he has ever lost a similar case or heard of anyone who has. If the lawyer recognizes the possibility but gives it an unrealistically low risk of occurring, ask in a curious tone how he arrived at his conclusion. You can also cite examples from your own knowledge. ("I hear that juries in Phoenix are. . .") Focusing on adverse outcomes lets you harness the power of loss aversion, discussed in Chapter Six; as disputants become more conscious of the risk that they may suffer a major loss, they will be more willing to agree to a compromise to avoid it.

Focus on the most likely outcome: a mediocre result. Another option is to draw a litigant's attention to the most likely outcome in the case, which is often a mediocre verdict rather than a clear victory for either side. Parties who see only two outcomes and focus only on the better one need to be reminded that many judgments fall somewhere in the middle. In a tort case, for instance, a mediocre outcome would be a ruling that the defendant is liable but that the plaintiff was contributorily negligent, resulting in a modest award. To the extent that a mediocre result replaces an outright win as the benchmark for evaluating a settlement, compromise will again appear more attractive.

For an example of exploring different damage scenarios, see Chapter 10 of the DVD.

Over-investment

People's tendency to be overconfident about their ability to assess the unknown is exacerbated once they invest in a prediction.

> *Example:* Experimenters asked subjects to handicap a horse race, then tested their confidence in their predictions of which horse would win. Some of the group were asked to place a small bet on their choice, while a control group did not.
>
> People who had placed a bet were found to be more confident, both that their horse would win and that they had estimated the odds correctly—that they were good handicappers—than subjects who did not place a bet.

In litigation, of course, parties and lawyers place large "bets" on "horses," in the form of the resources they invest in their cases. The "horse race" results suggest that litigants' investment will cause them to become even more certain that their predictions about outcomes are correct. A litigant who invests in a case because he is too confident will thus become even more sure that he has the best "horse" and plow more resources into the cause. In the language of gambling, litigants routinely place large bets and don't want to leave the table.

To respond to the impact of litigants' investments in their case:

○ Distance the "bettor" from his "horse."

Distance the "bettor" from his "horse." A mediator can reduce the "bettor" effect by making a party feel less invested in his prediction. You might, for instance, suggest that the money a litigant has spent on the case in the past—its "bet"—is a sunk cost. Money spent cannot be recovered regardless of whether one wins or loses, and is therefore irrelevant to decisions about the future. The real issue is whether to spend new money—place an additional bet—on litigation that has not been a clear "winner" so far.

b. General Suggestions

In addition to responses suggested for specific cognitive obstacles, the following techniques are helpful in reducing disagreements over legal issues. They progress from low-risk options to more forceful responses:

○ Ask questions.

○ Lead an analysis.

○ Draw attention to the cost of litigating.

○ Challenge overly optimistic assumptions.

Ask questions

The safest approach to misevaluation is to ask questions framed to help the disputants think through issues. Posing questions is particularly useful at the outset of a case, because you do not need to have completed your own analysis to do so. Indeed you can frankly admit that you are still feeling your way.

Open-ended questions. At the outset, use open-ended questions. (For instance, "What should I know about the case?" or "Tell me about your lost wages . . .") Pay close attention not just to words but also tone and how disputants react to it. Avoid "leading the witness"; ask, for example, "Have you checked that jurisdiction's attitude toward punitive damages?" rather than "It's true, isn't it, that the jurisdiction is hostile to punitives?" If a question could be construed as critical, don't pose it in joint session. Save it instead for a private meeting, and consider waiting until the disputants know you better.

Focused questions. As the process goes on, you should feel comfortable asking focused questions. ("Can you tell me more about the $500,000 claim for emotional damages? How would you present that in court?")

- If a question is potentially sensitive, try to phrase it so it comes from the opponent. ("They are arguing that at the April meeting your project leader admitted that the work was defective. They're pointing to an e-mail he sent on May 1. What should I tell them about that?")

- If possible, relate the question to something the listener has heard or seen. ("During the joint session you heard the defense stress that . . ." or "You probably saw in their mediation statement the argument that . . .")

- Bear in mind that if an issue was mentioned only in a private conversation or a document sent only to the lawyers, the parties may not know that an adversary has raised it. If so, alert them to its origin. ("When I talked to the other side, they asked why. . .")

- Phrase a question as a request for help, explaining that you're willing to present the party's argument to their opponent but need assistance to do so. ("When I talk with them, what do you think I should say about lost profits?" or "They're pretty certain to argue that . . . Can you give me anything I can take back to them?")

Confrontational questions. If gentler tactics do not work, you can make questions more pointed:

- To a plaintiff who has made a large money demand without substantiating it: "Can you explain how you calculated the $5 million in lost profits? Are there any documents I could look at to flesh that out?"

- To a defendant who claims that it has no exposure to multiple damages: "Is there a case that says that the court will have to throw out the punitives claim? . . . Can you give me a copy of it? . . . They're arguing that the appeals court ruled the other way; is that true?"

○ To a party who is ignoring a collection problem: "You're asking for $2 million in damages, but I only see insurance coverage of $250,000. How do you plan to collect that kind of judgment if you get it? Is it possible that the defendant will file for bankruptcy in response? What will you do if it does?"

Lead an analysis

Tougher questions can be combined with a more directive agenda. If questions do not expose the problem, then a point-by-point analysis may be necessary. A typical plaintiff, for example, must overcome four different hurdles to recover a money judgment:

○ Prove liability.

○ Overcome affirmative defenses.

○ Establish damages.

○ Identify assets to pay a judgment.

Each of these elements is composed, in turn, of subparts. Proving damages, for instance, can require submitting evidence on different components (lost wages, front pay, emotional distress, etc.) and providing an expert opinion on certain points. A structured analysis of a party's claims or defenses often illuminates weaknesses that the party has glossed over because of selective perception or over-optimism.

Lead a decision analysis. One way to conduct such a discussion is to use a technique known as "decision analysis," explained in Chapter Eight.

Look for receptive listeners. Some members of a bargaining team may be more realistic about a case than others. If so, you can work with a realistic member to persuade a less objective one. Occasionally the split is explicit—a lawyer may tell you privately that she is having a problem with a client—but more often you will have to assess each participant's attitude. Lawyers are usually more realistic than clients, because they have more experience with litigation and know that they are likely to be held responsible if the client loses. Some lawyers will pretend to disagree with a mediator, however, taking on a warrior role and counting on the mediator to argue for peace. Such advocates appreciate the fact that you are arguing for caution even while vigorously contesting what you say.

Written analysis. You can make your analysis more concrete by putting it down in writing. A written analysis can help focus disputants' attention on problems that remain obscure during verbal discussions. Putting an analysis in writing also objectifies it: you and the disputants can sit together analyzing a problem set out in front of you, rather than arguing with each other.

You can use a memo pad, but it is more effective to write the key points on a whiteboard or flip chart. Unless a participant affirmatively erases it or turns the page, the calculation will remain on display after you leave the room. It may prompt disputants to think more deeply about an issue and can give a realistic team member a springboard from which to work with other members while you are gone. You may return to find that your analysis has been marked up or replaced with a new one, advancing the discussion.

For an example of leading an analysis, see Chapter 13 of the DVD.

Draw attention to the costs of litigating

The legal system ordinarily does not reimburse parties for their legal costs, and in civil litigation these are often huge. Legal costs are in some ways even worse than bad outcomes, because while parties can hope to avoid a loss, they must ordinarily pay for their own legal expenses even if they win. The reality of litigation costs often makes parties' claims about the trial value of cases nearly irrelevant, because a plaintiff who wins a verdict will recover almost nothing after expenses, while a defendant who prevails will still be responsible for a very large legal bill. The more complex a case, legally or factually, the more significant the impact of litigation cost will be. Construction disputes, for example, are notoriously complicated to litigate because of the need to work through multiple claims and long series of decisions; as a result, legal costs often outweigh the merits in making settlement decisions.

Parties almost always understand the problem of legal costs in general terms, but often disregard it for purposes of settlement. They may hope to achieve a cheap victory or think that the specter of legal costs will force the other side to settle quickly. The effect is often that both sides in a case incur ever-higher litigation costs like competing bidders in an auction (unlike an auction, however, the loser in litigation also has to pay for its "bid").

You can sometimes move a party toward settlement by going over the future cost of litigating the case. Focus on the lawyer first, and allow her some leeway in responding—the issue of legal expenses can be a delicate one between lawyer and client. If a disputant's estimate of future costs appears unrealistic, apply the same methods as for legal claims generally: ask questions, lead a formal analysis, and explore various scenarios. When you discuss costs, be sure that the parties are inclusive in their analysis. A complete list of court costs, for example, includes not only lawyer's fees, but also the cost of items such as experts, deposition transcripts, and travel.

Don't raise the issue of legal costs immediately—as a rule of thumb, never mention it in the first caucus. Parties are often reluctant, even angry, to discuss costs early in mediation, feeling that it is unfair they should have to compromise simply because of legal costs. ("Why should I have to take less than I deserve just because the justice system is so expensive?") Disputants may also argue that their opponent will also save by settling, so it should be willing to compromise as well. Repeat players such as insurance companies worry that if they pay too much in one case simply to avoid defense costs, they will be hit with similar demands in others. Because of these factors, it usually is better to wait to raise the issue of litigation cost until the parties know that you have listened to them and the litigants have come to appreciate that simply arguing the legal merits is unlikely to produce a settlement.

For examples raising the issue of costs, see Chapters 13 and 16 of the DVD.

Challenge overly optimistic assumptions

Another option is to challenge a party's unrealistic assessment. Rather than posing queries, a mediator can explicitly state that he disagrees with the disputant's viewpoint. Directly challenging a party's opinion can shake its confidence in an unrealistic position, and if the person is bluffing, knowing that the mediator disagrees can make him less confident that he can pull it off.

Bear in mind that challenging a disputant is not the same as giving your own opinion about an issue. Thus to say "I'm afraid I don't share your optimism about getting punitive damages" is a challenge, while the statement "I think the likelihood that the court will award punitives in this case is 10 to 20 percent" is an explicit evaluation.

Offer an evaluation

If other methods do not work, a mediator can give a personal prediction of the likely outcome if the case is adjudicated—that is, an evaluation of the legal merits. Evaluation is an important, complex, and sometimes risky technique, and it is discussed separately in Chapter Eight.

A cautionary note

Before leaving the subject of legal analysis, let's consider for a moment what *not* to do.

Don't assume that an explanation will be enough. You might think that if an intelligent person hears a clear explanation from an unbiased observer she will be persuaded by it. You now know, however, that cognitive forces often make disputants partially deaf and blind even to neutral presentations. Don't assume that your analysis, however clear, will change a party's viewpoint.

Don't become an advocate for the "right" analysis. Your goal is not to make parties analyze a case correctly, but to help them reach an agreement. It's natural to feel frustrated when you present a thoughtful analysis and your audience doesn't seem to listen. But don't let yourself become upset. Your presence of mind and optimistic demeanor is your greatest asset. Remember that when disputants appear stubborn, it is often because they are unconsciously impaired by cognitive forces.

Don't expect the parties to reach consensus. Most parties who settle probably never agree about the case, despite the mediator's best efforts. Litigants settle for other reasons, such as to avoid the cost and risk of adjudication. Your goal in most cases is not to resolve the parties' disagreement about the merits completely, but simply to narrow the gap enough for compromise to appear sensible.

If the parties never fully grasp the issues but manage to agree, you have succeeded. If you lay out the merits with utter clarity but they remain in impasse, you have failed. Analyzing issues is merely a technique to reach a goal, not the goal itself. Don't let it get personal.

3. Concerns about Precedent and Reputation

Parties sometimes refuse to settle out of concern that an agreement will have a precedential impact, leading to pressure to make similar concessions in other cases. This is true whenever a case in mediation is similar to other disputes in which a party is involved. A company, for example, may worry that if it makes a large cash payment to a discharged employee in order to avoid legal costs, word will get around and it will face copycat claims. Alternatively, a lawyer may resist agreement for fear of harming his personal reputation for toughness. There are several possible strategies to deal with concerns about precedent or reputation:

○ Reframe terms to remove the issue.

○ Make sensitive terms confidential.

○ Recharacterize the issue so that the outcome appears unique.

○ Point out the risk of setting a public precedent.

Reframe terms to remove the issue

The most effective response to a precedential concern is to reframe terms so that there is no impact.

Example: An electric utility was mediating a dispute with consumer advocates over its request for higher rates. The company was resisting an agreement, however, because it was concerned that while a particular rate of return on investment was acceptable in that particular context, it might set a harmful precedent for future rate requests.

> In response, the mediator pointed out that the rate of return was only relevant as a step in adjudication. If the parties were settling the case, there was no need to replicate the adjudicative process. They could simply agree on a total dollar return and rates to achieve it, without specifying the components in the calculation.

Make sensitive terms confidential

A precedent-setting settlement is like Bishop Berkeley's famous falling tree: there is arguably no "sound" unless someone is present to hear it. Having outsiders hear about a settlement can sometimes be avoided by making the terms confidential. Defendants in particular, however, sometimes worry that plaintiffs will violate confidentiality guarantees. One option is to build compliance incentives or sanctions into a settlement.

> *Example:* A candidate for the ministry sued a church for allegedly discriminating against him. The church was willing to waive its legal immunity from suit and offer compensation to the claimant, but its lawyer was concerned that the waiver might set a precedent, exposing the church to demands in less worthy cases. An agreement was worked out under which compensation would be paid to the plaintiff over a two-year period, with a provision for forfeiture of part of the payment if he disclosed the terms of settlement.

Recharacterize the issue so that the outcome appears unique

Confidentiality is not a complete answer if the litigants expect to deal with each other over the same issue in the future. If the issue cannot be eliminated entirely, one option is to recharacterize it so that it loses some of its precedential impact.

> *Example:* Recall the homebuyer case described earlier, in which a couple sued a home relocation company when the company's seller refused to go through with the sales contract. The couple's claim to significant damages evaporated when they refused to hire an independent appraiser, but this did not make them give up. They continued to press for specific performance of the deal or, failing that, a large

amount of money. The mediator learned that the plaintiffs' tough stance was motivated in part by the fact that the husband, a lawyer, had promised his angry wife that he would "do whatever it takes" to get her the house.

The relocation company's inside counsel objected vehemently to paying a six-figure settlement, stressing that he had been able to settle other "disappointed buyer" complaints for an average of $20,000 apiece, one-tenth what the present plaintiffs were demanding. This couple had no more provable losses than other purchasers; how could he explain to his boss that he was paying them a huge amount just because they ignored reality?

The mediator responded that this case should be put in a separate category—"lawyer husbands"—that distinguished it from other cases. The company should expect to have a large "lawyer-husband" claim every few years, just as insurance companies had to deal periodically with hurricanes. A large payout for a hurricane, however, did not mean that an insurer would pay out excessively on routine claims. The lawyer began to joke about "crazy lawyers" and gradually appeared to carve out a special spot for the case on his mental map. The company eventually made the six-figure payment—still only half what it would have cost to litigate the case.

As this example shows, even a distinction that is somewhat arbitrary can be helpful if it permits a bargainer to convince himself or others in his organization that a settlement will not set a harmful precedent.

Point out the risk of setting a public precedent

If nothing else works, you can point out that a loss in court would establish a much more public benchmark than a confidential settlement. This is another example of emphasizing the worst alternative to a negotiated agreement to persuade a party to accept a mediocre outcome. It may be wiser, you can argue, to agree to a private compromise than to risk losing badly in public.

Conclusion

Disagreements about the legal merits strongly affect disputants' bargaining strategy and settlement decisions. The methods set out in this chapter will help you narrow these disagreements, making it easier for them to settle.

4. Summary of Key Points

Lack of Information
- Promote an exchange of data
- Suggest reliance on representations, with a right to verification
- Take advantage of confidentiality
- Suggest a neutral analysis

Poor Analysis of the Litigation Alternative
a. Responses to Cognitive Forces That Distort Judgment
- Selective perception
  - Encourage the parties to speak
  - Use charts and other visual aids
  - Explicitly question gaps
  - If you repeat, use different words and tone
  - Ask disputants to summarize the other side's key points
- Over-optimism
  - Discuss case outcomes generally
  - Question the special characteristics of the case
- Overconfidence
  - Discuss best- and worst-case scenarios
  - Focus on the most likely outcome: a mediocre result
- Over-investment
  - Distance the "bettor" from his "horse"

b. General Suggestions
- Ask questions
- Lead an analysis
- Draw attention to the cost of litigating
- Challenge overly optimistic assumptions

Concerns about Precedent and Reputation
- Reframe terms to remove the issue
- Make sensitive terms confidential
- Recharacterize the issue so that the outcome appears unique
- Point out the risk of an adverse public result

Chapter **8**

Merits Barriers: Evaluation and Decision Analysis

Marjorie C. Aaron and Dwight Golann

A mediator's ultimate weapon for influencing divergent case assessments is to offer an evaluation. Evaluation is an important, risky, and controversial tactic that should be carefully considered, structured, and delivered.

To understand the difference between evaluation and other mediator interventions, consider this metaphor. If mediators were doctors, fostering an information exchange might be the equivalent of recommending exercise and diet. Helping lawyers and parties to rigorously analyze their own views on disputed issues would be like administering medicine with potentially uncomfortable side-effects.

Mediator evaluation would be akin to surgery. Just as surgery can range from an arthroscopic procedure to a major operation, evaluation can vary from small and low risk to comprehensive and potentially threatening. Most people would not choose a doctor whose first response to every illness was to bring out a scalpel. At the same time, few would feel comfortable with a physician who refused to perform surgery regardless of need. The challenge for a mediator is to know when and how to perform evaluative "surgery" in the safest possible way.

What do we mean by *evaluation*? In this context it means forming and expressing one's views regarding a dispute. Evaluation can focus on a single issue ("It seems doubtful the statute of limitations defense will be successful") or the overall outcome ("The plaintiff is likely to win"). It can be expressed as a range ("I think damages could run between $125,000 and $175,000"), a numeric probability ("I would estimate a 40 percent chance of success"), or a precise number ("I predict a $500,000 award in this case in Randolph County"). An evaluation can be expressed with certainty ("I am fairly sure the plaintiff will win. . .") or left vague ("I have some doubts about how a jury might react to. . .")

The idea that parties and lawyers evaluate their own cases is not controversial. However, we have seen that a party's numbers may be seriously distorted or may be driven by emotional needs, the symbolism of dollar amounts, or what they want to receive without reference to their trial alternative.

Lawyers and parties who enter mediation often expect the neutral to evaluate the issues in dispute. The 2008 *Report of the American Bar Association Task Force on Improving Mediation Quality*, for example, reported that 80 percent of the users of commercial mediation believe that some analytical input by a mediator is appropriate in at least half of all cases, 60 percent of users think it is helpful to have a mediator predict the likely court result, and 84 percent think it is helpful for a mediator to recommend specific settlement terms.

Having educated a mediator about their case, disputants anticipate that she will think about what she has heard. Professional mediators are not "potted plants" and do, in fact, form judgments much of the time. Lawyers and parties are thus reasonable to think that they can ask a mediator "What do you think?" or "How do you see this argument?" or "Where do you predict the damages will fall out?"; if a mediator refuses to answer, it is understandable that they may feel frustrated.

On the other hand, many mediators can recount a time they provided an evaluation, were rebuffed, and soon thereafter the process ground to a halt. Experienced lawyers talk of frustration with mediators who announce a "reasonable settlement number" and then alienate or entrench clients by trying to push the outcome toward their opinion. Because evaluation can be powerful, both negatively and positively, it is critical for mediators to evaluate appropriately, skillfully, and with minimum collateral damage, just as a surgeon must choose the optimal technique to achieve his goal with minimum postoperative harm.

Some commentators reject evaluation entirely, arguing that mediators should limit themselves to "reality-testing" through strategic questions.

The very idea of reality-testing, however, assumes the questioner has formulated an opinion about what is "reality" in the case and what is not. In practice, we think litigants often perceive evaluation in what some would describe as mere reality-testing. A mediator could ask, for example, "What are your thoughts on the causation issue?" "Do you think there's a problem on causation?" "How would you answer the argument on causation?" "Don't you have a causation problem here?" These differences in phrasing alone communicate a viewpoint, and even when a mediator's phrasing is scrupulously neutral, her facial expressions, tone of voice, and body language may suggest a judgment.

If disputants can sense a mediator's opinion in any event, there is an advantage to neutrals in offering a viewpoint skillfully, and to lawyers in knowing when and how to request one. This chapter looks first at classic evaluation and then examines how a technique known as decision analysis can enhance an evaluative opinion.

1. Evaluation

a. Benefits and Dangers

Benefits. Evaluation can cause litigants to question and reevaluate their own judgments and "bottom lines." When a neutral who has listened thoughtfully to a presentation of facts and arguments disagrees with a litigant's prediction of victory, the party may be motivated to rethink its position. Evaluation can, for example, help overcome the impact of selective perception and other cognitive forces discussed earlier.

A mediator evaluation can also satisfy a litigant's emotional desire for "my day in court." An evaluation approximates the civil justice paradigm—both sides present their stories and arguments and a neutral renders a judgment—but within the safer, nonbinding confines of mediation. Having presented their cases to a neutral, even one without a black robe, parties may feel less need to do it again before a judge.

A mediator's evaluation can also provide psychological or professional cover to litigants who realize negotiation concessions are necessary, but who do not want to move from an entrenched position without a rationale. Business representatives, insurance adjusters, government officials, and even individuals who feel obligated to family members often use evaluations to protect them from after-the-fact criticism.

Example: A mediator was working on a dispute between a government loan agency and a borrower who had defaulted on his mortgage. As the mediation progressed, it became clear the original lender had handled the foreclosure process poorly, making it difficult for the agency that inherited the loan to collect it. The agency representative was concerned about being criticized by a review board, however, for not making sufficient efforts to collect bad debts.

In caucus, the agency's lawyer asked the mediator to give him a letter evaluating the case and endorsing the decision to compromise. The agency wanted to show the letter to his board to obtain approval for the settlement, but did not want it to be shown to the borrower's lawyer, in case the settlement effort failed. The borrower's counsel agreed, the mediator wrote the letter, and the case was resolved.

Lawyers can also use evaluations to justify settlement to stubborn clients. Mary Alexander, a former president of the American Trial Lawyers Association, explains this effect:

My practice focuses on personal injury cases. . .The single most useful service provided by mediators is to provide a reality check for clients. People often come into a lawyer's office with very real injuries, but unrealistic expectations about what they can obtain from the court system. They have heard somewhere about a large award and assume it is typical, when in fact it is not. Clients are often in dire financial straits and physical pain, making it hard for them to listen to a lawyer's warnings about trial risk.

When a mediator, especially a former judge, explains the realities of present-day juries—often in language that turns out to be very similar to what I had said earlier—it makes a real impression. Clients are able to become more realistic, and to accept a good offer when it appears.

Disputants can also use evaluation as a convenient scapegoat for a difficult decision, even when the disputant privately agrees with the assessment. ("Once the mediator said the case was worth $100,000, there was no way I was going to be able to settle it for any less. . .")

Dangers. Mediator evaluation can also create a serious risk of harm to the process, making settlement more difficult. First and foremost, mediators who evaluate risk damaging their credibility as neutrals. As long as litigants believe that a mediator is impartial, they are willing to consider options, listen to questions, and make painful compromises. When a mediator evaluates, however, a disputant may conclude the mediator has "gone over to the other side," assuming that because the mediator *thinks* the other side will win, the mediator must *want* settlement to be skewed in the other side's favor. When the mediator next asks for compromise in such circumstances, the disputant is likely to resist.

A mediator's evaluation also risks negative emotional impact. In *Beyond Reason: Using Emotion as You Negotiate*, Roger Fisher and Daniel Shapiro write of people's "core emotion concerns." One of these is "affiliation"— the feeling of being liked and having a connection with another. Mediators seek to develop this sense of personal affiliation with the parties and lawyers in their cases. Disputants, however, often fail to separate the intellectual process of case evaluation from their personal sense of connection with the mediator. When a mediator evaluates her case negatively, the disputant's feeling of affiliation with the mediator may evaporate. Feeling alienated from or betrayed by the mediator, the litigant will then filter even the most innocent comment through feelings of antagonism—the phenomenon of attribution bias described earlier.

If these risks are not enough, consider these additional concerns. A "global" opinion of case value may freeze the bargaining process because neither side wants to accept a settlement worse than the neutral's "right" number—even when it would be wise to do so. A defense representative, for example, may refuse to compromise further, for fear of being second-guessed by his employer if he offers more than the mediator's assessment of the litigation outcome. In these circumstances, a mediator's evaluation can become a take-it-or-leave-it offer to both sides.

A deal "worse" than the mediator's trial evaluation will often be desirable, however, because a litigant's business or personal interests would be harmed by continued litigation. A plaintiff in an age discrimination case, for example, may have a good chance of winning a better award two years hence, but what will she do in the meantime? How is the litigation affecting her marriage or the family's ability to pay college tuition? Is she less likely to be able to secure a comparable job while the case is pending? These factors are not part of the legal case, but may carry far more value for the litigants.

The expectation of a mediator evaluation can also discourage bargaining. After all, why confront painful decisions about concessions when the neutral may soon vindicate one's position? Disputants may also assume the mediator will place her evaluation between their last offers, and thus be concerned that offering additional concessions will simply shrink the zone in which they can "win" in the evaluation. In a more general sense, participants who expect an evaluation may feel less responsibility for resolution of their dispute, disengage from negotiation, and cease looking for ways to break impasse.

The expectation of an evaluation also changes the focus of the dialogue. Participants emphasize their legal arguments, seeking to persuade the mediator as judge and jury. This, in turn, can cause parties to become even more convinced of the strength of their arguments and angry at the other side's advocacy. Evaluations also tend to turn the parties' (and perhaps also the mediator's) attention away from nonlegal barriers to settlement and creative solutions. And if the real barrier to agreement is a party's unresolved feelings of grief or a similar nonlegal issue, evaluation will be irrelevant.

Evaluation also assumes certain "truths" about mediators that may not be accurate: that the mediator is in fact neutral, not "rooting" for one side or the other, and that the neutral's evaluation has greater claim to "reality" because his perspective is not corrupted by the psychological traps and tendencies discussed in this book. It is worth asking if all of these assumptions are true—for example, that neutrality renders mediators immune from psychological forces.

There is hubris in a mediator's confidence that his evaluation, because of his neutrality, is representative of what any or even most neutrals would say. Most mediators would deny they are conveying a point of view simply because it is theirs and would say, instead, that theirs is the neutral view—what experienced, dispassionate observers generally would say about the case. As the following experiment shows, this assumption is probably wrong.

Example: More than a hundred litigators from national law firms and corporations sat as arbitrators in a mock case. After reviewing stipulated facts, opening statements, excerpts of testimony, and closing statements, they were asked to render awards. The arbitrators' decisions regarding liability on contract and fraud theories diverged widely, and their awards also varied greatly, ranging from $100,000 to $6 million. These differences appeared even though the arbitrators were working from identical case files and were homogenous in their training and demographics.

In summary, evaluation can:
- Prompt a reassessment of an unrealistic case valuation.
- Satisfy emotional needs by providing a "day in court."
- Provide cover from criticism from an absent supervisor or constituency.
- Shield a lawyer or party from blame for a compromise.

However, it can also:
- Harm the mediator's credibility and destroy rapport.

○ Make disputants refuse to accept outcomes less favorable than the evaluation.

○ Freeze bargaining.

○ Distract disputants from focusing on the real obstacles to agreement.

○ Shift resolution toward the mediator's individual viewpoint.

Given its inherent dangers, our fundamental advice regarding mediator evaluation is this: "only when necessary, and with humility." To us, "necessary" means evaluation should be undertaken as a strategy of last resort, when it appears to be the only way to break a negotiation deadlock. At that point—even if all the risks of evaluation come to pass—they are of no ultimate consequence, because the case probably would not settle in any event. Of course when evaluation is necessary, the best practice is to capture its benefits *and* limit its risks. In the discussion that follows, we suggest ways to be as sure as possible that evaluation is necessary, the timing is right, and the opinion is tailored to minimize risk and maximize effectiveness.

b. Whether to Evaluate

When should an evaluative mediator not offer an opinion? The simple answer is this—when it is not necessary. Many apparent disagreements about legal issues do not require evaluation. It may be, for instance, that:

○ The problem is caused by lack of or differences in the parties' information.

○ A disputant is only pretending to disagree.

○ The disagreement is not driving settlement decisions.

Lack of information. The simplest and most common reason parties disagree about the merits, as explained in Chapter Seven, is that they are operating from different or incomplete sets of data.

> *Example:* In a case involving alleged injuries to the plaintiff's back and knee in a skiing accident, the parties had experts concerning the design of the ski lift, but neither side had consulted a medical expert about the plaintiff's back injury. Settlement positions were far apart because the plaintiff attributed his back problem to the accident and the insurer did not.
>
> When questioned by the mediator, the defense agreed that if the back injury was clearly caused by the accident, the plaintiff's settlement

range would be reasonable. The mediator responded by suggesting the defense consider commissioning an informal neutral medical review, or perhaps working out a settlement amount for the knee alone, pending further consideration of the plaintiff's back condition.

Disagreement is only feigned. When lawyers pound the table in caucus to emphasize unshakable optimism about their (mediocre) case, mediators may come to accept their sincerity, even if they doubt their intelligence. Or when a business principal asserts his 100 percent conviction that his "project manager's story will be believed by any jury in America," a mediator may assume his loyalty to his manager has rendered him deaf to the story's inconsistent ring.

Experimental data show, however, that absent highly specialized training, most of us are not very good at detecting lies, and hard experience has convinced us that mediation performances are often rehearsed to spin the mediator (Freshman, 2006). Some participants do know "deep down" that their witnesses are flawed or their legal argument tenuous, but they don't feel comfortable acknowledging it to the mediator. If a party has expressed unshakable faith in the merits of its case but offers a reasonable opening offer and keeps moving, there is simply no need for mediator evaluation.

Disagreement exists, but does not drive decision making. Parties may sincerely assess a legal case as "worth" only nuisance value or as virtually unshakable, but they may have reasons to pay more or accept much less than they think their case is worth. Their personal value system may, for example, find meaning in effectuating constructive changes, seeing demons get their due, or honoring individual contributions to an institution. An evaluation would be irrelevant to the decision making of these parties, but still risk alienating them. Before evaluating, therefore, ask what will motivate your disputants to settle. What do they hope to accomplish? If they did believe the risks of litigation were stacked against them, would it change their settlement decision? If not, then what would? Looking back from the future, what would make the participant feel settlement was worthwhile?

c. When to Evaluate

Delay an evaluation until as late in the mediation as possible. Waiting makes sense for three reasons: (1) it allows you to try other techniques and screen out false signals; (2) even where apparent impasse is caused by divergent views of the merits, the longer you wait the greater the chance evaluation will become unnecessary or less controversial; and (3) an evaluation delivered late in the process has greater power to move the parties toward settlement.

Waiting allows the participants time and reason to adjust their own evaluation of the case. People may come to recognize that weaknesses in their case are apparent to others. They may become more realistic about the case or at least about the other side's willingness to move. And as they invest more time in the mediation, people may become more committed to settling.

A later evaluation is also likely to be more powerful because the mediator has had time to gain the parties' trust and understand the issues being evaluated. Waiting also allows a mediator to learn more about the parties and their manner of thinking and speaking, allowing her to phrase the evaluation in more palatable ways. All this makes any opinion more persuasive.

Finally, waiting increases the chance the evaluation will yield enough movement to reach settlement. We find that evaluation gets us one "bump" in the parties' positions, and while the bump may be a substantial one, it cannot easily be repeated. If a mediator evaluates when the parties are still far apart, the resulting bump is unlikely to be enough to bring about a settlement, and the parties will slow down and lock in. If the same opinion is offered later in the process, after the parties have adjusted their expectations and closed some of the gap between them, it can inspire a bargaining leap far enough to reach agreement, or at least bring it within view. For all these reasons, evaluation should be a very late arrow in a mediator's quiver.

Suggestion: As a rule of thumb, never evaluate until:

- ○ You have completed at least one complete round of caucus meetings.
- ○ You have diagnosed and addressed other obstacles to agreement.
- ○ Bargaining is stalled or stalling.
- ○ You have talked with the disputants about offering an opinion.

There is one final "when" issue: should you obtain explicit consent from all parties before giving an evaluation? At one level, this is a matter of contract, which can be resolved by putting a sentence into the mediation agreement giving you the right to opine at your discretion (see the sample agreement in the Appendix). In practice, most civil litigators seem to expect a mediator to give an evaluation and would be disappointed if the neutral allowed a mediation to fail without doing so. Sometimes, however, disputants want to delay an evaluation because they do not want to focus on the merits and/or prefer to continue bargaining.

Example: A lawyer was pursuing a tort claim on behalf of a baseball coach at a private school who had recently died from unclear causes. The lawyer's theory was that the coach's death was due to "multiple chemical sensitivity" triggered by turf treatments. The school's position was that this theory was unfounded, but even if it was true such a claim was barred by the state workers' compensation law, which prevented employees from suing employers in tort. The school's representatives said, however, they were willing to offer special benefits to the coach's family as a purely voluntary gesture.

During the joint session, the plaintiff's lawyer played heavily on the "sympathy" card and at the same time threatened that the coach's widow was ready to rally alumni to attack the school for its stinginess. In response to the mediator's questions in caucus, the lawyer admitted privately to problems with his legal case. He asked the mediator not to opine about legal issues, however, because he thought as a tactical matter he would do better relying on a mix of threats and sympathy than his legal claim. The school, on the other hand, asked the mediator to point out to the plaintiff how weak the claim really was.

The mediator carried both sides' messages to the other. He privately suggested to the plaintiff that its legal case appeared to have serious problems, but did not give either side an explicit opinion about case value. The result was an agreement.

Suggestion: You have the following options when considering an evaluation:

○ Offer an opinion whenever it seems necessary, without seeking permission—provided the applicable rules allow this.

○ Check with both parties before evaluating. This is particularly appropriate if you wish to offer a global opinion ("I see the settlement value of this case as X because I see a trial value as in a range of Y to Z") or a comprehensive analysis of how you think the fact-finder would rule on each disputed issue.

○ Raise the option of evaluation with the party most resistant to bargaining further, as a way to prod it to consider whether it would prefer to make a significant move than to receive your opinion.

○ Offer each side a menu of options:

  • Continue the bargaining, provided someone makes a new offer.

  • Participate in a confidential listener exercise (described in Chapter Nine).

- Get evaluative feedback in the form of a settlement figure, a comprehensive analysis of the case, or less formal views on limited issues.
- Receive a mediator's proposal (also covered in Chapter Nine).

While indicating that we would be willing to undertake any of these options, we sometimes point out that the parties have successively less control as they go down the menu and that some, like the confidential listener exercise, require the assent of both sides. Presented with these options, many disputants decide to defer an evaluation and instead make a new offer or ask the mediator to play confidential listener.

d. Structuring the Evaluation

What issues?

The first question is what to evaluate. It is our sense that 20 years ago neutrals routinely provided flat opinions of "settlement value" or "what the case is worth." We believe mediators are now less apt to give bare, global evaluations and instead to think of evaluation as a means to jump-start a stalled negotiation—more like filling a "pothole," than building a road to a predetermined destination. The legal issue driving impasse may be relatively narrow, for instance whether the liquidated damages clause in a contract will be enforced. If so, there is no need to evaluate other issues on which the parties are closer to agreement. Indeed if the evaluator's view of other issues differs from that of the parties, an evaluation could worsen their disagreement.

Suggestion: If your evaluation is intended to stimulate bargaining, ask yourself:

- ○ What disagreements appear to be driving the impasse? For example, is the stumbling block liability or damages? What aspect of damages?
- ○ How specific an opinion do the disputants need to get over their impasse?
- ○ Do both sides need evaluative comments or only one? (Don't give an evaluation to a party who doesn't need it or is likely to react by toughening its position.)

Less may be more

A corollary to not evaluating unnecessarily is to build on the parties' opinions as much as possible, or "piggy-back." A plaintiff may have a more-or-less realistic take on liability but a highly inflated estimate of damages. If so, you might acknowledge the strength of the liability arguments, even if you do not entirely agree with them, and focus your evaluative comments on damages. It is easier to change a person's mind on one issue than two, and your concession on one point will often induce disputants to accept your viewpoint about another more significant issue.

Indeed, it is useful to highlight all of the elements of a party or lawyer's analysis with which you more-or-less agree before discussing where your evaluation differs from theirs. The fact that you accept the disputant's position on several issues makes it easier for it to listen to your somewhat different but well-reasoned analysis on a few (significant) other points.

If, however, you think a comprehensive settlement number is needed, you can provide one. This type of evaluation carries the greatest risk, however, and requires the most skill and diplomacy.

What standard to apply?

Prediction of the outcome in adjudication. Frame your evaluation as a prediction of how the likely adjudicator of the dispute would resolve a key issue or the entire case. If the alternative is a court, anticipate a judge; if it is a jury trial, a jury; if arbitration, the likely arbitrator.

Personal standard of fairness or the legally right result. Neutrals are sometimes tempted to focus on how they personally would decide the matter. Don't! Offering your own opinion about the "fair" or "legally right" outcome is dangerous, because it means personally rejecting the arguments of at least one side and perhaps both. Once a party learns that you believe her position is "less fair or right" than the other side's, she is likely at least to suspect your neutrality. And, in any event, your personal opinion is entirely irrelevant, because you are disqualified from ever adjudicating the case.

What it will take to settle. Another standard mediators sometimes apply is this: what will it take to settle this case? In other words, given the negotiation dynamics and the attitudes of the parties, what terms are likely to be minimally acceptable to everyone? Applying this standard, if one side were stubbornly unrealistic about the likely court outcome, a mediator would "bend" her opinion toward that view in order to secure an agreement. In doing this, the mediator is not actually evaluating legal issues, but rather the bargaining dynamics.

There is nothing inherently wrong with this approach, and it is often less risky than offering an evaluation of the legal merits. Disputants who might quarrel with a mediator's opinion about a legal issue will readily accept a neutral's assessment that its adversary will only agree to settle on unpalatable terms. After all, the mediator is merely recognizing what the party has been saying all along—that its opponent is unreasonable.

Interestingly, parties who would reject a settlement recommendation couched as an evaluation of the merits will sometimes accept the same terms if they are framed as a "what it will take" opinion, and vice versa. A party's reaction probably turns on whether it prefers to adapt to an opponent's unreasonableness or to a mediator's disagreement with its legal arguments. As a mediator your challenge is to assess which approach is most likely to be acceptable to a particular disputant.

It is hard for parties to disagree with the mediator's assessment of "what it will take," because it is unabashedly based on his reading of the other side. Moreover, as the bargaining progresses a mediator can offer several such opinions without contradicting himself, much like a weather forecaster who revises her forecast about the severity of an approaching storm.

How to prepare?

In some cases, an initial conference call with counsel will reveal that the participants hold widely divergent views on the merits and expect the mediator to give an evaluation. While a mediator should not necessarily commit to evaluate, she should prepare for it by asking for the critical documents on which the lawyers are basing their assessments. If lawyers place great weight on selected deposition testimony, court opinions, an expert's report, or critical correspondence, the mediator should review them. Early review of such documents is especially important, and easy to justify on a cost basis, in complex, high stakes cases.

One note of caution: while preparation is invaluable in a complex case, it is best to avoid forming any evaluation, even privately, on the basis of documents alone. We find the picture often changes dramatically after people present their case in joint session and a round or two of caucusing. If you have formed an opinion prematurely, you, like the disputants, will become subject to selective perception and may not be listening as well as you should.

Mediators commonly prepare their evaluations in the midst of the process, out of concern that adjourning will cause a loss of momentum. "Dead time," while waiting for a group to decide on its next offer, provides an opportunity to think through a simple analysis. In complex cases, however, you may need more time to formulate a good assessment and may have to call for an adjournment to do so.

In some cases, evaluation takes place through an informal dialogue. A mediator may ask if her input would be helpful, and if the answer is yes will explain her views, after which the caucus negotiation process continues. In such situations, the mediator hopes a relatively informal opinion will increase the party's willingness to move and influence its final settlement decision.

Evaluation may have more impact, however, if it is delivered in a distinctive, formal way. Particularly when the stakes are large, the issues are complex, and the mediation process has brought new issues to light or a participant wants a written opinion, lawyers may suggest the process be adjourned, allowing them time to brief key points and the mediator to prepare a formal "tablets from the mountain" opinion.

e. Delivering the Evaluation

What format?

Most mediators deliver evaluations to disputants in a caucus setting, to avoid humiliating a party in front of an adversary. Evaluating in caucus allows the neutral to articulate and even appear to accept a party's perspective, before turning to jointly analyze a significantly different question: what will some future decision maker do with this case? In caucus discussions, we often move deliberately to the disputant's side of the table to emphasize that we are jointly looking at a problem. We may concede the opposing side's key witness might well be lying, but then note that the witness has the demeanor and credentials to impress a lay jury. This is not something we could do with both parties present.

Another option is to hold a more formal session, creating more of a feeling of a "day in court." In this format, a mediator might ask the parties and lawyers to meet again in joint session and present summary arguments, with the mediator in the role of advisory judge. Going through this process may make parties more ready to settle. Doing an evaluation in a "moot court" format is dangerous, however, because it casts the mediator more firmly in the role of judge, making it seem the evaluation is a personal opinion, undermining the perception he is neutral, and making later interaction more difficult. Even if you hold semi-formal arguments, it rarely makes sense to deliver your "opinion" in the presence of both parties, as the following example shows.

> *Example:* A company that designed a software system for the Massachusetts welfare program sued the state for $9 million it had refused to pay under the contract, and the state counterclaimed for $15 million in federal reimbursements it said had been lost because of problems with the software. The case went to mediation with a neutral known for his work as an arbitrator.
>
> After a morning of unsuccessful discussions, the neutral announced that he would hear arguments from the parties and then give an advisory opinion. After listening to each side, the neutral retired briefly and returned to deliver his views. He said the state owed nothing under the contract, and the evidence on the counterclaim was not clear enough to reach a conclusion.

> The participants had assembled to hear the verdict, and as it was announced the claimant's CEO reacted as if he'd been hit with a two-by-four. The state welfare commissioner was affected as well. He had previously been anxious to settle the case with a small payment, but after hearing the evaluation was eager to collect his $15 million. It was only with much difficulty that the lawyers negotiated a walk-away agreement.

It is not necessary to evaluate the same issues with both parties. The fact that you give an evaluation of a particular issue to one side, for example, does not require you to give an evaluation of the issue to the other. Indeed if you think one side has an excellent legal case, there is usually no reason to tell them so—it will simply harden their position. You may cover liability and damages with the plaintiff if it seems overly optimistic on both issues, but focus only on liability with the defense because its take on damages seems reasonable.

However, if you do opine to both sides on the same ultimate issue, your bottom-line assessment to each must be the same. Although we try to adopt as much of each disputant's perspective as we can, we *never give different substantive opinions* to the different sides (for example, by telling each they are likely to lose).

Note that your view of an issue may be affected by your limited knowledge of the case. The party or her lawyer may know facts they have not shared; for example, a mediation statement may highlight a strong expert's report that affects the mediator's assessment, but counsel may know her witness, in fact, presents poorly.

It is often helpful to emphasize the areas in which you think a party's viewpoint is correct. As we have noted, communicating your honest assessment where it matches or is even a bit stronger than your audience's on a particular issue is good practice. A mediator might say, for example, "Look, I know people expect a mediator to harp on every weakness, but I would rather be clear. While anything is possible, I tend to agree with your point that provable damages are likely be fairly modest in this case. However, I see the chances on liability differently. . ."

When a mediator evaluates in private caucus, there is a risk participants will suspect him of giving different opinions in different rooms, telling each side bad news to encourage it to move toward the center. This is more likely to occur when participants have not worked with a mediator before, he has not had time to build trust, or he was imposed on the parties by a court. To dispel this suspicion, you may want to address it directly. Explain that it's not your practice to give different opinions to different parties, and that while you may phrase things differently, the substance of your evaluation will be consistent, as the lawyers will find out when they compare notes after the mediation is over.

One option is to put evaluations into writing on a notepad or whiteboard. This allows you to check your reasoning, visually reinforces the information, and makes it clear you are not "winging it" but have done your homework. We find it helpful to present numeric evaluations in the "scratch-pad" or decision-tree formats described later. We generally limit the written analysis to an outline, to leave leeway to adapt our oral explanation to the sensitivities of each side.

You may also note in passing that you have made a certain point in the other room. ("Now, I've said to the plaintiff I see real concerns about their ability to prove consequential damages, but I have to say I'm also concerned about your ability to avoid any liability at all...") Doing this confirms that you are balanced and the other side is being "taken to the woodshed" as well.

How? Tactfully, strategically, empathetically

As an immediate prelude to evaluating in caucus, consider summarizing silently, to yourself in the hallway, a party's perspective and arguments as well as your empathy for that side's predicament. The goal is for the participants in the room to feel you "get it"—that you fully understand their perspective. When you then turn to points where you differ, the participants will be more receptive. They can't easily tell themselves you didn't listen and dismiss your opinion. To hear someone articulate their views, and then thoughtfully explain why and where she disagrees with them, can be arresting.

When evaluating, be mindful of adapting your style of communication to your audience. Research confirms that "mirroring"—adopting another's body language, speech patterns, tone, and energy—can create rapport and positive emotion (Nadler, 2004). In a caucus room with informal, colorful participants (for example, representatives of an artists' collective suing their building's structural engineers), you can speak informally with colorful metaphors and expressive gestures. When meeting with the engineers, you would present your analysis in more precise and formal language, toning down your gestures and vocal range.

One reason to be careful about how you deliver an evaluation is that from the disputants' perspective the news is almost always at least somewhat bad, making the process a negative experience. Why does it matter if participants experience negative emotion in mediation? Research suggests negative emotions impair the ability to bargain by affecting cognition, thus reducing creativity, energy, and willingness to stick with a task (Shapiro, 2004). Because evaluation is likely to have a negative emotional impact, it makes sense to try to offset this as much as possible. This can be done through the manner in which you communicate and by expressing appreciation of a party's perspective and empathy for his circumstances.

The importance of distancing yourself

To reduce the likelihood participants will hold an evaluation against you, remember to emphasize that it is not your personal opinion about what is fair, but rather a prediction about how strangers—a judge or jury—would react to the case. You might stress that while these strangers will do their best to decide the dispute honestly, they won't know very much about the "real" situation and, if the dispute involves technical points, may have difficulty understanding it.

While acknowledging that the participants have superior command of the facts, you might note that your relatively superficial education about the case puts you in a position similar to the jury's. Precisely because you haven't probed the case as deeply as they have, you may be better able to appreciate the reaction of a more superficial observer like the future adjudicator. Again, use the language of prediction and do not claim certainty. By articulating your evaluation and acknowledging uncertainty, you encourage participants to acknowledge the uncertainty of their views as well.

As important as what you say, however, is what goes on in your mind: it is critically important that you not become invested in your evaluation. Having stated an assessment of a claim, it is natural to become annoyed when listeners don't "get it" and stubbornly persist in claiming a flawed case is bulletproof, a jury will sympathize with their unpalatable witnesses, and so on. Remember that the disputants may be rejecting your views for reasons other than their accuracy: agreeing with them, for example, may require accepting more of a loss compared to their hoped-for result than they are able to do at the moment. Or the opinion may call for a greater concession than their bargaining strategy allows. Or you may, just possibly, be wrong—after all, the parties or lawyers usually do know more about the case than you do.

> *Example:* In a recent case involving alleged fraud in a commercial contract, a mediator agreed liability was uncertain, but suggested that to prove the millions of dollars claimed in damages more proof would have to be offered. The case did not settle, and a year later the mediator received a triumphant e-mail from plaintiff's counsel, informing her of a $40 million damage award on not much more proof. As he had predicted, the local jury had decided to teach a lesson to the multinational corporate defendant, notwithstanding the slimmest of presentations on damages.

Remember that the case will only be tried once. Be humble when evaluating. No one can know the future. Becoming wedded to your evaluation and driving the bargaining toward that point will compromise your neutrality and create an adversarial relationship with people you are trying to assist.

One option is to express your prediction in probabilities ("I see an approximate 45 percent chance of winning on liability") and note that it will almost certainly prove wrong, because in any one trial, one side will win and the other will lose. To deal with this, consider putting your prediction in the form of multiple trial outcomes. ("If this case were tried ten times, I think you would win four or five times, but I am concerned you would also lose five or six times.") This allows you to agree with a party that it may in fact win, while also communicating that it is more likely it will lose.

For an example giving an evaluation, see Chapter 16 of the DVD.

f. After the Evaluation

Good evaluations do not necessarily settle cases. As noted, they are used more often to restart stalled bargaining processes than to propose a final set of terms. Mediators therefore need to think about what should happen *after* the evaluation to promote effective negotiations. Do the parties need time to reflect on what they have heard? To consult an outsider for more authority? In smaller cases, or when the principals are present, a mediator can give an evaluation and then ask for new offers. But if a case is complex or the evaluation surprises the listener or suggests a settlement range outside his authority, parties may need to adjourn to consider the implications.

Evaluation can be an effective tool to help break through merits-based barriers. You must next consider how to bring the negotiation to closure. If bargaining is to resume ask yourself these questions: Who should make the next concession? Are inventive terms possible that would obscure or cushion one side's defeat? Should you make a "what it will take" suggestion to take advantage of the impact of the evaluation, or cushion the result for the loser?

In conclusion, use evaluation only as a tool of last resort, and don't let it overshadow more facilitative techniques. But when facilitation fails and impasse looms because of parties' apparent unrealistic views of the merits, offering an evaluation may be the key to bringing the process to a successful result.

2. Decision Analysis

For most of us, the logic and procedure underlying the method known as "decision analysis" is quite natural and accessible. When faced with a decision, we inevitably choose among paths at the proverbial fork in the road. To choose wisely, we try to anticipate options and assess probabilities associated with each path. For a businessperson, the decision might be whether to maintain high cash reserves or make investments in product development or both. He would be wise to consider the likelihood of success in product development and to estimate the resulting revenues and costs. Litigants faced with deciding between settling or pursuing a litigation path should similarly consider challenges along the way, the likelihood of success at each step, and the range of possible results. Decision analysis uses the same logic and provides a quantitative method for considering the litigation path and comparing it to settlement options.[1]

Lawyers, clients, and mediators implicitly accept the logic of decision analysis when they argue about the merits of a case, discuss strengths and weaknesses, and relate them to a "reasonable" settlement figure. A lawyer whose defense client is *just about certain* to lose, and then be forced to pay *at least* $500,000 and *quite likely* between $700,000 and $1 million, will advise her client to offer much more in settlement than if she thinks the client has a *good chance* of avoiding liability, with a $300,000 award *most likely*, and only a *slight chance* of an award exceeding $500,000. This lawyer is considering different uncertainties in the case, and relating her assessment of probabilities and outcomes to settlement. However, because she is using inherently vague prose to express probabilities, she cannot communicate clearly the size of each risk or the impact of cumulative risks. (If you doubt this, ask a few people to write down, in percentage terms, what one of the italicized words means to them—we guarantee their percentages will be very different!) If the same lawyer were using decision analysis, she would assign numerical probabilities to her assessment of each risk and then estimate the monetary value of each possible case outcome, after deducting costs to be incurred before making a settlement recommendation.

Why work with decision analysis in mediation?

Decision analysis can help move participants toward settlement in mediation. Assigning numerical probabilities to possible twists and hard-dollar estimates to potential case outcomes can prove illuminating to participants who haven't related their lawyer's assessments, expressed in prose, to settlement value. Numbers tend to capture peoples' attention, perhaps by rendering the future more concrete. Using decision analysis enables participants to understand the cumulative impact of risk in the litigation, relating various theories to a precise outcome. It enables them to see the likelihood of each possible case outcome—whether, after all is said and done, there's a 10 percent chance of collecting more than $150,000, or less than a 30 percent chance of collecting more than $75,000, etc. By mathematically discounting each case outcome by its probability, decision

---

1. In litigation, decision analysis generally compares settlement to litigation risks that may be predicted but not controlled. Litigants analyze the risks and consequences associated with the litigation and decide whether to litigate or settle for a certain amount. While this chapter uses the term *decision analysis*, a purist may prefer using the narrower term *risk analysis* to the extent that the discussion focuses solely on the risks of litigation.

analysis yields a number both sides might view as "reasonable" settlement value.

Sometimes decision analysis is helpful not because of the numbers, but because discussion around the numbers helps participants detach—emotionally and personally—from their case. Decision analysis almost necessarily uses less emotional, less personal language than we often hear in mediation. No longer are parties arguing directly back to their lawyer's or mediator's suggestion that "your witness isn't very strong and you may lose this motion." Rather, they are looking at the numbers and discussing whether another witness, if located, could raise the percentage chance of winning a motion by 10 percent. The focus of attention is "mediated" by the easel, scratch pad, or computer on which the analysis is shown, and the task and tone become less oppositional and more focused on working with the problem.

Of course, the end numbers calculated through decision analysis can have power. When participants accept the logic of the method and recognize that the probability and payoff values in the decision analysis of their case are reasonably accurate, they may readjust their internal benchmark about what constitutes a fair settlement. The final discounted case value may thus have dramatic impact, providing reason or excuse for movement in negotiation toward settlement.

Do not assume that decision analysis should be limited to mediations involving engineers, business administrators, CFOs, and accountants. In our experience, a wide range of people, even many lacking post–high school education, can also understand it. No calculus is involved, just basic arithmetic. Most people do understand betting, and the logic of discounting for risk when making decisions. That is all you need. Even if a disputant does not follow the math, he will understand that a logical analytic method has been applied to his case, and its results may persuade him to adjust his settlement position. Whether introducing decision analysis will be productive in mediation depends less on whether participants will understand it—they will—and more on whether it will matter to them when making settlement decisions.

Two formats: scratch pads and tree structure

There are two ways of doing decision analysis. One we'll call a basic "scratch-pad" format. The other we'll refer to as "tree format" because it involves drawing horizontal treelike structures on paper or computer to demonstrate the interrelationships of the issues in the case. The two methods are logically identical, but they appear quite different.

Scratch-pad analysis may seem more familiar to people who are comfortable making quick bottom-line calculations. They may not need or care to see a map of the litigation and its flow or how one issue may affect another. As the name suggests, it requires a pen and a writing pad or whiteboard and marker. For more complex cases, an Excel spreadsheet can be used. One of the chapter authors generally uses the scratch-pad format, although will occasionally hand-draw full "trees."

The other author prefers the tree format as being more elegant and effective for people who process information visually. The tree method creates a map of the possible twists and turns in a case, using horizontal tree branches, generally moving over time from left to right, with the probabilities of each possible event carried on the drawing, ending with all the possible case outcomes at the far right. In relatively simple cases, a mediator can draw the decision tree entirely by hand on a regular note pad or easel. As with the scratch pad, a calculator makes the arithmetic easier. In more complex cases, analysis is best done on a computer using decision-tree software. (We use the TreeAge software available from TreeAge.com, but other software is available.) Printing it out is recommended if more than one or two participants will want to study and discuss it.

For examples of feedback in scratch pad format see Chapters 13, and in tree format Chapter 16, of the DVD.

A note on that final, calculated number—"discounted case value"

When using decision analysis in litigation, many people refer to the final number as the "settlement value" or the "reasonable settlement value" or the "case value." These terms suggest a normative claim—that someone is "unreasonable" by refusing to settle at or about that number.

In fact, the end number predicts the average result *if and only if* the event being analyzed will occur many times. When using this method for public health decisions that will be tested in large patient populations or business decisions to be tested over repeated consumer transactions, the number predicts a real average result. Remember, however, that when applied to litigation, the method still predicts the average of many, many hypothetical trial outcomes. *In fact, there will only be one trial.* The final calculated number from the decision analysis is not what will happen in that one trial; it is the *weighted average* of all the things that might happen. In reality, the trial will yield one and only one of the possible judgments or damages awards in the scratch-pad list or shown on the far right-hand side of the tree structure.

Because it cannot be said that a litigant should always settle for the "roll-back" or final, calculated number this analysis yields, we will not to refer to it as the "settlement value" here. We use the term "discounted case value" as reflecting the method's use of probabilities to discount the value for the various ways a case might end.

The analysis is only as good as the data

Whether using a scratch-pad format or formal decision trees, the outcome of any analysis is only as valuable as the input. This is true whether counsel is evaluating with prose such as "very likely" or "highly improbable" or with percentages. Carefully considered, experienced, and objective review of the probabilities in the case is essential.

Whatever the numbers, working through the process is valuable, because it forces you to explain and clarify your thoughts. Substituting alternative percentages and verdicts also helps identify which issues greatly affect case value and may therefore deserve close attention.

The method's central value is in revealing the cumulative impact of risk

If most mediation participants would agree that it makes sense to settle at a point that accounts for litigation risk, why do they so often cling to widely divergent positions? It may be due to perception bias and other psychological traps described in Chapter Seven, which cause them to estimate probabilities or damage awards optimistically. Yet often, when decision analysis is performed using participants' own estimates, the resulting discounted case value is far from their stated view of the "value of the case."

Successive hurdles. The central reason is parties' failure to consider the cumulative impact of risk in successive stages of the litigation. For example, a plaintiff's attorney may say he has a 60 percent chance of surviving summary judgment and also a 60 percent chance of prevailing at trial. The value of a verdict if the plaintiff wins, he says, will be $100,000, and the value of the case is therefore $60,000 (0.60 × $100,000). He has failed to appreciate that the likelihood he will both survive summary judgment and win at trial is much lower than 60 percent, because the risks on each event must be multiplied against each other. The chance of surmounting two risks in litigation, each with a likelihood of 60 percent, is 0.60 × 0.60, or 0.36, and the discounted value of litigating through trial in this case would be $36,000.

Suggestion: Whether using scratch pad or trees, when explaining the concept we sometimes analogize the situation to flipping a coin twice in a row. The chance of getting heads on any one flip is 50–50, but as even nonmathematical disputants appreciate, the chance of getting heads twice in a row is lower than 50 percent. Winning two separate issues in a case is like getting heads twice.

Using a scratch-pad format, we might make this notation:

0.60 × 0.60 = 0.36 chance of a plaintiff verdict
0.36 × $100,000 = $36,000 (discounted case value)

Using a tree structure format, we would first sketch it as shown in Figure 8.1.

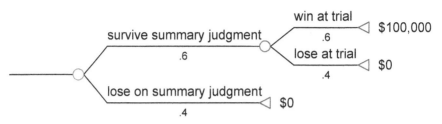

Figure 8.1

This tree records the lawyer's professional judgment that the plaintiff has a 60% (0.6) chance of surviving summary judgment by displaying 0.6 beneath that labeled branch. Thus, a probability of 40% (0.4) is displayed beneath the branch labeled "lose on summary judgment." The next phase of the litigation occurs after—to the right of—the "survive summary judgment" branch. (If the plaintiff loses, there is no next phase. For simplicity's sake, we have ignored any appeal option.) Having survived summary judgment, the next pair of branches would be "win at trial" or "lose at trial" with a 60 percent probability assigned to winning and a 40 percent probability assigned to losing. As in the scratch-pad example, we have assumed the "payoff" or damages will be $100,000 if the plaintiff wins and $0 if the plaintiff loses. The end node—the last thing that can happen in the litigation—is represented by the triangle symbol. The payoff number and its probability (shown as "P =") appears to the right of that node.

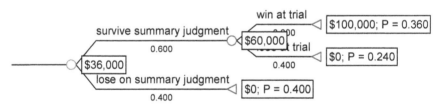

Figure 8.2

As depicted in Figure 8.2, to find the case's discounted value, the decision tree would be "rolled back," which means the values of all possible outcomes are discounted by their probabilities and summed. Calculations typically start at the right side. By multiplying the probability of plaintiff's verdict at trial by its payoff and multiplying the probability of defense verdict by its payoff and adding the two figures together, a discounted value of $60,000 is calculated (or "rolled back") and displayed beside the chance node that branches into the trial possibilities (win at trial or lose at trial), and after or to the right of the node "survive summary judgment." Thus, the expected value of the case after surviving summary judgment and before trial would be $60,000, as reflected earlier.

Any assessment of this litigation must also account for the summary judgment phase. Thus, the discounted value of the trial branches—$60,000—must be multiplied by the probability that the litigant will "survive" summary judgment (the opponents motion will be denied), 60 percent. The litigation's discounted case value is thus $36,000. The $24,000 difference reflects the additional discount for the risk of losing on summary judgment.

Different possible verdicts. The calculation of cumulative risk also affects the value of cases in which there are different possible verdict amounts. Assume the plaintiff in the preceding case has $100,000 in provable injuries but is also seeking punitive damages, which if granted will raise his recovery to $500,000—if he can collect it (punitive damages are generally not covered by insurance). Asked to put a percentage on the verdict possibilities, the plaintiff lawyer says the odds of obtaining a $500,000 verdict are at least one in three. He believes the case is therefore worth about $150,000 and will not settle for less. The lawyer's estimates of a high verdict seem optimistic to the mediator, but he plugs them into the model to see how they play out. The scratch-pad calculation goes as follows:

Likelihood of overcoming summary judgment: 60%
Likelihood of winning at trial: 60%
If these events occur, likelihood of damage awards is:

$100,000 – 66%
$500,000 – 34%

This yields the following valuation:

Liability:	Summary Judgment		Trial		Likelihood of plaintiff verdict
	.60	×	.60	=	.36

Damages:	.66 × $100,000 =	$ 66,000
	.34 × $500,000 =	$170,000
		$236,000

Discounted case value: .36 × $236,000 = $85,000

The decision tree drawn for this case would look like Figure 8.3.

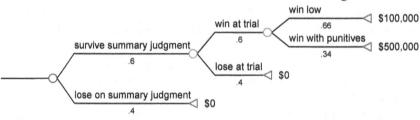

Figure 8.3

The discounted case value would be found by calculating or "rolling back" as shown in Figure 8.4.

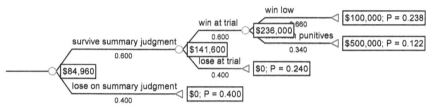

Figure 8.4

By setting forth these numbers and doing the math in scratch-pad or tree format, the mediator can demonstrate to the lawyer—and, equally important, his client—that even if the lawyer's assumptions are true, the discounted case value will be only about $85,000.

A lawyer may see the results on the motion and at trial as linked: "If I can convince the judge to deny summary judgment, the court will be rolling my way and our chances at trial will be more like 80 to 90 percent." The mediator can quickly redo the math, plugging in 85 percent in place of 60 percent for trial risk. This raises the likelihood of a plaintiff verdict to 51 percent (0.60 × 0.85). But 51% × $236,000 is still only a bit over $120,000, well below the attorney's $150,000 estimate. Implication? It may be time for the plaintiff to rethink its settlement goal.

> At this point the plaintiff might ask: "Try to persuade the defendant to come up to $150,000." The mediator might respond: "I would be happy to convey that you won't settle for less than $150,000. But if the other side won't meet that number, it probably makes sense, considering the risks, to accept a different number, as long as the offer is at least as high as your discounted case value."

A basic truth—the cumulative impact of risk—drives this example. Even aggressively optimistic litigants cannot avoid its effects. Assuming the plaintiff's chances of overcoming each hurdle are as good as his lawyer believes, the likelihood of surmounting all the hurdles and winning the large prize is still only modest.

Dealing with complex realities: multiple verdicts

Suppose a case in which the plaintiff has an 80 percent chance of surviving summary judgment and a 60 percent chance of winning on liability, making 48 percent the cumulative probability of success for the plaintiff. However, a liability finding could result in a range of possible verdicts. To keep the analysis manageable, we commonly assume three scenarios—excellent, poor, and average. In a commercial dispute these might be:

○ Out-of-pocket damages: $100,000.

○ Lost profits plus out-of-pockets: $250,000.

○ Punitive damages plus profits and out-of-pockets: $2 million.

As the number of possibilities increases, it becomes more and more difficult for lawyers and clients to estimate case value using "gut judgment." Decision analysis can help. Again, the mediator has a choice between using the parties' estimates or her own, but the method is the same. Assume the probabilities of each verdict are as follows:

○ Out-of-pocket damages: 50 percent.

○ Lost profits plus out-of-pockets: 45 percent.

○ Punitive damages plus profits and out-of-pockets: 5 percent.

What is the value of the case now? The likelihood of a plaintiff's win on liability is still 48 percent. We must now divide the victory into three parts, corresponding to the three possible verdicts. We can calculate the value of each verdict chance, then aggregate those values to arrive at the total verdict value, then multiply the result by 0.48. In scratch-pad format (again using a hand calculator) we would write:

Out-of-pockets	.50 × $100,000	=	$ 50,000
Lost profits	.45 × $250,000	=	$112,500
Punitives	.05 × $2,000,000	=	$100,000
	Average value of verdict	=	$262,500

Discounted case value = 0.48 × $262,500, or $126,000

Using a tree format, the analysis would look like Figure 8.5.

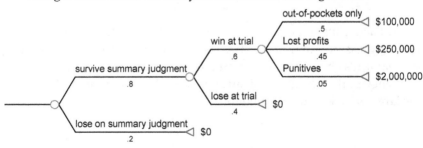

Figure 8.5

Of course, one case will yield only one outcome—zero if the plaintiff loses and either $100,000, $250,000, or $2 million if it wins. We remind

participants that this calculation means only that if the case could be litigated 100 times, the plaintiff would be predicted to win 48 times and lose,
recovering nothing, 52 times. Within the 48 times the plaintiff would win,
the verdict would come in at one of the three levels, with the likelihoods
as stated. Given these assumptions, analysis tells us the weighted average
of plaintiff's recovery over 100 cases would be $126,000, as indicated in
Figure 8.6.

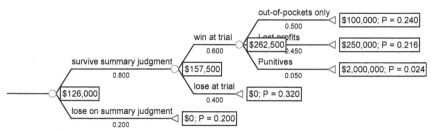

Figure 8.6

The tree format may be preferable for representing the complexities of reality

It may be that *no* format could represent every possible nuance and
future uncertainty. Is it possible that three jury members will be killed
on the eve of their second day of deliberations, requiring a mistrial? It is
possible the defendant CEO will be found to have a criminal record? Is it
possible a jury will disregard the damages theories presented and fashion
their own? The impossible does happen sometimes.

More often, there are many foreseeable twists and turns to litigation.
In a typical employment discrimination case, the plaintiff can survive
summary judgment or not; win or lose at trial; or be awarded back pay
only, emotional distress damages and back pay, or back pay plus emotional distress plus front pay. A wide range of years might be applied to
the front pay award. Punitive damages could be awarded in any or all
of these scenarios. Where a plaintiff was a commission salesperson, the
jury might use a higher or lower estimate of annual past or future lost
compensation.

If a litigant wants to assess her case, she might reasonably seek to estimate a range of numbers for each of these damages categories—back pay,
front pay, emotional distress, and punitive damages—and consider the
likelihood of each. At some point, the scratch-pad format may be difficult
to follow, and the visual mapping aspect of the decision-tree format may
prove more useful. The array of branches on the tree, building from back
pay only to back pay and front pay, accounting for a range of emotional
distress damages, a range of punitive damages, etc., more fully represents
the complexity of the case and makes it easier to track and to discuss it.

Sensitivity analysis

Particularly where the parties' assessments on one or two issues differ significantly from each other or from the mediator's, it is worth asking how important these disagreements really are—that is, how much difference would it make to the final value of the case if one person were correct or the other? It turns out, as you might expect, that not all components are equally important.

Sensitivity analysis asks the question: if we change the probability on a given issue or adjust a damages estimate, how much will it change the discounted case value? Participants inclined to argue every issue are sometimes surprised to learn that many of their disagreements don't much affect overall value. Sensitivity analysis identifies the issues that are worthy of greater attention ("drive the numbers").

Example: Assume in the preceding example that the parties disagree strenuously about whether the law allows the plaintiff to recover lost profits or limits him to out-of-pocket damages. The plaintiff estimates a 70 percent chance of recovering lost profits and only a 25 percent chance of being limited to out-of-pockets, while the other side sees the percentages as 50 and 45 percent, respectively. How much difference does this disagreement make to discounted case value?

A simple sensitivity analysis method is to recalculate with alternative numbers. Here, the discounted case value using the plaintiff's percentages would be:

Out-of-pockets	0.25 ×	$100,000 = $ 25,000
Lost profits	0.70 ×	$250,000 = $ 175,000
Punitives	0.05 ×	$2,000,000 = $100,000
Total verdict value:		$300,000
Discounted case value:	0.48 ×	$300,000 = $144,000

Sensitivity analysis shows that raising the likelihood of recovering lost profits by a full 25 percentage points increases the value of the case by less than $20,000 ($144,000 versus $126,000). However, it would also show that assumptions about the likelihood of punitive damages have a major impact. The mediator can point this out and suggest more careful focus on analyzing the risk of punitive damages, instead of arguing over lost profits.

Using a tree format, the two trees would be presented and contrasted as shown in Figure 8.7:

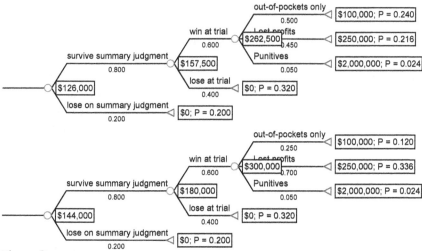

Figure 8.7

Decision analysis software enables you to easily generate a graph that shows the relationship between changes in one variable and the discounted case value (see Figure 8.8).

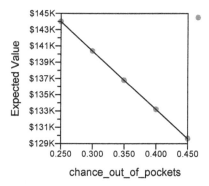

Figure 8.8

Decision analysis can facilitate more thoughtful evaluation by participants

After introducing the basic logic of decision analysis, the mediator can suggest that participants use it to analyze their own case. The mediator then guides the participants through a simple series of questions, such as: What could happen next? What are the chances of each possibility? If that happens, what could happen next? What are the chances. . .? Upon reaching the step of estimating final outcome, the mediator facilitates participants' consideration of various payoffs and subtraction of any costs that will be incurred from the present through the end point.

We might reasonably ask how decision analysis can be useful if participants (counsel or parties) supply the key estimates of probability, payoff, and costs. After all, can't participants be expected to offer unrealistic estimates? Won't that yield an unrealistically skewed analysis? The answer is, sometimes. However, even somewhat unrealistic probability estimates over several stages in litigation, applied to somewhat unrealistic outcome estimates, may yield a "discounted case value" far higher or far lower than a participant's current settlement position. Participants may be more willing to move from entrenched positions when *their own analysis* suggests it would be appropriate.

For an example of using decision analysis with estimates supplied by counsel, see Chapter 13 of the DVD.

Using decision analysis for mediator evaluation

Of course, where the participants' estimates are dramatically unrealistic, or they have failed to include important possible litigation twists, turns, and outcomes, their analysis may just confirm their entrenched positions. The mediator's evaluation, presented as probability and payoff or cost estimates, will reflect a very different picture.

To present an evaluation using decision analysis, the mediator reviews each step of a possible litigation path, discussing and recording what might happen next—summary judgment for the defense; no summary judgment; partial summary judgment on a particular issue; no liability; high, mid-range, or low damages; punitive damages; and so forth—and assigns the mediator's probability and damages estimates to each. If using a scratch-pad approach, the mediator can list the issues on a whiteboard or memo pad and then plug in the numbers, explaining how he arrived at each estimate along the way. Alternatively, the mediator might talk through the entire analysis verbally, then present the written scratch-pad calculation to back it up. Using the tree format, the mediator would draw the structure of the tree on a whiteboard, easel, or computer. She might insert and discuss probability estimates at each step, or draw the tree structure first and go back over it to fill in her estimated probability numbers and outcome values.

Whether using scratch-pad or tree sketches, we recommend a mediator think through his judgment of important percentages and values in the analysis outside the caucus room, before presenting his evaluation to the parties. This enables the mediator to anticipate which points are likely to be controversial with the audience and how to deal with them. Consistent with our advice that "less is more" in evaluation, we recommend the mediator "piggy-back" where possible. In other words, the mediator's analysis may incorporate a participant's probability or damages numbers that are not too far off, substituting the mediator's numbers only where his evaluation differs greatly.

Example: Consider again the example in Figure 8.3, and assume the mediator thinks that some of the advocate's estimates are skewed. In particular, she thinks the plaintiff is too optimistic when he estimates a 34 percent chance of collecting a large punitive award.

If the plaintiff wins on liability, the mediator puts the chance of a $100,000 verdict at 90 percent and a $500,000 verdict at only 10 percent. She thinks the plaintiff's estimates of 60 and 80 percent chances of success on the summary judgment motion and at trial are perhaps somewhat optimistic, but she decides to accept them and concentrate on the issue of punitive damages. The scratch-pad analysis would be:

Liability: 48%
Damages: 0.48×0.90 × $100,000 = $43,200
0.48×0.10 × $500,000 = $24,000
Discounted case value: $67,200

The analysis shows that the plaintiff's estimate of the probability of recovering punitives greatly affects the discounted case value. The mediator would explain her reasons for her different probability estimate, using the techniques discussed in the first portion of this chapter.

If using a tree format, the tree would look like Figure 8.9:

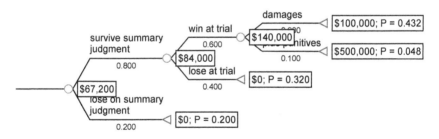

Figure 8.9

Choices in logistics and process for calculation

One of the authors writes out his numerical calculations (multiplying risk times payoffs, etc.) before entering the caucus room. This avoids the distraction of doing arithmetic while interacting with participants. The other author usually prepares a rough sketch of the decision tree outside of the caucus room, but prefers to enlist the participants in performing calculations, even when using the mediator's probability and payoff estimates. She might say to everyone in the room with calculators: "OK, what's 0.37 times $425,000?", write that number down on the tree, and then ask, "What's 0.20 times that. . .", and so forth. That way, participants are drawn into the calculation process and, perhaps, invested in the outcome of the analysis. Even if a mediator chooses to do some calculating outside the caucus room, however, it does not prevent him from changing the numbers and recalculating as part of a dialogue with the participants. (To facilitate calculations, it is helpful to carry a small calculator in your briefcase.)

The chances of that happening are . . .

Whether using a tree format or scratch pad, some litigants are unmoved by the discounted case value, because there will only be one trial. However, the calculated odds of particularly desirable or undesirable results may be compelling.

Imagine a case in which the plaintiff's counsel estimates an 80 percent chance of surviving summary judgment, a 60 percent chance of winning at trial, a 20 percent chance of a low verdict of $50,000, a 60 percent chance of a $120,000 verdict, and a 20 percent chance of a $200,000 verdict. Given these probabilities and dollar estimates, she would have a 52 percent chance of a $0 recovery, a 9.6 percent chance of recovering $50,000, a 28.8 percent chance of recovering $120,000 and only a 9.6 percent chance of recovering $200,000. A $45,000 offer might be more attractive when the plaintiff considers a 61.6 percent chance of getting $50,000 or less at trial (including a 52 percent chance of $0), and that the $45,000 offer is not much less than $50,000.

These may be shown on a scratch pad or using the tree format. On a tree, you would multiply just the percentages along each branch from left to right, and then multiply each possible outcome by its end percentage. The final possibility of each outcome is shown as "P =" on the far right-hand side, as indicated in Figure 8.10.

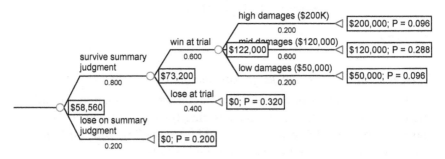

Figure 8.10

On the defense side, imagine the $120,000 payment, plus lawyer's fees that would be added to each end point, would render the defendant company unable to make payroll without risky borrowing. Apparent on the tree, the 38.4 percent risk of a $120,000 or higher verdict (plus fees) may be too substantial for her to bear, and may encourage her to increase her offer to $45,000 or more.

The method as mediator between mediator, parties, and decision

Introducing decision analysis in mediation helps distance the parties from the emotions, "principles," and other meanings wrapped up in their case. It enables the mediator to frame settlement as a decision problem and elevates the use of logic and careful, reasoned analysis. The language of the discussion almost inevitably becomes less highly charged. Even if an issue is potentially difficult—the credibility of a witness, the likelihood of punitive damages for malfeasance—participants' energy and focus are directed toward the scratch pad, the easel, or the computer. The dynamic becomes less argumentative. Even when the mediator presents a very different evaluation of an issue, disagreement tends to be directed toward the scratch pad, easel, or computer software intermediary.

Finally, for some participants, the rolled-back "discounted case value" number does seem logical and fair in the end. Or, at the very least, it provides a rationale for their movement toward settlement because the decision analysis—the formula calculations or the computer—pointed in that direction. They can bring it back to the office; put it in the file; show the boss, their spouse, or anyone who asks; and prove that they made a smart and logical decision.

Resolving Impasse and Closure

After you have worked with the disputants for hours or days and applied a variety of strategies, you will reach an endpoint—usually a settlement but occasionally an impasse. Whatever the situation, your work is not over. If the parties reach agreement, you can help them document it. If they fall into impasse, you can assist them to resolve it. This chapter explains how to deal with each situation.

1. Tactics at Impasse

You are likely to experience a range of emotions in your work as a commercial mediator. At the outset you will feel a real sense of pride: people with a difficult problem, advised by experienced lawyers, have selected *you* to help them resolve it. You will work hard to understand what is keeping the parties apart, and you can anticipate a real feeling of accomplishment at helping them solve a serious problem.

At some point, however—often during the late afternoon—you may find yourself silently wondering: how did I ever agree to become involved in this mess? This feeling arrives for me most often when the parties have stopped moving, not simply as a tactic or to consider a difficult decision, but in an apparent dead end. At that point I am often out of ideas and low on energy.

This chapter describes techniques I have used to move deadlocked lawyers and clients toward agreement. They vary from simple options such as challenging the parties to others, such as post-mediator proposals, that you may not have encountered. I begin with relatively simple approaches because they are my first resort, and then describe more esoteric tactics to apply if straightforward efforts fail.

a. Persevere

The first suggestion is simple: *persevere*. Many cases reach a point of apparent impasse, but it is only that—apparent. The disputants may be quite sincere, but the fact that a party has no intention of moving does not mean it won't do so later. Most cases reach impasse at some point. You never find out whether agreement is possible unless you push to find out.

Example: The dispute involved a Silicon Valley executive who sued his company after being fired. I continued to work even after each lawyer told me privately the case could not settle. Finally, at 9 PM, the parties reached agreement. As I went over the terms the defendant's lawyer exclaimed, "They kept beating you up and you just kept going. You were like . . . like . . . the *Energizer Bunny!*"

At first, as a professional mediator, I found the idea of being compared to a drum-beating pink rodent a bit demeaning. But as I thought more about it, the comparison was apt. A commercial mediator's job is to keep advocating settlement until the parties tell him unequivocally to stop, and he sees no plausible way to change their minds.

b. Ask for Help, and Wait

This advice may seem simple but it is counterintuitive to those of us who prefer to be active problem solvers. When parties are in an impasse, one option is to summarize the situation calmly and sympathetically and then wait. Ask the disputants for ideas and observe how they respond, while being prepared to nurture any initiative.

I have found, surprisingly, that when I step back and give responsibility to the disputants, they often take the initiative. Even when they don't, sitting back for a moment gives me a mini-break and lets me learn something from their reaction. I can also use the time to think about other options.

You can also ask disputants for advice. The natural people to ask are the lawyers, because they are often less emotionally involved than the parties and know a great deal about the controversy. Lawyers usually also have an interest in mediation succeeding, because they recommended their clients incur the time and expense to participate in it. Also, as a practical matter, it is easier to talk to a lawyer away from a client than to a client apart from a lawyer. Unless lawyers have become prisoners to their role as advocates, they can offer helpful insights.

If necessary, create an excuse to get a lawyer away from a party; for example, "Joan, a technical issue has come up and I wonder if you could come with me to talk to opposing counsel?" Once the lawyer is out of the caucus room, you can ask her for advice. You could also simply ask to talk with the lawyer alone, but doing so may make the party feel excluded. Excuses involve a bit of deception, but because it is done to achieve the parties' overall goal of settlement and does not involve taking sides, I find it acceptable.

c. Restart the Bargaining

To resolve an impasse you must either induce the parties to return to bargaining or make a proposal yourself. Let us first consider how to restart the negotiating process. You have the following options:

- Ask about interests, for a limited time.
- Push for linked moves.
- Make a special plea.

Ask about interests, for a limited time

The next suggestion is to try something mediators are taught to do as a matter of course—probe for interest-based options. As we have seen, stimulating interest-based bargaining is difficult in commercial mediation, but toward the end of the process parties are sometimes more open to creative ideas.

If discussing interests leads to a settlement, you're in luck. Keep in mind, however, that changing the subject can be helpful even when it yields no tangible result. Simply thinking for a few minutes about something other than the other side's obstinacy gives disputants a psychological breather, making them more flexible when they return to money bargaining. Someone who had earlier vowed to go no farther may now be willing to do just that, because a break allows her to change course with less feeling of contradicting herself.

One problem is that by the time they reach impasse, disputants often have little time or energy left to work on creative options. Again, you can limit this commitment by setting a time limit on consideration of interest-based terms.

Push for linked moves

When creative discussions are not successful, the other option is to continue pure-money bargaining. This is a good time to try linked moves such as "what if?", simultaneous steps, range bargaining, or parallel negotiations, each of which is described in Chapter Four.

Make a special plea

Personal request. You can sometimes obtain an additional concession by asking for it explicitly. ("If you could make special effort and make a move to break this deadlock, I'd appreciate it. I would tell the defense you had been adamant, and only agreed to this because I asked you.")

It is easier for a disputant to make an additional concession if it is portrayed as a special gesture to the mediator because it appears to be a one-time move rather than the start down a slippery slope. This means, however, that the tactic will only work once or twice; repeated requests are likely to be met with, "Why don't you ask *them* to be reasonable for a change?"

Final move. Parties will often agree to make an extra effort if they know it is the very last move you will ask them to make and not simply a prelude to further compromise. ("I'm going to ask you to go to $1.1 million. That's my last request. If this doesn't work, it's over, and I'll tell the plaintiff that. I won't come back to you again.")

This is a risky strategy because you cannot go back on your word—if you say you will not come back for more you can't, unless something truly unexpected happens. But a last-and-final plea will often produce an additional concession.

For examples of the presentation of a last-and-final request to both sides, see Chapters 20 and 21 of the DVD.

d. Modify the Mix or Structure

Changing the participants or the structure will sometimes restart the process. The simplest is to experiment with the format. If caucusing is not working, would another format be more effective? Options include:

- Disputants meet together.
- Key decision makers meet apart ("only you can do this . . .").
- Experts or lawyers only ("professionals confer").
- One person meets the opposing team ("into the lion's den").
- Participants meet in an informal setting.
- People are added to or subtracted from the process.

Any of these variations can unfreeze the process enough for parties to resume bargaining, and in unusual circumstances may resolve the case entirely.

Disputants meet together

In this option, all the disputants are convened in what amounts to a new joint session (assuming, as is usually true in commercial mediation, that they have been in separate caucus rooms). The purpose is not for each side to reargue its case; there may be a single issue that can be illuminated by a direct discussion.

Alternatively, you can assemble the disputants to deliver a message, for example, that the process is in peril and you are going to ask each of them for a special effort to avoid a breakdown. You could, of course, deliver the same message separately to each side, but calling a special meeting and saying it to everyone together makes it clear that the problem is real and no one is being singled out for blame. Laying out a situation in this way can also serve as a springboard for challenging disputants to come up with ideas, either together or in caucuses—a version of "ask for help, and wait."

Key decision makers meet apart

There is often a key decision maker for each party team. One option is to bring them together for a private conversation. The dynamic in these private meetings is often strikingly different than when groups talk with each other. A two-person meeting is likely to seem familiar and informal, much like a conversation outside litigation. Disputants chat, talk informally, and present at least an air of cooperativeness, particularly if they had a good relationship in the past. Lawyers often ask the mediator to be present at such meetings to ensure the discussion remains on a productive level or to guarantee confidentiality, but principals can also meet alone.

One of my colleagues, Eric Green, calls this the "Napoleon gambit," because he often adds an implied message to the process: "Only you have the wisdom, breadth of vision, authority, and decisiveness to end this conflict. This case is a difficult one, but you can . . ." Disputants with sizable egos are likely to rise to the challenge and take it as a personal goal to achieve a deal.

Example: In Chapter Eleven I give an example of a manufacturer suing its insurer for large amounts of money the manufacturer had spent to resolve mass tort class actions. The parties agreed to go to mediation. The insurer's CEO prepped intensively for the process, planning to have a point-by-point discussion of policy coverage and other issues with representatives of the manufacturer.

When the parties convened in joint session and the insurer's CEO tried to discuss the case, however, the manufacturer's inside counsel said he wasn't interested. He had listened carefully to his litigation team's analysis, he said, and saw no point in having a debate. The CEO was angry and frustrated by this, but at my request agreed to stick with the process. The parties adjourned into caucuses, and negotiations went forward painfully.

The turning point came months later when the manufacturer's counsel (the same lawyer who had refused to debate with the CEO) asked me to invite the executive to meet him in the bar of the hotel where the mediation was being held. As a dozen lawyers and I sat around conference rooms, speculating on what might be going on, the two key players talked for over an hour and cut a deal.

Experts or lawyers only

Sub-meetings need not be limited to parties; you can also put experts such as accountants or product managers together. When experts talk they tend to have the kind of conversation they are accustomed to in their daily work, often leading to disagreements being narrowed or at least the causes becoming clearer.

Lawyers are experts on the litigation process. If the lawyers have a good working relationship, it can be helpful to bring them together. Freed of the need to posture in front of clients, they sometimes talk candidly, admitting to risks, hinting at client-relations issues, and suggesting solutions. You can achieve some of the same effect by talking to each lawyer alone, but direct discussion is usually more effective.

One person meets the opposing team

You can also ask one person to meet with the entire bargaining team for the other party. This has a "Daniel in the lion's den" quality. The very act of going into the other caucus room without allies has symbolic impact, making the person's message more credible.

Example: A hospital filed a contract claim against an HMO. The hospital had agreed to treat members of the HMO in return for a payment calculated on the basis of the number of patients treated. At the end of the year the hospital sued the HMO, claiming it had been underpaid. The issue centered on an obscure contract provision that allowed the HMO to apply a "demographic correction" to its payment. The HMO said the correction was meant to adjust for the nature of patients treated: if the mix turned out to be younger than expected, for instance, the hospital would be paid less because young patients typically are less expensive to treat than older ones. The hospital, which had sued the HMO over another alleged underpayment three years before, saw this "correction factor" as merely an excuse to cheat it again.

After a day of bargaining, the parties narrowed the gap from $7.5 to $2 million, but then reached an impasse. As the mediator listened, it seemed the hospital team still did not understand how the HMO applied its correction factor, and—in the absence of knowledge—was making worst-case assumptions.

The inside counsel for the HMO asked why the analyst couldn't simply explain this to the hospital team. The neutral thought the analyst was a good witness, and he appeared to have a working relationship with his counterpart on the hospital team. It was agreed that the analyst would offer to go, accompanied by the inside counsel but not the HMO's litigator, a self-described "mad dog."

The analyst arrived under ground rules that limited him to discussing the disputed issue and limited the session to no more than 15 minutes. The hospital team peppered the analyst with questions, however, turning the meeting into an informal, sometimes heated discussion of the entire case. After 30 minutes the mediator looked questioningly at the HMO lawyer, but she signaled that she was fine with what was happening.

> After the session, the parties adjourned and the next day the hospital dropped its demand substantially. After a week of telephone discussions through the mediator, the HMO doubled its offer and the case settled.

Participants meet in an informal setting

Sometimes the key to breaking an impasse is to change the physical setting. Most commercial mediators work in conference rooms, but at times other settings can be effective because they make participants more comfortable or have positive connotations.

> *Example:* A doctor sued a high-tech company, arguing it had illegally diluted his interest in the company by issuing stock to new investors without his permission. There seemed to be a very personal element in the case: the doctor felt he had played a crucial role in sponsoring the startup and that the young CEO, a friend of his daughter, had betrayed his trust. Settlement discussions reached an impasse and we adjourned.
>
> With the defense's assent, I suggested visiting the doctor at his home before work one day. He beamed as he showed me his porcelain collection and mementos of his medical achievements while his wife watched. Over coffee and grapefruit, the doctor talked about the dispute in a much more relaxed way, and a few days later we had a settlement.

People are added to or subtracted from the process

It is sometimes useful to change the mix by adding people or taking them out of the process. It is usually easier to add players than subtract them; suggesting a participant leave is often interpreted as a judgment that he is being unreasonable or, if made by an opponent, as an effort to "push us around." It is sometimes possible to eliminate a problem player indirectly, by suggesting that both sides bring in someone from a higher level. ("Perhaps if we could get the plaintiff to bring in its CFO and you did too, we could explain your thinking on damages . . .")

e. Offer an Opinion

At this point in the process, the participants should have enough trust in you, and enough frustration with dealing with each other, to accept your advice. Consider offering some, or sharpening advice you have already given. You can offer an opinion about what offer to make next, or about what will happen if the case is tried.

Bargaining advice

If the parties are, or claim to be, at their bottom lines they will probably not welcome advice about further compromises. Equally often, however, parties refuse to move further because "the other side hasn't been reasonable" or "they haven't shown they're committed to settle." When this happens you can sometimes jump-start the bargaining by suggesting a linked move, as described earlier.

Legal analysis

Another option is to offer an evaluation of the court alternative. The first step should be to emphasize the cost of continuing in the litigation process; parties may not welcome the reminder, but they should by now be willing to take account of it. If that is not enough and you have not yet given a "hard" evaluation, this may be the time to do so. You can:

- ○ Evaluate more of the case (for example, going past stating a view about a single issue to give an opinion about a party's chance of winning on liability).

- ○ Make an opinion more definite by replacing a characterization such as "you'll have difficulty winning on liability" with "I think you have a 30 to 40 percent likelihood of prevailing on liability at trial."

- ○ Give a global evaluation, setting a specific monetary valuation on a claim ("probably a $200,000 case in this county").

- ○ Make an evaluation more forceful by putting it in writing.

f. Manage the End Game

Play confidential listener

Toward the end of a process, you can probe for the parties' bottom lines. One way to do this is to play "confidential listener." This involves asking each side privately how far it will go to get an agreement, then giving all parties a verbal characterization of the gap. This technique allows parties to give the mediator and each other a signal about their willingness to compromise without having to make a "public" concession to the other side. Effectively applied, the confidential listener tactic can give both you and the disputants a clearer sense of each side's actual goal.

Don't ask disputants for their last-and-final number. Parties almost never give it and asking puts them under pressure to mislead you. Worse yet, if a party does answer sincerely, it may feel it has to stick with the number for the sake of consistency, even if later it becomes willing to stretch farther. You are likely to get more candid answers if the parties fear failure from seriously gaming the process. It makes sense, therefore, to wait until disputants are close to impasse and to characterize the technique as one of the last things you can do to find a solution. I would introduce the option in this way:

> Your offers are a million dollars apart, but I think you are in fact much closer. Let me try something I call "confidential listener." I'll ask each of you to give me what I'll call your "next-to-last number"—a number one step away from the lowest you'd accept or the most you'd pay to settle this case.
>
> I won't reveal either side's number to the other, or give you a numerical statement of how far apart you are; if I did, each side could calculate what the other party's number was. Instead I'll call the lawyers together and give a verbal assessment of the gap, such as "very close" or "far apart." That keeps anyone from being locked in. I'll be back in a few minutes to ask for your number.

You'll note that I ask for each party's "next-to-last number" rather than its "final number" or "bottom line." As a practical matter, few lawyers will disclose their final number to a mediator playing confidential listener—if indeed they even know what it is at that point—because they expect that there will be more bargaining and that they will be asked to compromise from the number they give. The next-to-last formulation is a suggestion from mediator Marjorie Aaron, designed to avoid forcing lawyers to lie.

Once you have gotten the parties' numbers, you can give them a characterization of the gap between them. For example:

- ○ "The gap is substantial, but I think it can be bridged."
- ○ "You are closer than the cost for each of you to litigate this case through trial, so it's worth continuing to talk."
- ○ "You are very far apart. Unless someone changes their view of what the case is worth, it'll be hard for you to agree. Should we consider getting an expert opinion?"

After giving verbal feedback you have an additional option, which is to ask each side for permission to reveal its number to the other on a mutual basis. ("I'm going to ask both sides if you would agree to let me disclose your number to the other side, on the condition they authorize me to tell you theirs.")

For an example of the confidential-listener technique, see Chapter 14 of the DVD.

Offer a mediator's proposal

Under a mediator's proposal, the neutral suggests a set of terms to both parties to which they must respond under the following ground rules:

- ○ Each litigant must tell the mediator privately whether or not she would agree to the proposal, assuming the other side has agreed as well.

- ○ The terms must be accepted or rejected unconditionally; in other words, no "nibbling." For example, "We'll accept, but the warranty has to be three years, not two" would be treated as a rejection.

- ○ Each side must answer without knowing the other's reply. If a party rejects a proposal, it never learns whether its opponent would have accepted it.

- ○ Usually each side will answer within 5 to 20 minutes. However, if accepting would require a party to go beyond its authority, it may be necessary to set a response deadline for the next day or several days later. (If one side asks for repeated extensions there is sometimes a problem: it becomes apparent the other side has said yes—otherwise why would the mediator extend the process?)

Mediators' proposals give parties the hope they may be able to achieve complete peace by saying yes, but if the effort fails their bargaining position will not be impaired. My practice is usually to require both sides to answer, even if one side quickly rejects the proposal. My thinking is, first, that these are the ground rules, and second, it is useful for parties at impasse to think hard about how far they will go to get a deal.

Many mediators avoid this technique, perhaps because it involves presenting terms on a take-it-or-leave-it basis and thus taking over the bargaining process. I believe, however, that parties often reach a point at which they want a third person to take over responsibility. Doing so relieves them of the "water torture" of positional bargaining, in which they have to make one painful concession after another without knowing whether it will get them a deal. It also allows parties who expect to be second-guessed by outsiders to use the mediator as a scapegoat. ("This lousy compromise wasn't our idea, it was the mediator's.") I find mediator's proposals are successful at least two-thirds of the time.

If you decide to make a proposal, how should you decide what the terms will be? My proposals do not reflect an evaluation of the parties' legal cases, and I tell them that. (Doing so reduces the risk a party will feel I have ruled against them on the merits.) I am likely to say:

In framing the proposal my goal is not to please either side. I could suggest terms you would be very happy with, but it would be a waste of time because the other side would reject them. For the same reason, I can guarantee my proposal won't make them happy either. I'm afraid we're at the point where any proposal has to balance the pain each side will feel in accepting it. My goal is to find a set of terms that both parties will decide, however reluctantly, is better for them than litigating the case through trial.

For an example of a mediator's proposal, see Chapter 18 of the DVD.

If a proposal fails. Assume the parties have rejected your mediator's proposal. Is this the end of the road? No. You can ask the rejecting party to take the initiative. ("I understand you can't accept my proposal, but what do you need to make it minimally acceptable?") Parties usually reply by giving a new number that often falls between your proposal and their last offer. ("We won't go to 500, but we could go to 400.") You can then ask to present the party's new number to the other side. ("Can I tell them you'd settle if they would go there?") Often a party that had refused to make any further concessions will now agree to put forth a new offer.

It may seem strange a party would offer compromises beyond its announced bottom line, but this may be due to what is called the "contrast principle": a further concession looks good compared with the "unacceptable" proposal you have made. Or it may be that a party who has rejected a proposal feels it should make a gesture to preserve its relationship with the mediator. Or the fact the other side has rejected a mediator's proposal may convince the party it must go the "last mile" to avoid failure. Whatever the motivation, the failure of a mediator's proposal often sets the stage for new offers that had been unavailable before.

Successive proposals. It is sometimes possible to make two mediator's proposals.

Example: A plaintiff is adamant that the defendant, if pushed hard enough, will pay $150,000 to settle a case. You privately think the defendant will reject that number, but the plaintiff believes it will take it, and as long as he does he will not settle for less. You therefore make a proposal to both sides at $150,000. The plaintiff accepts but the defendant immediately turns it down.

You can then meet with the plaintiff team and say: "I made the proposal at $150,000, to hold their feet to the fire and see if they were bluffing. But they've turned it down flatly. They just won't go there. I think we now have to consider a different strategy. I'm willing to keep looking for a deal, or even make another proposal, but it'd have to be at a lower number. Sticking with $150,000 would just be beating our heads against the wall. What do you think we should do?"

Challenge the parties

If all these techniques fail you can once again challenge the parties to take the initiative. Simply asking the parties for ideas as described earlier is a gentle challenge, but you can also pose a question more bluntly. ("It looks like we have a real problem here. We may be at the end of the road. What do you want to do next?") And wait . . .

For an example of a mediator using silence to prod a party, see Chapter 18 of the DVD.

g. Adjourn and Try Again

Mediation often requires parties to accept deals much worse than they had expected going into the process, and litigants sometimes cannot quickly adjust to the resulting feelings of loss. Even when emotions do not block a decision there may be other problems: a party may not have enough authority to settle, for example. Some forms of mediation occur over a series of sessions, which provide breaks to deal with such issues. Commercial mediation, however, is typically scheduled for a concentrated time period, leaving little time for adjustment and consultation.

Adjournment, of course, carries dangers. Parties make difficult concessions in part because they hope to achieve peace. Once they leave, there is a risk they will become discouraged or decide they have gone too far. In practice, however, this does not often happen. I have rarely seen a commercial mediation fall apart because of an adjournment. If there is failure, it is usually because an impasse that existed at mediation cannot be overcome, not because anyone backpedaled or suddenly gave up.

Indeed, commercial mediations increasingly seem to require more than a single day. When the process cannot be completed within the originally scheduled time, you have these options:

- ○ Arrange status calls.
- ○ Schedule another meeting.
- ○ Use telephone and e-mail diplomacy.
- ○ Conduct a time-block session by telephone.
- ○ Pursue the disputants.
- ○ Set a final deadline.

Arrange status calls

The easiest option is to ask lawyers to participate in a status call. ("I'll call each of the lawyers on Wednesday morning to talk about next steps.") Agreeing to a status call does not commit people to make decisions or guarantee an interactive process, but it does give you a chance to gather information and then propose a structure for further discussions.

I find that it is almost always better to talk with each side privately, rather than have a joint call. A private call permits disputants to give more honest information about obstacles and to signal flexibility without hurting their bargaining position. The key point is to create a timeframe and expectation of further discussion.

Schedule another meeting

The next option is to set up another meeting. Before suggesting one, ask yourself these questions:

- ○ Are all the parties ready to move forward? Does a litigant need more time to calm down, or do the parties need to do additional investigation?

- ○ If there is another meeting, how should it be structured? In particular, can the process be set up in a way that makes it less likely that it will simply repeat the last session?

I often make some of the following points when proposing another meeting:

- ○ Because each side has already argued its case, it will not be necessary to hold a second opening session. (This is usually greeted with expressions of relief.) It may make sense, however, for the parties to meet together for a specific purpose, such as to hear the defendant's critique of the plaintiff's damage analysis.

- ○ There is usually no need to commit to another full day. (Indeed, doing so may give a signal that the parties are still far from a settlement and should wait to make their final concessions.) Given the progress made so far, two to four hours should be enough for a follow-up session. I often suggest the parties agree to meet after lunch, or to go only until noon. (Setting a short timeframe does not mean the process cannot continue longer, and often it does. Doing so does signal it is moving toward closure and disputants should come prepared to make hard decisions.)

- ○ I may go further, emphasizing it is time to "cut to the chase" and I expect everyone to be ready to make final decisions at the session.

Use telephone and e-mail diplomacy

Often it is not possible to schedule another meeting quickly. Disputants may have flown in for the first meeting and are not able or willing to return for another one, or they may need time to confer with colleagues or gather data. Luckily there is usually less need to meet in person a second time because the mediator has built a working relationship with the disputants. Once a session has been held, it is much easier to carry on follow-up discussions by telephone or e-mail.

Electronic communication has disadvantages of course. Over the telephone, participants cannot see each other's body language and with e-mail cannot hear each other's voices. With e-mail, in particular, there is a danger messages will seem harsh because they are in writing and have no body language or tone of voice to soften their impact. The biggest disadvantage of electronic communication may be the loss of focus and continuity—people drop a case and then pick it up again, often reading a message or taking a call when they are distracted by other matters.

Another option is to arrange for videoconferencing. In theory, this is a solution for problems convening disputants, allowing people to see and communicate with each other in real time while separated by thousands of miles. To date, however, it has not caught on—parties and lawyers seem to prefer either to make the commitment of traveling to meet personally or to take advantage of the convenience of telephones and e-mail. Similarly online dispute resolution, or ODR, has not proven popular except in small disputes between widely separated parties (eBay is by far the largest user of ODR at present). All this, however, may change in the future.

Conduct a time-block session by telephone

One way to inject focus into a process conducted electronically is to set up "time-block mediation." Disputants agree that during a certain time period, say from 2 to 5 PM one afternoon, all of the lawyers and decision makers in a case will be at a telephone, ready to receive a call from the mediator. They may work on other matters, but will interrupt it to respond to the neutral's calls. The mediator can then conduct shuttle diplomacy. The advantage of time-block mediation is that it is less subject to interruption, and the existence of a time limit motivates parties to make hard choices.

Pursue the disputants

Remember that one of the traits lawyers say they most value about mediators is persistence. The time and willingness to follow up is a key advantage a new mediator has over "star" neutrals, who must go on to a new case almost every day. Even if the parties do not ask for a follow-up process, call the lawyers on your own initiative within a few days of an unsuccessful session to ask their thoughts and sound them out about next steps. Almost no lawyer resents such a call.

Remember that you are the guardian of optimism about the process. Disputants tend to assume the worst and look to you for signals about whether it is worth continuing. Unless you have no realistic hope for the process, keep a positive tone.

Set a final deadline

The only thing that will motivate some people to make difficult decisions is a firm deadline. You can create one by setting a time at which you will declare the mediation over and stop acting as mediator. The parties can continue to negotiate alone, of course, but the implicit message is, "If you have not been able to reach agreement with assistance, why should you think you will be able to do so by yourselves? And if you don't settle, is your litigation alternative really as rosy as you have been claiming?" A polite warning that you will end the process can cut through posturing and put pressure on the parties to make a final effort.

To avoid making disputants feel that you are pushing them around, stress that you are not setting the deadline to coerce anyone, but simply are recognizing the reality of the situation—at some point everyone has to make decisions and move on.

After you have attempted in all possible ways to bring about a settlement, there are two basic possibilities. By far the most likely is that the parties settle, but the other is that they do not. The next two sections describe how to handle each possibility.

2. Managing Settlements

a. Confirmatory Acts

When the participants in a dispute finally say "yes," you may be tempted to think your work is over. Everyone involved is often fatigued, and disputants may be reluctant to focus on precise terms for fear of upsetting the deal. It is important, however, that you ask them to confirm the terms of settlement. Before the key players leave, do some or all of the following:

- ○ Confirm the agreement in both sides' presence.
- ○ Commit key terms to writing.
- ○ Affirm the agreement symbolically.

Confirm the agreement in both sides' presence

My usual practice is to move directly into drafting a memorandum of the agreement. Another option, however, is to call the lawyers together, summarize the agreement, and ask each lawyer whether you have stated it correctly. When the details are technical or the representatives get along well, it may be appropriate to ask one of the lawyers to perform such a summary. Be careful, however, of allowing one side to do so when people are being adversarial. In such situations, a party may insert "details" or "implied terms" that the other considers controversial or inconsistent.

Commit key terms to writing

Once a verbal deal is reached, I suggest the lawyers draft a memorandum of agreement (MOU) to confirm it. The MOU is typically handwritten, although if a computer and printer are available, lawyers will sometimes type it on a laptop or even bring a draft agreement with the amount of money left blank. An MOU covers the key terms of agreement and contemplates that the parties will later execute formal settlement documents such as releases of liability. Once an MOU has been drafted, the parties or the lawyers sign it and the mediator distributes copies.

Sometimes participants suggest they leave with a verbal agreement only and exchange written drafts in a few days. It is an article of faith in the mediation field that disputants should never leave mediation without signing an agreement, even an informal one. In practice, however, parties sometimes do not or cannot execute agreements on site; for example, an insurance adjuster may have left for the airport and assented to the final terms over a cell phone.

In fact, I have mediated dozens of cases in which the parties did not sign an agreement immediately and no such settlement has ever fallen apart. Once parties and lawyers have verbally agreed to settle a dispute, they seem to commit psychologically to a resolution and virtually always find a way to agree on formal settlement documents. The fear a deal will fail if it is not written up immediately thus seems overstated.

Leaving a settlement in verbal form does, however, increase the risk the parties will later fall into a dispute about exactly what they agreed to. In the few cases when this has happened, I have been able to mediate the differences and save the settlement. Of course even signing an MOU is not an absolute guarantee; parties can still argue over the wording of the documents that implement it. Still, the better practice is to have disputants sign a written memorandum before they leave a mediation.

Affirm the agreement symbolically

Apart from signing documents, people often take symbolic actions to confirm their agreements. For Americans the most familiar signal is a handshake. Some disputants will shake hands and others will not, depending in part on how bitter the conflict has become. In unusual cases, parties draft a public statement announcing that they have settled.

> *Example:* A mediator was working with two partners in a small design firm to agree on terms to dissolve their business relationship. After several meetings, the parties reached a verbal agreement. The mediator asked each partner to initial the notes the mediator had made about the deal. The notes themselves were largely illegible even to the neutral, but he told the parties that by initialing them they would be confirming to each other the controversy had been resolved. The two partners then went out and bought ice cream cones; they said this was their traditional way of celebrating when they completed a project.

b. Drafting

Memorandum agreements

It is not your job as a mediator to draft a legally binding settlement agreement—that is the responsibility of the lawyers. Indeed, you may annoy a lawyer if you advocate specific language. At the same time, you do have an interest in ensuring a deal does not fall apart because a key element is missing.

The requirements for a binding contract are generally set by the law of the state in which it is signed or which the parties have designated in the document. As long as a document identifies the conflict and the parties, states that they intend to enter into an agreement to resolve it, outlines each significant term well enough for a court to enforce it, and is signed by the parties or their lawyers, it need not ordinarily use legal terms or "magic words" to be a binding contract. In particular, settlement documents need not cover every detail or contain the actual language of final documents to be effective. A competently written MOU fulfills these requirements.

You can outline the parties' deal on a pad of paper and then give it to both lawyers to read over, or read it aloud and ask if anything has been left out or misstated. If the document is acceptable, ask either the parties or the lawyers to sign it. Typical points of a memorandum of agreement include:

○ A title (for example, "Memorandum of Agreement") and date.

○ An indication the document memorializes an agreement (for example, "Jones and Smith agree that . . .").

○ Identification of the dispute (for example, the title and docket number or court of the legal case).

○ That the defendant will pay a certain sum (or provide goods or services) to the plaintiff.

○ That the plaintiff will give a general release to the defendant or the parties will mutually release each other.

○ Undertakings about confidentiality, nondisparagement, and other nonmonetary items.

○ A stipulation that pending litigation will be dismissed, usually with prejudice.

○ A deadline or schedule for when each of these steps will occur.

○ In certain jurisdictions (notably, California), a statement that the memorandum is intended to be a binding agreement or may be introduced in court or is not subject to confidentiality provisions.

Formal settlement documents

Lawyers sometimes bring a draft of formal settlement agreements to mediation or create them on a laptop. They can also provide drafts of supporting documents such as releases of liability. If the other side believes documents are being offered in good faith, such drafts can allow parties to leave mediation with an executed final settlement agreement. One party may, however, see another's draft as a tactic, or a client may feel her own lawyer should have had a draft ready as well. In such situations, a mediator may have to discourage an over-eager draftsperson. More often, an informal memorandum is signed at the mediation and the lawyers exchange drafts of a formal agreement, releases, indemnifications, and other settlement documents over a period of days or weeks following the mediation.

The role of the mediator

The process of committing an agreement to writing is itself a negotiation, in which the selection of words or the addition or omission of provisions can benefit one side or another. In an ideal world, parties and lawyers would resolve drafting issues themselves, and whenever possible you should leave the task to them. In practice, however, mediators often have some role in the drafting process, either to serve as scribe or mediate the process itself.

You may have to take on a mediative role for several reasons. Bad feelings and adversarial tactics can continue into the post-settlement stage. Or the participants may not foresee problems involved in implementing a settlement and fall back into conflict. Because of the credibility you will have built up, you will be well positioned to help disputants resolve problems of drafting and implementation.

If you agree to write up the settlement memorandum, be sure neither party thinks you are proposing or endorsing terms favorable to the other. Instead, present yourself as a "mere scrivener" and begin by asking the lawyers or disputants what they want in the agreement and what words they would suggest to express it. For example,

- ○ On timing, it would be appropriate to say, "Do you want to put in a timeframe?" but probably not, "Shall I put in 'The payment shall be made in 15 days?'" or "How about 15 days for the defendant to pay?"

- ○ Once parties have agreed on a timeframe, it is appropriate to propose noncontroversial phrasing to implement it ("So, you are OK with payment within 30 days . . . That would be the end of September . . . Should I write 'The defendant shall make payment on or before October 1?'")

If a settlement is endangered because the parties cannot agree on wording or if the players ask you for help, you can assist them to reach agreement on documentation issues as on any other aspect of the dispute. I suggest using the following approach:

- ○ Encourage the disputants to negotiate directly with each other. If you place an issue on the table, prompt the disputants to resolve it together. This is particularly important if the parties will have to work together to implement the agreement.

- ○ Raise sensitive issues in private before placing them before both sides jointly.

- ○ If you make a specific drafting suggestion, suggest that it is meant to accomplish a neutral goal such as increasing the ease of implementation or the durability of the result.

- ○ If possible, support potentially controversial suggestions with a reference to common practice or a neutral model.

- ○ *Do not* offer legal advice or express an opinion over the legal effect of language, especially when parties are not represented by lawyers. Advise parties without a lawyer to consult one before signing an agreement, then make a file note that you gave the advice, and/ or confirm it in a letter or e-mail to the pro se litigant.

- ○ Be careful about proposing you continue as the monitor or adjudicator of disputes that may arise during implementation of a settlement. You may well be the most qualified person for the role, but suggesting yourself may be seen as self-promotion and carries other dangers (as discussed later).

c. Ratification

Sometimes the participants in mediation do not have authority to bind their side to a settlement. Their power may be limited to recommending terms to a supervisor or negotiating a package a constituency can vote up or down. In these situations, it is appropriate and may be helpful for a mediator to advocate the settlement to outsiders. Outside players can include a company's board of directors, a regulatory commission, advocacy groups, or anyone else whose approval of or neutrality toward a settlement is needed to ensure it is effective.

The task of "selling" the settlement is similar to other aspects of a neutral's role. You should inquire about who is key to the approval process and will ordinarily work with the disputants to help them present the settlement effectively. Occasionally, it makes sense to become involved yourself; you might offer, for instance, to meet with a ratifier if the bargainer thinks this would be helpful.

In other situations, your most useful role may be as the scapegoat for a compromise, making it politically feasible for a governing board or constituency to accept an unpalatable deal. Parties sometimes select a prominent person as a neutral precisely in the hope he will be able to persuade their constituency to accept a compromise or serve as a lightning rod for criticism. This is one of the less pleasant aspects of a mediator's role, but if a scapegoat is necessary you should accept the role with grace.

> *Example:* The general counsel of a large technology company mediated a patent dispute with a Japanese corporation. He found that his counterparts refused to make concessions directly to him, apparently because doing so would constitute "giving in" to an opponent. The Japanese negotiators readily agreed, however, to compromises recommended by the mediator, appearing to have much less difficulty accepting a neutral outsider's judgment.

Recommendation authority. If bargaining representatives do not have final authority to agree to a settlement, an alternative is to ask them to commit to "recommendation" authority as described in Chapter Three.

d. Implementation

In the flush of good feeling that sometimes accompanies a settlement, parties may be reluctant to confront the possibility they will disagree again. Indeed merely talking about remedies for a future dispute can be taken as an indication that one is expected. If the settlement terms are simple and the parties do not expect to have a future relationship, disputes are unlikely and provisions to deal with them unnecessary. In other cases, however, such as controversies involving patent licensing, environmental cleanups, and contract restructuring, implementation may be complex and the parties' interactions will continue into the future. In such situations, the risk of disputes should be addressed as part of the settlement. The most effective way to do so is to build a dispute resolution clause into the agreement. Such clauses may be very simple or quite complex.

Simple clauses

A simple implementation clause designates a person to serve or a set of rules to govern arbitration of any disputes that arise over implementation. To discourage needless quarrels, the clause may state that the parties will attempt to agree on an outsider, but if they cannot then the mediator will serve as arbitrator.

Summary arbitration

When speed, low cost, and finality are more important than full due process, consider suggesting a "summary arbitration" clause as part of a settlement. In this form of arbitration, the parties agree that if they have a controversy over implementation of their agreement, they will notify a designated arbitrator or alternative dispute resolution (ADR) organization. The arbitrator is often the mediator, but this is not essential. The summary arbitrator:

○ Will give both sides a reasonable opportunity to present their viewpoints and respond to points made by the other in an informal manner, over the telephone if feasible, and will receive informal written statements.

○ Will not authorize discovery beyond production of crucial documents or ordinarily conduct an evidentiary hearing or take live testimony.

○ Will render a written decision within a brief, specified time, such as ten business days. The decision need not contain a statement of reasons and may be delivered by e-mail.

○ At the parties' option, the arbitrator may be authorized to award lawyers' fees, and the award may be restricted to a stated monetary limit.

The characteristics of summary arbitration—speed, low cost, and finality—can convince a doubtful party a settlement will be quickly enforced, often by someone whom they have come to know and who is familiar with the course of bargaining.

Multistep clauses

In more complex cases, parties may adopt a multistep ADR clause similar to those used in corporate contracts. Such clauses provide that disputes will be resolved through successive steps of negotiation, mediation, and arbitration. Information about multistep clauses for business contracts is available from websites such as www.cpradr.org.

3. Dealing with Final Impasse

Assume the worst has occurred—you have applied every conceivable tactic but the parties still have not been able to settle. At this point two basic options exist: terminate the mediation with the possibility of recommencing, or help the parties transition to an efficient form of adjudication.

a. Termination with the Possibility of Recommencing

One option is to terminate the process. It is worth noting, however, that despite the draconian warnings you may have given to the disputants in order to create a deadline, until the matter is finally resolved you retain the option of seeking to revive settlement discussions. In particular, you can call or e-mail participants at any time to ask whether another try at mediation would be worthwhile. Good mediators—like the relentless Inspector Javert in Hugo's *Les Misérables* or even the Energizer Bunny—will let the dust of a failed process settle, then try again.

b. Litigation Plans

If the obstacle to agreement is uncertainty about how a court will decide a particular issue, it may be advisable for parties to seek a judicial ruling on that issue and then return to mediation. Mediators can also serve as special masters to resolve discovery or scheduling issues, although doing so places the mediator in the uncomfortable role of limited-purpose arbitrator. Each of these approaches, as well as others familiar to experienced litigators, can greatly reduce costs if a decision in the case is necessary.

c. Binding Arbitration

If mediation fails it does not follow that the parties should return to court. A mediator can sometimes help the disputants by encouraging them to enter binding arbitration.

Example: A contractor and a state agency were involved in a dispute over 74 separate claims arising from a highway project. After two days of mediation, the parties were able to settle 59 minor claims, but 15 other items were unresolved. At that point, the mediator suggested the parties place the 15 claims, which the contractor had offered to settle for $1.1 million but on which the highway department had offered only $500,000, into arbitration.

The mediator proposed an expedited arbitration process. A construction expert would hear the claims over a two-day period and render a decision within 30 days. The mediator suggested that the arbitrator's award be bracketed by the parties' offers during mediation: the state would not pay more than $1.1 million and the contractor could not receive less than $500,000, regardless of the arbitrator's decision. This framework eliminated any risk of an extreme result, making the parties more willing to use an expedited process.

Through the combination of mediation and expedited arbitration, the parties were able to resolve all the claims and avoid a six-week trial in five days of ADR.

The key is to remember that even an impasse does not mean mediation has been unsuccessful. By waiting and trying again or suggesting arbitration, neutrals can add value even when parties reach an impasse.

4. Summary of Key Points

Persevere

Ask for Help, and Wait

Restart the Bargaining
- Ask about interests, for a limited time
- Push for linked moves
- Make a special plea

Modify the Mix or Structure
- Disputants meet together
- Key decision makers meet apart
- Experts or lawyers only
- One person meets the opposing team
- Participants meet in an informal setting
- People are added to or subtracted from the process

Offer an Opinion

Manage the End Game
- Play confidential listener
- Offer a mediator's proposal
- Challenge the parties

Adjourn and Try Again
- Arrange status calls
- Schedule another meeting
- Use telephone and e-mail diplomacy
- Conduct a time-block session by telephone
- Pursue the disputants
- Set a final deadline

Ethical and Legal Issues

To talk of a "law" of commercial mediation is in some ways a contradiction in terms. While mediated discussions often focus on legal issues, mediation as a process has few rules. Unlike, for example, lawyers and psychologists, mediators do not have to obtain a license to practice. Nor are they bound by mandatory ethical standards akin to lawyers' Model Rules of Professional Responsibility. Practicing ethically is nevertheless important, and there are significant legal rules that govern confidentiality, compulsory participation in mediation, and enforcement of agreements. This chapter provides you with a working knowledge of these topics.

1. Mediating Ethically

It is difficult to discuss ethics issues without preaching. I will try to avoid this, first by focusing on situations that mediators have encountered in practice and second, by assuming that you have good personal values.

That does not mean that you will never confront an ethical issue, but it does suggest that when you do it will probably not be a simple one.

The most difficult ethical issues in mediation arise when two ethical principles, each valid in itself, come into conflict and a mediator cannot fully satisfy both. Imagine, for example, that you are mediating with a distraught litigant who is about to make what seems to be a very bad settlement decision. He does not have a lawyer to advise him. Ethical standards tell mediators to respect each disputant's right to make his own choices and also say that mediators are responsible for ensuring that the process has integrity. In this situation, how can you accomplish both?

I cannot tell you how to resolve such situations because, by their very nature, there is no perfect solution. There is, however, a real advantage to thinking about problems *before* you are confronted with them in practice. That is the purpose of this section.

a. Ethical Codes and Guidance

As noted, there is no state or federal licensing system for mediators, and they are not subject to a mandatory system of ethical rules, although mediators who join an organization or court program may be required to comply with its rules. There are two national sources of standards in the field, and one source of guidance.

1. *The Model Standards.* Recognizing the value of self-regulation, several mediation organizations have drafted voluntary ethical standards. The best known are the Standards of Conduct for Mediators, known as the "Model Standards." The Model Standards were promulgated jointly by the American Arbitration Association, the American Bar Association, and the Association for Conflict Resolution.

2. *The Uniform Mediation Act.* The Uniform Mediation Act, or UMA, has been proposed by the National Conference of Commissioners on Uniform State Laws and adopted by several states. The UMA focuses on confidentiality and is not intended to define a comprehensive set of ethical standards. That said, Section 9 of the UMA covers one ethics issue: the disclosure of conflicts of interest. The Reporter's Notes to the UMA provide interpretation of its provisions.

Ethics guidance. The ADR Section of the American Bar Association has established an ethics committee to respond to inquiries from mediators. The committee's opinions, posted on the Section website, www.abanet

.org/dispute/home, may provide useful guidance about how ethical standards apply to specific situations.

b. Problems from Practice

The basic problem with the Model Standards, and to a lesser extent the UMA, is that they are too general to be of assistance in specific situations. To fill this gap, I provide here examples of ethical issues that have arisen in actual cases, followed by excerpts from the relevant Model Standards and comments about how I personally would respond to the problem.

Problem: Pro se litigant asking for legal advice

In private commercial mediation, parties almost always appear with lawyers; as a result, it is rarely necessary for a mediator to worry about whether they are agreeing to unacceptably bad deals. When I do become concerned, I remind myself that the lawyer knows much more about both the case and her client than I do. I almost always defer to the lawyer, and if I have a serious question, talk it over with her privately. In court-affiliated and pro bono mediation programs, however, pro se litigants are more likely to appear.

Example: You are participating in a volunteer court program mediating landlord–tenant cases. You are referred a case involving a pro se tenant facing eviction. The landlord, a corporation, is represented by counsel. The tenant seems to have little understanding of what will happen in court if he does not settle. At one point shortly before lunch, the landlord makes a "final offer": he will allow the tenant two months' occupancy, provided that all past rent is paid, future rent is escrowed, and the tenant agrees to the entry of judgment for eviction at the end of the two months. If the plaintiff does not accept the offer by 1 PM, he will go back to court and ask that the tenant be ordered to vacate within seven days.

The tenant is unsure what to do and in a private caucus asks you, "Are they right about the law here? What do you recommend?" You privately believe that if the tenant offers to pay rent into escrow, it is very likely that the court will give him at least six months to move, although for a judge to grant the landlord's request is not completely inconceivable.

Model Standard II. Impartiality: A Mediator Shall Conduct the Mediation in an Impartial Manner.

The concept of mediator impartiality is central to the mediation process. *A mediator shall mediate only those matters in which she or he can remain impartial*[1] and evenhanded. If at any time the mediator is unable to conduct the process in an impartial manner, the mediator is obligated to withdraw.

Standard VI. Quality of the Process: A Mediator Shall Conduct the Mediation Fairly, Diligently, and in a Manner Consistent with the Principle of Self-Determination by the Parties.
     A mediator *shall work to ensure a quality process* and to encourage mutual respect among the parties...

Comment: The primary purpose of a mediator is to facilitate the parties' voluntary agreement. This role differs significantly from other professional–client relationships: *a mediator should therefore refrain from providing professional advice . . .*

5. The role of a mediator differs substantially from other professional roles. *Mixing the role of a mediator and the role of another profession is problematic* and thus, a mediator should distinguish between the roles...

What would you do? What are the problems in answering the question?

Comment: Pro se litigants raise two kinds of issues. The first is that they often ask for legal advice. If a mediator provides such advice, however, she is putting herself in difficulty because she may be practicing law. Second, the pro se litigant may misunderstand the advice or not follow it, and not remember accurately what the mediator said.

Some have suggested that the comment to "refrain from providing professional advice" is intended to express disapproval of mediators evaluating legal issues. Commercial mediators generally do not read the Model Standards to prohibit evaluating legal issues, but some court programs have rules that forbid neutrals from doing so.

The practical danger, I think, is not so much in giving a view of the likely court outcome (assuming that you are competent to do so) as long as it is clear that you are not acting as the litigant's lawyer. Rather, it is the risk that if a court does rule against the tenant he will not remember

---

1.   The italics in this and other rules are added to emphasize key phrases; they do not appear in the original rule.

that you said this was "not completely inconceivable." To avoid these problems,

○ Don't give legal advice to an unrepresented party.

○ Suggest that the litigant consult a lawyer, and offer to adjourn to permit this.

○ Establish a record of what you say by making a note and, if feasible, sending a follow-up e-mail to the party.

Problem: semi-competent litigants

A related problem occurs when a party appears to be too upset or impaired to make a good decision, but insists on going forward. This is more likely with pro se's, but may arise when an emotional party is represented by a weak or indecisive lawyer.

> *Example:* In a private mediation of a partnership breakup, one partner appears without a lawyer and the other has counsel. As the process goes forward, the pro se party becomes progressively more upset, sometimes making illogical arguments and reversing decisions unexpectedly. The mediator suggests that the mediation be adjourned so that he can rest and consult a lawyer, but he expresses determination to "get it over with," saying that "outside factors" make it important he resolve the case quickly. He will not explain what they are, but the mediator suspects he is involved in a divorce and needs cash badly.
>
> The other party's lawyer, sensing this, drives a very hard bargain. She demands that her client receive more than 75 percent of the assets, despite a partnership agreement that provides for a 50–50 split. The process continues for several hours. The pro se partner becomes increasingly upset but refuses to stop. At one point, early in the evening during a private caucus, he says to the mediator in an agitated tone, "I know about the agreement and all, but this can't go on any longer! I guess I've got to take their offer."

This situation implicates Model Standard II, impartiality, Standard VI, the quality of the process, and Standard I, self-determination.

> **Standard I: Self-Determination**
> A. A mediator shall conduct a mediation based on the principle of party self-determination. Self-determination is the act of coming to a voluntary, uncoerced decision in which each party makes free and informed choices as to process and outcome. . .

1. . . . *a mediator may need to balance such party self-determination with a mediator's duty to conduct a quality process . . .*
2. A mediator cannot personally ensure that each party has made free and informed choices to reach particular decisions, but, where appropriate, a mediator should make the parties aware of the importance of consulting other professionals . . .

Standard VI: Quality of the Process
A . . . 10. If a party appears to have difficulty comprehending the process, issues, or settlement options, or difficulty participating in a mediation, the mediator should explore the circumstances and potential accommodations, modifications or adjustments that would make possible the party's capacity to comprehend, participate and exercise self-determination . . .
C. If a mediator believes that participant conduct . . . jeopardizes conducting a mediation consistent with these Standards, a mediator shall take appropriate steps including, if necessary, postponing, withdrawing from or terminating the mediation.

What would you do here? Would you terminate this mediation? What if the party had explicitly asked you for advice about whether he should take the offer?

Comment: I have never faced such a situation, but my instinct would be to urge the pro se participant to take the time he needed to regain his composure. If necessary, I would adjourn the mediation to allow him to do so. I would already have strongly suggested that he talk with a lawyer, pointing out that a short consultation would be a good idea given what is at stake, and he would be free to reject the advice. And I would make a note of what I had said.

If this did not work, I would try to draw him out again about the "outside factors" that made him feel that he had no choice but to settle. If I concluded that he was irrational, I would end the process or, if the parties did not agree to stop, withdraw from it.

Problem: sympathy for a disputant

Mediators are taught to develop rapport with participants, and it is natural to feel sympathy with people in difficulty in any event. What should a mediator do in the following situation?

Example: You are contacted by a lawyer at a large firm about mediating a sexual harassment complaint brought by a nurse against a manager at a hospital. You talk ahead of time with the plaintiff's lawyer, a young woman with a solo practice, who maintains that the claim has merit but sounds uncertain about litigating it. The lawyer for the hospital is very confident.

The mediation begins. The plaintiff seems sincere and the facts she relates are bad, but the hospital has legal defenses. After discussing the case at length the plaintiff makes an opening demand of $150,000. You go to the defense and ask them for an offer. The hospital lawyer smiles and says, "$2,500." You raise your eyebrows questioningly. "We think this case can be had for ten or less," she says. "I want to send a signal. Let's see what she does." After some discussion you agree to take the number to the plaintiff.

When you convey the offer, the plaintiff nurse looks with distress at her lawyer. The lawyer projects doubt. "Well, I guess they have to start somewhere," she says. After some discussion they decide to drop to $110,000. The defense then goes up to $5,000.

The bargaining continues, the defense responding with thousand-dollar moves as the plaintiff drops by tens of thousands. As offers are exchanged, you discuss the case with each side, concluding that the plaintiff has a triable claim but also that she does not want to litigate it. You feel badly for the plaintiff, because you know that it will cost the hospital well over $100,000 simply to defend the case and the claim appears to have merit. If the plaintiff holds firm, your experience suggests that the defense will move at least into the mid-five-figures; you have seen the same defense firm do so in other cases. You do not disclose your view of the situation, however. The plaintiff eventually settles for $9,500.

This situation presents a potential clash between Standards I, self-determination, II, impartiality, and VI, quality of the process. As a mediator, you are bound to remain impartial, but at the same time you might strongly sympathize with the plaintiff here, who seems to be getting a bad outcome in a process you are facilitating. Would you intervene? What would you say if the plaintiff or her lawyer asked you for advice?

Comment: In the actual case I did not intervene. The plaintiff lawyer appeared to be basically competent, and I did not know all the circumstances that might be motivating the client to settle at a very low number. The plaintiff's most serious apparent problem, which was that she and her lawyer lacked the resources and the will to litigate against a large institution represented by a major law firm, was not one I could solve. I felt badly about the outcome, but believed that as long as the process itself was fair (the plaintiff had professional advice and adequate time to think), I could facilitate it. I also did not think that the plaintiff would be better off if I withdrew from the case. It was a situation in which there appeared to be no good choices.

Problem: connections to disputants

You will receive cases as a mediator because lawyers and perhaps other professionals know of you. Inevitably, however, this means that you will encounter cases in which you have a significant personal or professional tie to a participant.

Example: You provide mediation and training services in addition to your law practice. These services make up a small but significant percentage of your income. An old colleague, who is now a partner in a large law firm, asks you to present a lunch program to his firm on mediation advocacy. You arrange with the firm's professional education coordinator to receive a $1,000 honorarium and give the program. Afterward, the firm's training manager talks about doing a longer training for $5,000.

You suddenly realize that you have agreed to mediate a dispute next month in which a different lawyer in the same law firm represents a large pharmaceutical manufacturer who has been sued by a patient claiming severe side-effects from the defendant's medication. The plaintiff is represented by a suburban practitioner.

As you review briefs in the case, you realize that a lawyer for the Public Justice Foundation, a liberal legal group, is assisting the plaintiff lawyer (it could also have been a conservative advocacy organization assisting the defense). You are a dues-paying member of the group, but have not participated actively in it.

Standard III: Conflicts of Interest
A. A mediator shall avoid *a conflict of interest or the appearance of a conflict* of interest during and after a mediation . . .
C. A mediator shall disclose, as soon as practicable, all actual and potential conflicts of interest that . . . *could reasonably be seen as raising a question about the mediator's impartiality* . . .
F. Subsequent to a mediation *a mediator shall not establish another relationship* with any of the participants in any matter *that would raise questions about the integrity of the mediation.*

Note: The Uniform Mediation Act, Section 9, imposes a similar conflict of interest rule.

Do you need to disclose anything about your training work for the large firm or your membership in the advocacy organization? If so what would you say?

Comment: The plaintiff would probably consider it material that you received, and expect to receive, a significant payment from the other party's law firm. Similarly, each side would want to know that you are a member of a group that supports the other. The fact that you are not actually influenced by any of these items is irrelevant; what matters is whether a party might (allowing for the suspicion that pervades litigation) be concerned that you were. In the actual case I disclosed both issues, although not the dollar amounts of compensation. Neither lawyer asked follow-up questions or expressed any objection to my continuing as mediator.

If you agree that disclosure would be appropriate, try sketching out what you would have said in this situation.

Problem: lack of experience

Mediators sometimes encounter cases in areas in which they have not practiced or previously mediated—indeed, as their practice expands such situations are nearly inevitable. What obligation does a mediator have to disclose his lack of expertise to parties who inquire about his services?

Example: You are a litigator with ten years' experience who occasionally acts as a mediator. You have handled a total of 15 mediations as a neutral and participated in dozens more as an advocate. You have been asked to mediate a bitter employment dispute involving an employee who says that she was sexually harassed by her supervisor and that management knew of the problem but swept it under the rug.

You do not handle employment cases and have never mediated one, but you do read summaries of appellate decisions in your local legal newspaper, which sometimes include court and agency decisions in employment cases. You have skimmed these cases, but do not consider yourself versed in employment law.

Standard IV: Competence
A. A mediator shall mediate only when the mediator has the necessary competence to satisfy the reasonable expectations of the parties.
   1. Any person may be selected as a mediator, provided that the parties are satisfied with the mediator's competence and qualifications . . .

> 3. A mediator should have available for the parties' information relevant to the mediator's training, education, experience and approach . . .

> Standard VII. Advertising and Solicitation
> A. *A mediator shall be truthful and not misleading* when advertising, soliciting or otherwise communicating the mediator's qualifications, experience, services and fees.

What, if anything, should you say about your experience in this area?

Comment: Oddly, Standard IV does not appear to require a mediator affirmatively to disclose potential issues of competence to the parties, as in the case of conflicts of interest (it is phrased "should have available," not "should disclose") and assumes that a mediator will determine his own competence.

To me, a key question is the nature of the obstacles to agreement. If the barrier is a dispute about what award an antidiscrimination agency is likely to make or a difficult area of law, expertise is probably necessary. If, as is more often true, the focus of disagreement is "he said/she said" allegations or abrasive bargaining techniques, then a general familiarity with litigation and process skills are more relevant. I would talk with each lawyer about the case and then make a decision about whether to take it and what to disclose about my background.

Problem: respecting confidentiality between caucuses

Caucus-based mediation puts a mediator into arguably conflicting roles. On the one hand she is supposed to keep discussions within each party caucus confidential, but on the other, a basic purpose of mediation is to facilitate communication between parties, which in a caucus-based process requires the mediator to transmit information. How to carry out both tasks well poses significant practical issues, which are explored in the next section of this chapter, on confidentiality.

Problem: sleazy or illegal deals by disputants

> *Example:* After a fierce bargaining session in which you have used your entire bag of tricks, the defense has come painfully to a final offer of $180,000, but the plaintiff refuses to accept less than $200,000. A key issue, from the plaintiff's perspective, is that he needs to come out of the process with $100,000, after paying his lawyer a one-third

contingency fee and taxes. The primary claim is for lost pay, however, and any settlement will be treated by the company as back pay subject to tax withholding. The effect is that a $200,000 payment would net the plaintiff only about $70,000. The plaintiff has also asserted a general claim for emotional distress, but federal law bars plaintiffs from receiving settlement money tax-free unless their injury was physical in nature. "Mere" emotional distress is not sufficient to avoid a tax bite.

Suddenly the plaintiff lawyer asks the mediator to take an idea to the defense. In a spell of depression caused by the firing, he now remembers, the plaintiff suffered from erectile dysfunction. Counsel didn't make it an explicit part of the claim because of the embarrassment factor, but it was a physical injury. The lawyer proposes allocating most of the settlement to this injury, which would allow the plaintiff to receive a $100,000 net payment. You have never heard of this allegation and see no basis for it in the documents.

Standard I: Self-Determination
A. A mediator shall conduct a mediation based on the principle of party self-determination. Self-determination is the act of coming to a voluntary, uncoerced decision in which each party makes free and informed choices as to process and outcome . . .
   1. . . . a mediator may need to balance such party self-determination with a mediator's duty to conduct a quality process . . .

Standard IX: Advancement of Mediation Practice
A. A mediator should act in a manner that advances the practice of mediation.

Is there any problem for you as a mediator here?

Comment: It seems likely that the plaintiff's "physical injury" is an after-the-fact inspiration rather than a serious claim. I would probably take advantage of the shelter of Standard I, self-determination, and decide that if both sides' counsel approved the plan, there was no reason for me to object (my only option would be to withdraw). However, the agreement seems uncomfortably close to tax evasion, and I would be concerned about actively helping to put it together. I would also not wish to sign a memorandum of agreement memorializing the arrangement.

The Model Standards also cover other issues, but I do not discuss them here because they are unlikely to arise in commercial practice. The full Standards appear in the Appendix.

Rules for lawyer–mediators

Special issues arise for mediators who also practice law, involving conflicts between their role counseling clients in mediation and as advocates in law practice. Lawyers in large firms who work part-time as mediators encounter conflicts of interest frequently. One problem is issues that arise from past work by the firm, but such concerns are at least apparent at the time the lawyer–mediator takes a case. More troubling to many firms is the possibility that they will be excluded from a lucrative piece of litigation in the future, because one of their lawyers had made an unsuccessful effort to settle the dispute, or perhaps a related matter, as a mediator in the past.

Lawyer–mediators should comply with Model Standard III for mediators. In addition, an ABA Model Rule for lawyers deals specifically with intrafirm conflicts.

ABA Model Rule of Professional Conduct 1.12: Former Judge, Arbitrator, Mediator or Other Third-Party Neutral

(a) . . . a lawyer shall not represent anyone in connection with a matter in which the lawyer participated personally and substantially as a . . . mediator . . . unless all parties to the proceeding give informed consent, confirmed in writing . . .

(c) If a lawyer is disqualified by paragraph (a), no lawyer in a firm with which that lawyer is associated may knowingly undertake or continue representation in the matter unless:

  (1) the disqualified lawyer is screened from any participation in the matter and is apportioned no part of the fee therefrom; and

  (2) written notice is promptly given to the parties and any appropriate tribunal to enable them to ascertain compliance with the provisions of this rule . . .

---

2. The Law of Mediation

The primary legal issue with which commercial mediators must deal is confidentiality, so we begin with that. We also discuss enforcement of participation in the process and enforcement of settlements.

a. Confidentiality

Confidentiality issues in mediation arise in two fundamentally different ways. The first is when a person discloses information generated in mediation to persons *outside* the process, usually a court. The second occurs when a mediator makes an inappropriate disclosure *within* the process by communicating information provided by one litigant to another without consent.

(1) Disclosures outside the Process

Some practical advice

The most important thing to know about avoiding disclosures of confidential information outside the mediation process is that as long as you follow some basic rules, it should not be a problem. Throughout hundreds of mediated cases, I have received virtually no complaints from disputants that an opponent breached confidentiality and none that anyone was harmed by a disclosure. Other neutrals report the same experience.

This is not surprising when we think about how mediation works. A very large proportion of mediated cases settle, and once cases are resolved, the most significant reason to breach confidentiality, to gain a tactical advantage in litigation, disappears. It also seems that when disputants enter into explicit agreements they keep their word. The process itself may have something to do with this: when parties engage in a civil discussion led by a neutral person, whom they feel is genuinely striving to "bring peace into the room," they respect the rules of the process even when it does not succeed.

Three suggestions will protect you from most problems with confidentiality:

1. *Be clear about the rules.* Say what is and is not permitted to be disclosed outside the mediation, who is covered, and any exceptions. Put the ground rules governing confidentiality into writing, preferably in an agreement signed by each party or its lawyer.

2. *Don't overstate the degree of protection.* Describe what the mediation agreement or an applicable rule commits parties to do. ("You have all agreed that . . ." or "The rules of the court program require that . . .") Don't, however, make general statements about what rules will apply ("Nothing said here can be repeated outside this room") unless you are sure that the governing law will back you up—and remember that a future problem may arise in a different state or court system.

3. *Remember that there are two forms of confidentiality.* One involves what participants can reveal *outside* the mediation process; the other governs disclosures *within* a caucus-based process. Be clear about both.

A primer on the law of confidentiality

There are five primary sources of law governing the confidentiality of information disclosed in mediation:

○ Rules of evidence.

○ Privileges.

○ Other confidentiality guarantees.

○ Mediation agreements.

○ Positive disclosure obligations.

Rules of evidence

Virtually every jurisdiction has adopted a rule of evidence to protect the confidentiality of settlement discussions. The key federal provision is Federal Rule of Evidence 408.[2] About two-thirds of the states have evidentiary rules patterned on Rule 408. The first point to note about Rule 408 is that it is a rule of evidence, not a guarantee of confidentiality. Rule 408 is intended to limit what litigants can offer in evidence in a court proceeding and does not control disclosures outside a courtroom. The rule does not, for example, bar anyone from disclosing what is said in a deposition, nor does it apply to a media interview. In addition, Rule 408 applies only to court proceedings; it may not have any effect in less formal settings such as administrative hearings and arbitrations. Whether a mediation conversation will be admissible in another forum will depend on its rules and the philosophy of the presiding officer.

Even in court, Rule 408 may not prevent information about settlement discussions from being disclosed. The rule covers only evidence showing that a person offered or agreed to accept "valuable consideration" to compromise a claim, not everything said in settlement discussions. Thus, for example, the rule does not protect a trade secret from being introduced into evidence, unless it was part of an offer to settle. Indeed, even an offer of compromise is not necessarily sacrosanct under Rule 408, because the rule has many exceptions; for example, it does not bar use of settlement offers to impeach a witness.

Other uncertainties arise from the fact that only the party against whom evidence is offered can make a Rule 408 objection. The rule, in

---

2.   The text of the rule is as follows:

Rule 408. Compromise and Offers to Compromise. Evidence of (1) furnishing or offering or promising to furnish, or (2) accepting or offering or promising to accept, a valuable consideration in compromising or attempting to compromise a claim which was disputed as to either validity or amount, is not admissible to prove liability for or invalidity of the claim or its amount. Evidence of conduct or statements made in compromise negotiations is likewise not admissible. This rule does not require the exclusion of any evidence otherwise discoverable merely because it is presented in the course of compromise negotiations. This rule also does not require exclusion when the evidence is offered for another purpose, such as proving bias or prejudice of a witness, negativing a contention of undue delay, or proving an effort to obstruct a criminal investigation or prosecution.

other words, is designed to prevent a party from being shot in court with certain types of ammunition that it has provided to the other side during settlement discussions, not to keep all discussions confidential.

Privileges

There is no general federal mediation privilege, but about half the states have enacted general statutes covering mediation (there are other laws that apply to particular forms of the process, such as marital mediation). Most of these general statutes create formal legal privileges. It is important to realize that while a privilege bars evidence from being admitted in adjudication, like an evidentiary rule it does not prevent persons from disclosing information outside of court. A privilege is, in essence, a stricter form of an evidentiary rule. Privileges are less subject to evasion than Rule 408, because they bar admission of evidence regardless of the purpose for which it is offered and violations can expose the violator to a tort claim for damages.

One point to bear in mind is that only persons who are designated as "holders" of a privilege are entitled to invoke it. Typically, the parties in a case are "holders" and can prevent disclosures, but a mediator may not be entitled to use privilege as a shield.

The Uniform Mediation Act also creates a legal privilege, stating that communications made during mediation are not "subject to discovery or admissible in evidence" in a legal proceeding. (UMA §4) The UMA thus prevents the use of mediation communications in adjudicatory proceedings, subject to a list of exceptions for evidence of a plan to commit a crime, situations involving child abuse, and so on. Like Rule 408, the UMA leaves disputants free to disclose mediation information outside the litigation process, although the UMA provides that disputants can explicitly agree otherwise. Mediators in a UMA jurisdiction who want to be sure that communications remain confidential should therefore enter into a written confidentiality agreement.

Other confidentiality guarantees

Many of the state laws governing mediation go beyond establishing an evidentiary privilege to make the entire mediation process "confidential." This usually means that participants may not disclose what occurred in any context, in or out of court. A Massachusetts statute, for instance, states that any communication during a mediation "shall be confidential," and California statutes have similar provisions. (See Mass. G.L. c. 233, §23C; Cal. Code §§1115-1128.)

Neither Congress nor the federal courts have provided any general federal confidentiality guarantee to mediation, but confidentiality provisions exist in specific statutes. In addition, each federal district court is required to have local rules providing for the confidentiality of mediations that occur in its court-affiliated programs.

State court and private mediation programs also typically have rules stating that mediations held under their auspices will be confidential. The rules of such programs rarely define, however, what they mean by "confidential." In one sense, a party's incentive to comply with the rules of a court-affiliated program is strong, because if it violates a rule it may incur the wrath of the judge who will hear the case. This is not to say, however, that a party has a legal remedy if an opponent violates a court rule.

Mediation agreements

Mediation agreements are the surest way to keep information from "leaking" out of the process. My practice is to offer a standard confidentiality clause in my mediation agreements (a sample appears in the Appendix). Lawyers almost never ask for changes in it.

The biggest drawback of mediation agreements is that they are only contracts and, therefore, bind only those persons who enter into the agreement, not outsiders. This means that third-party litigants are not bound and can serve subpoenas on mediation participants. If a breach does occur, a party's only remedy under a contract is usually to sue for monetary damages, if any can be proved. This said, however, I have rarely heard a disputant complain that an opponent has violated a confidentiality agreement.

Positive disclosure obligations

Public policy sometimes bars secrecy concerning settlement negotiations. Some states have case law or statutes that require persons who become aware of certain matters such as child abuse to report them to authorities. Both individual states and the federal government also have public record and "sunshine" laws that require documents and certain meetings involving government officials to be open to the public. As a result, when regulatory issues are mediated, the process may have to be open to outside observers.

(2) Disclosures between Caucuses

People almost always talk about confidentiality in terms of disclosures outside mediation, but in caucus-based processes the most delicate problems for a mediator involve communication between caucuses. This is because of a tension mentioned earlier: parties are assured caucus discussions are private, but at the same time a mediator's key function is to facilitate communication.

There is no general statute governing disclosures between parties within the mediation process, but Model Standard V states the following:

Standard V: Confidentiality

B. *A mediator who meets with any persons in private session* during a
   mediation *shall not convey directly or indirectly* to any other person,
   any information that was obtained during that private session without
   the consent of the disclosing person.

Practical advice

How can one comply with Standard V and at the same time mediate
effectively? Again the key is clear ground rules. I suggest telling disputants that:

- ○ If they believe information is sensitive, they should flag it and I
  will keep it confidential just as I would if I were their lawyer.

- ○ Even if they do not say anything, I will use my judgment and
  not disclose things I think they would consider sensitive without
  checking back with them. But, I say, it is easier if they warn me
  about hot-button issues.

These rules protect me from the risk that I will forget to check with
parties, and allow me to exercise judgment about how to conduct the process, which, after all, is what parties hire mediators to do.

Trickier questions arise when an assertive lawyer asks questions
about what is going on in the other caucus room. To what extent can a
mediator respond to such queries without prejudicing the absent party?
For example, if one side asks you the following questions in a caucus conversation, how should you deal with them?

- ○ "How is Smith feeling now? Is he as upset as he was in the opening session? Is he ready to bargain?"

Comment: I would feel comfortable giving information that I thought
would support constructive bargaining, such as that Smith had calmed
down or was ready to negotiate. I would not provide information if I
thought it might place Smith at a disadvantage—for example, that he was
distraught at the accusations against him, suggesting that he might give
in rather than go to trial.

- ○ "Who's taking the tough line in the other room? Is it the client, or
  is the lawyer calling the shots?"

Comment: I would be very wary of answering this kind of question,
because it suggests a strategy of finding weak points in the opposing
team or exploiting differences of opinion. I would make an exception
if I thought that the absent party would not object to my explaining its

situation. A lawyer might, for instance, want its adversary to know that her client was adamant. In fact, if the absent side appeared to be pretending to be emotional in order to play "good cop/bad cop," then a literal answer might deceive the party asking the question. In that situation, the best response might be to answer with a qualification, "I don't know what they are thinking, but the client is certainly taking a hard line."

○ "Have they shown any flexibility on the counsel fees issue? Without that resolved, talking about these other things is a waste of time!"

Comment: It's a party's call whether it wishes to show flexibility on an issue. I would not indicate flexibility without a signal that I should do so. I would, however, be willing to offer my own predictions or even speculate if I thought that it would advance the bargaining process and it would be clear that the opinion was my own. I might, for example, say, "They haven't so far. Of course, counsel fees routinely come up in discrimination cases, and in my experience defense counsel usually expect a plaintiff to raise the issue, but we'll see . . ."

b. Enforcement of Participation in Mediation

Requirements that parties go to mediation arise from three general sources: contracts, rules and statutes, and ad hoc judicial orders. More and more commercial contracts contain dispute resolution clauses that require parties to mediate as a precondition to filing suit, and many court systems have adopted rules that require litigants to go through mediation as a prerequisite to getting to trial. Judges sometimes also issue ad hoc orders to parties in specific cases to go to mediation. State programs and rules often require that parties mediate "in good faith" or send representatives with "full settlement authority," imposing additional ambiguous requirements on participants.

Practical advice

The best advice for a mediator (advice for lawyers appears in Chapter Twelve) is probably the following:

○ Do not take sides in disagreements between parties over an obligation to mediate.

○ If parties are entering mediation under a requirement, consider asking them for deposits, subject to forfeiture if they cancel.

○ As the process goes forward, be careful to monitor whether each party is committed to participating and address any problems.

Don't take sides in disputes over obligations to mediate by interpreting or attempting to enforce requirements. If, however, there is a dispute about participation or attendance, you can mediate it. It is possible to evaluate such issues, but be careful not to be seen as acting in your personal interest, for example, by pushing for a mediation to take place for which you will be paid.

Once in the process, monitor the parties' commitment. Parties rarely state explicitly that they do not intend to participate; for one thing, saying so might put them in violation of the very requirement that forced them to attend. You will usually have to infer this from the disputants' behavior. This is difficult, because behavior that indicates lack of commitment can be very similar to the tactics of someone who is simply angry or playing negotiation "hardball."

If you sense that a party does not want to mediate, the best option is to confront the issue. Ordinarily, you should do so in private. Try to discover why the disputant does not want to participate and what might persuade it to do so. If, for example, the reason is lack of information or suspicion about the other side's sincerity, address the problem. If the reluctant party needs a court decision on an issue, it may be possible to bargain for that. If a party wants to use the litigation process for delay, you can explore whether this can be accomplished more effectively by agreement. If the purpose is to inflict pain, you might explore whether the cost is worth it.

c. Enforcement of Mediated Settlements

When mediation is successful the parties usually enter into a settlement agreement. Settlements can, however, provoke new controversies over issues such as the following:

- ○ Did the parties actually reach a final agreement? If so, what were its terms?
- ○ Should the agreement be invalidated on grounds such as duress, mistake, unconscionability, or lack of authority?

Practical advice

Best practice is to do the following:

- ○ Strongly encourage disputants to sign a memorandum that sets forth key terms of their agreement, as outlined in Chapter Nine, before they leave the mediation site.
- ○ Comply with any special laws or requirements that apply to mediated settlements in your jurisdiction.
- ○ Do not become involved in evaluating whether or not a settlement complies with the law, especially if one of the parties is not represented by a lawyer.

A primer on the law

The existence of an agreement. Most courts test mediated settlement agreements by the standards that apply to contracts generally. Where a court has refused to enforce an oral agreement reached in mediation, it has usually been because of special procedural rules that go beyond the requirements of the common law.

One common issue is whether disputants may testify about the existence of an oral settlement, or whether the mediator can be called as a witness on the issue. Section Six of the Uniform Mediation Act prevents participants from testifying about agreements reached in mediation, but exempts agreements that are in writing and signed by the parties or electronically recorded (for example, when counsel appear in court to report a settlement). The net effect of the UMA is to bar enforcement of oral settlements, but permit enforcement of written or recorded ones.

Grounds for invalidation. Suppose that lawyers draw up a settlement agreement and the parties sign it. Is that enough to ensure that a settlement will be enforced? Generally the answer is yes, but not always. Again there are potential concerns, some of which are formal in nature.

First, settlement agreements must contain the essential terms of the parties' bargain. Where, for example, a settlement provided that "the parties shall exchange mutual general releases," a court would probably find the language adequate to form a binding agreement. If, however, a settlement stated that a defendant will make payments "in installments" but did not specify a schedule, it might well be rejected by a court. Some jurisdictions also require that mediated settlements of pending litigation be approved by a court.

The most serious basis for invalidating mediated settlements is a substantive one: That the process of mediation itself was so poor that the resulting agreement is invalid. It seems less likely that a bad settlement would result when a neutral person presides over the negotiation, but aspects of commercial mediation that push litigants to confront unpleasant realities may also create stress that inhibits good decision making. For a leading decision that authorized an invasion of mediation confidentiality to assess a plaintiff's claim that she was browbeaten into signing an agreement, see *Olam v. Congress Mortgage Co.*, 68 F. Supp. 2d 1110 (N.D.Cal.1999) (after review, the court upheld the settlement).

3. Mediator Liability

Only rarely do disputants charge that a mediator has engaged in malpractice. Professor Michael Moffit (2003) conducted an exhaustive survey and found only one reported case in the past quarter century in which a verdict was entered against a mediator for improper conduct—and the result in that case was overturned on appeal. Moffit concluded that, "Despite the thousands, if not millions of disputants who have received mediation services, instances of legal complaints against mediators are extraordinarily rare."

Even allegations of misconduct are very unusual. In Florida during the late 1990s, for example, state courts sent more than 100,000 cases per year to mediation, but the state board created to investigate complaints against court-certified mediators received only 49 complaints in its first eight years of operation.

The absence of malpractice verdicts against mediators may be due in part to the fact that they are largely immune from suit. Mediators acquire immunity either through court rules or mediation agreements (the agreement in the Appendix, for example, contains a partial immunity clause). Even if mediators were not immune, however, disputants would find it very difficult to prove that an act of misconduct had caused them to lose money. Parties to commercial mediation, after all, almost always have lawyers. As a result, absent factual misrepresentations, it would be hard to prove that a mediator overrode a lawyer's advice and caused a disputant to make a bad decision.

The first defense against liability is, of course, to practice ethically. The next is to obtain insurance. Because of the paucity of claims, the cost of mediator malpractice insurance is very low. As of late 2008, the most prominent issuer of mediator liability policies, Complete Equity Markets, quoted a premium of less than $300 per year for a $100,000/$300,000 policy covering commercial cases (in a few states, the cost ranged up to $400, still not a large sum). Whether due to high ethical standards, difficulties of proof, or legal immunity, lawsuits against mediators are very infrequent.

4. Additional Sources of Information

This chapter is intended only to provide an overview of the legal issues that can arise for mediators. The following sources provide additional information about these issues:

○ For a comprehensive discussion of the law of mediation, see Cole et al., *Mediation Law, Policy and Practice* (2004).

○ For an analysis of court decisions concerning mediation and mediators, see James Coben and Peter Thompson, "Disputing Irony: A Systematic Look at Litigation about Mediation," 11 *Harvard Negotiation Law Review* 43 (2006).

○ For an updated listing and analysis of mediation cases around the United States, see www.hamline.edu/law/adr/ Mediation_Case_Law_Project.

Representing Clients in Mediation: Advice for Lawyers

To this point, this book has been written for mediators. Part III is meant for lawyers who represent parties in mediation. The next two chapters explain how lawyers can use the special powers of mediators and the structure of the process to more effectively achieve their settlement goals.

Traditionally, lawyers have seen mediation simply as a method of facilitating traditional bargaining over money. In this vision, a mediator's primary role is to carry offers back and forth between the parties and serve as a buffer to cushion the impact of hard bargaining tactics—in effect a combination of "telephone" and "boxing glove." When money bargaining breaks down, such lawyers expect a mediator to give clients a dose of reality, in the form of an evaluation of the case, and perhaps also make a settlement proposal. Some lawyers still favor this approach, but it does not take full advantage of what a mediator can do.

Mediation is a different process from direct bargaining. The key difference is the presence of the neutral, which turns a two-sided process into a more complex interaction.

Mediators sometimes claim they "have no power," but that is not really true. They cannot compel parties to settle, but they do influence the process of bargaining. They are like referees in a sports contest: they don't score points themselves, but they affect the tempo and content of the game litigators play, and their decisions can boost—or lower—a lawyer's final tally.

Wise lawyers understand how a mediator can help them. As one mediator remarked about a litigator, a note of admiration in his voice, "She moved me around like a chess piece!" And not just a pawn, either. Good mediators are like chessboard knights—they have many capabilities and, properly deployed, can multiply the effectiveness of a lawyer's bargaining strategy.

Mediators can enhance a lawyer's bargaining in several ways. They can, for example, improve communication with the other side by explaining what an offer means. ("Tell them we're at 25 thousand, but are prepared to talk seriously once they drop their claim to double damages.") Mediators can also provide information about the attitude of people in the other camp ("Has the plaintiff calmed down?") or influence the format of bargaining ("I think it would be helpful if we could set up a discussion between my client and their CFO").

Advocates can use mediation to enhance both competitive and cooperative bargaining strategies. An extreme opening offer that would send the other side out the door in a direct negotiation, for instance, is less risky in mediation because the mediator is present to cushion the impact of the tactic ("scrape them off the ceiling"). Or a lawyer can use mediation to support a mixture of toughness and cooperation by pressing for the best possible money deal and at the same time asking the mediator to explore on his own initiative whether the other side is open to a creative solution.

Particularly toward the end of the process, a lawyer is likely to find herself in a three-sided negotiation, with the other side and also with the mediator. Advocates can, for example, negotiate over how and when the mediator uses an impasse-breaking technique. ("Before you give your own view about liability, I'd appreciate it if you would ask them if . . .") A lawyer cannot expect a mediator to favor her side at the expense of the other, but if a tactic is facially neutral, the mediator may well agree to use it.

The key lesson? Don't approach the process passively. Instead, use mediation affirmatively to enhance your clients' interests. Based on my own experiences of being "spun" by savvy counsel, I offer suggestions in the next two chapters of how lawyers can "borrow" a mediator's powers.

How to Borrow
a Mediator's Powers

This chapter looks at the range of ways lawyers can use mediators to advance their bargaining strategies.

1. Manage the Structure and Flow of Information

Experienced advocates know that mediators have influence over the format in which mediation occurs and the way information is exchanged, and use this to their clients' advantage. Lawyers can use a mediator to:

O Influence the structure of the process.

O Focus discussion on specific issues.

O Gather information or convey it to an opponent.

O Use confidentiality to manage the flow of data.

Influence the structure of the process

Chapter Nine discussed ways in which a mediator can avoid an impasse by changing the format of the process. As an advocate, you do not have to wait for the mediator to suggest changes, however. Before mediation begins, ask yourself: am I content with the usual structure, or would I do better in another format?

The most common option is to suggest that a subset of the disputants meet with each other—principals only, experts only, or lawyers only. This can happen at any point in the process. When principals meet alone, lawyers often ask the mediator to attend so as to prevent confrontations and ensure confidentiality, but this is not essential. Here is an example:

Example: A manufacturer and a trucking company had a productive relationship for more than a decade, with the trucker distributing the manufacturer's products throughout the southern United States. Then their relationship went sour. The manufacturer sued the trucking company, claiming it had fraudulently inflated its costs by overstating mileage and padding other charges. After two years of intense litigation, the parties agreed to mediate.

The mediation process began with an unusual twist: the plaintiff's lawyer called ahead of time to suggest I ask the defense whether we could dispense with the usual opening statements by lawyers and instead have the two CEOs meet privately. I raised the issue with defense counsel, who agreed, subject to my being present during the conversation.

The three of us retired to a room, leaving the lawyers behind. The plaintiff executive opened the discussion by retracing the companies' earlier good relationship and their later problems. He suggested the breakdown had been provoked in part by a wayward manager he had hired away from the trucking company but had recently let go. The executive then made a settlement offer. The defendant CEO said he needed to run it by his lawyers.

The parties went into caucuses and bargained intensely for hours, reducing an initial $900,000 gap to $30,000—a demand of $300,000 against an offer of $270,000. At that point, however, the defense refused to make another offer, expressing frustration at the plaintiff's unreasonableness.

As I searched for ways to break the impasse, the defendant CEO suddenly pulled a quarter out of his pocket. "See this?" he asked. "You check—It's an honest quarter. I'll flip him for it!" "For what?" "The 30," he replied. "Let's see if he's got the ****s to flip for it!" I looked at the trucker's lawyer: was this serious? The lawyer shrugged his shoulders; "It's OK with me. Why don't you take Jim down and present it to them. But you should do the talking; Jim's feeling really frustrated by all this." Why not? I thought; it was better than anything I had to suggest.

I led the defendant CEO into the plaintiff's conference room and, with a smile, said, "Jim has an idea to break the deadlock. It's kind of . . . unusual, but you might want to listen to it." In a calm voice and without anatomical references, the CEO repeated his coin-toss offer.

The plaintiff executive grinned. "OK," he said, "But you didn't answer my last move, so the real spread is 50, between my 320 (his last offer before dropping to $300,000) and your 270." They argued over what should be the outcomes for the flip, showing some exasperation but also bits of humor. When the discussion stalled, I suggested options to keep it going ("Why not give the 20 to charity?"), but in the end they could not agree and the defendant CEO walked out.

As he left, I walked with him down the hall. "Suppose I could get him to drop to a flat $290,000," I asked. "Would that do it?" As it turned out, it did.

In this mediation, both lawyers' initiatives proved important to settlement. The plaintiff lawyer's proposal that the process begin with a parties-only meeting created an informal connection between the executives that smoothed their later bargaining. And the CEO's idea of a coin toss, which I learned later had been concocted with his lawyer, was key to shaking the parties out of their stalemate.

As we saw in Chapter Nine, advocates can also put an expert or lawyer from one side together with the other side's team. Still another option is to arrange for the mediator to meet with an outside advisor or with your opponent. If you think this would be helpful, alert the neutral to the issue and urge him to set a meeting up.

Example: A town refused to pay a contractor for its work on a new high school, arguing that the construction was defective. The contractor sued for payment and the case went to mediation. The parties made some progress but eventually reached a stalemate and adjourned.

The contractor's lawyer suspected the town's negotiating team had been unable to make a decision because of internal conflicts provoked by the chairman of the school board. Her client said he had developed a good relationship with the town manager during another construction project and thought that if he could connect with the manager on a one-on-one basis, he could resolve the personality issue and reopen negotiations.

The lawyer asked the mediator to contact defense counsel and ask for permission for the contractor to have breakfast with the town manager. The defense lawyer agreed, and the case was resolved.

To summarize:

○ Ask a mediator to vary the mediation structure.

○ Consider suggesting that one person, or part of a team, meet with an opponent.

○ Seek advice about what structure is likely to work. Don't be afraid to ask the neutral to stay out of a meeting or join it.

Focus discussion on specific issues

Some lawyers let mediators determine the agenda, but others take a more active stance: they tell the mediator what they want discussed in joint session or stressed to an opponent, and in this way influence the focus of the process.

Example: Experienced advocates were filmed as they mediated a commercial warranty case. The setting was a large contractor's claim for $1.5 million in damages against a supplier, based on the allegation that the defendant had sold the contractor defective antifreeze, severely damaging the cooling systems of two dozen of its heavy trucks and placing many more at risk.

The plaintiff did not have an expert opinion pointing to a specific problem with the antifreeze. Instead it relied on a *res ipsa locquitor* theory: it had put the suspect antifreeze into 70 out of its fleet of 150 vehicles, and almost immediately some of the treated trucks showed extraordinary damage to their cooling systems. Trucks at other depots that had not received the defendant's antifreeze had no problems.

The defendant had an expert test the antifreeze sample and found nothing wrong with the product, nor had any of the defendant's other customers reported problems with antifreeze from the same batch. This made the defendant sure the cause lay in the trucks. Defense counsel saw causation as a key defense, and at the end of his first caucus meeting raised the issue with the mediator:

Defendant's counsel: We hope you'll raise with them that we see the crux of settlement as hinging on the fact that we don't see any evidence to support their case on causation . . .

Mediator: But if they have evidence, that might influence your bargaining position?

Counsel (smiling): Yes, and if they don't, we hope it influences theirs.

The mediator raised the issue in his meeting with the plaintiff side:

Mediator: Suppose an outside expert reports there is no foreign substance in the antifreeze and the expert is credible . . . How does that affect the case?

> *Plaintiff counsel:* Well, it's a problem, no question about it. We recognize it's the weakest part of our case.
> *Mediator:* What percentage chance would you place on liability?
> *Counsel:* 50 percent.
> By the conclusion of the discussion, the plaintiff team agreed to discount its chance of success on liability to 40 percent.

The defense lawyer in this example persuaded the mediator to focus part of his discussion with the plaintiff on her issue, and in doing so took advantage of the plaintiff's inclination to be more candid with the neutral.

It is also possible, at least temporarily, to shift attention from an issue that is unhelpful or embarrassing.

> *Example:* Your client is outraged at the other side's alleged fraud, but you see the evidence of intentional misconduct as weak, and believe the fraud claim is doomed. Your client, however, refuses to face the fact that it will be necessary to severely compromise or even abandon his claim to punitive damages. Even discussing the issue makes him angry.
>
> In a pre-mediation call, you alert the mediator that focusing on the fraud claim will impair everyone's ability to make progress on other issues and ask her to defer discussion of punitive damages until late in the day, when your client will have had time to become more realistic.

To summarize:

○ Harness a mediator's influence over the discussion agenda.
○ Ask the mediator to focus discussion on a key issue, or avoid a sensitive one.

Gather information or convey it to an opponent

Sophisticated bargainers consider exchanging information an important aspect of any negotiation. Information exchanges have to be handled differently in commercial mediation, however, because parties separated in caucuses must rely on the mediator to convey data back and forth. Experienced advocates take advantage of this to ask a mediator to provide, and sometimes to obtain, information.

Gathering information about the merits. Lawyers' most common question is for information about factual issues. You can ask a mediator to gather specific data, arguing, for example, that if an adversary is relying on a particular theory to bolster its case, it should be willing to support it with data. If it does not, you can say, the mediator should appreciate why you give the argument little credence.

> *Example:* Recall the case discussed in Chapter Seven, in which frustrated homebuyers sued an executive relocation company for damages after the company canceled a house sale and prevented them from acquiring their "dream" home. The plaintiffs alleged the sale price was far below the fair market value of the house, giving rise to a large claim for damages. The defendants, however, argued that the plaintiffs had bought at the market price and therefore would recover almost nothing, even if they prevailed on liability.
>
> The mediator suggested the two sides obtain a confidential appraisal of the property, but the plaintiffs refused to agree, tacitly admitting their damage claim was inflated. In that case, the mediator took the initiative to suggest the appraisal, but defense counsel could have coached the neutral to do so.

Probing an opponent's state of mind. Advocates can ask a mediator about the other side's attitudes and feelings.

○ If a plaintiff seems agitated in the opening session, defense counsel might later ask the mediator, "Has Smith calmed down?" or "If his lawyer recommends a deal, do you think he'll listen?"

○ A lawyer could also inquire about the other side's decision making: "Do you think her client will listen if she recommends settling?" "Is this her first time representing this client?" "Do we need to adjourn and get the adjuster here in person?"

○ Another option is to ask a mediator to explore an adversary's reaction to a potential deal: "Would you try to get a sense of whether they'd drop to six figures?" or "Can they go to $125,000? I can't talk to my client about making another concession if it's a moving target."

Questions about what the other side is thinking pose tricky ethical and practical issues for mediators because of the tension between maintaining confidentiality and facilitating the flow of information, but that does not mean you shouldn't ask.

Be aware, however, that if you ask a mediator for information about your opponent, the neutral is likely to interpret it as permission to give the other side the same kind of data about you. Discuss with a mediator what he will say to your opponent, and if you are concerned something sensitive might be disclosed, make it clear how you want it treated. In general, it is easier to ask that something not be revealed at all than to control how a mediator presents an issue if she does talk about it. As in direct bargaining, information exchange is a two-way street. That does not mean, however, that asking questions is not helpful, and the mediation structure can amplify your ability to do so.

Convey information to an opponent. Lawyers also use mediation to convey data. They know that through credibility and phrasing a mediator can deliver a tough message—either about substantive issues or bargaining—and at the same time reduce an opponent's anger at hearing it.

> *Example:* You have strong evidence that an opposing witness is lying, but you are concerned that if you raise the issue directly with your opponent, she will dismiss the information out of hand. You decide to go over the data in private with the mediator and ask him to discuss it with the other party.
>
> You know that evidence presented by a mediator is less apt to be summarily rejected, and even if information has no impact on the other side, the fact that you highlight it will focus the mediator's attention on the issue.

Another option is to transmit a message about your bargaining intentions.

> *Example:* A plaintiff has decided to go to its bottom line, but is concerned its opponent will take offense at receiving an ultimatum. It decides to make the statement through the mediator: "Tell them we've thought it over and $90,000 is our last and final offer."
>
> At a minimum, the mediator can cushion the message, making it less likely the other side will react angrily. If the neutral believes the plaintiff is sincere, she may go further and accredit it: "I've been talking to them for hours. You can never be sure, but my sense is they can't go below $90,000 . . ."

In practice, most lawyers designate few facts as confidential and expect a mediator to reveal at least some of what they say in private caucuses. Experienced lawyers know, in other words, that while mediators will not reveal sensitive data to an opponent, they will usually feel authorized to go beyond simply repeating what a party says. Think about what message you want the mediator to send about your intentions and state of mind. Tell the neutral what you want communicated, and in what tone. Exactly what the mediator says is up to her, of course, but the likelihood the mediator will convey your message as you wish is higher if you tell her what you want said and how.

> *Example:* A plaintiff lawyer might tell a mediator, "$500,000 is as low as we'll go at this point. You can tell them 500." The lawyer knows the neutral will interpret this to mean she can tell the other side the plaintiff is reducing his demand to $500,000 and will probably be willing to go significantly farther ("at this point") if the defendant makes an appropriate response.

You can ask or, as in the preceding example, by implication prompt, a mediator to convey a viewpoint as her own and not attribute it to you. Communicating intentions in this way has two advantages. First, the listener may be left a bit unsure as to what signal has been given, giving you leeway either to reinforce or back away from it in light of the response, similar to the way government officials float trial balloons to the press. Second, the fact that the mediator is the one making the interpretation makes it appear less manipulative, and therefore less subject to reactive devaluation, than if you give the same signal directly.

In summary, to take advantage of the mediator's ability to transmit information:

- Ask the mediator to gather or convey information that supports your bargaining strategy.
- Ask the mediator questions about the other side's attitude and emotional state, including questions about specific team members.
- Convey messages about your own intentions, discussing with the mediator what you wish said.

Use confidentiality to manage the flow of data

Mediation is, of course, a confidential process. Confidentiality rules were discussed in Chapter Ten; for purposes of advocacy, what is important is that confidentiality is not only a cloak that can protect, but also a tool that can make your bargaining more effective. One way to accomplish this is to give the mediator information privately, not allowing her to disclose it or permitting disclosure only under specified conditions.

Information given to the mediator alone. The most common tactic is to show or describe evidence to a mediator but refuse to allow her to disclose it to an opponent. In this way, a lawyer can reveal a piece of evidence he argues will be a "silver bullet" at trial, hopefully influencing the mediator's view of the merits without forewarning the other side. Similarly, defense lawyers might cite a "killer" defense but forbid a mediator to tell the plaintiff about it:

○ "Look at the data we've turned up on the profits of this 'troubled' company over the past three years—but you can't tell them we have it."

○ "He claims to be disabled, but our investigator saw him playing basketball last month! Just wait until we cross-examine."

○ "They didn't send the required demand letter before suing, and in a week it'll be too late. If this doesn't settle today we'll move to dismiss."

"Silver bullet" allegations pose troubling problems for a mediator because they require the neutral to predict how an adversary might rebut evidence. For this reason, mediators often discount evidence that a party will not allow them to discuss with an opponent. That said, there is little downside to providing information in this way as long as you trust the mediator to keep it confidential.

The fact that you provide information to the mediator on a confidential basis does not, of course, prevent you from disclosing it later in the process. Lawyers sometimes forbid disclosure at the outset but allow information to be revealed later if the mediator thinks it is likely to bring about a settlement. ("You can show them the affidavit if it will tie down a deal.")

Conditional disclosures. Advocates can also make partial or conditional disclosures, authorizing evidence to be given to an opponent but using the structure of mediation to prevent or hinder its use in litigation. Chapter Seven discussed how a mediator can use confidentiality to facilitate an information exchange. Advocates have other options, however, that a mediator would probably not suggest because they involve one side using the rules to its advantage.

Example: Each side has been wooing a witness to testify about a crucial meeting. The defense obtains an affidavit from the person that confirms its version of what happened. Counsel knows disclosure of the affidavit will help convince the plaintiff to settle but is concerned that if she shows it to the other side and the mediation fails, it will lose its status as lawyer work-product, allowing her adversary to use it on cross examination.

She decides to show the affidavit to the mediator privately, allowing him to read it and transcribe key passages in his own handwriting. The mediator is allowed to comment on and even read passages from his notes to the plaintiff. ("Here's what Smith's affidavit says . . .") The neutral does not receive a copy, however, and cannot show it to the opponent. In this way, the lawyer hopes to influence an adversary by disclosing the contents of a document, while at the same protecting its status as work-product and shielding it from discovery.

Example: Two parties' disagreement about a claim turns, in large part, on the credibility of a witness who is no longer available for deposition. The lawyer who controls the witness allows the mediator to question him privately and give the other party her impressions of the witness's credibility. The effect is to use the witness in the mediation without giving the other side a "free look" at the witness, which could assist it if the case has to be tried.

In summary, to take advantage of mediation confidentiality,

O Present evidence to the mediator privately. Ask the neutral to give his impressions of the evidence to your opponent, but not to disclose it.

O Allow an opponent to view documents, but have the mediator personally label them confidential.

O Show a document, but bar an opponent from making notes or copies.

2. Influence the Bargaining Process

Advocates can also use mediation to improve their effectiveness in the give-and-take of bargaining. This can be done whether one is using positional or interest-based techniques. Among the options are to:

O Ask for advice.

O Enhance your offers.

O Support a hard bargaining strategy.

O Explore hidden issues and options.

O Take advantage of a mediator's flexibility.

Ask for advice

In a typical mediation, a neutral will spend hours talking privately with your opponent, giving the neutral a unique perspective on the other side's bargaining style and settlement priorities. As a result, the mediator can be a helpful bargaining consultant.

> *Example:* An elderly tourist on a tour of Europe fell on a castle stairwell and died as her family watched. The tourist's estate sued the U.S. company that had set up the tour, and after lengthy litigation the parties went to mediation. The tour company's insurer made a first offer of $20,000, but the plaintiff's lawyer replied that until the defendant came up to "six figures or close to it," it would not consider dropping from its opening demand of $650,000. The mediation adjourned with no progress.
>
> Defense counsel decided to involve the mediator in calls with his adjuster, who had not been at the mediation session. The mediator gave his impressions of the case and why he thought it would be sensible to settle in six figures. Following lengthy discussions, the defense lawyer was given the authority to raise his opening number by an unspecified amount and to settle in the $150,000 to $175,000 range. Defense counsel was not sure, however what offer would meet the plaintiff's demand without inflating its expectations. In the meantime, the judge in the case was close to deciding a motion that might greatly increase the tour operator's liability exposure.
>
> Defense counsel held another conversation with his adjuster and the neutral and discussed how to present the next offer. The mediator said he saw two options: either offer $70,000 to $80,000 on the theory that this would be "close" to $100,000 and would not give the plaintiff an inflated expectation about the final result, or offer a flat $100,000 and let the defense's next offer signal that despite the large move, it saw the case as worth only in the low six-figures.
>
> Under either option, the mediator said, he would offer the plaintiff an explanation of the number. If the offer were $100,000 he would say the defense had been inclined to start lower but had reluctantly been "talked up." If it were $70,000 to $80,000, the mediator would stress that while the offer might be low, he believed there might be significantly more money available. The lawyer decided to put $100,000 on the table as a sign of good faith.

In this example, the defense made a low opening offer because a new adjuster had recently taken over the file and did not appreciate his insured's exposure (in particular, that the judge in the case had made cutting comments from the bench about the tour operator's "irresponsibility"). Defense counsel was aware of the risk and therefore favored making a higher opening offer, but at first was not able to convince his adjuster to authorize one. In a direct negotiation, the defendant might well have refused to "bid against itself," by putting a better offer on the table before the plaintiff made a concession. Indeed, the parties had been in litigation for three years without serious negotiations because each was using tough positional tactics. In mediation, however, the lawyer used the neutral's views to persuade his adjuster to give him more authority, then used the mediator as a consultant to decide how best to use it.

Enhance your offers

Experienced lawyers instinctively understand the concept of reactive devaluation—that an idea presented by a mediator as his own will be given consideration, while an identical offer coming from them will be viewed with suspicion. Assume, for example, two parties are stuck at offers of $75,000 and $120,000. Defense counsel suggests to the mediator, "Why don't you tell them you think you might be able to get us to $90,000? Six figures is impossible, but we might be able to be persuaded to go as far as $90,000 if it would finally resolve the case. I might be able to push my client that far if it would truly get it done."

In this example, the lawyer is trying to do several things. First, he hopes the mediator will take responsibility for the proposal to protect it from reactive devaluation by the plaintiff. Second, he is making it hypothetical so the other side will not escalate its demand in response. Finally, he is negotiating with the mediator about what the settlement target will be.

Authorship. Lawyers may also ask mediators to take authorship of a proposal to protect it from devaluation. Here is one example:

Example: In the filmed experiment described earlier involving a construction company's claim that a supplier had harmed its trucks with defective antifreeze, defense counsel suggested that the client, who had sold the plaintiff diesel fuel for years, give the plaintiff a discount on fuel purchases for a five-year period, but no cash. She knew that the plaintiff would be upset with a "coupon only" offer, and therefore tried to persuade the mediator to present the proposal as his own.

Mediator: I've told you the plaintiff is willing to move significantly from their opening demand. This isn't just the mediator reading tea leaves—they gave me explicit permission to tell you that . . . But if I go back now and say, "They're willing to give you a discount but . . . *that's*

> *it*," it's going to be a hard sell . . . But if that's what you think is the best way to move this forward, then I'll try it.
>
> *Outside counsel:* No, I don't think those words are the best way, and I don't think that's the way you would want to phrase it. I'm confident you would say to them that you decided after talking to us that it wasn't fruitful to talk in terms of how many dollars we would give them to settle—that *you* came up with the suggestion for a discount program . . .
>
> *Mediator:* Well . . . I'll phrase it however I'm going to phrase it.

In this example, the mediator refused to take ownership of the discount offer, out of concern that doing so would damage his credibility. But the defense lawyer was not bashful about asking. Later, by adding a small amount of cash to the offer, she obtained an excellent settlement for her client.

Endorsement. If you cannot persuade a mediator to assume authorship of a proposal, a second-best alternative is to ask the neutral to endorse it. You could, for example, ask the neutral to tell an opponent that she sees your latest concession as a reasonable step forward. Another is to bargain with the mediator, offering to increase a concession if she will endorse its reasonableness. ("If I could convince my client to go to 'X,' would you be willing to tell the plaintiff you think it is a significant step and ask them to go to "Y?' ")

In summary, to take advantage of a mediator's perceived neutrality:

○ If you think a proposal could be viewed as fair or an argument as convincing, ask the mediator to take authorship of it.

○ If the neutral will not take authorship, ask him to endorse it as worthy of consideration.

○ Bargain with the mediator, offering a larger concession in turn for an endorsement.

Support a hard bargaining strategy

Books about mediation rarely mention one important effect of the process: it allows negotiators to take tougher stands than would be possible in direct bargaining. The fact that the process is difficult to convene makes parties reluctant to walk out, even when the other side uses "hard," or even improper, tactics. In addition, mediators can cushion the impact of abrasive bargaining by calming a party when it erupts at an adversary's stubbornness. Lawyers take advantage of this dynamic to play "bad cop," knowing the mediator will instinctively take on the role of "good cop" to keep the process alive.

Example: A manufacturer was in a dispute with its insurer over the insurer's refusal to pay nearly a billion dollars in claims arising from product liability. The parties agreed to go to mediation. The insurer's CEO prepped intensively for the process, planning to have a point-by-point discussion of policy coverage and other issues with representatives of the manufacturer.

When the parties convened in joint session and the CEO tried to discuss the case, however, the plaintiff's inside counsel said he wasn't interested. He had listened carefully to his own team's analysis, he said, and saw no point in having a debate with the insurer. The lawyer went on to say that he would not make any concessions at all until the insurer first agreed to pay the full amount due under what he called an "incontestable" section of the policy. That amount, the lawyer said, was slightly under $130 million.

The mediation was held in a conference room at an airport, and in a direct negotiation the insurer's team would very likely have been on the next flight out. The manufacturer's lawyer believed, however, that I—as the mediator—would respond to his tactic by cajoling, even begging, the CEO to ignore his opponent's obnoxiousness, look at the big picture, examine the legal risks—and put up a very large amount of money. That is exactly what I did. After hours of talking, the CEO strode into the manufacturer's conference room, wrote "100" on the board, and walked out.

Now it was my job to convince the plaintiff team that although $100 million might seem paltry in light of its claim, from the insurer's perspective it was a huge step forward. To counter feelings of loss or frustration over the insurer's not having met the manufacturer's precondition, I suggested the right way to assess the offer was to count up from zero rather than down from the original $130 million demand. After an hour's discussion, the plaintiff reluctantly agreed to continue.

Months later the case settled. As mentioned earlier, the turning point came when the manufacturer's counsel (the same lawyer who had refused to debate with the CEO) asked me to invite the executive to meet him in the bar of the hotel where the mediation was being held and talked privately, and cut a deal.

In this instance, the plaintiff lawyer relied on the fact that both parties had committed to mediation to impose a precondition, demanding a high offer from the other side before he would bargain. He coupled this with a procedural snub—which was also a demonstration of his willingness to walk out if he did not get a good offer—by refusing to listen to the CEO's arguments. The lawyer knew, however, that I as mediator would work to smooth over the confrontation he had provoked and that this tactic would probably succeed in securing a much larger opening offer than if he had let the defendant select the number.

The plaintiff's strategy pushed the defense into an uncomfortable position and created a favorable foundation for later bargaining. Later in the same process, the plaintiff lawyer short-circuited the caucusing structure to ask for a private meeting with the CEO he had snubbed, something that would have been difficult to arrange outside the mediation process.

In the travel-death case described earlier, defense counsel used the mediator to do the opposite, convincing his adjuster to abandon an overly tough position and make a new offer at a higher level.

In summary, to enhance your strategy in positional bargaining:

○ Use a mediator to cushion the impact of a hard positional tactic.

○ Allow, or ask, a mediator to persuade your client to change a position.

For an example of a lawyer taking a hard position and relying on a mediator to cushion its impact, see Chapter 6 of the DVD.

Explore hidden issues and options

Mediators can also be used to support creative approaches to bargaining. As discussed in Chapter Five, once in conflict people often lose their ability to "think outside the box." Plaintiffs in particular tend to be concerned that mentioning interests will imply they are not committed to their money demands. Mediation allows lawyers to have it both ways: they can press strongly for the best possible money deal, while simultaneously asking a mediator to explore interest-based terms. The effect is to have bargaining take place on two levels, one involving an exchange of money and the other over other priorities.

Example: A Chicago investment advisory firm, Pilgrim Advisors, sued a large Michigan bank, Pilgrim Financial NA, that had entered the Illinois market and begun to market investment services under the name Pilgrim Consultants. The Chicago firm argued that the bank's use of the word "Pilgrim" violated its trademark and caused customer confusion, particularly because, it claimed, the financial community referred informally to both firms as "Pilgrim." The Chicago firm sued the bank and asked for an injunction against its use of the name Pilgrim in Illinois. The judge sent the matter to mediation.

Although the legal case focused only on the bank's use of the Pilgrim name in Illinois, the real stakes were larger. The plaintiff planned to expand its own services into Midwestern states which were already served by the Michigan bank. The plaintiff's strategy, in other words, put it in danger of having a victory in the Illinois case used as a weapon against it in states where it was the newcomer.

In its mediation statement the Chicago firm argued that the only relevant issues in the process were the terms of an injunction and the amount of damages. Before the mediation, however, the firm's inside counsel called the mediator and asked him to explore a more comprehensive settlement that dealt with use of the Pilgrim name throughout the region. After three weeks of intensive telephone and e-mail negotiation, the parties worked out a broad understanding that avoided conflicts over the name throughout the Midwest.

To summarize, use mediation to enhance your ability to negotiate interest-based solutions by asking a mediator to:

- Raise business, personal, and other nonlegal issues with the other side.
- Explore imaginative options while you focus on legal claims and money demands.

Take advantage of a mediator's flexibility

Mediators do not need to worry about maintaining a judge's reserve or showing a litigator's resolve. As a result, they have freedom to do what it takes to bring about a settlement. When advocates encounter nonlegal problems in a case, they should inform—and, if necessary, prod—mediators to take on unusual roles to address them.

Example: Recall the example in Chapter Three of two siblings, Barbara and David, who were fighting over the business empire of a deceased uncle. David frustrated everyone during the first day of mediation by making offers and then reneging on them. Defense counsel suspected David was secretly consulting his wife, a bookkeeper at a local store. At the end of day one of the process, he suggested that before the next day's session the mediator drive out and talk with her.

The mediator took up the suggestion, and early the next morning went to talk with the wife in her basement office, listening to her story and then inviting her to come to the mediation.

With his wife present to advise him, David became much more decisive. The case settled with a multiyear agreement under which the couple cashed out their stake in the store, conveying their stock to Barbara in return for a schedule of payments secured by the firm's assets.

> The tentative deal almost foundered, however, because David's family did not trust Barbara to make the payments on time. To deal with this concern, David's lawyer suggested the mediator take on the role of arbitrator to resolve any disputes over implementation. With that assurance, the settlement went forward.

The mediation of this dispute would almost certainly have failed had defense counsel not shared his private knowledge about his adversary's situation and made an out-of-the-box suggestion about how the neutral should respond to it. At the end of the case, the other lawyer's request that the mediator take on the role of arbitrator of disputes over the settlement quieted his client's anxiety about whether the defendant would implement the agreement.

These roles are, if unusual, at least dignified. Mediators can be asked to take on less attractive roles if necessary.

> *Example:* A defense lawyer once berated a mediator in front of his client for "mistakenly" communicating a concession to the other side. It was an offer he had in fact authorized the neutral to make. His client, however, was apparently experiencing "buyer's remorse" over it. The neutral apologized for the misunderstanding and told the other side it had been a mistake on his part.
>
> By making the offer and then having the mediator disavow it, however, the defense counsel sent a signal to his opponent. The deadlock was broken and the case settled. A few months later, the same lawyer who had berated the mediator asked him to handle another large case.

Taking blame, even unfairly, for painful steps is all in a day's work for a mediator. To exploit a mediator's role flexibility:

- ○ Alert the mediator to hidden issues and missing decision makers.
- ○ If necessary, suggest that a neutral use unorthodox techniques or act as scapegoat for a difficult compromise.

3. Achieve Closure

A mediator can also be helpful at the end of the bargaining process, especially when parties are locked in impasse. Chapter Nine described a range of techniques a mediator can use in such situations. This section looks at some of the same options from an advocate's perspective, asking how to take advantage of each method to get the best possible outcome. Among a lawyer's options during the "end game" are to:

○ Bargain over impasse-breaking techniques.

○ Educate an unrealistic opponent—or client.

○ Ask for help if mediation fails.

Bargain over impasse-breaking techniques

A mediator's most important attribute when faced with an apparent impasse is the willingness to plug on. If neutrals falter, however, lawyers should urge them to keep going, perhaps offering the neutral a small concession as a "carrot" with which to work. Mediators are likely to try one or more of the following options, listed in order of intrusiveness:

○ Tactics to stimulate positional bargaining, such as "what if?", range bargaining, and hypothetical offers.

○ Tactics to estimate the size of the gap, such as confidential listener.

○ Interventions to change the parties' state of mind, for instance, extending the time or changing the format or participants.

○ Methods to change a party's assessment of its no-agreement option, such as evaluation.

○ Techniques that take control of the bargaining process, such as a mediator's proposal.

Keep in mind two important things about such methods. First, there is no set order in which they must occur. Mediators ordinarily use less-intrusive options first—for example, proposing confidential listener before giving an evaluation—but if a different sequence would better suit your needs, ask the neutral to use it.

Second, it may be worthwhile to bargain with a mediator over what process to use. If, for example, you want to increase your client's share of the "settlement pie," you will want to promote the best process to accomplish this. If your process differs from what the mediator is considering, and the mediator needs your assent to move forward (for example to conduct range bargaining, confidential listener, or a mediator's proposal), you can bargain with the mediator over the tactic as a condition to agreeing to it.

Restart positional bargaining

As noted, mediators use techniques such as "what if?" questions, range bargaining, and hypothetical bargaining to deal with positional impasses. Advocates can influence how each of these tactics are used.

What if? ("What if I could get them to go to seven figures?") is an attractive tactic for mediators because it avoids reactive devaluation and can be applied repeatedly if it fails ("Well, what if I could get them to 1.2?"). As an advocate, you can respond to it in several ways:

- First ask yourself whether you want the mediator to use it.
- If so, consider preemptively suggesting a favorable number. ("If you can get them to seven figures, we'll consider moving again . . .")
- Bargain with the mediator over the number. ("$1.2 million won't do it. They'd have to go to at least $1.5 million.")
- Probe the mediator about how confident she is the other side will move—how much of a hypothetical is this, in other words?

Range bargaining can be useful because it allows simultaneous moves. Given the tendency of bargainers to settle near the midpoint of a range, however, the endpoints are important. You may be able to bargain with a mediator about what endpoints she will propose. ("I could see agreeing to go to $420,000 if they dropped to $600,000, but not if they stay at $650,000.")

Hypothetical bargaining. Here the mediator asks each side to move in response to assumed concessions of the other. ("Assume they are now at $1 million . . . Just for my private information, where would you go if they did that?") This can be useful when the parties cannot agree about where each other should be. Be careful, however, about making substantial disclosures to a mediator about where you will go before getting at least a sense about whether the other side has been similarly candid with the neutral.

Change the parties' psychological framework

We have talked about how mediators may declare a recess or adjournment, hold the parties' feet to the fire, or take other steps to change the dynamics of a process. The issue for an advocate is: what option best meets your client's goals at a given point? Is it to break, press on, or change the mix of people? Advocate for the option you want, whether or not the mediator is doing so. If you don't think a tactic will be helpful, however, don't be bashful about saying so.

Estimate or communicate the size of the gap

One method to gather better information about the real gap between two parties is confidential listener, in which a neutral asks each side to disclose privately how far it would go to settle. In thinking about whether to suggest or agree to this technique, keep in mind that mediators usually do not expect the tactic to settle a case; rather the goal is to get parties to communicate, in an intentionally ambiguous way, more realistic offers.

What should you tell a mediator playing confidential listener? Your situation is similar to a bargainer in a positional negotiation: you want to give a number far enough "out" to set up a favorable compromise, while at the same time good enough to motivate the other side and the neutral to continue.

Unless you are in the unusual situation in which the mediator states that he wants your bottom-line number *and you believe he truly means it*— that is, unless the numbers given by the parties actually touch or overlap, the mediator will terminate the mediation—*do not* give the mediator your actual bottom line. Doing so will put you at a disadvantage later in the process when parties are asked to compromise further. Asserting a bottom-line position may also lead your client to dig in prematurely. Consider instead using these tactics:

○ Ask the mediator for an opinion about what is needed to keep the process going. Do so only if you trust the neutral, however, because it is in the mediator's interest for each party to make as large concessions as possible.

○ Provide not only a number, but also an indication of your intentions. ("Our number is $100,000. We might go a little farther, but that's close to our endpoint. Let's see what they come back with.")

○ After giving both sides a verbal statement of the gap between their numbers, a mediator will sometimes ask for permission to disclose each side's confidential number to the other. Keep this in mind when formulating your number.

Take control of the bargaining

Mediator's proposal. A mediator may make a "take it or leave it" offer to both sides; this is usually done through a mediator's proposal. Such proposals usually work, but the effect is that the mediator rather than the parties dictates the final terms of agreement. By intervening actively, however, you may be able to affect what occurs.

Suppose, for instance, a mediator signals that she is considering making a proposal. You can take the initiative to negotiate with the mediator about what the proposal will be. In effect, you will be preemptively defining how far your side is willing to go to settle. ("We reject their $400,000 offer, but if you made a proposal at $500,000, I would try to convince my client to take it.")

A neutral should not give special influence to either side in formulating a proposal, but the idea of starting with one "yes" vote in one's pocket can be attractive, and mediators may be willing to bend a proposal slightly if you signal that doing so will ensure its acceptance by your side.

For an example of a lawyer bargaining over a last-and-final proposal, see Chapter 20 of the DVD.

If a proposal fails. We have seen that when a mediator's proposal fails, it is not the end of the process. Good neutrals just keep going. ("If you won't take that, what would you take?" "Do you want to propose that?" "What data would you have to see in order to change your mind?") If you expect that the mediator will continue if a mediator's proposal is rejected, you may want to respond to it in a different way.

You might, for example, allow a mediator to make a proposal that you intend to reject, in order to motivate your opponent to make a mental adjustment. You could turn down the proposal and then make a new offer, moving the opponent farther toward your position. If worst came to worst, you could probably return to the original proposal, although at that point you would not be able to hide your willingness to take it.

In summary, to make best use of a mediator's impasse-breaking techniques:

○ If a mediator appears ready to quit, ask him to keep going. Bear in mind, though, that the mediator may interpret this as a signal of your willingness to compromise.

○ Ask a mediator to use, or avoid, specific tactics.

○ Before responding to a tactic, consider how your reply will affect later bargaining.

Educate an unrealistic opponent—or client

Litigators are often more realistic than their clients about what can be achieved in a case. The problem is that when a party is unrealistically optimistic its lawyer is put in an uncomfortable position, because a pessimistic assessment may anger the client or lead her to doubt the lawyer's loyalty. One way to avoid this is to ask a mediator to give your side an evaluation.

A mediator's opinion can help a lawyer deliver bad news—that a case is not as good as the party thinks it is, or even as the lawyer may have suggested at the outset. By having the mediator take on the role of realist, lawyers can maintain their clients' confidence, sometimes even arguing against an assessment that they privately know is correct.

As we have discussed, disputants sometimes use mediators as shields or even scapegoats to avoid criticism. ("Once the mediator pegged damages at that level, it was impossible to convince the defense to go any higher!") Whenever a lawyer turns to me as a mediator during a discussion and asks "What's your view of this case?" or stops me in the hallway to suggest that I give her side a perspective on a legal issue, I know that I'm being enlisted in the difficult task of client education and management.

Even if lawyers do not ask for an evaluation, however, commercial mediators may well take the initiative to offer one. This may occur at any stage of the process, but as parties approach impasse, neutrals are more likely to give "hard" or "global" evaluations, ratcheting up the precision and scope of their opinions. Your challenge is first to decide whether you want an evaluation at all and, if so, what kind. Then ask for it or, if it would help your client for the process to be delayed or avoided, work to arrange this.

For an example of a lawyer allowing a mediator to give an evaluation to an unrealistic client, see Chapters 15 and 16 of the DVD.

Two questions to ask. Before requesting a mediator's evaluation, ask yourself two questions:

○ Is the primary obstacle to settling this case really a disagreement about the court outcome or some other problem that evaluation can address? Or is the barrier something else? If the latter, deal with the real cause and don't ask for an evaluation—at least not yet.

○ If the mediator evaluates the merits, are you confident that it will be helpful? If you are not sure what the mediator will say, consider sounding him out privately before he opines to both sides.

Preparing for an evaluation. Once you have decided to seek an evaluation, the next issue is how to structure the process. The questions you should ask are similar to those a mediator must consider, but there are differences that flow from your role as advocate. The major difference is that the mediator is focused only on breaking the deadlock, while you want the best possible outcome.

Use an outside evaluator? One issue is whether an evaluation should be performed by a mediator or an outsider. In theory, there are advantages to having an outsider, but as practical matter, lawyers rarely opt for them except in the largest cases. Doing so requires adjourning, agreeing on a new person, and briefing in the new evaluator. For these reasons, lawyers almost always ask their mediator to perform evaluations.

What issue to evaluate? Like a mediator, you should think about what issue should be evaluated. Don't simply say "the case"; a prediction limited to a single issue is often enough to put the parties back on the path to settlement. The question then should be: what specific aspects of the case do you want evaluated?

The answer lies in your diagnosis of what is causing the impasse. Your task is similar to a mediator's, but with some important distinctions. It may be, for example, that the disagreement turns on an argument that you know you will lose but have pursued to humor a client. Or you may suspect that regardless of the other side's chances in court, it does not want to litigate for fear of exposing trade secrets. If you are raising an issue for a reason other than its legal merits, you will not normally want to have it evaluated and should make that clear to the neutral.

How specific an opinion? As noted in Chapter Eight, good mediators see evaluation as a spectrum of interventions rather than a single event, and rely on shadow techniques more frequently than explicit statements. You probably know better than the mediator what level of specificity and emphasis your client needs at a certain point in the process. It may be that the client is not ready to hear the unvarnished truth, and if so you should ask the mediator temporarily to pull her punches or avoid certain issues. Or the contrary may be true: someone needs to be hit with the mediation equivalent of a baseball bat. If you need an opinion to convince a supervisor or other outsider, you may want it to be put in writing or at least explained by the mediator. If so, tell the mediator this.

Getting a good evaluation is in some respects like ordering a meal: your chances of obtaining what you want are much better if you specify your wishes than if you leave the choice to the chef's discretion.

What data should the mediator see? The next question is what data the mediator should review in reaching an opinion. Bear in mind that a mediator's views about a case will usually be based solely on the briefs and documents she reads, augmented by observations of the people present at the mediation. This means that like trial, mediation has:

○ A *primacy* effect: the evidence and people that a mediator actually observes are more vivid, and thus usually have more impact on decisions, than data she merely hears about.

○ A *melding* effect: when a mediator cannot personally observe a witness, she is likely to place the person in a category ("nurse," "retired accountant," etc.), and then make an assumption about how a fact-finder would react to a typical member of that group.

If you want a mediator to give full weight to a witness or piece of evidence, you should give her the actual document or allow her to observe the person directly. Take care to ensure that the mediator takes the time required to consider your evidence. Don't assume, for example, that a mediator has read every document given to her; mediators often receive thick piles of paper that they must review without knowing what will turn out to be relevant in the mediation process.

If the neutral is busy or concerned about keeping costs down, she is likely to skim through voluminous materials and wait for the parties to tell her what is important. Mediators are also reluctant to take long breaks in midst of a mediation to review evidence, for fear of losing momentum.

You should therefore organize the evidence you give to a mediator much as you would for a judge. A neutral assisted in this way is less likely to jump to a bad opinion with which you will then be stuck. If you have documents or decisions that may be important to the mediator's evaluation, bring copies to the mediation room and highlight the key language in them.

You may want to have the mediator meet a witness. If so, you can usually arrange for the mediator to talk with the witness in a private setting, without incurring an obligation to expose the witness to your opponent.

In summary, to use evaluation effectively:

- ○ Before asking for an evaluation, decide whether a disagreement about legal issues is a primary cause of the impasse.
- ○ Identify the issues and level of specificity you want in the evaluation.
- ○ Direct the mediator to key evidence, and make it easy to digest.
- ○ Look for a mediator who uses evaluation sparingly, but who is willing to use it when necessary.

Ask for help if mediation fails

Prod the mediator to pursue an agreement. Suppose that your case does not settle at the mediation session. As you know, good mediators will contact the parties afterward and attempt to restart the settlement process. Your mediator, however, may not take the initiative, either because that is not his style or he is too busy. If your client would benefit from follow-up activity and the mediator does not take the lead, prod him to do so.

Example: An inventor sued a company for patent infringement. The company hired a large law firm to represent it, but was aware that litigation costs could easily exceed a million dollars and that in the meantime its business strategy would be in limbo. The company therefore decided to explore settlement. Its lawyers suggested early mediation, the plaintiff agreed, and the parties selected a retired judge as the mediator.

At the end of the first day, the defense had offered almost $5 million, but the plaintiff refused to accept it. The mediator indicated that the parties were too far apart and said that the process should be terminated. The company's counsel, however, asked the mediator to adopt a different approach: adjourn for a week, after suggesting to the plaintiff that he think about what he would do with the money on the table if it were in his bank account. A few days later, the case settled at a figure close to the company's offer.

Ask the mediator to organize a more efficient litigation process. Sometimes settlement is simply unachievable, at least at that moment. Even then, a mediator can be of use, helping counsel work out a better process of adjudication. A mediator might, for example, facilitate negotiations over an efficient discovery plan or broker an agreement for an expedited adjudication process.

One thing to consider in negotiating such plans is that there is a tendency for parties to suggest that the mediator play a central role in any new process. If, for example, you want your mediator to be the arbitrator you can play on this feeling, although you must do so subtly in order not to stimulate reactive devaluation by your opponent. If you do not, then you should push for a process that will produce a new person, for example by suggesting that a selection be made from a panel of neutrals.

To take advantage of a mediator's abilities when settlement is not currently possible:

○ Suggest that the mediator follow up.

○ Ask the mediator to facilitate agreement on a more efficient process of adjudication.

○ If you opt for arbitration, think about what role you want the mediator to play in the process.

Conclusion

Mediation is an active process with almost infinite variations. Good lawyers know that a mediator can help them bargain more effectively and are not bashful about asking for help. By doing so, they achieve better outcomes for their clients.

4. Summary of Key Points

Manage the Structure and Flow of Information
- Influence the structure of the process
- Focus discussion on specific issues
- Gather information or convey it to an opponent
- Use confidentiality to manage the flow of data

Influence the Bargaining Process
- Ask for advice
- Enhance your offers
- Support a hard bargaining strategy
- Explore hidden issues and options
- Take advantage of a mediator's flexibility

Achieve Closure
- Bargain over impasse-breaking techniques
- Educate an unrealistic opponent, or client
- Ask for help if mediation fails

Advocacy at Specific Stages

This chapter explains what an advocate can do to get the maximum benefit at specific stages of mediation. Let's begin with an account of a case, the only one in this book to use the names of the actual parties.[1]

1. A Case Example: The Death of a Student

In August, Scott Krueger arrived for his freshman year at the Massachusetts Institute of Technology (MIT). Five weeks later he was dead. In an incident that made national headlines, Krueger died of alcohol poisoning following an initiation event at a fraternity. Nearly two years later, Krueger's parents sent MIT a demand letter stating their intent to sue. The letter alleged that the university had caused their son's death by failing to address what they claimed were two longstanding campus problems: a housing arrangement they said steered new students to seek rooms in fraternities and what their lawyer called a culture of alcohol abuse at fraternities.

---

1. Confidentiality is, of course, an important attribute of mediation. Disclosures in this account have been approved by lawyers for both parties.

MIT's lawyers saw the case as one that could be won. An appellate court, they believed, would rule that a college is not legally responsible for an adult student's voluntary drinking. Moreover, under state law the university could not be required to pay more than $20,000 to the Kruegers (although the limit did not apply to claims against individual university administrators). University officials felt, however, that a narrowly drawn legal response would not be in keeping with its values. They also recognized there were aspects of the institution's policies and practices— including those covering student use of alcohol—that could have been better. MIT's president, Charles M. Vest, was prepared to accept responsibility for these shortcomings on behalf of the university and felt a deep personal desire for his institution to reach a resolution with the Krueger family.

MIT also recognized that defending the case in court would exact a tremendous emotional toll on all concerned. The Kruegers would be subjected to a hard-hitting assessment of their son's behavior leading up to his death, while MIT would be exposed to equally severe scrutiny of the Institute's culture and the actions of individual administrators. Full-blown litigation in a case of this magnitude was also sure to be expensive, with estimated defense costs well in excess of $1 million. The question, as MIT saw it, was not whether to seek to engage the Kruegers in settlement discussions, but how. The university decided to forego a traditional legal response and reply instead with a personal letter from President Vest to the Kruegers—that noted the university's belief that it had strong legal defenses to their claims, but offered to mediate.

The Kruegers responded with intense distrust. Tortuous negotiations ensued. The parents eventually agreed to mediate, but only subject to certain conditions: at least one session would have to occur in Buffalo, where the Kruegers lived. MIT would have to offer a sincere apology for its conduct; without that, no sum of money would settle the case. There would be no confidentiality agreement to prevent the parents from talking publicly about the matter, while at the same time no settlement could be exploited by MIT for public relations purposes. The Kruegers would have the right to select the mediator. And President Vest would have to appear personally at all the mediation sessions. The university agreed to most of the conditions, and the mediation went forward.

MIT's lawyers believed it was important the Kruegers' lawyers and the mediator understand the strength of the university's defenses, but plaintiff counsel knew subjecting the Kruegers to such a presentation would make settlement impossible. To resolve the dilemma, the lawyers bifurcated the process. The first day of the mediation, which the Kruegers did not attend, focused on presentations by lawyers and was held in

Boston. The mediator questioned both lawyers closely about the legal and factual issues, creating a foundation for realistic assessments of case value later in the process.

One week later, the mediation resumed at a conference center located a 40-minute drive outside Buffalo, this time with the Kruegers present. Their counsel selected that location so "no one could leave easily." On the second day, the Kruegers met President Vest, and the parties exchanged settlement proposals.

Counsel had decided the mediator should begin the second day by having a private breakfast with Mr. and Mrs. Krueger and their lawyers. The Kruegers vented their anger, first to the neutral and later at the joint session to President Vest. "How could you do this?" they shouted at Vest, "You people killed our son!" They also challenged Vest on a point that bothered them terribly: why, they asked him, had he come to their son's funeral but not sought them out personally to extend his condolences? Vest responded that he had consulted with people about whether or not to approach the Kruegers and was advised that, in light of their anger at the institution, it would be better not to do so. The advice was wrong, he said, and he regretted following it.

Vest went on to apologize for the university's role in what he described as a "terrible, terrible tragedy." "We failed you," he said, and then asked, "What can we do to make it right?" Mrs. Krueger cried out again at Vest, but at that point her husband turned to her and said, "The man apologized. What more is there to say?" Their counsel later said he felt that "There's a moment . . . where the back of the case is broken. You can feel it . . . And that was the moment this day."

According to the plaintiff's counsel, the mediator's greatest contribution was the way he responded to the Kruegers' feelings:

> What he did most masterfully was to allow a lot of the emotion to be directed at him. He allowed it almost to boil over when it was just him with the Kruegers, but later he very deftly let it be redirected at President Vest and the university . . . He also prepared Charles Vest for the onslaught . . . Mediation can be like a funeral—especially with the death of a child. He mediated the emotional part of the case, and then let the rest unfold on its own."

The mediator gradually channeled the discussion toward what the Kruegers wanted and the university could do. The initial money offers put forth by each party were far apart, but the mediator put them into context so neither side gave up in frustration. Hard bargaining followed, much of it conducted through shuttle diplomacy. By the end of the day, the parties had reached agreement: MIT paid the Kruegers $4.75 million to settle their claims and contributed an additional $1.25 million to a scholarship fund the family would administer. And President Vest offered the Kruegers a personal, unconditional apology on behalf of MIT that no court could have compelled. At the conclusion of the process, Vest and Mrs. Krueger hugged each other. For MIT the settlement, although expensive, made sense: it minimized the harm contested litigation would have caused the institution. More importantly, the university felt it was the right thing to do.

Although the mediator contributed a great deal, it was the lawyers who designed and implemented a process for the case that differed in key respects from the usual mediation format. By doing so, they were able to work through intense emotional issues, significant legal questions, and the tensions generated by difficult money bargaining and find a resolution. As we discuss advocacy at stages of the process, I will return to the *Krueger* mediation, noting ways in which the lawyers customized it to increase its chances of success.

2. Structuring the Process

How should you structure the process? Ask yourself these questions:

○ What kind of mediator do I want?

○ Who should be present?

○ What should be in the mediation agreement?

○ What format do I want?

○ If mediation is mandatory, what options do I have?

What kind of mediator do I want?

The most important single issue in setting up a mediation, apart from deciding who will attend, is to select the right neutral. Mediators vary greatly in their qualifications and approach to the process. You will want to find a person with qualities that match your case.

Again it is important to think about what is preventing the parties from bargaining effectively. If, for example, the major obstacle is your opponent's abrasive manner, then a mediator with strong process skills is needed. If the issue is that your client needs cover to justify a difficult decision, then someone with strong evaluative credentials may be better. If the focus is on repairing a relationship, then a neutral with excellent interpersonal skills may be called for. Usually more than one barrier exists, calling for a mediator with a blend of qualities.

The most important criterion among qualified mediators is how well they relate to the parties. Will your client connect better with a business-person or a litigator? Will a key player on the other side defer instinc-tively to an ex-judge? If necessary, ask for a telephone conversation with your candidate; all except the busiest mediators are usually willing to talk informally with lawyers interested in hiring them.

In the right case, you may want to allow opposing counsel to select the mediator. To lessen the risk, you might retain a veto or ask the other lawyer to draw up a short list of candidates from which you will select. It may seem odd to cede the power of selection, but your goal is to persuade the other party, and your opponent is more likely to listen to someone it chose.

> *Example:* In the *Krueger* case, the defense decided to allow plaintiff counsel to choose the mediator. The plaintiff looked for a mediator who had litigated personal injury cases for claimants but who was also known to defendants as being realistic about evaluating claims.
>
> The student's family had specific demands about how the process should be structured, so the lawyer also wanted a mediator who would be flexible about format. He knew the discussions would be extremely emotional, and it was therefore crucial the mediator have the ability to absorb and manage intense anger and grief. The mediator's final quali-fication was unique: the lawyers learned that he had also once lost a college-age son.

Who should be present?

We have seen that the presence of the right people is crucial to media-tion success. This issue is arguably more important than the identity of the mediator, but I have placed this issue second, because lawyers can enlist a mediator's help to get people to the table.

Who the right people are will depend again on your objectives. Pos-sibilities include:

- ○ *Principals.* If the primary goal is to repair a personal relationship, then the presence of the principals themselves—to talk out their problems and regain the ability to relate with each other—is usu-ally essential. The same may be true when the outcome is intensely important to a party, as in a "bet the company" case.
- ○ *Experts.* If the objective is to work out an imaginative solution, you will need people capable of thinking outside the box and experts

who know enough about nonlegal issues to develop and assess options.

○ *Bargaining authority.* If the parties no longer have a relationship and there are no emotional issues (for example, when a company makes a routine claim against an insured defendant), the primary concern should be that the other side's bargainer have enough authority to settle the claim.

Example: In the *Krueger* case, the lawyers invited only lawyers to the first session, which focused on MIT's potentially inflammatory legal defenses. For the second session, the lawyers thought it crucial the principals in the dispute, the parents of the student and the president of the university, attend.

Ensuring adequate authority. You may need to bargain for the presence of people at the table with the authority to make difficult decisions. We have seen that a mediator can help with this. Mediators, however, will not know there is an issue unless you tell them, and busy neutrals may need to be prompted to act.

When you ask a mediator for assistance, you benefit from several factors. First, having agreed to mediate, your opponent will feel an interest in maintaining a good relationship with the neutral. Mediators, too, acquire a stake in the process and have a bias toward inclusion. Better, a mediator will think, to bring in someone who later proves unnecessary than to find oneself lacking a key decision maker at crunch time. You can take advantage of a mediator's feeling of investment in the process to obtain the participation of a key player.

Example: Recall the example in Chapter Three of a high-tech company that sued a former employee, arguing that he had violated a noncompete agreement by recruiting his former team to join him at a competitor. The competitor was not a party to the litigation but was essential to a settlement because it had agreed to indemnify the employee for the liability. The competitor's general counsel refused to attend the mediation, however, saying it was too far to travel and in any event her company was not a party.

Knowing this, the plaintiff's lawyer agreed to mediate, then lobbied me, the mediator, to persuade the lawyer to come. In doing so, he stressed how important the general counsel would be to the success of "our" case. I eventually persuaded the general counsel to join the process by conference call.

What should be in the mediation agreement?

Mediation agreements are usually form documents, and counsel rarely bargain over them in detail. The most common disagreement is over how to share the cost of the process. Suppose, for example, there are four parties—one plaintiff and three defendants. Does sharing the cost "equally" mean one-half for the plaintiff and one-half for the three defendants as a group (one-sixth per defendant), or a one-quarter share for each party? There is no obvious answer. If, for example, you represent all three related defendants, a parent company and two subsidiaries, you may argue that you are only one actual party and should not pay a larger share simply because the plaintiff engaged in shotgun pleading. It can make sense to argue over cost allocation for the following reasons:

○ To confirm the other side is serious about settling.

○ To set a pattern for sharing the cost of settlement.

○ To save money.

Example: A homeless person died in a state facility from an undiagnosed illness, after being referred by physicians at a city hospital. Her estate sued five doctors, two from the city and three from the state, for negligence. The parties agreed to mediate.

The plaintiff lawyer suggested allocating the costs on a "per party" basis, which would result in the estate paying one-sixth, the city two-sixths (two defendants), and the state three-sixths (three defendants). As the lawyer for the state, I disagreed—arguing that the plaintiff should pay two-eighths and the city and state three-eighths each. I did this to push the plaintiff lawyer to admit that he was seriously interested in settling the case. I pressed for an even allocation among the two defendant groups to set a precedent for dividing the cost of settlement. The other lawyers agreed and the case settled, with each defendant group assuming half the cost.

If necessary you can ask the mediator to become involved. While mediators are usually reluctant to negotiate over fees, they may be willing to facilitate the resolution of a dispute over allocation, provided the total amount of the fee is not at issue and they therefore have no personal interest in the outcome.

What format do I want?

Mediation can occur in a wide variety of formats. Again, the choice depends on your objective.

○ If your goal is to repair a relationship, you will probably want the clients to have as much opportunity to talk together as possible, suggesting a longer opening session and/or private meetings between the principals.

○ In a very emotional case, it may be useful for a party to meet with the mediator ahead of time and for the neutral to carefully structure the party's interactions with the other side.

○ In factually complex cases, it may be necessary to arrange for advance meetings between the mediator and each side and lengthy opening statements, perhaps supported by expert comments.

○ Where the condition of property is at issue, as is true in construction and environmental disputes, it may make sense to take a site view.

Think through the following issues in advance:

○ Do you want to meet with the mediator before the process starts? If so, should you meet with the neutral alone or with your client?

○ Do you want to have an opening session? If so, do you want the mediator to steer the discussion toward or away from any topics?

If you see a reason for changes in the usual format, alert the mediator before the process begins.

Example: In the *Krueger* mediation, the lawyers modified the format in several ways. In addition to dividing the process into two days, they included the following:

- To satisfy the Kreugers' need to feel the University was coming to them, counsel agreed that the second meeting would be held near the parents' home.
- To discourage a walkout and set an informal tone for the second session, the advocates selected a rural conference center.
- To create an opportunity for the parents to express their anger and grief, the second session began with the mediator having breakfast with Mr. and Mrs. Krueger and their lawyers.
- Later the same morning, there was a joint session in which the parties could speak to each other.
- After an emotional opening session, the mediation evolved into more typical caucusing.
- At the end, the Kreugers and President Vest came back together and hugged.

Very few cases are as emotional as the death of a child, but the modifications made in the *Kreuger* case give a sense of how much freedom imaginative lawyers have to vary the format of mediation to achieve their objectives.

Timing. You and your opponent need to agree on a timeframe for the mediation session. Should you schedule it for a few hours, a full day, several days, or a series of sessions over a longer period? The quandary is between allowing enough time for the process to work and not allowing parties to put off tough decisions. Here are some guidelines:

○ One day is usually right for a typical commercial contract or employment case.

○ A half-day may be enough to resolve smaller personal injury lawsuits, if the plaintiff's lawyer effectively controls the client's settlement decision.

○ Two days are often necessary for construction cases, because they usually include several parties and involve multiple "mini-cases" over various issues in a project.

○ For unusually complex disputes, such as antitrust cases, mass-tort class actions, and environmental contamination claims, several meetings over a period of weeks or months may be needed.

This said, you should—in general—err on the side of allowing more time. You can always settle early, but there are often substantial delays and costs involved in reassembling the parties for another session.

If mediation is mandatory, what options do I have?

The discussion to this point has assumed you have freedom to design the process in cooperation with the other side. Sometimes, however, your client is required to engage in mediation by a contract clause or court order. Some courts impose significant requirements on the process. Litigants may be able to opt out of restrictions by agreement, but in the context of adversarial litigation this can be difficult.

If you have a case subject to mandatory mediation, assess whether the process is adequate for your case and if not, how to avoid it. In particular:

○ Will you have a role in choosing the neutral? Some programs require parties to select a mediator from a panel, while others assign mediators to cases.

○ Who must be present? Many program rules require the parties to send representatives with "full settlement authority," but do not define what this means. Such requirements can create serious problems for companies with large numbers of cases pending in different court systems.

○ Will you have an opportunity to brief the mediator in advance? Some programs discourage parties from submitting statements or talking with neutrals ahead of time.

○ Will you be required to pay for the process? Some programs are free, relying on volunteer lawyer–mediators, while others use private neutrals at market prices, and still others offer mediators at below-market rates.

○ Will you be required to mediate within a specific timeframe? Court processes range from one hour to a full day. If the process is time limited, the mediator is likely to feel pressure to "cut to the chase," reducing your ability to explore nonmonetary issues.

○ What confidentiality guarantees does the program offer?

○ Can you change the structure by agreement with the other side?

If you do not want to mediate, or conclude the mandated process is inadequate, consider these questions:

○ Is it possible to opt out (for example, by applying for an exemption)?

○ If not, what is the minimum you have to do to comply?

○ Are there penalties for nonparticipation or noncompliance? For example, will the mediator make a report to the court about your noncooperation?

3. Preparing to Mediate

The next issue is preparing to advocate effectively in the mediation itself. This requires developing a negotiating plan, defining roles for yourself and your client, and perhaps exchanging information.

Developing a negotiating plan

Texts often speak of mediation "advocacy," but as you know, mediation consists primarily of negotiation. Lawyers usually make presentations at the outset, but the rest of the process consists of discussions and bargaining. You should plan for mediation in much the same way you would for a direct negotiation, while looking for ways to incorporate the mediator in your strategy.

Exchanging information

One of the key aspects of any negotiation is exchanging information. This process often begins well before the disputants actually meet to mediate. To plan this phase, ask yourself two questions:

○ What data do I need to bargain well and make a settlement decision?

○ What information will help persuade my adversary to agree to my terms?

> *Example:* Recall the case from Chapter Three in which a town sued a contractor over a defective sewage treatment plant. As the parties prepared to mediate, it became clear that while the town had carefully laid out its theory of liability, it had provided almost no information about its $3.5 million claim for damages. The mediator noticed the problem and asked the plaintiff to supply a breakdown of damages before the mediation; defense counsel could also have prompted the mediator to do so.

Educating the mediator

You will usually have an opportunity to orient and begin to persuade the mediator before you meet to mediate. These communications can take the form of organizational discussions, conversations, meetings, and written statements.

Organizational discussions. In complex cases, mediators sometimes schedule conference calls and/or meetings with counsel to discuss questions such as who will be present at the mediation, the schedule for filing statements, and so on. Such meetings are usually limited to lawyers, but in the right case you may want to have a client or expert participate as well.

Private conversations. Mediators should take the initiative to talk with advocates before the mediation, but if a mediator does not schedule a conversation, consider asking for one. For a preview of the questions you might ask, see Chapter Three.

Lawyers usually devote pre-mediation calls primarily to presenting their legal arguments. This is usually a mistake. The mediator will have trouble assimilating a long oral presentation, and your arguments will usually become clear from the mediation brief and discussions during the process itself. Instead of making detailed arguments, use the conversation to shape a mediator's overall "take" on the dispute.

Meetings. You have the option to ask for a pre-mediation meeting between your client and the mediator. You might do so to:

○ Allow your client to begin building a relationship with the neutral.

○ Permit a client to begin the process of working through emotions.

○ Present sensitive data or float proposals privately.

Written statements. Except in some court programs, parties almost always file written statements and/or documents with the mediator in advance. In doing so, think about these issues:

○ Do you want to prepare a customized statement or use an existing document? A customized document has obvious advantages, but particularly in small cases or when mediation is scheduled on short notice, you can use existing documents or pleadings. Most mediators are also willing to receive statements in letter format.

○ Should you submit the statement on an ex parte basis or exchange it with opposing counsel? Mediators usually prefer to have lawyers exchange statements, but doing so does not ordinarily prevent you from raising a sensitive issue privately through a letter or telephone call.

○ In complex cases, should you agree with your opponent on a common set of documents to give to the mediator so she does not have to juggle multiple copies? Or would you rather submit your own set, so you can mark key passages?

What should be in a mediation statement? The mediator is likely to be interested in knowing answers to the following questions:

○ How did the dispute arise?

○ Who are the important players?

○ What are the key factual and legal issues? What are the most important points of agreement and disagreement? Are there non-legal concerns in the case?

○ What barriers have made direct bargaining difficult?

○ Without reciting every event, what is the history of the legal proceeding?

○ Has there been any bargaining? What are the last offers, and whose turn is it to move?

○ Is there a possibility of an interest-based solution or a need to exchange information?

○ What documents should the mediator review in advance, and what parts of lengthy documents are most relevant?

If you don't want to commit all of this information to a document exchanged with the other side, put some of it into a private conversation or side letter to the neutral.

Imposing preconditions

Lawyers sometimes attempt to take advantage of the other side's wish to mediate by imposing preconditions on attending. The condition can be either procedural ("We won't mediate until I have a detailed statement of damages") or substantive ("Until they get into six figures, we won't mediate"). Again, it is less risky to impose conditions in mediation than in a direct negotiation, and procedural demands are less likely to offend than substantive ones. For a discussion of how mediators are likely to respond to this tactic, see Chapter Three.

Preparing the client

Mediation is a process of negotiation, but one that varies in significant ways from direct bargaining. Parties are ordinarily present; at the same time, participants typically spend most of their time isolated in caucuses, interacting only through the neutral. And, of course, the mediator is a key participant. Because of these structural differences, you will need to cover the following topics with a client, in addition to those you would address in preparing for a direct negotiation.

- How the format of mediation differs from that of ordinary negotiation, including:
  - The expected procedure (for example, will there be an opening session?).
  - The client's role in the opening session.
  - The confidentiality rules that will apply and exceptions to them.

- How the client should interact with the mediator and the other side, including:
  - The mediator's background, personality, usual style, and the likelihood the mediator will change styles as the process moves forward (for example, from empathic listener to evaluator).
  - The allocation of roles between you and the client. For instance, will one of you talk and the other listen? One play "good cop" and the other "bad"?
  - How the client should respond to questions from the mediator (that is, what the client may want to volunteer or should not reveal). Tell your client it is appropriate to decline to answer questions from opponents or even the mediator. The client should also know that lawyers regularly disagree with mediators, and you have the option to ask the mediator to leave so you can talk privately.

- The possibility the client will be invited to meet privately with the other principal.

- The role you will play. Explain that your overall goal—getting the best possible outcome—remains the same, but you will adapt tactics to the setting. In particular, you will take a different tone in mediation than you would in a courtroom, being relatively conciliatory and "pulling punches" to promote a settlement. You may also conceal favorable evidence to save it for trial.

4. The Opening Session

Once mediation begins, your options increase. We have seen that commercial mediations typically start with all parties together. You may be tempted to avoid the opening session or to treat it as a formality, but what happens here can help you achieve your goals later in the process. To use the opening session to advantage consider these questions:

○ What is special about an opening session?

○ How can I structure it for maximum impact?

○ How can the mediator help me?

What is special about an opening session?

An opening session resembles a court hearing, in that lawyers engage in advocacy in the presence of a neutral moderator. Unlike a judicial hearing, however, mediation is a "cool" medium. It usually takes place in a room smaller and less imposing than a courtroom. Parties are seated only a few feet away from each other, and the mediator sets an informal tone. As a result, a subdued style of advocacy is usually more effective than courtroom rhetoric.

A cooler, less formal presentation also makes sense because of the nature of the audience. Unlike a court hearing, you have two different audiences: the opposing party and the mediator. The mediator is very willing to listen but has no power to make a decision. Your opponent does have the ability to decide, but will usually resist hearing what you say.

Decision makers from both sides will also be personally present, something not always true in direct negotiation. This is probably the only time in the litigation process you will have the opportunity to talk directly to the principal on the other side, presenting facts and arguments you think he should consider in deciding whether to settle the case.

How can I structure it for maximum impact?

When thinking about what to say during an opening session, consider the following issues:

What tone to project. Sessions in mediation typically have the feeling of tough business negotiations rather than courtroom arguments. That said, your tone should be consistent with your client's goals. If your client wants to repair a relationship, set a relatively cooperative tone and focus on personal or business issues as much or more than on legal points. If your client wants the best possible money deal, emphasize the strength of your legal case and your determination to persevere.

The nature of the dispute is also important: a claim of negligence, for instance, is very different in tone from an allegation of intentional misconduct. Finally, the nature of the audience matters: you will want, for example, to speak differently to an insurance adjuster than to an accident victim.

How to frame your presentation. Once you have decided on a focus, you need to think through the elements that will implement it most effectively. The structure gives you great freedom to customize your presentation. For example, you can:

○ Restrict yourself to legal issues, or cover other topics as well.

○ Rely on a spoken presentation or incorporate media such as PowerPoint slides.

○ Take as much time as you need, within broad limits.

If you plan to say nothing or take an unusual length of time, will need special equipment, or have unexpected elements in your presentation, alert the mediator so she can facilitate your approach and warn you about any problems.

Exhibits and video are likely to have a greater impact in mediation than in court because viewers are closer to the screen and documents can stay "on the table" for hours. Evidence also cannot be excluded; if a document is inadmissible, your opponent will probably point it out, but evidence that will never get before a court can still have an effect, especially on a lay party.

> *Example:* A plaintiff lawyer identified an embarrassing e-mail sent by the defendant's CEO. She had it blown up on a 2-foot by 3-foot foamcore board and set it up as she talked. The words seemed to fill the conference room, to the discomfort of the defendant's executives.
>
> When she finished she left the board up. The defendants' lawyer took the board down and set it facing the wall. When the plaintiff counsel began her reply, she put the board back up, underlying the fact that the words would return to bedevil the defense.

Again, keep in mind that persons or items physically present will have much more impact than absent witnesses or documents. In the context of mediator evaluation, Chapter Eleven described the "primacy" effect— that evidence a person sees has more impact than information a person merely hears about—and the "melding" effect—that if a person cannot see a witness, he will tend to place the witness in a general category. These effects apply in the opening session as well; it is in the opening session that the mediator gets his first look at the people whose persuasiveness as witnesses he may have to evaluate. The opposing party may have seen the witness, but the mediator will not and must imagine whatever she cannot see.

Conversely, the mediator will usually have reviewed key documents, but the decision maker on the other side may not have seen them or understood their significance. If you have a person or document that strongly supports your case, bring it into the mediation room and make it part of your presentation.

Remember also that once the mediation session begins, the mediator will not have much time to read through new documents or court opinions. If you must present a document for the first time at mediation, highlight or make a copy of key passages.

Who should speak. Unlike opening statements at trial, openings in mediation can include several people—lawyers, parties, experts, and/or witnesses. Take advantage of this freedom to use whoever is most likely to have a useful impact on the other side and on the neutral.

Consider giving your client a role. Your opponent will listen much more carefully to a party than a lawyer. You can, for example, summarize the legal arguments and ask the client to describe key facts, or cover liability and let the client describe the financial effect of events on her. Or your client can focus on nonlegal factors, such as the effect of the defendant's actions on her family or business.

If you want your client or the other party to speak, prompt the mediator in advance to encourage the principals to comment. If you don't want your client put on the spot, warn the mediator of this. If your client is inarticulate, shy, or not an attractive witness, you have no obligation to put him on display.

Example: In the case described in Chapter Eleven arising from the death of a tourist in Europe, the plaintiff lawyer announced he would not bring his client, the decedent's daughter and executrix, to the mediation. He explained this in terms of her emotionality: she would accept his settlement recommendations, he said, but was likely to get "out of control" if she had to listen to the tour company's excuses for her mother's death.

The mediator eventually accepted her absence, given the lawyer's guarantee that he had full authority. The defendant's lawyer said, however, that the real reason for the executrix's absence was she was an irritating "whiner" whose presence would hurt the plaintiff's case. Whatever the truth, the lawyer was able to keep his client-witness out of the process, despite the mediator's initial wish to involve her.

Go over with your client in advance what he will say and how best to present it as you would with a trial witness. In particular,

- ○ Remind your client that the setting is informal and he can take a break to consult with you at any time. Work out ground rules about how you and the client will interact, for example how to signal a need for a break.
- ○ Alert him that he may be asked questions or given the chance to speak, but he has no obligation to do so.
- ○ If you don't want your client to answer a question, intervene and respond yourself. If you don't want to answer at all but don't wish to seem rude, say you would prefer to discuss the issue with the mediator in caucus.

How can the mediator help me?

Shaping the agenda. Chapter 11 described how a mediator can influence the mediation agenda. Again, if you would like an issue discussed, ask the mediator to encourage it. If you don't want to raise a topic yourself, ask the mediator to do so. You may also want to avoid issues. It is difficult to avoid a topic entirely, but if your client will be upset by a topic, you can alert the mediator to discourage or contain discussion of it.

Mediators can also help with issues of timing and structure. If, for example, you want a recess between an opponent's presentation and your own, ask the mediator ahead of time to suggest a break.

Muting adversarial reactions. A mediator can explain your role as an advocate to the parties, lessening their instinctive negative reaction. If, for example, you need to accuse the other side of misconduct, the mediator can partially "defang" your role and make it easier to present the issue.

Example: An American pharmaceutical company terminated its relationship with its Indian distributor, alleging that its sales were disappointing and asserting it had the right to cancel the contract on 90 days' notice. The distributor filed suit in state court, alleging that the American company had allowed it to invest two years of effort to obtain state approval of new drugs and promote the company's products in local markets. Then, just as the distributor was beginning to enjoy success, the pharmaceutical company hired away the distributor's chief salesman and put him to work soliciting the same clients. An Indian court had ruled this violated the salesman's noncompete agreement with the distributor.

The distributor's lawyer told the mediator his client had e-mails showing that the American company's executives had begun talking with its salesman a full two months before he joined them. The distributor planned to argue that the U.S. company had stolen its employee. Recognizing that the American company's executives might take umbrage at these charges, the distributor's lawyers asked the mediator to frame the discussion.

In his opening comments, the mediator said, "I've asked each lawyer to state his case unvarnished and with the gloves off. The parties may find what they say upsetting, but I've asked them to do this because we have to be aware of what will happen in court if this case does not settle."

Gathering information. If you want to gather information during the opening session, ask the mediator to:

○ Raise issues at the session.

○ Suggest the parties ask questions or discuss the case.

Example: A contractor was sued by an owner for allegedly mis-pouring the concrete slab on which a building had been erected. Before the mediation, the lawyer told the mediator, "We cannot figure out how the plaintiff got its figure of $750,000 to fix the foundation. Even assuming it's our problem, our contractors are coming in with figures in the $300,000 range. This is the major element of damages, so the difference is really driving our assessment of what we'd pay to settle. Can you ask them to flesh out their estimate, or suggest it would be useful to have a discussion in the joint session about the calculation of the repair costs?"

5. Caucusing

The suggestions made in Chapter Eleven focus on caucusing, and I will not repeat them here. Here are some general suggestions about what an advocate can expect.

a. Early Caucusing

You can expect the following to occur in a first caucus meeting:

○ The mediator will focus on listening and asking questions. He will seek to gather information, both to help the parties understand their opponent's perspectives and eventually to lower their confidence about prevailing in court. Offer supportive data and supply ammunition for the mediator to use with your opponent.

○ A mediator will tend to use a principled, "let's be reasonable" bargaining style, trying to avoid tough positional tactics such as first offers intended to jolt the other side. She will expect you to show some cooperation and offer a concession to help the process get going. She will be looking for possible openings, or at least a private indication of flexibility. Be prepared to offer something or to explain why it is not appropriate.

In planning for early caucusing, lawyers should ask themselves these questions:

○ If I have confidential information that might sway the mediator's analysis of the merits, should I disclose it early in the process or wait?

Comment: It is usually better to offer evidence as early as possible while the mediator is focused on gathering information. If you wait until late in the process, the new data will be mixed with the bargaining. You might say, for example, "We've located another salesman whom they tried to solicit in violation of his contract with us. They don't know we know this, but it will really make them look bad at trial. Given that, we really can't justify going below . . ." Evidence presented later in the process, during the bargaining phrase, risks sounding like an excuse for refusing to compromise. The mediator also may fail to give it full weight because he is focused on managing the bargaining.

○ Should I direct the mediator to take a tough line with the other side, but tell her privately that we are willing to compromise?

Comment: Your strategy should flow from your goals. That said, it is usually a good idea to let the mediator know your strategy in general terms, so he can warn you of problems and think about how to present it to the other side.

○ Should I make an offer in the first caucus meeting?

Comment: It may or may not be the best strategy. If not, don't let yourself be pushed to act prematurely. Instead of making an offer, say you would prefer to wait, for example, because you want to talk more about the issues before making decisions about bargaining.

○ Will the mediator be offended if I ask her to leave the room or don't explain my bargaining goal or strategy?

Comment: Don't be bashful about asking a mediator to leave so you can confer with your client, especially if the mediator asks you for a concession. Mediators expect parties to talk confidentially with their lawyers. Indeed, the fact that you want to do so suggests you have listened to what the mediator has said. You might say, "This has given us some things to think about. Can we have a few minutes to talk?"

Mediators also understand that lawyers will not disclose their entire strategy because advocates and neutrals do not have the same goals. They expect that if a lawyer makes a factual representation it will be accurate, but not that lawyers will confide in them about tactics.

b. Later Caucusing

As caucuses progress, mediators become more active in expressing viewpoints and press harder on the costs and risks of litigation and reasons to compromise. Keep in mind the following points:

○ Be prepared for harder reality testing. Warn your clients that the mediator may ask tough questions and disagree; assure them that this is a normal part of the process. Remind your client that the neutral is also presenting your arguments and taking issue with the opponent in the other room.

○ Be ready to suggest changes in the format, such as a joint meeting or conversations between subsets of disputants. Ask the mediator to advise you whether the other side is receptive to talking directly.

○ If your client is becoming discouraged, consider asking the mediator for an assessment of how the process is going. If your client is becoming tired or irritable or is being pushed too hard, ask the mediator to adjourn to allow the client to rest.

○ As the process nears an end, be ready to bargain with the mediator about whether and how the mediator will use the tactics discussed in Chapters Nine and Eleven.

○ If you sense that the mediator is planning to make a proposal, consider preempting him by telling him what you want done, or bargain with the mediator over what the proposal should contain.

6. After the Mediation

If a case settles, mediators will typically give the process back to counsel and move on to their next case. If you represent the defendant, it is your responsibility to ensure that the case is dismissed with prejudice and releases are executed and delivered to you. If you are counsel to the plaintiff, you will probably press for paperwork to be completed and your client paid. Implementing a settlement is the lawyers' responsibility, but don't hesitate to ask the mediator for assistance.

If the case does not settle, the mediator should follow up, making inquiries, scheduling another session, and/or using shuttle diplomacy. Don't be bashful about prodding a mediator if he is not following up as he should. Remember, the mediator is there to help you achieve your goals.

PART IV

Specialized Areas of Practice

The techniques described in this book can be applied to a wide variety of cases, but certain subject areas pose special challenges. They may require a mediator to focus on particular obstacles, such as strong emotions, or emphasize tactics, such as evaluation or process management. In some instances, it requires enlisting the judge in the case as an active partner.

In the chapters that follow, experts in five specialized fields—employment, insured, intellectual property, environmental, and "mega" cases—discuss how to respond to the special challenges that arise in their subject area.

Chapter 13

Employment Disputes

Carol A. Wittenberg, Susan T. Mackenzie, and Margaret L. Shaw

The use of mediation to resolve employment disputes is on the rise. Increasingly, federal district courts are referring discrimination cases to mediation; similarly, administrative agencies charged with enforcing anti-discrimination laws are experimenting with mediation programs. Mediation is well suited to resolving employment disputes for a number of reasons.

1. Special Issues

Emotionality

Employment disputes usually involve highly emotional issues. It is said that loss of one's job is the third most stressful life event, next only to death and divorce. Whether one's livelihood is at stake, as in a wrongful termination case, or the issue involves a professional relationship that has gone awry, as in a sexual harassment claim, the dispute occurs in a charged atmosphere. A mediator can help parties vent their anger and frustrations in a nonjudgmental setting that allows them to feel that their positions have been heard and to move on to a more productive, problem-solving viewpoint.

Example: One of us had the experience of being asked by a plaintiff after several hours of mediation if a one-on-one meeting with the mediator was possible, and counsel agreed. After telling the mediator that she reminded her of a former boss who had been an important mentor, the plaintiff talked about how upset the case had made her. She also talked about how much the negotiations over dollars were leaving her feeling disassociated from the process, and what she was personally looking to accomplish. The mediator was able to help the plaintiff identify her feelings, think through what she really wanted out of a resolution, and work within the process to accomplish that result. The case settled shortly after their caucus.

Confidentiality

The privacy and confidentiality that mediation affords may be important to employees and employers alike. For example, in many of the cases involving sexual harassment claims we mediate, a primary focus of claimants is to have an unpleasant situation stop, stop quickly, and stop permanently. Individual respondents, too, unless they are looking for vindication, may want to get on with their lives and put the incident behind them. Most employees are concerned about their reputations and want their careers to continue uninterrupted. Employers, for their part, are almost always interested in confidentiality. This is particularly true in discrimination cases because publicity can affect the employer's reputation in the marketplace. Employers are also concerned that without confidentiality, settlements will create precedents or "benchmarks" for future complainants, or encourage "me-too" complaints.

Creativity of outcomes

Mediation's creativity is particularly important in employment disputes, where the impact of the controversy can have profound effects on the parties' lives. We find that in many of the litigated disputes we mediate, nonlegal and nonmonetary issues are barriers as significant to resolution as the financial and legal aspects of the case. For example, in one age discrimination claim we mediated, the settlement called for the employee to retain his employment status without pay for a two-year period, so as to vest certain benefits afforded retirees. In a gender discrimination case, the terms involved keeping the employee on the payroll for a period of time with a new title to assist her in securing alternative employment. In a breach of contract case involving a senior executive, part of the settlement involved a guaranteed loan to invest in a new business.

Cost savings

Practical considerations also make mediation of employment disputes an attractive alternative to litigation. The process is likely to be much less expensive than litigation, or even arbitration. One lawyer who frequently represents plaintiffs in discrimination cases observed that, as of the mid-2000s, the litigation cost of a discrimination claim to individual claimants was roughly $50,000, as compared with $2,000 to $4,000 for mediation. A study in the early 1990s estimated the cost to defend a single discrimination claim at $81,000, a figure that is now almost certainly much higher.

Note also that the monetary cost of litigation does not take into account the indirect, personal, and emotional costs to all parties of a court proceeding. All workplaces have informal information channels; we often hear from individual mediation participants about the disruptive effects of the case on fellow employees. For instance, at one company with which we worked, speculation was rampant about who would be let go or reassigned in the event the case resulted in the reinstatement of a discharged employee.

Speed

Mediation is also likely to be significantly faster than litigation. This is of particular importance in the employment context, given the dramatic increase in antidiscrimination claims. In our experience, mediation of a routine employment case involving an individual claimant generally can be concluded in one day (or sometimes two). Although some parties are unable to reach complete closure in the mediation sessions, additional follow-up telephone conferences with one or both sides will often bring about a settlement. An evaluation of the Equal Employment Opportunity Commission's (EEOC) pilot mediation program, for instance, showed that mediation resolved charges of discrimination less expensively and more quickly than traditional methods, with closure in an average of 67 days as opposed to 294 in the regular process.

Questions

Are there disadvantages to mediation in the context of employment disputes? Of course there are, although we believe that some of the "dangers" are often overemphasized. Some employers are concerned that the availability of mediation will encourage frivolous complaints. Others are concerned that mediation simply adds a layer of time and expense when a case does not settle. Certain lawyers have also expressed a concern that an opposing party might merely be using mediation as a form of discovery. There are, of course, specific cases that are inappropriate for mediation, cases that upon analysis are without any apparent merit and call for the employer to take a firm stance.

2. Challenges for the Mediator

There are some distinctive characteristics of employment cases that can challenge a mediator and require special approaches.

Disparity in resources

While parties in other kinds of cases may have unequal resources, in employment disputes a lack of parity can make it difficult even to get the parties to the table. Employment claimants are often out of work or face an uncertain employment future. They may balk at the added expense of a mediator, particularly when the outcome is uncertain. While some employers will agree to pay the entire mediation bill as an inducement to a plaintiff to participate, others are concerned that without some financial investment a plaintiff will not participate in the process wholeheartedly. In these circumstances, we have found several approaches effective. If, for example, the employer is worried about the employee's investment in the process, the mediator can explore the nature of that concern and whether verbal representations by the claimant or claimant's lawyer might allay them. As an alternative, a mediator can suggest having the employer assume most of the cost, while requiring the employee to pay something.

Timing

The timing of mediation can affect both the process and its outcome. Where it is attempted shortly after a claim has been raised, the claimant may need extra help in getting beyond feelings of anger or outrage, while an individual manager or subject of a claim may feel betrayed. If little or no discovery has occurred, the lack of information about the facts on the part of one or both parties can hamper productive negotiations. At the other extreme, when a case has already been in litigation for an extended period of time, positions can become hardened and the parties even more determined to stop at nothing short of what they perceive to be "justice."

Example: In one case we handled, an age discrimination claim referred by the court, the plaintiff's lawyer had done little investigation prior to the mediation and thus was unaware of circumstances that called into question the plaintiff's integrity during his final year of employment. Assisting the lawyer to become more realistic about the chances for a recovery at trial became the challenge of this mediation.

In another case that involved a sexual harassment claim, outside counsel for the employer, who had recommended mediation, was unaware of some of the conduct of the individual manager who was the subject of the allegations. That case required us to mediate between the employer and the manager, the individual manager and the claimant, and the claimant and the corporate entity as well.

Imbalances of power

In certain employment disputes, such as those involving sexual harassment claims, a perceived or real imbalance in the power relationship between the parties may itself constitute an impediment to settlement. We have found that as a general proposition, particularly in dealing with an individual who feels at a power disadvantage in mediation, movement is better accomplished by pulling than by pushing. For example, in one case where the facts underlying the claim were perhaps unconscionable but not legally actionable, helping the claimant recognize the benefits of moving forward with her life was more effective than trying to convince her that she had a legally weak case.

When an issue of power imbalance is articulated or apparent, it is helpful to take the time to consult with the parties before the "real" mediation begins in order to structure the process. We typically discuss, for example, whether the complainant or the lawyer wants to make an opening statement. We have observed that complainants who prepare a statement for the initial joint session tend to feel a degree of participation that engenders a sense of control and dignity in the process that is not otherwise possible. At times, having a family member or close friend attend a session is helpful. We also attempt to establish in advance whether it will be necessary to keep the complainant and individual respondent apart, at least initially. We routinely schedule pre-mediation conference calls with all persons involved in the case to work through these kinds of issues.

Desire for revenge

Complainants who feel they have been wronged will sometimes look for a way to make the employer or the individual charged with harassing or discriminatory behavior "pay." Such a focus on revenge can present a major obstacle to settlement. There is no simple way to deal with this in mediation. Sometimes, particularly in cases where the complaint has already prompted the employer to take preventive measures, explaining the full impact that the complaint has already had on workplace policies or on the careers of others can help the complainant recognize and change to a posture more conducive to resolution. Another approach may be to have the individual respondent contribute out of his or her own pocket to a financial settlement.

Negotiation by numbers

In some employment mediations, one or both parties may become fixed on a settlement figure and refuse to budge. Finding a new framework for analysis that appears objectively fair can help parties stuck on numbers save face and ultimately agree on a different figure to settle the case.

Nonlegal and personal issues

At times both parties will fail to realize that a nonlegal problem is the root cause of an employment dispute.

Example: In one case we handled a personality conflict between the head of accounting and his most senior employee had festered for years. The working relationship between the two had deteriorated to the point that they routinely hurled racial and sexual epithets at one another. At that point, management could see no alternative to dismissing one or both of them. With the mediator's assistance, each party was able to shift focus from placing blame on the other to recognizing their mutual interest in continuing to be employed, and mutually acceptable procedures for personal interaction in the office were identified and put in writing. During the mediation, the parties also came to recognize that a contributing, if not overriding, cause of the deterioration of their relationship was an outstanding loan from the department head to the bookkeeper. While the department head had treated the loan as forgiven years ago, in reality the bookkeeper's failure to repay it had continued to bother the department head. The resolution between the parties included a repayment schedule for the loan.

"Outside" barriers to resolution

In some employment cases, the real barrier to resolution may be an individual who is not a direct party to the dispute.

Example: In one case we mediated involving a disability claim by an airline manager with more than 25 years of service, the claimant was moving toward resolution. However, as the mediation progressed, it became clear that his spouse, who was also present, was so angered by what she perceived as unconscionable treatment by the employer that she considered all offers of settlement by the employer insulting. Egged on by his spouse, the claimant became more obstinate and refused to budge from his initial position. The mediator dealt with this situation by giving recognition to the wife's feelings, and by helping her understand that her anger was fueled at least in part by resentment over the amount of time her spouse had spent on his job rather than with his family over the years. The spouse was also afforded an opportunity to air her position directly to the corporate representatives who were present. Once she had communicated her feelings, she was able to reorient her focus from the past to the future and to consider the potential impact of lengthy litigation on her husband's deteriorating health and well-being. Both she and the complainant were then able to focus on what could be accomplished in mediation, and the elements of a mutually acceptable package fell into place.

3. Preparing for Mediation

Once selected, the mediator routinely schedules a conference call with the lawyers. The purpose is to determine the lawyers' familiarity with the process, set ground rules for the mediation, and answer questions or resolve issues that may create barriers to settlement. This step can be particularly useful in employment cases because of the often perceived, if not actual, imbalance of power of the two parties.

The mediator generally describes the mediation process, including requirements for confidentiality. The mediator may review an agreement to mediate over the telephone and advise the parties that they will receive a copy of the agreement in time to go over and sign it before the mediation session. The parties will be asked whether they wish to make written submissions to the mediator prior to the session to familiarize the mediator with the nature of the dispute and, if so, whether these submissions will be shared with the other side as well as with the mediator.

The mediator will also ask the parties who will be attending the mediation session. Parties want to be assured that there is someone involved in the process on the other side with the ability to respond to issues that may arise in mediation as well as with the authority to settle. Although the ultimate decision maker may not be able to attend the session, it is important that everyone understand the extent of the mediation participants' authority.

Lawyers or their clients are expected to make a brief statement at the mediation session, setting forth the essential elements of their case. If the lawyers make a statement, we encourage them to present their case in a way that allows the other side to hear the client's concerns without creating an offensive or defensive reaction. In our experience, an adversarial posture at the outset is rarely conducive to fostering productive settlement discussions. The mediator may also discuss whether the claimant will be more fully involved in the process if he or she makes a brief statement.

At the start of mediation, the mediator explains the general process to be followed to everyone present. We often use this opportunity to describe our style of mediation as well. We alert participants that we may utilize joint or separate sessions or speak to a lawyer privately during the day as needs require. Advising participants of procedures at the outset creates clear expectations.

4. Combining Mediation with Other ADR Procedures

In our experience, mediation can be used effectively in combination with other alternative dispute resolution (ADR) procedures, such as fact-finding or facilitation to address specific needs in particular employment disputes.

Example: One of us served as a member of a neutral team under a procedure developed by all parties to resolve a hostile environment/sexual harassment claim. Under the agreed-upon procedure—embodied in a document that was signed by the parties and the neutral team—the team first conducted interviews with the claimant and the individual alleged to have created the hostile environment. Any other employee the team deemed relevant was also made available for interview, and interviews could be conducted by one or both of the team members at their discretion. The team also had access to personnel files and any other corporate records.

Under the procedure, the team was to mediate the dispute after conducting interviews, either in joint sessions with both individuals or through separate meetings with each party. If mediation efforts were not successful, the team was to draft a report, with findings of fact on several specific charges. That report was to be shared with the complainant and individual respondent, but not the employer, and was to be followed by a further attempt at mediation. Only if a second mediation attempt proved unsuccessful did the procedure call for submission of a fact-finding report to the employer.

In the actual case, the parties did not negotiate realistically during the first round of mediation. Only after reading the neutral team's findings of fact did each party express an interest in moving from previously expressed "final" positions. The parties were able to reach resolution during the second round of mediation, rendering moot the issuance of the fact-finding report to the employer.

Mediation can be combined with fact-finding in other ways as well.

Example: We were asked to mediate a case that involved a sexual harassment claim by a management trainee against two senior vice presidents of a bank. Investigation by the bank's lawyers had found sexual contact between the complainant and one bank executive, but concluded that the incident was consensual. The bank's lawyers also concluded that the complainant was not being sexually harassed or retaliated against by the second bank executive, who was her boss. Mediation was difficult because the complainant and her lawyer had little faith in the investigation conducted by the bank's lawyers, who also represented the bank in mediation. The bank's lawyers were unwilling to engage in serious settlement discussions without independent support for some of the complainant's allegations.

The mediator adopted the role of fact-finder under agreed upon conditions. The names of the other individuals the mediator interviewed would remain confidential, although the substance of their observations would be made available to the bank. The mediator interviewed several of the complainant's coworkers as well as her therapist and shared her preliminary findings with the parties. Mediation then resumed, and the parties were able to resolve the matter.

In another instance involving claims by several employees against one employer, a settlement was reached in mediation that called for the continued intervention of the mediator, but in the role of facilitator. We have also been asked to participate in procedures for evaluating the effectiveness of settlement agreements that address ongoing relationships. For example, one of us agreed to participate in a six-month review and "fine-tuning" of settlement terms resolving a dispute between the two chief executives of a membership organization.

5. A Case Example: Wrongful Termination and Race Discrimination

Mary Beth Lee, a 28-year-old African American female, was terminated from her position as makeup artist with a clothing designer, after seven years of continuous employment. At the time of her termination, Mary Beth earned a base salary of $55,000 and bonus of $12,000. The clothing company is known both for its couture women's clothing and for its makeup products.

Until the last eight months of her employment, Mary Beth had excelled in selling makeup at a number of the company's store locations and had developed sales in one ethnic neighborhood store to exceptional levels. Mary Beth was then transferred to a midtown store. She accepted the transfer for two reasons: (1) her boss, Suzanne Kay, was taking over management of the midtown store and asked Mary Beth to join her, and (2) she would be eligible for a promotion in six months.

The midtown store was a challenge. Historically, it had been poorly managed and sales were flat. Suzanne left the company three months after Mary Beth's transfer, as did one of Suzanne's managers. Mary Beth asked for a promotion at that time and was not interviewed for the position. Instead, the company transferred Beverly Tam, a Caucasian woman, from another store into the position Mary Beth was seeking. Beverly brought Laura Bay, another Caucasian woman, with her to the midtown store. Laura had previously worked with Beverly as a makeup artist.

Things did not go well for Mary Beth from the time Beverly and Laura joined the midtown store. Mary Beth felt that she was being unfairly criticized for poor sales. In addition, her time was being scrutinized in ways she had never before experienced. Mary Beth also noticed that Beverly started replacing other African American makeup artists with Caucasian and Asian makeup artists. Beverly, a demonstrative person, would often hug others, but was cold and aloof to Mary Beth. After six months at the store, Mary Beth received a midterm performance appraisal of "less than satisfactory," the first negative performance appraisal Mary Beth had received in seven years.

Two months later, the company announced a reduction in force of 50 employees. There were two layoffs at the midtown store and Beverly was given the authority to select those to be laid off. Beverly selected Mary Beth and another woman who had only joined the company within the last year. Although Mary Beth had seven years of service with the company, she had the second least seniority at the store.

Mary Beth filed suit against the company a few weeks later, charging race discrimination and wrongful termination. She opened a full-service salon in her local neighborhood, which included makeup and providing related services. That salon had yet to turn a profit one year later. Mary Beth insisted that she had looked for makeup artist jobs, but that she believed that her reputation had been harmed in the industry, making it impossible for her to find a comparable job. She also claimed that she suffered emotional distress as a result of her termination.

After the initial joint session, the mediator met separately with Mary Beth and her lawyer. Mary Beth was extremely angry about her treatment by the company. She felt that she had accomplished much in her seven years, and that Beverly set her up for termination because of her race. She was particularly upset that she had not even been interviewed for the supervisory position at the midtown store, and pointed out that Laura had no supervisory experience when she was brought to midtown by Beverly.

Company representatives, who viewed Mary Beth as an employee at will and one of 50 employees who lost jobs as a result of the decline in sales, did not appear to understand Mary Beth's perspective. The company stressed Mary Beth's poor performance and claimed that she disappeared frequently from the store during the day.

The mediator spent much of the day exploring Mary Beth's goals in mediation and the basis for her anger, including her feeling that she had devoted herself to the company since college graduation and that she had been humiliated by her performance appraisal and selection for layoff. Mary Beth was seeking a significant settlement to compensate her for the startup time it would take to make her salon successful, demanding $250,000, based in part on her belief that there were two former employees who also worked with Beverly who would testify to the manager's racist comments.

The mediator then met with company representatives to explain Mary Beth's substantive and emotional position and to explore the company's response. The company wanted to settle the case, but also believed that it was not a "six-figure" case, particularly because Mary Beth had chosen to open a salon rather than to seek other employment. The company was insistent that Beverly was a strong and fair manager and that her performance appraisal of Mary Beth was defensible. The company acknowledged that Beverly hired more Caucasian and Asian makeup artists for the store counter, but insisted that her actions did not constitute race discrimination. The company also questioned whether Mary Beth's witnesses would actually be willing to testify against the company. Nevertheless, the company offered Mary Beth $50,000.

The mediator returned to meet with Mary Beth and her counsel. They discussed the company's offer, which Mary Beth thought was an "insult." The mediator explored some potential weaknesses in Mary Beth's claim, including her failure to search for an equivalent position after her layoff and the lack of medical treatment for emotional distress. Mary Beth's lawyer acknowledged that even if she were to prevail in court, she might not be awarded the amount she was seeking. The mediator discussed with Mary Beth the emotional toll that a trial would take and her need to move on with her life.

The mediator continued with the negotiations between the two sides. After a long day, Mary Beth agreed to accept $125,000, which she viewed as a significant compromise. She was concerned about having to wait for money she needed for her salon. The mediator was convinced that Mary

Beth's position was firm. At that point, the company had offered $100,000 and was adamant that it was not going to increase its offer because of the limited value it placed on the case. Nonetheless, the company was concerned about defending the charge of racism.

The mediator had been impressed during the day with the way Mary Beth presented herself; she was impeccably dressed and her makeup was perfect. She mentioned several times that losing her job and struggling to establish a business on her own affected her ability to "dress for success." As a means to bridge the gap, the mediator discussed with the company its willingness to offer Mary Beth a gift certificate to purchase designer clothing. Because of the high markup on couture clothing, the company could offer Mary Beth a significant benefit that would cost the company a fraction of the face value. The company agreed to the idea, but insisted that the gift certificate be no more than $15,000. The mediator presented the idea to Mary Beth, who was excited about the prospect of being able to obtain designer clothing. She accepted the $15,000 gift certificate in addition to the $100,000. Mary Beth's lawyer agreed to base his fees on the $100,000 alone and the case was settled on those terms.

Chapter 14

Insured Claims and Other Monetary Disputes

J. Anderson Little

1. Limitations of the Problem Solving Method

Mediators who want to facilitate the settlement of civil litigation should be aware of the fact that a large percentage of lawsuits, particularly those in state courts, will be settled with the payment of a sum of money by one party to another. Mediators also should be aware of the fact that monetary resolutions will be achieved through an arduous process, in which the parties become increasingly frustrated with one another as they make concession after concession in an effort to settle the case.

The resolution of insured claims is characterized by positional, or traditional, bargaining. This is true because of the nature of the disputes themselves. Plaintiffs want as much money as they can get; defendants want to pay as little money as they can get by with. There is little in monetary disputes that has to do with working relationships that allows parties in other types of disputes to craft creative solutions or make beneficial trade-offs that work to strengthen the ties between them.

The concept of positional bargaining is well known to anyone who has negotiated the sale or purchase of a house or automobile. Those negotiations involve a lot of "haggling" and are seldom enjoyed by the participants. As prevalent as positional bargaining is in our daily life, it is also responsible for a great deal of the arguing and fussing that goes on in work and family settings.

In their landmark book, *Getting to Yes*, Fisher and Ury alerted mediators to the pitfalls of positional bargaining and urged another approach to negotiation that has revolutionized our thinking about how to resolve disputes. In advocating an interest-based form of negotiation, Fisher and Ury sought to reframe "negotiation as bargaining" into "negotiation as joint problem solving."

The mediation world embraced this notion of interest-based negotiations and incorporated it into the model of mediation that was already at the heart of mediation theory and practice—the problem-solving model. We have been taught to help the parties solve problems by helping them identify their needs and interests, and we invent elegant solutions for mutual gain. To this day, the literature of mediation is dominated by the problem-solving approach, although many commentators are beginning to recognize some of its limitations. Nowhere are those limitations more apparent than in the mediation of lawsuits in the trial courts across this country, particularly those that involve the settlement of insured claims. In those cases, mediators quickly realize that the process of mediation they were taught to employ often collides with the realities of positional bargaining.

Civil trial court mediators should be aware of the fact that positional bargaining will occur in the settlement of insured claims whether we mediators want it to or not. That type of bargaining is characterized by a number of phenomena that I will highlight briefly in the rest of this chapter.

2. Important Features of the Mediation of Insured Claims

Withholding information

During the mediation of insured claims, parties typically withhold from each other information about the strengths and weaknesses of their positions. The reason is simple. If they reveal information about the weaknesses in their case, they diminish the bargaining power they have in their negotiations. If they reveal strengths in their case during a negotiation they don't think will result in a settlement, they give up the element of surprise that lawyers like to hold for use at trial.

Reluctance to talk

As a consequence of our first feature, the parties in civil trial mediations are reluctant to talk with each other openly and directly in general session and would rather spend their time in private sessions with the mediator. There they can discuss the strengths and weaknesses of their case in safety and work confidentially on bargaining positions and negotiation strategy, without giving away bargaining advantage to the other side.

Dominance of case analysis

In the mediation of insured claims, case analysis will dominate the early stages of discussion, and the primary participants in that conversation will be the professional negotiators in the room, that is, the lawyers and insurance claims representatives. The major topic of conversation early in the settlement conference will be "the value of the case": the result if the case is tried to a judge or jury. Conversation about the value of the case involves a discussion of the evidence likely to be admitted at trial, the law governing the controversy, verdicts in similar cases, the costs of prosecuting the case, the skill of the advocates, the tendencies of the judge who will be presiding over it, and many other factors.

Lawyers and claims representatives tend to dominate the discussion of case value in private sessions. In their minds, the negotiation is about the "value" of the case, and their goal in the negotiation is to maximize that value. Conversation about the needs and interests of the litigants themselves will rarely occur at the beginning of the mediation, and only then at the initiation of the mediator.

Monetary nature of proposals and proposal swapping

In the settlement of insured claims, the proposals made by the parties will be monetary in nature. The process of negotiation will be one of positional bargaining. Rarely will there be proposals with multiple elements and requests for nonmonetary or personal results. Additionally, as the process of proposal swapping begins to occur, case analysis discussion begins to fade into the background. The parties begin to engage in what I call the "used-car sale" stage of mediation, in which the negotiation is dominated by round after round of proposal swapping. In the mediation of insured claims I conduct, it is the norm that the parties spend more time making, reacting to, and sending monetary proposals to the other team than they do discussing the merits of the case.

Responding to a disliked proposal

Finally, the parties often become angry with each other when they receive monetary proposals that are "out of the ballpark" of settlement. As a result, they spend enormous amounts of time and energy trying to decide whether, or how, to respond to such a "ridiculous" proposal. This emotional reaction has an impact on the proposal they make in return; and typically, they will be inclined to make one of three responses: pack up and walk away, demand that the other side give them a more realistic number, or send a proposal of their own that the other side will experience as a low-/high-ball proposal.

This type of response is often counterproductive and tends to invoke the same type of response from the other side. After several rounds of such proposals, the parties typically conclude that the negotiation is fruitless, that the other team is "negotiating in bad faith," and that the parties are "too far apart" to settle the case. As a result, they often terminate the negotiation prematurely. Without the intervention of a skilled mediator at these points, the negotiation will fall apart at an early stage—even though both sides have more room to move and would move if they thought it would settle the claim. The plaintiff quits before his lowest number is proposed and the defendant quits before her highest number is offered.

This is the stage of negotiations about money that lawyers, claims representatives, litigants, and mediators alike despise and avoid. To the litigant, the "haggling" feels demeaning, to the pros in the room it seems like a waste of their time, and to the mediators it feels childish and leaves them feeling useless. I often hear the complaint from many new civil trial mediators that they feel "little more than a messenger" at this stage of the mediation.

3. A Working Model for the Mediation of Insured Claims

So what is it that mediators can do to assist the parties in negotiations that they themselves detest and in which they feel so ill equipped? I have tried to answer that question in great detail in a book called *Making Money Talk: How to Mediate Insured Claims and Other Monetary Disputes*. In it I set out a framework, a model if you will, for mediators who work in the context of civil litigation in general and insured claims in particular. It's a framework that works well for facilitating disputes that are dominated by positional bargaining, and it consists of three principal elements:

○ Facilitate the flow of information.
○ Facilitate case analysis.
○ Facilitate movement when negotiations stall.

Facilitate the flow of information

Mediators know that the development of information is an important factor in the successful resolution of conflict, and we work to help the parties uncover important, and sometimes neglected, information. In addition, many of us bring an ideological or professional bias toward openness and candor to the mediation process. However, mediators who work in the context of civil trial mediation must be careful about this subject. We must learn to blend our instincts for openness with the realization that the parties and lawyers in civil litigation consider information to be a valuable commodity and the release of information to be a strategic decision.

Mediators should be mindful of the fact that litigators tend to hold on to information reflexively, fearing that the release of it will give up strategic advantage at trial. They will withhold information unless they are prompted to consider whether it would benefit the settlement process to release that information. Mediators should also be aware of an important fact of human nature in this regard: most of us hold tightly to anything someone else wants from us. With regard to giving away that which someone else wants, whether it be information or anything else, we humans tend to react reflexively rather than thoughtfully.

Mediators can assist negotiators at this point by promoting a discussion about the nature of the information, the pros and cons of holding or releasing it, and the likely consequences of either decision. As a result of such a conversation, parties will often release information that is important to the settlement process, when their first reaction was to withhold it.

Mediators should give the decision to release information the same importance as we give to the ultimate decision to settle the case. In keeping with the notion that we should be facilitative rather than directive, mediators should never try to sell disclosure as the best or right decision. Lawyer–mediators are often accused of practicing directive mediation in this type of situation and, generally, in mandatory civil trial mediation. This does not have to be true. If mediators truly believe that the decision to withhold or convey information is the clients' to make, we will do everything in our power to help the parties make thoughtful and informed decisions and not direct the outcome of their decision making.

The timing of information exchange is important to the settlement process as well. Many lawyers, particularly on the plaintiff's side of the negotiation, do not understand the importance of providing information well in advance of their settlement negotiations. As a consequence problems develop at mediation because the defense lawyer has not had the opportunity to examine important information such as the plaintiff's medical and billing records.

Mediators in the civil trial court context would do well to keep these dynamics in mind before the mediation is convened. We should also keep in mind that the administrative tasks of scheduling and choosing a location for the conference present us with many important mediation moments and opportunities. During these times, we can inquire about the readiness of the parties to negotiate. We can discover whether any of the parties need additional information before they can negotiate intelligently, and we can help the parties gather that information. If the parties do not have the necessary information, we can continue a scheduled mediation or seek additional time from the court within which to schedule it. In doing these things, we help the parties understand the process needs of the other side and understand how those needs affect the prospects of settlement. Mediators who understand the importance of information and the timing of its development make a major contribution to the parties' settlement efforts.

Facilitate case analysis

Many lawyers and their clients are well prepared to articulate their case analysis when they show up for a mediated settlement conference. They have thoroughly discovered their case, the lawyer has formed an opinion about the value of the case based on the evidence and her legal analysis, and the lawyer and client have formed a common understanding about the case and have decided upon an appropriate range of settlement.

Regardless of how good a lawyer is or how well prepared she may be, mediators and litigators must reckon with an important fact of human nature that affects the ability of the parties to be fully prepared. Most of us cannot think of everything that could possibly go wrong with a case or every interpretation of the facts or law that cuts against our own view of the case. Thus some case analysis discussion will be appropriate and helpful, even when the parties have thoroughly prepared.

While most lawyers are well prepared to negotiate, their clients often are not. Sometimes the lawyer has not done as good a job of educating his client about the case as he has done in educating himself. However, my experience suggests that most lawyers diligently try to educate their clients and are sometimes unsuccessful in reaching a common understanding of the value of the claim. Frequently, it is the plaintiff who has the hardest time coming to grips with the value of his case, because most plaintiffs have no experience with or understanding of how cases are analyzed by courts, lawyers, claims representatives, and juries.

Case analysis, or risk analysis, is fundamentally important in a traditional bargaining setting—for both the claimant and the defense. It provides the framework within which we will negotiate and a touchstone for decision making. In simple terms, case analysis helps negotiators know when a proposal should be accepted as a good deal or discarded as an inadequate one.

If I value my case at $80,000 and the best and final offer of the defendant is $7,400, why would I accept such a proposal? The best offer of the other side is far lower than what I can get at trial. The outcome of the case, or the value of the case, provides a touchstone for the negotiation. It is how people become grounded in the negotiation. If I don't know the value of my case, I don't know when to accept an offer and when not to accept an offer. I don't know what kind of offers to make. So it is important for people who are negotiating the settlement of claims for money or insured claims to know the value of the claim. Of course, valuing a case is not an exact science, but prior to a settlement conference, the parties and their lawyers should work to discover the case, compare it with similar cases that have produced settlements and verdicts, and reach a conclusion about its value (more accurately, the range of value into which the case will fall).

Mediators can help lawyers and their clients by posing questions about the case. The answers to those questions help the parties articulate and come to grips with the evidence and, thus, the realities of their case. Case analysis questions form the core of my work with lawyers and their clients in private sessions at the beginning of any mediation. Those questions fall generally within four categories of inquiry:

- ○ What do you get if you go to court? (Or, what is the likely result in monetary terms?)
- ○ What are your chances of obtaining that outcome?
- ○ What does it cost you to get that outcome?
- ○ What are your chances of collecting a judgment if you obtain one?

In legal parlance, these questions can be translated into questions about damages, liability, costs, and collection. They are the four fundamental case evaluation questions that lawyers wrestle with in order to arrive at their opinion of value. As a reminder, let me add that a discussion of any of these areas should be undertaken by mediators in private sessions, because a discussion of case analysis involves strategic, and therefore, private information.

Mediators can assist the parties in their case analyses by asking important and probing questions; by attending to all the parties to the negotiation, so they understand what the professionals are saying; by clearly summarizing and reframing the information heard and statements made; and by translating the thoughts of one side to the other in such a way that the one side can hear and consider the analysis of the other. The goal of this work is to assist the parties in articulating at a conscious level a clear understanding of the strengths and weaknesses of their case so that they become grounded in the realities of their case, thereby providing them with a realistic range of settlement.

Facilitate movement when negotiations stall

When parties try to settle monetary disputes through traditional bargaining, they find the process difficult at best. They often have a hard time starting the process ("Who goes first?"), they have a hard time keeping it going when they find that their ranges vary widely ("They just aren't moving fast enough!"), and they grow discouraged and resentful as they make concession after concession in an effort to settle their case ("I think this is just a waste of my time!")

Most of the time and energy spent by negotiators in the settlement of civil litigation is spent in the proposal making and swapping part of the positional bargaining process. And yet, this part of the process has received little attention in the literature of negotiation and mediation. Not surprisingly, negotiators themselves neglect this important part of the process as they think about how to settle their cases.

When it comes to the task of making offers and counteroffers during the course of a negotiation, even experienced negotiators often fail to recognize that they have not planned their negotiations as well as they have the rest of their case. Instead of having a plan for their movement from position to position, they react reflexively to the other side's movement by walking away, demanding that the other side bid against itself, and throwing low- and high-ball proposals back to the other team. More often than not, they react in ways that impede the progress of negotiation and make settlement impossible.

Over the years I have collected a variety of responses that negotiators make in reaction to monetary proposals from the other team during the proposal-swapping stage of mediation. They are so prevalent that I have come to call them the "settlement conference clichés" of civil trial court mediation. They typically signal that the speaker believes the proposal received from the other team is so far out of the ballpark of settlement that the other side "is wasting my time." Or it means that the proposal is so outrageous that it calls into question the speaker's competence or discredits the injury complained of in the case. Here are some examples:

- ○ "I'm not going to bid against myself!"
- ○ "That's insulting. Is that what they think my leg is worth?!"
- ○ "That's insulting. Who do they think they're dealing with?!"
- ○ "Go tell them to give me a realistic number!"
- ○ "I'm not even going to dignify that number with a response!"
- ○ "I'm out of here!"
- ○ "They're just not here in good faith!"

Negotiators who have these reactions usually formulate their counterproposal in reaction to the other side's proposal. Proposals made "in the heat of the moment" are usually less generous than those made more carefully and thoughtfully. As a result, the other side will have similar reactions, make similar statements, and formulate similar proposals. Left to their own devices, negotiators will continue in this reactive mode until movement between proposals slows, stalls, and ceases altogether. Proposals made in reaction to the movement of the other side inevitably lead to impasse unless a skilled mediator intervenes.

Unfortunately, however, many mediators who work to settle civil litigation are not equipped to provide skillful intervention during the proposal swapping stage of positional bargaining. Many of us, in fact, did not like that kind of haggling as practicing lawyers and felt that publishing an ever-changing series of proposals diminished our credibility in the eyes of our clients and colleagues. Our experience and temperament may have also conditioned us to dislike this part of the process.

Additionally, civil trial mediators have not been provided the necessary tools to assist them with the difficult situations that characterize this stage of mediation. Many mediators have reported to me that they feel useless at this stage, good only for walking from room to room toting numbers for the parties. They often say about their role at this point that, "I'm just a messenger."

Many mediators feel ill equipped to handle the emotional outbursts of parties who perceive the proposals of the other side to be "ridiculous" or "outlandish." With no other recourse, many of us resort to highly directive statements and techniques to "get control" of our clients and keep them in the negotiating game. There is even a tendency on our part to admonish the participants for engaging in "childish" outbursts and "juvenile" behavior during this stage of the process.

In reality, there is much mediators can do to intervene in the cycle of reaction and counterreaction that occurs during the proposal swapping, or "used-car sale," phase of traditional bargaining. The first is to realize that the positional bargaining that occurs at this stage is entirely appropriate and constitutes the only way the parties can communicate about the most important component of the negotiation—the range in which the case can settle.

The second is to realize that the emotional reactions of the parties are not an act; they are real emotions brought on by the perception that the other side's proposals are out of the realm of settlement. Many mediators are offended by the emotional outbursts of the parties and are inclined to chastise the parties for childish behavior. Others do not recognize the real emotional expressions of the parties and try to "talk them out of their reactions" by resorting to case analysis conversation.

The first thing mediators should do at this point is to take the outbursts seriously and deal with the emotions of the moment. Once we take the emotional reactions of the parties seriously and understand their source, we can proceed to the next important step: commiserating with the reacting party in the moment.

Over the years I have come to realize that the parties' emotions are stirred up by a few well-defined perceptions. In the defendant's room, an angry outburst occurs in reaction to a proposal from the plaintiff that is "out of the ballpark." The thought process is this: "the plaintiff's too high; we're too far apart; the plaintiff is wasting my time." The reaction in the plaintiff's room to a low-ball proposal of the defendant may be the same but more typically it is slightly different. That thought process is this: "the defendant is too low; he's jerking us around and insinuating that my injuries aren't real; his proposal is an insult." For the plaintiff, the defendant's low-ball offer is perceived as discounting the plaintiff's injury or as an attack upon the plaintiff's credibility.

The most important thing a mediator can do when the parties react strongly to the other side's proposal is to understand the basis of the reaction and to reflect that basis back to the participant in such a way that she knows you understand. ("So, that proposal says to you that we'll never get this case settled?") Litigants and their lawyers are more likely to calm down and get back to the business of proposal making if they have the experience of being understood and taken seriously by the mediator.

The second thing a mediator can do is to help the reacting party identify a number of ways of dealing with the situation other than by leaving, making no proposal at all, or making a low- or high-ball proposal. Parties who react strongly to a proposal from the other side lose sight of the fact that they have many tools at their disposal to further the objective of settlement. Thus, one of the things I try to accomplish with a reactive negotiator is to get him to discuss the many ways of handling the situation and the many proposals he could make. A list might include:

○ Walking out.
○ Sending the mediator back to the other side to get a "realistic" proposal.
○ Giving an equally "ridiculous" proposal (for example, $1.50).
○ Making a token offer.
○ Making a proposal that is less than what he had planned to make.
○ Making the proposal she would have made if the other side had been "reasonable."

Invariably, a discussion about other options will generate a discussion about the negotiator's goal for the mediation and how his proposals further or impede those goals. Some of the goals negotiators identify include:

○ Keeping the other side in the negotiation game.

○ Keeping the negotiation moving.

○ Communicating that the other side's proposal is too high or low.

○ Encouraging the other side to make a move.

○ Educating the other side about the proper range of settlement.

○ Settling the case within an acceptable range of negotiation.

○ Saving some money if that's possible.

Discussing goals and options will have a calming effect on most negotiators and will bring them back to a more thoughtful process of proposal making. As a result, their proposals will keep the bargaining process moving, make their communications about the proper range of settlement more clear, and, often, inspire the other side to do likewise.

Those discussions may also have the effect of inspiring one party or the other to develop a plan for movement. A plan for movement puts the negotiator in control of her agenda, makes her less reactive to the other side's movement, and eliminates much of the agony she experiences during the used-car sale phase of the process. Negotiations conducted by parties who have a plan of movement are less likely to stall out or impasse before the parties have reached the end of their negotiation ranges.

4. Develop a Variety of Mediation Models

Making Money Talk grew out of a one-day advanced mediation program that I have been teaching for many years. In it, I wrote extensively about the problems of movement that occur in the settlement of civil litigation and the models and techniques mediators can use to help parties avoid impasse. In doing so, I have been described by a few as encouraging and promoting the use of positional bargaining. Nothing could be further from the truth.

Like many of you, I was trained in the problem-solving model of the negotiation/mediation process. I believe in that model and seek to employ it whenever possible, including the mediation of civil litigation. I carry with me into every mediation a firm determination to find ways to encourage problem-solving and interest-based discussions, even in those cases that resist it the most—the personal injury cases that dominate our state courts.

It is reality in that context, however, that those cases resist the application of an interest-based approach and that the parties' negotiations are characterized by positional bargaining. When, not if, that occurs, mediators who are equipped only with a problem-solving model of the process will find their work exceedingly frustrating. Things will improve for them only if, ironically, they take a problem-solving approach to their work and recognize that this model does not fully arm them to meet the challenges they face. Mediators will need to revisit positional bargaining to study its dynamics and to develop skills, models and techniques to handle the peculiar phenomena that kind of negotiation present. Only then will mediators be able to help parties take a thoughtful approach to settlement through positional bargaining rather than the reactive approach that so quickly leads to anger, frustration, and premature impasse.

Chapter 15

Intellectual Property Cases

David W. Plant

1. Characteristics of Intellectual Property Mediation

Some consider mediation to be the same process regardless of the subject matter of the dispute or the characteristics of the players.[1] That is, mediation is mediation is mediation. Undercutting this view, intellectual property (IP) disputes often exhibit unique characteristics and call for special variations on the mediation theme.

A dispute as to the appropriate royalty rate for rights to IP may not pose unusual problems. But if the royalty rate is affected by a most favored licensee clause, rulings about construction of patent claims, doubts as to the proper royalty base, concerns about technology obsolescence, geographic considerations, varying competitive situations from market to market, or

---

[1]. This chapter includes some of the thoughts set out in the book *We Must Talk Because We Can—Mediating International Intellectual Property Disputes*, published by the International Chamber of Commerce in Paris in 2008.

the need to incentivize licensees to succeed, mediation of the dispute may require the extraordinary, creative attention of all concerned.

Even more challenging are disputes as to who developed an invention, what the invention is, who has rights under it, what those rights are, and whether the rights are commercially valuable. These issues frequently give rise to unusual problems, calling for especially creative work. Similar complexities arise in connection with trademark and service mark issues, copyrights, and trade secrets.

Complexities may increase as disputes focus on:

○ Whether to protect IP (for example, to apply for government grant or registration).

○ Whether to enforce IP rights (for example, to bring an action for infringement, misappropriation, or breach of a license agreement), and against whom.

○ Whether to ignore, avoid, challenge, or negotiate for rights under IP.

○ Whether or not to exploit IP rights commercially, and, if so, how.

Intellectual property disputes are typically complex because of the subject matter, the number of players, the disparate business and personal interests and needs of the players, emotional concerns, cultural disconnects, changes in technology, and changes in the market place.

2. Preparing for Mediation

All of these considerations and complexities should cause the mediator and every other player to prepare, and to prepare well, for mediation. Especially in intellectual property mediations, the dispute is never about what the dispute is about. This has been apparent time and time again, as ill-prepared parties and counsel have stumbled toward impasse, and as poorly informed mediators have made counterproductive moves.

This leads to the first of 13 steps that should be undertaken in preparing for IP mediation, from the moment any party senses a dispute is in the making. These steps should be undertaken by every player (whether the mediator, the lead negotiator, the CEO, a laboratory manager, or a marketing head). The steps may be undertaken in the order set out here. But as preparation proceeds and the ensuing mediation unfolds, engaging in one step will cause the mediator or a party to revisit a prior step or jump to a later one. This is inevitable. No matter how the preparation develops, the participants should seek to ensure that, at least for purposes of the mediation at hand, the hard-nosed litigators, proud inventors and authors, and bitter competitors are transformed into well-informed, joint problem solvers.

Step 1: Identify the problems

The first step is to identify the problems as one understands the situation. This is not the end of the inquiry. As a mediator continues to prepare and goes through the mediation process, he must frequently check his view of the problems in light of new information that unfolds. At the outset of all IP mediation, the problems may appear to be legal and technological. But as the mediation evolves, the problems will almost always entail business and emotional issues, and all concerned should focus as much on these as on the legal and technology issues.

Step 2: Identify the players

All players—that is, both party players and nonparty players—and their roles in the genesis and development of the problems must be identified. As with identifying the problems, the identities of the players are likely to change as the preparation and the mediation itself proceed. For example, during the course of the mediation, it may become apparent that people not at the table should participate (such as a CEO, banker, investor, vendor, licensor or licensee).

> *Example:* In a recent mediation in a patent infringement action between two family-owned businesses, the disparate interests of an absent family patriarch, an absent exclusive customer, and an absent potential purchaser of the defendant's business were all material to a resolution of the dispute.
>
> In an unfair competition mediation in the United States, after many days of mediation over many months, the dispute was resolved after one party received telephonic approval to sign the agreement from the principal's absent rabbi—in Jerusalem.

Step 3: Identify the material facts

The third step is to identify the material facts as the neutral understands them and as she believes the disputants understand them. The trade secret owner's team may believe that the secret is of great commercial value and has plainly been stolen. The accused misappropriator may believe that, whatever the other side believes the trade secrets to be, they are in fact of no value, are known to the world at large, and were not in any way misappropriated. A nonparty may play a role if it developed the same technology independently of the purported trade secret owner.

Step 4: Identify further information

The next step is to identify further information needed by the mediator and by each party—from the party's own team, from other parties' teams, and from other sources—to confirm, test, or augment the "material" facts. A party's financial situation and its near-term and long-term plans may be crucially important to finding a solution to the problem. For example, in one patent infringement mediation the need for the patent owner to enhance the value of its company by obtaining recognition of its patent emerged as an important fact only after the mediation was well under way.

Step 5: Identify the players' real interests and needs

The real interests and real needs of all players—every party and every nonparty—should be identified. In intellectual property mediation, parties and their counsel tend to focus, and get stuck on, the technical and legal merits and the right and wrong of each participant's position.

> *Example:* Some time after a mediated settlement of a software dispute between a U.S. corporation and an Indian company, the U.S. payee surprisingly returned the settlement amount to the Indian company. The American corporation explained that money was really not what it needed—but acknowledgment of its U.S. patent, which the settlement provided, was.

For example, litigants may want to settle to:

○ *Create IP rights:* to establish a defensive or offensive IP portfolio to protect or enlarge market share.

○ *Assign IP rights:* to be relieved of the burden of ownership and enforcement, to receive compensation, or to comply with a contract.

○ *Grant a license to IP rights:* to acquire cash to pay debts or invest in capital equipment; to comply with an obligation; to acquire rights under the licensee's IP portfolio; to obtain an acknowledgment of the value of the licensed IP; or to avoid pouring money, energy, and time into litigation with uncertain results.

Assisting the parties in this critical endeavor is a critically important chore for the mediator.

Step 6: Identify no-agreement alternatives—(BATNAs)

In IP mediation, like other mediations where the sticking point is money, parties and their counsel often come to the mediation with a pre-set bottom line above or below which the party will not budge. Thus, the no-agreement alternatives for each party must be identified. For example, the party will not take a penny less (or will not pay a penny more), or will not take less than full ownership of, or exclusive rights to, the property in question (or will not grant more than nonexclusivity in a limited field or geographic area, for only a limited time), or the party will not grant terms more favorable than those granted to others (or will destroy the other party's IP or the other party's market share before the party pays the same as others). A mediator can assist each party in identifying and assessing the availability and merits of its alternative, as compared with the potential deal being negotiated.

Step 7: Identify objectives

The seventh step for each party is to identify its own objectives and the objectives of the other parties and relevant players. A party's objective is a solution that will (1) satisfy its real interests and (2) equal or exceed its no-agreement alternative. Each party and player must understand the objectives of every other participant. Any number of combinations of terms may comprise objectives; the trick is to find the combination that satisfies everyone's real interests and exceeds everyone's alternative.

Step 8: Explore options

The next step is to explore options, both substantive and procedural. In preparing for mediation and in going through the process, every party ought to explore options repeatedly. Unanticipated business deals often are substantial components of resolutions of IP disputes. Considering rights that were not directly, or originally, in dispute often assists the parties to enlarge the pie. Assessing the prospects of doing business in a new way with another party (or a nonparty) may create an even bigger pie, even if the new business has nothing to do with the IP at issue.

The mediator must help the parties in exploring options. He may be the first to suggest these options, and is likely to be more directive in this exercise than would be the norm for mediators.

Example: In one dispute, the parties appeared stuck and were at the edge of breaking off discussions. The mediator intervened and asked them to pause and consider brainstorming. With the parties' assent, the mediator proposed two or three possibilities for consideration. Seeing these possibilities listed on a whiteboard triggered further proposals by the parties. Ultimately, they solved their problem.

Step 9: Identify emotional issues

In intellectual property disputes emotions run deep. It is safe to say that every such dispute has an emotional component. Inventors take pride in their inventions; authors tout their creations; designers believe their trademarks are unique; software creators are confident that their programs will propel users to "the next level." Creators of "trade secrets" are jealous of their formulas. Research and development partners feel betrayed when expectations are not met. Innocent designers are outraged when charged with infringement or misappropriation. Competitors are morally offended by perceived misconduct by each other, especially when market share and price are affected. It goes on and on.

Simply because IP often entails scientific or technical matters does not insulate such disputes from dark clouds of emotion. Indeed, emotions often outweigh monetary considerations. One party's acknowledgment of another's scientific contribution or innocent design, for example, may be worth large amounts of money. An apology for misunderstanding another's motives may carry great weight. An acknowledgment that another party may have the better of the argument on the merits may move a mediation past impasse.

Step 10: Identify cultural issues

Each of us is, to some degree, culturally different from every other person, even if we have grown up in the same town in the same country. These differences are magnified when we must deal with people from other places and backgrounds. Cultural issues are particularly strong in intellectual property disputes, and mediators must be aware of cultural differences between teams, of cultural differences within each team, and of cultural differences between players and the mediator.

A third world infringer, for example, may not accept a pharmaceutical company's assertion of a patent. A European businessperson may not understand unique characteristics of the U.S. patent system. In addressing damages, royalty, or valuation questions, a U.S. party may not be familiar with local accounting rules or the tax laws applicable to the adversary's business. A U.S. party may not be comfortable with another party's negotiating style. These and many other differences between parties compel them to understand each other's backgrounds—and compel a mediator to be sensitive to nuances. Ignoring cultural differences can easily derail a mediation.

Step 11: Identify difficult people and difficult situations

Arrogant or aggressive (read "Rambo" litigation) counsel often offend other participants. ("We have no incentive to let the other side live. They are abusing the patent system.") A principal may refuse to be in the same room with the principal's counterpart. Participants engage in ad hominem attacks. ("We regard people like you as patent terrorists.") An infringer dominant in the field for years resents the patent owner's invasion of the territory. ("We developed this market for 50 years. They have no right to take our customers [even though 'they' own a valid patent]") Mediators must become skilled at identifying difficult people and situations so as to diffuse them.

Step 12: Outline potential solutions

The twelfth step for each party is to come to the mediation with an outline of potential substantive solutions—even a draft term sheet. In a recent patent licensing and joint development dispute, for example, counsel projected potential terms on a screen and modified them as joint discussion unfolded, expediting the closing of the deal. In addition to facilitating agreement at the mediation, pre-mediation drafting compels a party to think carefully about the problem and the participants' needs, alternatives, objectives, needed information, and options.

Step 13: Expect the unexpected!

The thirteenth step is to prepare for the unexpected. This is not a matter of anticipating all surprises; they will occur regardless of the thoroughness of preparation. This step comprises preparing to deal with surprises when they arise, by anticipating the parties' reaction to, and how they will deal with, any of a variety of possible events.

3. Other Important Considerations

a. Confidentiality

Confidentiality in intellectual property mediation means different things to different people. It may mean that the mediation process itself is private. It may mean that anything said or done by a participant is "privileged" (that is, it cannot be used against the participant or the participant's party in later proceedings). It may mean that within the mediation, a party's proprietary information can be seen only by specified people under specified circumstances.

Confidentiality in IP mediations is not always easy to maintain. This is especially so with regard to intellectual property that is imbued with the public interest, such as patents, trademarks, and copyrights. In short, the public's interest in the resolution of a dispute may trump mediation confidentiality. A mediated IP solution and underlying considerations may have to be disclosed to government agencies, licensees, investors, bankers, or creditors.

> *Example:* In a patent infringement mediation, the paying party was a small publicly held company. A major concern in working out the agreement was what would be regarded as "material," and thus requiring filing of the agreement with the SEC.
>
> In another patent infringement mediation, the settlement agreement had to be disclosed to the infringer's insurer.
>
> In yet another mediation, taxes on future payments had to be approved by foreign tax authorities. The basis for the payments was to be the settlement agreement, which would have to be disclosed to the tax authorities.

b. Mediator's Qualifications

A mediator's qualifications are the subject of debate in the IP world. Familiarity with the nuances of the matter at issue is, of course, helpful. But is it a sine qua non? Given the legal and technology complexities of such mediation, we could argue that familiarity is required.

Often, the intellectual property mediator (and thus the mediation process) will benefit from familiarity with the law, procedures, and jargon peculiar to the IP world. "Markman" hearings are unique to U.S. patent infringement actions. "Prosecution estoppel" and the "doctrine of equivalents" are unique to U.S. patent prosecution. The role of the Court of Appeals for the Federal Circuit, and that court's track record, are usually material to patent mediations. How "likelihood of confusion" is measured and established at trial of a trademark infringement action is a sensitive matter. What is incontestable about an "incontestable" U.S. trademark registration is not always straightforward.

If the parties are well informed and well advised, and if they need evaluation from the mediator, a mediator's familiarity with IP issues will be necessary. If the principal role of the mediator is to herd cats, calm damaged feelings, help business objectivity replace emotion, and assist parties to learn to talk with another, a person skilled in managing human relations is likely to be required.

Comediation may answer issues as to appropriate qualifications. The parties and their counsel may agree on a skilled process mediator and a skilled IP professional to work together. This can work, but the parties, their counsel, and the mediators must understand that relationship complexities may increase exponentially. The two mediators must learn to work together in a seamless and productive manner. Each mediator must develop a relationship of trust and respect with each participant. It is best if the two mediators are both present at every joint meeting or conversation and private caucus or conference, because it is likely to complicate communication if a mediator confers alone with one party (or both) at one point and the other mediator confers alone with another party on another occasion. Any perceived advantage of having all parties fully occupied in meetings with a mediator is easily offset by the need for the mediators to coordinate, compare notes, and understand each other's interpretation of what has happened to date. For example, it is hardly likely that in every situation each mediator will draw the same inferences or retain the same impressions as another mediator in the same situation.

c. Communication and Culture

IP disputes are often transnational, embracing people of different cultural backgrounds and different language skills. We see time and again how culture and language limitations fundamentally affect ways of thinking about the world, and thus limit the ability of parties from disparate backgrounds to communicate. The parties may be well equipped to communicate about scientific issues, through numbers and symbols and even the English language. However IP issues are nuanced, because rights are viewed differently in different countries (and even in different companies from the same country). Right and wrong may be viewed differently. Common sense for one person may be nonsense to another.

Interpreters and translators may be necessary, but in cross-cultural IP mediation, it is often difficult to determine whether interpreters are translating correctly, adding their own shadings, omitting significant parts, or simply negotiating with other interpreters. This taxes the mediator's active listening, empathetic listening, looping, and reframing skills.

G. B. Shaw surely had intellectual property mediation in mind when he said, "The greatest single problem with communication is the illusion it has occurred."

4. Intellectual Property Mediation Works

The lessons learned from hundreds of IP mediations include—(1) thorough preparation is crucial, and (2) no matter how bitter the feelings at the outset or how deep the despair at apparent impasse, parties of goodwill, with a real need to control their destinies and not hand over the futures of their businesses to the expensive crap-shoot called U.S. litigation, will almost always be able to create and claim value in a manner that meets everyone's interests and at least equals each side's no-agreement alternative. This does not happen in every IP dispute, but when it does, all parties have won.

Chapter **16**

Environmental Contamination Disputes

Carmin C. Reiss

1. Characteristics of Environmental Contamination Disputes

This chapter focuses on the mediation of environmental contamination disputes, one segment of the broader world of environmental dispute resolution. These disputes arise chiefly from the pollution of land and water. The issues involved include how to choose the remedy, allocate the cost, and compensate those affected. Typically, environmental contamination disputes are legal disputes, subject to binding resolution through the state and federal courts. Related types of disputes, involving environmental insurance, personal injury arising out of contamination, or professional liability alleged against environmental consultants, are often in the background.

The world of environmental dispute resolution beyond the limitations of this chapter is varied indeed, including land and natural resource utilization disputes (for example, fishing rights), facility siting controversies (landfills and nuclear waste facilities), negotiated rule making (drinking water quality standards), environmental impact controversies (design and construction of massive public transportation projects), permitting (expansion of a hazardous waste operation), and environmental justice controversies (disproportionate impact of environmental harms and hazards upon minority and low-income communities). These controversies are often capable of binding global resolution only through the political process. At least some of the affected parties may be stakeholders without standing, possessed of a political voice and perhaps economic power, but few legal rights.

What differentiates environmental contamination disputes from other controversies? The disputes are like the contamination itself: not readily confined or defined in time or space, tangled and uncertain in history, multiple and varied in their impact on numerous parties, subject to constant movement and change in character horizontally and vertically, plagued with scientific and economic uncertainty, subject to regulatory change, governed by unsettled legal principles, expensive, high risk, and a seemingly unavoidable part of doing business.

Disputes over environmental contamination require people to make expensive decisions based on what they do not know ("How many meters down into acres of bedrock does the aging plume of spilled solvents go?"), what they cannot reliably predict ("Will vacuum extraction reduce the contaminants to maximum allowable concentrations within ten years?"), what they cannot explain ("How is the contamination getting to the other side of the stream if the dye test shows no hydrological connection, and why does only well #1 sporadically show high levels of pollutants?"), and what they do not remember and cannot reconstruct ("What type of solvent did we use in the manufacturing process from 1952 through 1973, how much did we use, and what did we do with spent solvent?").

Multiple uncertainties on facts and science, exacerbated by a retroactive liability scheme, distinguish environmental contamination disputes from other types of cases, such as construction or product liability, where the factual and scientific parameters are usually better defined. The great number of unsettled legal issues also sets these disputes apart. ("What is the appropriate measure of damage to property due to pollution?" "Do parties sued not by the federal government but by other private parties receive contribution protection if they settle directly with the government?" "Can such plaintiffs recover lawyer's fees?") Another defining characteristic is the regular spawning of related horizontal (for example, among contributors to a landfill or neighbors in an industrial park) and vertical (for example, between successors in interest, clients and consultants, policy holders and insurers) claims. Finally, because of the combined effects of factual and scientific uncertainty, unsettled law, multiplicity of parties, and spawning of related claims, contamination disputes carry very high transaction costs (lawyers, experts, and company personnel).

From the mediator's perspective, these typical characteristics present some daunting obstacles to settlement. However, they also mean that the average contamination dispute is far removed from the "zero-sum" situation in which the mediator can only work with the parties to divide up a fixed pie. The environmental mediator is likely to find significant opportunities to create value and maximize joint gain, as will be discussed later.

2. Common Obstacles to Settlement in Environmental Contamination Disputes

The obstacles to settlement encountered in environmental contamination disputes include the same types of process, psychological, and merits issues that arise in other kinds of cases. And, as is also true in other contexts, any single dispute will most likely have multiple barriers. However, some settlement obstacles are particularly common, if not unique, to environmental contamination disputes; these are discussed in this section.

a. Process Issues

Settlement authority

Settlement authority issues are particularly important in an environmental contamination dispute. Real or affected limitations on authority are more likely to crop up as an obstacle to settlement in cases in which there are vertical disputes (for example, predecessor and successor liability claims, insurance disputes) and multiple parties, because of the frequently accompanying tendency of some parties to try to become "free-riders," the large dollars at stake, or the need to consider in-kind exchanges (for example, indemnification agreements, performance of work) in order to put together a settlement package.

In addition, it may not be possible, especially when dealing with parties with highly structured decision-making mechanisms such as governmental units or agencies, large corporations, or insurance companies, for a mediator to solve potential authority problems by securing the presence of the real decision makers at the table. Even so, the mediator should do her best to ensure that, consistent with institutional limitations, the people at the table have levels of authority commensurate with the stakes involved and that there is parity of representation among the parties.

One often useful approach is to hold a pre-mediation meeting or conference call and have each party identify its mediation representative, describe his position, and explain the party's final decision-making process and timetable. Each party will be committed at least in a moral sense by what it has represented. In addition, any problems or disparities in authority will become apparent, and the mediator can address them privately.

The free rider

The free rider phenomenon, generally seen in multiparty cases, is almost inevitable in large environmental contamination disputes. One or more of the parties alleged to have contributed to contamination will try to position itself as a small player, and then take a "free ride" on the coat-tails of those forced forward as the big players. Sometimes a party's claim to small-player status is based on lesser liability or culpability. ("They sent PCBs; we just sent empty, nontoxic paint cans." "They ran the service station for ten years longer than we did and may have altered their inventory records to hide product losses.") Sometimes the small-player claim is based on a lesser ability to pay. ("The other defendants are a big oil company and a *Fortune* 500 company; we're just a 'mom and pop' enterprise.")

The free rider phenomenon is a challenge to the mediator. It affects not only the availability of resources for an ultimate settlement, but also the mediation process itself. The rider may, for example, lobby for process parameters that validate its small-player status and deflect attention. ("We already have enough information on our historical involvement with the site—let's concentrate on remedy and damage" or "What's really necessary here is some litigation risk education for the Big Player"), while other parties insist that the rider is not a small player at all. Once engaged in the process, the rider may be the least candid and most intransigent party with which the mediator must work—hanging back, resisting analysis of its litigation exposure, repeating a refrain ("We can't afford to pay another nickel" or "We don't belong in this case"), and holding out for the smallest settlement share. Such an attitude can undermine the commitment of other parties to the mediation process and become a serious obstacle to settlement. The other participants will, at a minimum, resent the rider and express real or feigned outrage over its behavior. They may condition their movements toward settlement on some action by the rider, or may demand that the mediator deliver certain messages or take particular steps to deal with the rider.

The key in designing and managing process in the free rider situation is to strike a balance, and perhaps even more importantly, to make the parties feel that a fair balance has been struck, between the big-player and the small-player views of the principles that should govern the conduct of the mediation. The big-player view is that everyone has high risk, broad exposure, and enormous legal and expert fees in an environmental contamination dispute; no one should be allowed to hide; every party should pay its fair share. The small-player view is that the high clean-up costs and expansive process requirements are driven by the big players; the small players should not be asked to bear a disproportionate share of the process (cost, time, and effort) or the ultimate settlement. Although there is no formula that will work in every mediation, there are some possible approaches a mediator can keep in mind.

At the outset, if there is disagreement among the parties as to the categorization of players as big and small, there may be a need for a limited, carefully defined information exchange to form the basis for a consensus. Parties that object to an information exchange must be reminded of the need to get basic information on the table in order to make settlement possible and of the unattractiveness of their litigation alternatives. Dismissals and grants of summary judgment are rare in environmental contamination disputes, and no party is likely to avoid discovery. Alternatively, it may be possible for the mediator to facilitate agreement on a pragmatic working arrangement to allow the process to go forward, and negotiations to begin. ("We'll accept for now No Money Corp.'s representation that it has no money and agree that there is no point in developing information about its liability, but any settlement will have to be contingent upon review of its financial situation.") The mediator can question the parties, on a confidential basis, to avoid a working arrangement likely to prove completely unjustified later and thus to derail settlement discussions far down the track.

Once the process is under way, the mediator should probe regularly for frustration levels that may threaten the process and be prepared to change the management of the process or to persuade the parties to make process adjustments to address rising frustration. It may be appropriate, for example, to separate out one or more small players and reserve negotiations with them until the participants in the main event have assembled the major building blocks of a settlement. Or it may be appropriate well into the mediation process for the parties to agree to an exchange of information or the briefing of a legal argument narrowly focused on the exposure of a party asserting that it is a small player.

The mediator should keep in mind the value of simple acknowledgment of the legitimacy of different points of view. ("You're a small fish caught in a big net here, and I understand completely what the legal and mediation fees mean for a company of your size." Or "You're perceived as a 'deep pocket' and I understand that, as a matter of principle and economics, you can't settle claims on the basis of that perception.") In these cases, as in others, the party that feels "heard" is far more likely to trust the mediator, to regard the mediation process as one that addresses its needs and interests, and thus to fully engage itself in the process.

b. Psychological Issues

It might be concluded that, because they typically involve business-people, business decisions, scientific issues, and money, environmental contamination disputes are probably unlikely to present much in the way of psychological barriers to settlement. Not so. For example, "sticker shock" (that is, paralysis or a refusal to deal in the face of an astonishing clean-up price tag) is an often-encountered barrier to settlement. Disbelief and indignation upon confrontation with the retroactive liability scheme under CERCLA[1] and its various state counterparts is another familiar psychological barrier. Take, for example, the manufacturer asked by the state and federal governments to make a seven-figure contribution to the cleanup of a solvent recovery or drum recycling site that held a state license for many years. How, it asks, can it possibly be legal or fair for the manufacturer to be given a huge bill after what it sees as ten years of failures by the regulators?

Different attitudes among the parties toward contamination may also form a barrier to settlement. It is not unusual to hear a commercial property owner insist that despite its connection to the municipal water supply, it is entitled to have its property clean enough to drink the water beneath the ground, while the accused source of the contamination insists that every commercial property in an industrialized area has some level of contamination and that, relative to other problems, this one is not worthy of attention.

Part of the mediator's job is to identify and diffuse psychological barriers through confidential discussion and the setting of process parameters. The mediator must allow the party afflicted with sticker shock the opportunity to probe the reality and veracity of the sticker, the opportunity to vent outrage, a vehicle for exploring possibilities for bringing the price down (for example, identification of less costly alternative technologies), and some time to adjust. A mediator experienced in environmental law can, at the right moment, help the disbelieving party or the inexperienced lawyer appropriately reevaluate alternatives, by providing both some empathy and a reality check on the workings of the environmental liability scheme. The mediator can give the manufacturer that has tried to be a good corporate citizen acknowledgment of its efforts and good intentions, sympathy with its perceptions of unfair treatment, and some discussion about the legislative policy decisions that have led to its current position. In these ways, mindsets can be changed.

---

1. The Comprehensive Environmental Response, Compensation, and Liability Act, 42 U.S.C. §9601 et seq.

Perhaps most importantly, the mediator can help the parties look for ways to address their attitudes or interests in the context of settlement. For example, the homeowners concerned about potential family health impacts of contamination levels deemed acceptable under state regulations may need to have this concern addressed in order to agree to a settlement (for example, through a commitment to pay for medical checkups over time), even though they know they are unlikely to recover for this concern in litigation. These types of issues will often be more important to a resolution than the parties realize.

c. Disagreement over Scientific Issues

It is not uncommon for environmental disputes to present hotly contested scientific issues requiring expert testimony. Such an issue may be determinative on liability, allocation of responsibility, selection of remedy, or calculation of damages. For example, an oil company may argue that product "finger-printing" has identified an oil additive that it never used and thus proves that the oil in the ground belongs to someone else. A past operator of a plant may perform a "fate and transport" analysis to show that chemical leaks during its long-past watch have now naturally attenuated or biodegraded, thus demonstrating that the current owner bears the primary responsibility. Field x-rays (a technology for delineation of ledge borrowed from oil drillers) may be used in an effort to chart a "plume" of contamination—information that may be relevant on source of contamination or choice of remedy. Or the plaintiff's expert and the expert hired by a group of defendants may advocate radically different approaches to cleanup.

If a scientific issue is a primary obstacle to settlement, the mediator should encourage the parties to involve their respective experts in the process, either indirectly through exchange of reports or letters or directly through presentation or presence at the mediation session. The informality and confidentiality of the mediation process allows an opportunity for a beneficial direct interaction between experts that may be unavailable otherwise. Experts in the same field speak the same language and will typically get better information from each other faster than even the best-tutored lawyer. They belong to a scientific community with a tradition of peer review and thus often tend to moderate their views in each other's presence, thus narrowing the gap between their positions. When the experts are brought together, there is also a potential for joint problem solving, going so far as an actual teaming of opposing experts to develop additional data and solve technical problems.

Litigators may resist the involvement of experts in a mediation process because they fear that a loss of trial advantage will result from giving the opposition a direct opportunity to question its expert. This is a variant of the usual litigator's tension: to litigate successfully (which I may have to do later), I should hold my cards close to the vest, but to mediate successfully (which my client would like to do), I should lay my cards on the table. There can be little doubt that parties are more likely to reach settlement if they have more information about their alternatives. If a dispute centers around a scientific issue, the persuasiveness of the other side's expert, personally and analytically, is key in evaluating the likely outcome at trial. If a party has a strong expert, it will negotiate a better resolution if it shows him off. If a party declines to bring its expert, the other parties may conclude that the expert is weak and evaluate their litigation alternatives accordingly. If a technical issue is key, the parties are almost always best advised to involve their experts in the mediation process.

d. Disagreement over Allocation among Defendants

Allocation disputes in the environmental contamination arena range from the two-party problem (for example, how the present and former owners of the same manufacturing facility should divide the cost to clean up contamination caused by both of them) to the two-hundred-plus–party problem (for example, how the 175 trash generators and 25 trash haulers should divide the cost to clean up a contaminated landfill).

With small numbers of parties and relatively straightforward allocation issues (for example, how much of the single contaminant was released during the first party's watch and how much during the second party's watch), it is possible for the mediator to work with everyone simultaneously in the same process. In disputes involving larger numbers of parties or thornier allocation issues (for example, many facility owners, decades of operations, changes in activities over time, missing records, and various cross-indemnification agreements), it may be necessary for the mediator to break the mediation up into separate phases (for example, dealing first with the plaintiff and all the defendants as a group, next with allocation among the direct defendant generators, and last with allocation among the third-party generators) and to work with a comediator or an assistant.

Phasing

There is no rule of thumb on how to phase mediation of an unwieldy allocation problem. There does need to be a consensus among the parties that phasing the process is the right thing to do and that a particular manner of phasing (whether suggested by the mediator or by the parties themselves) is a sensible way to proceed. There also needs to be flexibility, with the mediator and the parties prepared to make adjustments in the order of the process as new information comes forward and new developments take place. Factors to keep in mind in developing an approach include:

○ *Interest groups.* (Is there a big-player group? A de minimis group? A group of municipalities? transporters? schools or public institutions?)

○ *Degree of prior group organization.* (Are some parties organized into a well-functioning group and others not?)

○ *Parties' relative levels of information development and prior involvement with the site.* (Are some parties brand new PRPs [potentially responsible parties]? Have some parties been cooperating with the government for some time? Has a particular group already spent substantial money?)

○ *Activities in the field.* (Is there a remedial investigation/feasibility study about to be undertaken? Are there immediate opportunities for participation in cleanup decisions or joint gains in reduction of cost?)

○ *Status of government enforcement activities.* (Is the government about to commence litigation or issue an order? Has it already settled or is it about to settle for portions of investigation or work? Is there a litigation timetable?)

○ *Time requirements for work on various aspects of an overall resolution.* (How long will it take for an information exchange among parties new to the site? How many meetings with the municipalities will be necessary? How much realistically can the mediator accomplish in a given time?)

In considering these factors, the mediator may discover, for example, an immediate opportunity for shifting responsibility for work in the field that could offer substantial cost savings benefiting all parties. Such a chance for joint gain could be the cornerstone for a broad settlement. It would demand that the mediation be structured to put the necessary parties into a dialogue on transferring control of the work at the earliest possible time, with work on other damage claims or allocation issues to take place simultaneously or to be deferred. The mediator may learn that the information needs of one particular group will require more time to meet than those of others, thus dictating that allocation efforts within that group be taken up later in the process.

Comediation

Working with a comediator on a large allocation dispute is an excellent idea. It is challenging if not impossible for a single mediator to maintain the level of accessibility and regular communication with all parties the process requires to succeed. It is also difficult for a single mediator to have a finger on the pulse of every party in a large group, to anticipate every problem likely to be encountered, and to work with individual parties on collateral issues (for example, successor liability or indemnification or insurance disputes) that may affect ability to settle. There may be a benefit in working with a comediator of a different background (for example, a lawyer may wish to work with an environmental engineer or accountant), depending on the obstacles to settlement expected to be encountered. And, of course, two heads are better than one when it comes to brainstorming about solutions to various obstacles to settlement, giving evaluative feedback, and supplying the level of energy to the process necessary to keep all the parties engaged.

Allocation versus mediation

Often, parties to an allocation dispute will want a neutral collection and analysis of data on relative contributions to the site, resulting in a nonbinding allocation of responsibility among the parties, in order to reach a settlement. (This "number crunching" exercise is typically referred to as "an allocation.") The skills necessary to perform an allocation are not the same skills necessary to mediate a dispute over allocation.

An allocation takes on a life of its own once it is circulated and can be either an impetus or an obstacle to settlement, depending on how it is viewed by the parties. An allocation generally perceived as internally consistent, free of obvious errors, based on all key information, sound in its working assumptions, and reasonably fair in its principles may move the parties much closer to settlement. An allocation oppositely perceived, which leans heavily toward some to the benefit of others, may lock the parties into adversarial positions and prevent settlement. An allocation is probably most valuable to the parties when there has been the maximum possible consensus in advance on the data to be obtained, the methods of collection, the handling of the inevitable gaps, the assumptions to be used in analysis (for example, whether dumpsters are assumed to have been full when delivered to the landfill), and the principles to be observed in developing the nonbinding allocation of responsibility among the parties (for example, whether parties that sent PCBs should be assessed a greater share of responsibility for overall clean-up costs).

Although the parties may benefit from building an allocation into the mediation process, they probably do not want the mediator to develop it. Allocations tend to be provocative and often result in some or all of the parties being critical of and angry with the allocator. If the allocation itself becomes an obstacle to settlement, the individual who created it probably cannot help the parties get past it. An exception to the presumption against the mediator serving as allocator might be made for a process in which the neutral first endeavors to facilitate a resolution and then, only if agreement is not achieved, offers a nonbinding allocation of responsibility as a last-ditch attempt to push the parties to resolution. This approach to incorporating an allocation in the process will be workable in many situations, but not when the parties regard the gathering and analysis of liability information in a matrix format as a necessary precondition to settlement discussion, as they often do at large Superfund sites.

Chapter 17

Mega-Disputes and Class Actions

Eric D. Green

1. Why Mediation of Mega-Cases is Different

Mediation has outgrown its origins in family, community, and small claims courts and has achieved ubiquity in American civil litigation over the past 25 years. As a result, there is an increased effort to utilize it even in the most complex, difficult, lengthy, and high-stakes legal disputes. Mediation is now being attempted regularly in class actions, multidistrict litigation, mass torts, bankruptcy, antitrust, multiparty construction, intellectual property, and financial fraud cases. These cases present major challenges, not only for the disputants and their lawyers but also for the neutrals who must manage them. The traditional models developed for routine disputes requiring a passive and detached judge and a nonevaluative mediator need to be replaced by a more expansive and flexible paradigm to accommodate mega-cases.

What do I mean by *mega-cases*, and why are they different for purposes of mediation from routine cases? Millions (or billions) of dollars in dispute, dozens or hundreds of parties, simultaneous litigation in multiple jurisdictions (including cross-border), long durations, and legal fees and expenses reaching eight or nine figures are now common. Managing and resolving these mega-cases requires a very different approach and set of tools than the typical cases that mediators deal with on a daily basis.

Every case is unique and important to the disputants. Mega-cases are "uniquely unique." What special challenges do mega-cases commonly present? First, the underlying subject matter often involves complicated, cutting-edge knowledge or technology, such as application programming interfaces and communications protocols for operating system software; client/server interoperability; or the effect of magnesium stearate excipient and a few millimeters of polymer coating on the rate of decay for time-release pharmaceutical delivery. Few mediators are knowledgeable in the fields relevant to such issues.

Second, these cases also often involve specialized, some would say "esoteric," subject matter that is beyond the normal encounter of the generalist lawyer, judge, or mediator but is intellectual putty in the hands of the high-powered legal experts retained by the parties who tend to dominate the particular field. These boutique legal powerhouses are all too willing to bedazzle the poor mediator with finely honed discourse, sprinkled with leading cases known to the cognoscenti. Few judges or mediators are masters of these many different legal spheres.

Third, in many mega-cases, mathematics, statistics, and economics are important; economists and other technical experts are often heavily involved. The mediator has to deal with these experts, which usually consists mostly of listening to them or plowing through their reports. Even if a mediator can get up to third gear (or can fake it) on the underlying subject matter and governing legal doctrine, making sense of the experts is often more difficult. Of course, the parties always present these experts as objective and independent. They are typically introduced with the sermon about being retained for their independence no matter which way the chips may fall. Rarely, if ever, do the chips fall on the other side.

Fourth, the stakes are very high, often in the hundreds of millions or even billions of dollars. Sometimes, however, the risk is virtually unquantifiable, as when major structural or conduct remedies are at issue. This means that cases often take on a "bet the business" intensity that changes normal disputing and settlement dynamics. For one thing, the heavy hitters of each party come to bat, with judicial outcomes and settlement possibilities influenced and handicapped by their big reputations and commensurately big egos.

Fifth, most mega-cases involve multiple parties with complicated and diverse interests, even among the participants nominally on the same side. For example, consider an antitrust mediation involving many separate cases consolidated before a multidistrict litigation judge. The plaintiffs may consist of a class of direct purchasers, individual direct purchasers who opted out of the class, a class of indirect purchasers, and individual indirect purchasers or opt-outs commonly including state attorneys general. On the other side of the *"v"* are the various alleged conspirators in their spun-off, resold, acquired, and combined afterlives. Further, it is not uncommon for there to be differences of opinion even within the individual parties, or among their representatives for that matter. Coalition breakdown on one or both sides of the case can create particularly sensitive problems when it occurs among plaintiffs' lawyers, *Fortune* 100 companies, or worse, sovereigns.

In addition to the extra challenges unique to mega-cases, the mediator must recognize and overcome all of the usual barriers to settlement present in the typical simple bilateral mediation. These obstacles can include communication failures, wrong participants, lack of necessary information, extrinsic linkages, bad timing, inaccurate assessment of the likely legal outcome, lack of resources, and poor negotiation skills.

Why do lawyers, parties, and judges believe that mediation could possibly help in these cases? Mega-cases seem impossible to mediate, but often these cases are resolved—sometimes partially, sometimes completely. Experience with several of these cases suggests that the key to successful mediation of the mega-case is a deep respect for, and understanding of, the *roles* that those present at and absent from the table must take on, and a willingness to adapt those roles to the specific demands of the case, even if this means departing from conventional mediation wisdom. Fortunately, mediation is a wonderfully flexible process that can be adapted to almost any situation, including the mega, complex, multiparty case. However, structuring a mediation for these cases requires an appreciation by the parties, their counsel, and the mediator of the roles that each of them must play.

Sometimes too much deference to the various players at the wrong time can be fatal to resolution. The mediator must exercise process leadership throughout and be ready to step in to help when experts, lawyers, or parties are on the wrong track for settlement and need to be led back. In particular situations, the mediator must recognize the potential need for judicial involvement, the appropriate level and the risk of the timing of involvement, and the means and methods of actually using the judge so as to obtain the greatest benefit at the least risk to the judicial process.

Opportunities abound. For example, in the telephone equipment Sherman antitrust cases *(Bell Atlantic Corp. v. AT&T Corp.)*, the mediator had an opportunity to work alongside some of the most creative and skilled businesspeople and negotiators in crafting significant win–win commercial deals. Mediation facilitated the creation of joint gains that would continue to flow both to the parties and to the consuming public for many years.

Unfortunately not all complex cases lend themselves to this kind of joint gains, facilitative mediation that results in textbook outcomes, even in the antitrust area. There is a great deal of variance in antitrust mediation issues, structure, and dynamics. For example, a group of vitamin price-fixing cases *(Bristol-Myers Squibb Co. v. Teva Pharmaceuticals USA, Inc.)* involved purely dollars, and the mediation challenge in those cases was handling the problems created by having a multitude of parties, on both sides of the case, with different viewpoints and sharply differing damages analyses. Some cases present both large dollar issues and structural, behavioral, or commercial issues to negotiate. For example, the telephone equipment antitrust cases (mentioned above) were not purely about dollars; they cried out for a settlement that dealt with the manner in which the equipment suppliers and the phone companies would do business in the future. Antitrust cases involving credit card merchants and issues *(Wal-Mart Stores, Inc. v. VISA U.S.A. Inc.)* presented claims totaling billions of dollars but even more significant behavioral issues. On the other hand, *United States v. Microsoft Corp.* involved no dollars but immense structural and behavioral issues, while the follow-up private actions against Microsoft involved both large money claims and commercial arrangements. These case variances, among others, require a great deal of mediation flexibility and adaptability. It is useful to understand the specific obstacles to settlement that these cases posed in order to better understand the importance of structuring the roles of the participants in each mediation to meet the particular needs of a specific case.

2. Facilitating Roles

United States et al. v. Microsoft

The Microsoft antitrust enforcement action brought by the Department of Justice (DOJ) and joined by more than 20 states is a good example of how careful attention to roles in complex mediation is critical to success. On May 18, 1998, the United States filed a civil antitrust case against Microsoft, alleging that the company had restrained competition in violation of the Sherman Act. On the same day, 20 states and the District of Columbia filed a similar complaint, and the court consolidated the cases at Microsoft's request.

Microsoft was and is the world's largest supplier of software for personal computers; its Windows operating system has overwhelming monopoly power in the market for Intel-compatible personal computer operating systems. Microsoft also dominates the market for many software applications, most notably with its Office suite of products, which includes Word, Excel, and PowerPoint. In the mid-1990s, as the Internet became more and more important, Microsoft engaged in robust competition (to say the least) over control of this critical technology, heavily promoting its Internet Explorer browser against Netscape Navigator and other products. Competitors and some public officials believed that Microsoft crossed the line between lawful and unlawful competitive behavior in many ways. However, the lawsuit was controversial from the start; some antitrust experts contended that it should never have been brought because it penalized the most successful innovator of the silicon age for its success while ultimately hurting consumers. Others maintained that the case was the most important antitrust enforcement action since the original telephone system cases.

The essence of the complaint was that Microsoft unlawfully maintained its operating system monopoly by engaging in a variety of exclusionary, anticompetitive, and predatory acts in violation of the Sherman Act: in particular, to monopolize the market for Web browsers. They also argued that some actions taken by Microsoft as part of its attempt to protect its operating system monopoly, such as tying Internet Explorer to its operating system, constituted unreasonable restraints on competition.

The case was first tried in the District Court for the District of Columbia. After the district court entered its findings of fact, but before it entered its conclusions of law, a four-month attempt at court-ordered mediation before Judge Richard Posner failed to produce a settlement. The district court ultimately concluded that Microsoft had violated the Sherman Act. However, the appellate court affirmed in part, reversed in part, and vacated the Final Judgment against Microsoft that (discussed below). In addition, the trial judge who had made the initial findings of fact and conclusions of law was disqualified for serious judicial misconduct during the trial, and the case was remanded to the district court, where it was reassigned to a new judge for further proceedings.

The decision of the appellate court had a profound impact on the case that was never completely appreciated by the anti-Microsoft crowd. The appellate court affirmed the district court's finding that Microsoft had monopoly power as well as the conclusion that Microsoft had illegally maintained its operating system monopoly. The appellate court also agreed with the district court that Microsoft had engaged in a variety of exclusionary acts designed to protect its operating system monopoly.

The appellate court also, however, reversed and remanded some of the district court's rulings. Most significantly, the appellate court vacated the district court's judgment breaking up Microsoft and remanded the case for further proceedings. This ruling dramatically changed the posture of the case. Consequently, upon remand, all the plaintiffs (federal and state) stated that they no longer intended to pursue a structural remedy—that is, breaking Microsoft up. The appellate court's decision, and the reconfiguration of the case by the plaintiffs in response to that decision, significantly changed the nature of the proceedings.

In late September 2001, the new judge, Judge Colleen Kollar-Kotelly, met with the parties and entered a scheduling order that strongly encouraged them to try to settle the case. The original scheduling conference had been set for September 11, 2001, but had been postponed because of the terrorist attacks on the United States that day. Judge Kollar-Kotelly referred to the events of September 11 as making the benefits that would be derived from a quick resolution of the case "increasingly significant." However, the parties did not think that more mediation would be particularly helpful in light of their prior unsuccessful mediation experience with Judge Posner. Instead, they requested an opportunity to explore settlement through face-to-face negotiations. Judge Kollar-Kotelly acquiesced to this request and gave the parties two weeks to try to reach a negotiated resolution. Despite intense efforts, the parties could not make much progress. Accordingly, the parties reported to the court that their own negotiation attempts had failed and asked the court to appoint me as the mediator. The judge entered an order giving us three weeks to reach a settlement, after which she would move the case forward along the litigation track. A mere three weeks to settle such a complex case seemed a nearly impossible task. I immediately sought reinforcements in the form of a comediator, Jonathan Marks.

The mediation sessions were intense, protracted, detailed, and difficult. All three parties (Microsoft, the federal government, and the states) participated fully. The mediation consisted of joint-facilitated negotiation and drafting sessions, usually with four or five representatives from each side at the table; some ex parte caucuses between mediators and party representatives; some direct discussions between representatives of some or all of the parties (with and without the mediators); and time-outs for frequent consultations between the parties' mediation representatives and other members of their organizations.

Like all tough mediations, the process had its ups and downs—two steps forward, one step back. Slow progress was made until a compromise was reached on a critical issue over which the parties had been at impasse. Ironically, this key issue was not even in the original case that had been brought by the government. It emerged much later in the settlement negotiations because the ways in which people used computers and software changed over the course of the litigation. The mediation problem was that Microsoft, not surprisingly, took the position that any settlement should not concern itself with issues that were not formally in the case. However, as a very practical matter, considering how technology had evolved, this issue had become an important interest for the governmental parties to address in any settlement. Finally, two days before the court-imposed deadline for mediation to conclude, the parties agreed that the settlement would address this issue. Some of the governmental parties saw Microsoft's concession on this issue as a major achievement. With this issue now resolved, the pace of negotiations on the remaining open issues rapidly accelerated. Settlement became imminent: each side now felt that it had achieved more than it might possibly obtain if the case went to judgment.

On the last day allowed for mediation, the mediators reported to the court that Microsoft, the United States, and most of the states had reached a settlement, which they presented to the court in the form of a Proposed Final Judgment. Nine states and the District of Columbia indicated that they did not agree to the Revised Proposed Final Judgment and would continue to litigate. Eventually the federal courts approved the settlement after full review and challenge by the nonsettling states.

Reflecting on the Microsoft mediation, one essential element of the process was that mediation could only succeed if the mediators focused on facilitating solutions to negotiating barriers and resisted the temptation to control everything and impress their own evaluation or solution on the parties. At the time of this mediation, nearly every academic and industry commentator had a view on the case—and sometimes it seemed as if they all had published them. It would be unrealistic for the mediators not to have formed some substantive opinions on the case and perhaps some views on how it should be resolved. But the mediation called for a much more complicated and nuanced facilitative role, in which the key to success was orchestrating the talents, interests, influences, and decisions of the many others involved in the case, rather than an evaluative, highly directive role. Stepping back from control of the mediation process in order to move forward with the process—renouncing power to have more power—was critical to success.

In the *Microsoft* case it was especially important that the mediators be flexible enough to know that they couldn't possibly contribute more than a tiny thimble of substance to the content of a settlement. Meeting management, agenda making, communication clearing, and fair presiding took priority over steering, evaluating, manipulating, and persuading. Most of all, the mediators understood that the only way the case would settle was if everyone played their proper role; only in that way could the barriers that had prevented settlement be overcome. In this respect, the mediators were fortunate to come into the case at a time when all of the other players necessary to reach a settlement were prepared to play their necessary roles. Timing is everything in mediation.

3. The Importance of Timing

Enron/Arthur Andersen

The *Enron/Andersen* case in some ways was even more of a challenge to mediate than the *Microsoft* case, but for different reasons. As was later reported, Jonathan Marks and I ultimately had to inform the court that, except for a settlement between the plaintiffs and Andersen Worldwide (Arthur Andersen's Swiss parent), the parties were at an impasse. The impasse was largely caused by the parties' inability to resolve some important issues created by the proportionate liability provision of the 1995 Private Securities Litigation Reform Act (PSLRA). In addition, by the time mediation started, Arthur Andersen had been indicted for obstruction of justice and was facing a criminal trial that clearly threatened its continued existence as a "Big Five" international accounting firm, as well as massive claims from many quarters for its audits of Enron and others. At the same time, its international components, tax, and consulting practices were either up for sale or withdrawing and making separate deals, while its captive insurance program itself faced insolvency.

If timing is everything in mediation, for *Enron/Andersen* the mediation effort was both too late and too early. The mediation effort was too late for Arthur Andersen, which was already fatally wounded by the government's indictment of the firm, and too early for the shareholder plaintiffs class—the class action lawyers' focus on the billions of dollars worth of claims against the investment banks virtually precluded a front-end settlement with Arthur Andersen, because it would be too risky under the PSLRA's proportionate fault, judgment reduction provision.

Enron/Andersen is an example of a situation in which legal and economic obstacles created a settlement barrier based on sequence or timing problems. These problems can be severe to the point of being unsolvable. In this case, these problems were partially overcome through a relatively minor settlement covering only the offshore Andersen Worldwide component. Unfortunately, the opportunity to resolve more of the case was lost.

More recently, and with great difficulty, we were able to find a potential solution to the PSLRA judgment reduction problem in mediating a settlement between the Enron creditors and shareholders on the one hand and the outside Enron officers and directors on the other hand. This settlement managed to preserve for settlement what remained of Enron's officers' and directors' liability insurance while at the same time providing for some personal contributions from defendants based on their sales of Enron stock—a fairly unusual attribute of securities class action outcomes. The lesson from this later settlement is that given enough and the right time, mediation can find a solution to nearly any problem.

The judge's role in the *Enron* mediation was to push hard for the appointment of a mediator, to keep as much pressure on the parties to settle as was consistent with a separate and detached judicial role, and to accommodate, where possible, the settlement process over an extended period of time. Sometimes, however, the judge's role has to be larger than it was in the *Microsoft* and *Enron* cases.

4. Judicial-Mediator Cooperation

MasterCard/Visa

The *MasterCard/Visa* antitrust case, which settled in May 2003, presents an interesting contrast to the mediation of the *Microsoft* and *Enron* cases. In many respects, the *MasterCard/Visa* case was more complex and difficult to settle. The issues at stake arguably affected even more people than those in the *Microsoft* case—everyone who uses a credit card or a debit card, the thousands of banks that issue them, and the millions of merchants that accept them. It involved a class action of 5 to 7 million merchants, big and small—such as Wal-Mart, Sears, Safeway, Circuit City, The Limited, and Bernie's Army-Navy Store—suing the credit card behemoths MasterCard International and Visa U.S.A. for allegedly violating antitrust laws by forcing retailers to accept their debit cards as a condition of being able to accept their credit cards—a classic tying arrangement according to the plaintiff class, with attempted monopolization counts thrown in for good measure. According to press reports and official filings, the eventual settlement of this case resulted in $3 billion in payment by MasterCard and Visa to the plaintiff class—a record-shattering amount for any antitrust settlement—as well as fundamental structural changes in the way the credit card companies do business, with potential economic ramifications for merchants and the bank members of the credit card companies far in excess of the amounts paid in monetary compensation.

The case was in litigation for years, one theater of battle in a war waged between consumers' and merchants' lawyers, public officials, and the banks and credit card companies over a little-understood but critical component of our economic system. The federal district judge in charge of the case encouraged the parties to discuss settlement and to consider mediation, but the parties remained so far apart in their assessments of the merits of the case that no significant settlement dialogue ensued until the final stages of pretrial preparation. At that point, the parties privately engaged in mediation. However, the legal differences were still so extreme and the stakes so huge that settlement seemed unlikely until the court ruled on a critical motion for partial summary judgment, dealing with market definition and monopoly power, three weeks before the trial was set to start. This judicial ruling was the necessary spark that ignited intense mediated settlement efforts, which continued almost uninterruptedly through jury selection and into the first week set for trial, eventually culminating in a settlement with MasterCard and, soon thereafter, with Visa. But the decision on the summary judgment motion alone was not enough to produce a settlement. The parties were still far apart, even after the court's ruling, primarily because of differing assessments of likely jury trial outcomes.

Unlike the *Microsoft* case, the trial judge in the *MasterCard/Visa* case, at the mediators' suggestion and with the parties' explicit consent, played a role in the mediated settlement discussions by hosting and participating in mediation sessions in the courthouse virtually around the clock, even on weekends and in the evenings. Given that there were no prior findings of fact or appellate opinions on the issues in the case, as there had been in the *Microsoft* case, the mediators understood that the impressions of the trial judge as a kind of "thirteenth juror," although tentative and subject to change after hearing the evidence, could be extremely valuable to the parties in assessing their no-agreement alternatives and hence their settlement positions. This was a role that no one—not even objective, experienced neutrals—could fill as well as the actual trial judge. It was the mediators' challenge to recognize this ingredient as the necessary catalyst to settlement and then to bring together the remaining parts of the mixture—the parties' legal advisors and trial lawyers, economics experts on damages, and the key principals necessary to make hard settlement decisions on both sides. Critically, the parties were willing to allow the trial judge to participate in the mediation in this manner and the trial judge was willing to do so. This mediator/judicial mediation partnership differed dramatically from the mediation structure in the *Microsoft* and *Enron* cases, and from the traditional mediation paradigm.

5. Science and Mediation

Toms River

The *Microsoft* case may have been greater in terms of public profile, but the *Toms River* childhood cancer mediation was in many respects a more significant mediation breakthrough and achievement. The residents of Toms River, New Jersey, had waged a lengthy and contentious battle against several corporations that allegedly had contaminated the groundwater (and hence the drinking water) and the air by releasing various chemicals from manufacturing facilities located in the town. Mass tort litigation ensued, involving thousands of plaintiffs seeking damages for personal injuries, medical monitoring, and property damage; there were also regulatory actions by state and federal environmental agencies. In the midst of this battle, 69 families with children who allegedly contracted cancer from chemical exposure banded together to find answers and seek redress. It would have been easy and conventional for the families to join one of the many lawsuits threatened (and later filed), or, for that matter, to start their own lawsuit. But despite their pain and anger and the ready availability of professional gladiators, they did not. Guided by an extraordinary team of highly capable and experienced plaintiffs' lawyers, the families instead decided that it was more important to try to find out what was really happening to their children and why, and that some process other than litigation would be more likely to provide those answers.

In the *Toms River* case, the families and the companies did not litigate, but they also did not enter into "mediation," at least not at first. Rather, the families and the companies decided to engage a neutral with experience and expertise in process design to help them think through what kind of process they should follow. The result of those discussions, again, was not mediation. Instead, the families and the companies decided to engage in a moderated scientific dialogue in which they each would bring the best knowledge they could obtain on subjects such as hydrology, drinking water distribution modeling, toxicology, epidemiology, occupational hygiene, childhood medicine, and public health. They agreed to conduct this scientific dialogue in a nonadversarial manner and to table any litigation that might throw the process off track. They also agreed to have the process moderated by a mediator who, for these purposes, was described not as a "mediator" but as the "Institutional Memory."

The scientific dialogue took place for about 12 total days spread out over several months. While the presentations by, and questioning of, various experts focused on tough scientific and factual issues and exposed expected sharp differences of opinion on transport, toxicity, and causation, the participants still managed to implement the scientific dialogue in the spirit in which it was conceived. In fact, the parties and lawyers who designed and engaged in the *Toms River* scientific dialogue were able to reverse the proportion of "heat" and "light" that usually obtains in such mass tort cases. Much was learned; much was acknowledged; and even though many differences remained, a much greater appreciation of the fundamental scientific and factual issues was obtained by all participants through a civil and respectful process.

But what then? What would this process produce beyond information and perhaps greater understanding? What would be the result for the families and the companies? What was the Institutional Memory's responsibility as far as guiding the participants to the next phase? The participants had not asked for mediation and had not agreed to engage in it. Did this mean they did not want it? Did this mean they did not need it? These questions needed answers. At the very least, the neutral serving as the Institutional Memory had to ask the questions and help the participants find the answers.

As the scientific dialogue entered its final sessions and neared conclusion, there was a slow turning of the wheel by the parties toward the possibility of a facilitated resolution under the auspices of the neutral, now finally shifting in his role from Institutional Memory to mediator.

Soon thereafter, settlement of the *Toms River* childhood cancer cases was reached relatively easily. How did this come about when the parties to the dispute initially could not even bring themselves to say they were engaging in dispute resolution? The reason was that from the start the process was grounded in the scientific information exchange that preceded actual mediation. When mediation came, the parties' first settlement proposals were based so much on the scientific exchange that they were immediately perceived as legitimate, coherent, and even elegant. When it became clear that both sides were operating with reciprocal reasonableness based on the scientific and technical information exchanged by the experts, the remaining differences between the parties were "bridgeable" through the use of conventional mediatory processes. Because no lawsuit had been filed, the only judicial involvement in the *Toms River* childhood cancer cases was the shadow of law.

In the *Toms River* cases, the participants overcame the low odds of success because the scientific process created positive momentum and goodwill, which carried them through the transition from dialogue to resolution. Incrementally, the mediator introduced suggestions and steps that might lead to a resolution growing integrally out of the scientific process. When these suggestions were positively received, the foundation was laid for more conventional mediatory procedures that ultimately led to a complete global resolution of all the childhood cancer cases, utilizing a methodology founded on the scientific dialogue in which the participants had so strongly invested. Once the parties entered the conventional mediation phase of the process, resolution was almost inevitable.

6. The Evolving Role of the Judge in Complex Mediation

The most interesting lesson from these complex mediations is how far commercial civil mediation has come in the past 25 years—from a novel, pioneering, and radical idea welcomed by only a few innovative senior counsel to the dispute resolution mechanism of choice in nearly all of the most significant cases of our time. As these cases demonstrate, mediation is a flexible and powerful tool capable of resolving even the seemingly impossible dispute. The process has shown a remarkable adaptability to the various demands of individual cases, responding to the needs and expectations of each contextual environment.

In particular, based on the experiences described in these and other mega-cases, as well as conversations with mediators and judges wrestling with similar kinds of disputes, the conventional wisdom about the mediator's and the judge's roles in mediation requires reassessment. According to the conventional wisdom, there should always be a firm wall between mediation and the court that judges should not cross, except perhaps to encourage or appoint a mediator. This fossilization is unfortunate; as we gain experience in applying mediatory techniques to mega-cases, we should take advantage of the variety of roles that judges and mediators can and should play to meet the particular needs of specific cases.

Judges need to consider playing a much more active role in the mediation of mega-cases than has generally been thought appropriate. Mega-cases often require specialized case management plans custom-tailored to the particular dispute, rather than the standard orders entered automatically in typical cases. Likewise, these cases often require that the judge be prepared to engage more aggressively in settlement activities—from suggesting mediation to encouraging, ordering, managing, and even engaging in mediation. This does not mean that a presiding judge should actually attempt to be the sole mediator in the case, as most judges are neither prepared nor inclined to take on this role (although there are notable exceptions). Nor is it to suggest that judges should feel free to engage in mediation without careful consideration of appropriate ethical constraints and rules of good practice. But within well-defined rules designed to protect the integrity of the adjudicatory process and the perception of unbiased courts, judges can and should play a much more active and positive mediatory role in mega-cases, working in conjunction with professional mediators.

As a team, a nonjudicial mediator (selected by the parties or appointed by the court) and a judge can often complement each other. Together, they supply more of the ingredients needed to help the parties in a mega-case evaluate dispute resolution options and implement them in a well-informed and efficient manner. Teamwork between a mediator and the judge can be synergistic because certain settlement tasks are better allocated to the mediator—for example, organizing and meeting with the disputants; orienting participants to the settlement process; identifying interests and options; conducting multiple, joint, and ex parte settlement meetings; fixing communication problems; and facilitating the early- and mid-stage offer–exchange process.

Other tasks may require the judge's involvement and can be better accomplished by a jurist willing to engage actively in the settlement process. Most importantly, after the mediator has received the parties' permission, the judge can provide informal and nonbinding feedback on critical legal and factual issues that the parties need to evaluate in calculating their no-agreement alternatives and hence their reservation prices. Further, when suggested by the mediator, based on assessment of the status and timing of settlement talks, the judge can provide views about the benefits, costs, and risks of settlement versus trial, which may be more meaningful to the disputants than the mediator's views, no matter how compelling. The judge is the judge; the mediator is not. By pairing judge with mediator in a mega-case, disputants receive the highest competencies of both in their respective areas of expertise.

The timing, mechanics, and operational details of judicial involvement in mediation vary from case to case. However, in most cases in which the judge operates as a member of the mediation team, the judge's entry into the mediation process is at the suggestion of the mediator or the parties' counsel, with agreement by counsel and the mediator that it would be a good idea to involve the judge. The mediator then approaches the judge to explain the request for judicial assistance and ascertain the judge's willingness to participate. Typically, the court then discusses the request with counsel for the parties and satisfies itself that all parties consent to the court's involvement; usually the court requires counsel to indicate their consent in writing or on the record. Once judicial involvement has been established, the judge works closely with the mediator to make sure that the judge's involvement is most effectively focused and timed. While not a conventional comediation, the mediator–judge combination is a team effort. This arrangement should mitigate, if not eliminate, criticisms of judicial involvement in mediation based on competency concerns.

In seeking to strike the right balance in specific cases in which a more active judicial role in the mediation process is considered, the following factors should be considered:

- ○ Are there specific aspects of the settlement or mediation dynamic in the particular case that will benefit from judicial involvement, such as a need for the parties to receive feedback from the trial judge on legal or factual questions?
- ○ Is the judge capable of providing helpful feedback on the specific issues blocking settlement, and can the judge do so without compromising her judicial role should the case not settle?
- ○ Is the case ready for active judicial involvement?

○ Are the parties amenable to judicial involvement in the settlement effort, and will they agree on the record that the judge can be involved without threat of a recusal motion or other delay to the trial process if the case does not settle?

○ Are there specific factors in the case that render such judicial involvement particularly inappropriate?

○ How should the judge and the mediator coordinate their settlement efforts?

With careful consideration of these and other case-specific factors, mediators, with the active assistance of judges, can successfully mediate even the most complex of legal disputes.

Appendix

1. Documents

a. Engagement E-Mail

Dear counsel,

I understand that you have selected me to assist you with the ___/___ dispute. Thank you very much for your expression of confidence. I will do my best to assist you.

- **Date:** I understand that we will mediate on _____. I will assume that we will start at 9:30 AM and go as long as necessary unless you advise me differently. In particular, if that start time should be changed, please let me know.

- **Location:** We will mediate at _____ in _____. Please send the names of all persons attending to _____, _____@_____, so that she/ he can give the names to security and arrange for appropriate rooms.

- **Agreement:** I am attaching my standard-form mediation agreement; I hope you will let me know if you have any questions or concerns. If not, each of you please sign a copy and return it to me.

- **Deposit:** The agreement notes that a deposit of $___ is due from each side at least one week before the date of the mediation. Please send the check to my office or e-mail for wire instructions.

- **Participants:** You should check with each other to satisfy yourselves that each side will have an appropriate decision maker present. If you have any concerns about this, please let me know as soon as possible.

- **Briefing:** It would be helpful to read in advance any material that you think might assist me to understand the situation. The material need not be prepared expressly for the mediation. I will leave it to you to decide what materials, if any, would be suitable. It would be preferable if you could see each other's material so that we can discuss it freely, but I would also be willing to receive material on an ex parte basis.

If possible, please get your materials to me by ____, _____ at my office at _____ in _____. If you would like to fax it, my fax number is _____, or it can be e-mailed.

- **Pre-mediation conversations:** I would like to talk with each lawyer a day or two before the mediation. My purpose is not to ask about the merits, which I will learn about from the statements, but rather to learn about any nonlegal factors that you think may have an influence on the negotiation.

I would be happy to answer any questions that you or your clients may have, and look forward to working with you.

Dwight Golann

b. Mediation Agreement

Mediation Agreement
_____ (Plaintiff) and _____ (Defendant) agree to mediate the dispute pending between them, and any issues arising from or related to that dispute, with _____ as the Mediator.

Purpose
The purpose of the mediation is to attempt to arrive at a mutually acceptable resolution of the dispute in a cooperative, informal manner.

Mediation Process
Representatives of the parties with full settlement authority will attend the mediation. The parties will follow the recommendations of the Mediator regarding the agenda most likely to resolve the dispute. The Mediator may review written information, have private conversations with the participants, and conduct a mediation session with representatives of the parties and their counsel. If it appears to the Mediator that discussions

after the mediation session will be useful, the parties and/or their representatives will make themselves available for them. The Mediator may, in his discretion, provide an evaluation of the likely resolution of the dispute if it is not settled. The parties agree that in doing so, the Mediator is not acting as a lawyer or providing legal advice to any party.

Confidentiality

The entire process is a compromise negotiation. All offers, promises, conduct and statements, whether oral or written, made in the course of the mediation by any of the parties, their agents, employees, experts and lawyers, or by the Mediator are confidential. Such offers, promises, conduct, and statements shall not be disclosed to third parties, including without limitation any judge or other person who participates in the adjudication of this dispute. They are privileged and inadmissible for any purpose, including impeachment, under Rule 408 of the Federal Rules of Evidence and any applicable federal or state statute, rule, or common law provision.

Upon request by any party, the other parties and the Mediator shall return to the requesting party the original and any copies of any documents and other materials in their control that were provided by the requesting party in connection with this mediation. However, evidence that is otherwise admissible or discoverable shall not be rendered inadmissible or not discoverable as a result of its use in the mediation.

The Mediator may engage in separate and private meetings with the parties and their counsel. If a party or counsel informs the Mediator that information is being conveyed by the party to the Mediator in confidence, the Mediator will not disclose that information.

Disqualification of Mediator and Limitation of Liability

The parties agree not to call the Mediator, and agree that he will be disqualified, as a witness or expert in any pending or subsequent litigation or arbitration involving the parties and relating in any way to the dispute. They agree that the Mediator is not a necessary party in any arbitral or judicial proceeding relating to the mediation or to the subject matter of the mediation, and undertake to defend the Mediator from any subpoenas from outside parties arising out of this Agreement or mediation. For purposes of this agreement, employees of the Mediator shall be deemed Mediators as well.

The parties understand that the Mediator may have mediated, or may presently be mediating, disputes involving counsel or parties who are also involved in the present dispute. They agree that such activities do not disqualify the mediator from acting in this case. They also agree that the Mediator shall not be liable for any act or omission in connection with this mediation, other than for acts of gross negligence or bad faith.

Compensation

The Mediator will be compensated at the rate of $ ____ per hour for the time he spends conducting the mediation, and for his reasonable out-of-pocket expenses if any. Unless the parties otherwise agree in writing, these costs will be divided in equal shares between the parties. Time expended shall include time reasonably spent reviewing documents furnished by the parties and private conversations, conference calls, or meetings conducted outside the formal mediation sessions.

Each side shall provide a deposit of $____ in advance. The deposit is neither a minimum or maximum charge. Each deposit will be applied to the charges attributable to the party furnishing it. Additional statements or refunds will be sent to each party at the end of the mediation. Checks should be made out to ____ and sent to _____.

Notice of any change in date or cancellation of the mediation should be given to the Mediator and other parties by telephone or e-mail. A party who cancels less than seven days before the mediation date, or who does not appear at the mediation, is subject to forfeiting its deposit unless the Mediator is able to reschedule the time.

Miscellaneous

This is a voluntary, nonbinding process of assisted negotiation. The parties agree to participate in good faith in the entire mediation process. However, any party may terminate its participation at any time and for any reason by notifying the Mediator.

_____   _____

Counsel for   Counsel for

_____   _____

Date: _____   Date: _____

c. Opening Comments

The following are typical comments that a mediator can make at the start of a mediation.

Good morning. I'm _____. I don't know everyone, so before we go any further I'd appreciate it if you would introduce yourself and indicate who you're with.

Comment: It is often useful to sketch the shape of the table and write down each person's name and role.

Some of you are familiar with mediation, but for others it may be a new experience. Let me describe what we'll be doing, then turn it over to you for opening comments.

Comment: Participants often are doubtful about protocol (for example, whether there will be a time limit on statements). It's best for lawyers to discuss these issues with the mediator in advance, but a confirmation at the outset is also useful.

The purpose of mediation is to help people negotiate. My only role here is to help you find a solution to this dispute. I am not a judge, and I have no power to decide this case. By signing the mediation agreement, you have agreed that I am disqualified as a witness and will never play any role in the case if it goes to trial. That leaves me entirely free to focus on one thing: helping you find a settlement. My goal is that if an agreement is possible, and the large majority of the time it is, I don't want it to be left on the table because of an accident or misunderstanding.

In cases like this, my experience and that of other mediators is that more than three quarters of the time parties *are* able to reach agreement. That means that the odds of obtaining a settlement are strongly in your favor. The fact that you have all come here is evidence that everyone wants to find a solution and that you are willing to make compromises to bring it about. However, ultimately it's up to you whether you agree.

Comment: Promote optimism, but do not misstate the terms of anyone's participation.

One of the key aspects of this process is that it is confidential. You have all signed the mediation agreement and agreed not to disclose anything said during this process. You've agreed to confidentiality on two levels. First, both sides agree that nothing said here can be used at trial: the other side cannot ask you in court, "Didn't you say X at mediation, and now you're saying Y?" Second, you've agreed that you won't discuss anything said here with outsiders such as a reporter or a neighbor. It's understood that if you are with an organization you may have to talk with others to confirm a settlement, and if you are an individual you may want to talk with an advisor or family member. But aside from consultations about settlement, no one will discuss what occurs here with anyone outside this room. That gives us more freedom to talk frankly about possible solutions.

> *Comment:* Focus on what the parties have agreed to, and do not attempt to state what laws will apply.

I understand that we have as long as we need today [or: until ____ PM], and if we keep focused I believe that we can get it done. If you don't mind, as this is an informal process, I'll proceed on a first-name basis and I hope you'll do so with me.

> *Comment:* Some participants may feel demeaned by being called by first names. If there is a question about this, check as to how each person wishes to be addressed. If in doubt, proceed formally at first.

I would like to begin by asking each side to present its perspective on the situation. It's useful for me and for the other side to know your views on the legal issues, but I also would welcome ideas about how we can get to a resolution. I've asked each side to present its views frankly so everyone knows what will happen if you can't settle this case. But I've asked the lawyers not to give the kind of full-scale presentation that they would at trial.

Mr. [party] and Ms. [party], I will ask you to take a special role. You each have experienced lawyers who will handle the legal issues. I'd like you to sit back and simply listen. Ask yourself this: if I were a judge or juror hearing this story for the first time and didn't know what actually happened, how would it sound? As you listen, feel free to take notes, but please don't interrupt. I won't take the fact that you are listening politely as meaning that you agree with anything that you're hearing. I know that you disagree, or you wouldn't be here.

Parties' Opening Comments

Does anyone have any questions about the process or what I've said so far? If not, let's go ahead. I'll ask the plaintiff to go first, and then we'll hear from the defense.

[If the client does not speak:] Mr. ____, your counsel has covered the legal aspects of this dispute, but I wonder if there is anything of a

nonlegal nature that you'd like to say, or that you think we should have in mind as we go forward? If you'd rather not, or would like to wait until later, that's fine, but if you do want to say anything, I hope you'll feel free to do so now.

Joint Discussion

[*After each side has spoken and replied to the other*] Often, especially when people mediate early in a dispute, there is information that each side needs to know. You should keep in mind that you are each asking the other to make a very difficult settlement decision. If there is something they need to know to make that decision, I'd encourage you to provide it. Does anyone have any questions?

[*If parties do not want to talk or fall into unhelpful argument, you can say the following:*] It's clear that there is a disagreement about what happened. Given enough time we might be able to reach conclusions about the facts, but you're here to avoid a trial. I suggest that we go forward with discussions and work to reach a resolution.

Transition to Caucuses

[*When productive discussions are over:*] At this point I suggest that we go into caucuses so that I can talk with each of you privately. We do this because it's usually easier for people to discuss the pros and cons of legal issues and think imaginatively about options if the other side is not sitting there listening while they do it. I usually start with the plaintiff, so I'll ask the plaintiff side to come with me to the other conference room, and the defense can remain here.

There is an additional rule of confidentiality that applies to the caucusing process. If you tell me in caucus that something is confidential, I will not disclose it to the other side, just like a lawyer–client discussion. Even if you don't say anything, if I sense that something is sensitive I will check with you before discussing it with the other side. But it is much easier for me if you flag items that you want to keep confidential.

I should warn everyone now about one basic rule of caucusing: time always passes more slowly for whoever is waiting for the mediator. Please keep in mind that if I spend a long time with the other side, it's usually because I'm explaining your point of view and they are disagreeing, or I am asking them questions so that I can bring you their responses. Also, the first meeting with each side is usually longer than later ones because there is more new information to cover. I'll be back with you as soon as I can.

2. Model Standards of Conduct

a. Model Standards for Mediators

Model Standards of Conduct for Mediators

American Bar Association—American Arbitration Association
Association for Conflict Resolution

The *Model Standards of Conduct for Mediators* was prepared in 1994 by the American Arbitration Association, the American Bar Association's Section of Dispute Resolution, and the Association for Conflict Resolution. A joint committee consisting of representatives from the same successor organizations revised the Model Standards in 2005.[1] Both the original 1994 version and the 2005 revision have been approved by each participating organization.

Preamble

Mediation is used to resolve a broad range of conflicts within a variety of settings. These Standards are designed to serve as fundamental ethical guidelines for persons mediating in all practice contexts. They serve three primary goals: to guide the conduct of mediators; to inform the mediating parties; and to promote public confidence in mediation as a process for resolving disputes.

Mediation is a process in which an impartial third party facilitates communication and negotiation and promotes voluntary decision making by the parties to the dispute.

Mediation serves various purposes, including providing the opportunity for parties to define and clarify issues, understand different perspectives, identify interests, explore and assess possible solutions, and reach mutually satisfactory agreements, when desired.

Note on Construction

These Standards are to be read and construed in their entirety. There is no priority significance attached to the sequence in which the Standards appear.

The use of the term "shall" in a Standard indicates that the mediator must follow the practice described. The use of the term "should" indicates that the practice described in the Standard is highly desirable, but not required, and is to be departed from only for very strong reasons and requires careful use of judgment and discretion.

---

1.   Reporter's Notes, which are not part of these Standards and therefore have not been specifically approved by any of the organizations, provide commentary regarding these revisions.

The use of the term "mediator" is understood to be inclusive so that it applies to co-mediator models.

These Standards do not include specific temporal parameters when referencing a mediation, and therefore, do not define the exact beginning or ending of a mediation.

Various aspects of a mediation, including some matters covered by these Standards, may also be affected by applicable law, court rules, regulations, other applicable professional rules, mediation rules to which the parties have agreed and other agreements of the parties. These sources may create conflicts with, and may take precedence over, these Standards. However, a mediator should make every effort to comply with the spirit and intent of these Standards in resolving such conflicts. This effort should include honoring all remaining Standards not in conflict with these other sources.

These Standards, unless and until adopted by a court or other regulatory authority do not have the force of law. Nonetheless, the fact that these Standards have been adopted by the respective sponsoring entities, should alert mediators to the fact that the Standards might be viewed as establishing a standard of care for mediators.

Standard I. Self-Determination

A. A mediator shall conduct a mediation based on the principle of party self-determination. Self-determination is the act of coming to a voluntary, uncoerced decision in which each party makes free and informed choices as to process and outcome. Parties may exercise self-determination at any stage of a mediation, including mediator selection, process design, participation in or withdrawal from the process, and outcomes.

    1. Although party self-determination for process design is a fundamental principle of mediation practice, a mediator may need to balance such party self-determination with a mediator's duty to conduct a quality process in accordance with these Standards.

    2. A mediator cannot personally ensure that each party has made free and informed choices to reach particular decisions, but, where appropriate, a mediator should make the parties aware of the importance of consulting other professionals to help them make informed choices.

B. A mediator shall not undermine party self-determination by any party for reasons such as higher settlement rates, egos, increased fees, or outside pressures from court personnel, program administrators, provider organizations, the media, or others.

Standard II. Impartiality

A. A mediator shall decline a mediation if the mediator cannot conduct it in an impartial manner. Impartiality means freedom from favoritism, bias or prejudice.

B. A mediator shall conduct a mediation in an impartial manner and avoid conduct that gives the appearance of partiality.
    1. A mediator should not act with partiality or prejudice based on any participant's personal characteristics, background, values and beliefs, or performance at a mediation, or any other reason.
    2. A mediator should neither give nor accept a gift, favor, loan or other item of value that raises a question as to the mediator's actual or perceived impartiality.
    3. A mediator may accept or give de minimis gifts or incidental items or services that are provided to facilitate a mediation or respect cultural norms so long as such practices do not raise questions as to a mediator's actual or perceived impartiality.

C. If at any time a mediator is unable to conduct a mediation in an impartial manner, the mediator shall withdraw.

Standard III. Conflicts of Interest

A. A mediator shall avoid a conflict of interest or the appearance of a conflict of interest during and after a mediation. A conflict of interest can arise from involvement by a mediator with the subject matter of the dispute or from any relationship between a mediator and any mediation participant, whether past or present, personal or professional, that reasonably raises a question of a mediator's impartiality.

B. A mediator shall make a reasonable inquiry to determine whether there are any facts that a reasonable individual would consider likely to create a potential or actual conflict of interest for a mediator. A mediator's actions necessary to accomplish a reasonable inquiry into potential conflicts of interest may vary based on practice context.

C. A mediator shall disclose, as soon as practicable, all actual and potential conflicts of interest that are reasonably known to the mediator and could reasonably be seen as raising a question about the mediator's impartiality. After disclosure, if all parties agree, the mediator may proceed with the mediation.

D. If a mediator learns any fact after accepting a mediation that raises a question with respect to that mediator's service creating a potential or actual conflict of interest, the mediator shall disclose it as quickly as practicable. After disclosure, if all parties agree, the mediator may proceed with the mediation.

E. If a mediator's conflict of interest might reasonably be viewed as undermining the integrity of the mediation, a mediator shall withdraw from or decline to proceed with the mediation regardless of the expressed desire or agreement of the parties to the contrary.

F. Subsequent to a mediation, a mediator shall not establish another relationship with any of the participants in any matter that would raise questions about the integrity of the mediation. When a mediator develops personal or professional relationships with parties, other individuals or organizations following a mediation in which they were involved, the mediator should consider factors such as time elapsed following the mediation, the nature of the relationships established, and services offered when determining whether the relationships might create a perceived or actual conflict of interest.

Standard IV. Competence

A. A mediator shall mediate only when the mediator has the necessary competence to satisfy the reasonable expectations of the parties.

   1. Any person may be selected as a mediator, provided that the parties are satisfied with the mediator's competence and qualifications. Training, experience in mediation, skills, cultural understandings, and other qualities are often necessary for mediator competence. A person who offers to serve as a mediator creates the expectation that the person is competent to mediate effectively.

   2. A mediator should attend educational programs and related activities to maintain and enhance the mediator's knowledge and skills related to mediation.

   3. A mediator should have available for the parties' information relevant to the mediator's training, education, experience, and approach to conducting a mediation.

B. If a mediator, during the course of a mediation determines that the mediator cannot conduct the mediation competently, the mediator shall discuss that determination with the parties as soon as is practicable and take appropriate steps to address the situation, including, but not limited to, withdrawing or requesting appropriate assistance.

C. If a mediator's ability to conduct a mediation is impaired by drugs, alcohol, medication, or otherwise, the mediator shall not conduct the mediation.

Standard V. Confidentiality

A. A mediator shall maintain the confidentiality of all information obtained by the mediator in mediation, unless otherwise agreed to by the parties or required by applicable law.

   1. If the parties to a mediation agree that the mediator may disclose information obtained during the mediation, the mediator may do so.

2. A mediator should not communicate to any non-participant information about how the parties acted in the mediation. A mediator may report, if required, whether parties appeared at a scheduled mediation and whether or not the parties reached a resolution.

3. If a mediator participates in teaching, research, or evaluation of mediation, the mediator should protect the anonymity of the parties and abide by their reasonable expectations regarding confidentiality.

B. A mediator who meets with any persons in private session during a mediation shall not convey directly or indirectly to any other person, any information that was obtained during that private session without the consent of the disclosing person.

C. A mediator shall promote understanding among the parties of the extent to which the parties will maintain confidentiality of information they obtain in a mediation.

D. Depending on the circumstance of a mediation, the parties may have varying expectations regarding confidentiality that a mediator should address. The parties may make their own rules with respect to confidentiality, or the accepted practice of an individual mediator or institution may dictate a particular set of expectations.

Standard VI. Quality of the Process

A. A mediator shall conduct a mediation in accordance with these Standards and in a manner that promotes diligence, timeliness, safety, presence of the appropriate participants, party participation, procedural fairness, party competency, and mutual respect among all participants.

1. A mediator should agree to mediate only when the mediator is prepared to commit the attention essential to an effective mediation.

2. A mediator should only accept cases when the mediator can satisfy the reasonable expectation of the parties concerning the timing of a mediation.

3. The presence or absence of persons at a mediation depends on the agreement of the parties and the mediator. The parties and mediator may agree that others may be excluded from particular sessions or from all sessions.

4. A mediator should promote honesty and candor between and among all participants, and a mediator shall not knowingly misrepresent any material fact or circumstance in the course of a mediation.

5. The role of a mediator differs substantially from other professional roles. Mixing the role of a mediator and the role of another profession is problematic and thus, a mediator should distinguish between the roles. A mediator may provide information that the

mediator is qualified by training or experience to provide, only if the mediator can do so consistent with these Standards.

6. A mediator shall not conduct a dispute resolution procedure other than mediation but label it mediation in an effort to gain the protection of rules, statutes, or other governing authorities pertaining to mediation.

7. A mediator may recommend, when appropriate, that parties consider resolving their dispute through arbitration, counseling, neutral evaluation, or other processes.

8. A mediator shall not undertake an additional dispute resolution role in the same matter without the consent of the parties. Before providing such service, a mediator shall inform the parties of the implications of the change in process and obtain their consent to the change. A mediator who undertakes such role assumes different duties and responsibilities that may be governed by other standards.

9. If a mediation is being used to further criminal conduct, a mediator should take appropriate steps including, if necessary, postponing, withdrawing from or terminating the mediation.

10. If a party appears to have difficulty comprehending the process, issues, or settlement options, or difficulty participating in a mediation, the mediator should explore the circumstances and potential accommodations, modifications, or adjustments that would make possible the party's capacity to comprehend, participate, and exercise self-determination.

B. If a mediator is made aware of domestic abuse or violence among the parties, the mediator shall take appropriate steps including, if necessary, postponing, withdrawing from, or terminating the mediation.

C. If a mediator believes that participant conduct, including that of the mediator, jeopardizes conducting a mediation consistent with these Standards, a mediator shall take appropriate steps including, if necessary, postponing, withdrawing from, or terminating the mediation.

Standard VII. Advertising and Solicitation

A. A mediator shall be truthful and not misleading when advertising, soliciting, or otherwise communicating the mediator's qualifications, experience, services, and fees.

1. A mediator should not include any promises as to outcome in communications, including business cards, stationery, or computer-based communications.

2. A mediator should only claim to meet the mediator qualifications of a governmental entity or private organization if that entity or

organization has a recognized procedure for qualifying mediators and it grants such status to the mediator.

B. A mediator shall not solicit in a manner that gives an appearance of
partiality for or against a party or otherwise undermines the integrity
of the process.

C. A mediator shall not communicate to others, in promotional materials or through other forms of communication, the names of persons
served without their permission.

Standard VIII. Fees and Other Charges

A. A mediator shall provide each party or each party's representative
true and complete information about mediation fees, expenses, and
any other actual or potential charges that may be incurred in connection with a mediation.

   1. If a mediator charges fees, the mediator should develop them in
   light of all relevant factors, including the type and complexity of
   the matter, the qualifications of the mediator, the time required,
   and the rates customary for such mediation services.

   2. A mediator's fee arrangement should be in writing unless the
   parties request otherwise.

B. A mediator shall not charge fees in a manner that impairs a mediator's impartiality.

   1. A mediator should not enter into a fee agreement which is
   contingent upon the result of the mediation or amount of the
   settlement.

   2. While a mediator may accept unequal fee payments from the
   parties, a mediator should not allow such a fee arrangement to
   adversely impact the mediator's ability to conduct a mediation in
   an impartial manner.

Standard IX. Advancement of Mediation Practice

A. A mediator should act in a manner that advances the practice of mediation. A mediator promotes this Standard by engaging in some or all
of the following:

   1. Fostering diversity within the field of mediation.

   2. Striving to make mediation accessible to those who elect to use it,
   including providing services at a reduced rate or on a pro bono
   basis as appropriate.

   3. Participating in research when given the opportunity, including
   obtaining participant feedback when appropriate.

   4. Participating in outreach and education efforts to assist the public
   in developing an improved understanding of, and appreciation
   for, mediation.

5. Assisting newer mediators through training, mentoring, and networking.

B. A mediator should demonstrate respect for differing points of view within the field, seek to learn from other mediators, and work together with other mediators to improve the profession and better serve people in conflict.

b. Uniform Mediation Act (excerpt)

Section 9. Mediator's Disclosure of Conflicts of Interest, Background

(a) Before accepting a mediation, an individual who is requested to serve as a mediator shall:
  (1) make an inquiry that is reasonable under the circumstances to determine whether there are any known facts that a reasonable individual would consider likely to affect the impartiality of the mediator. . .and
  (2) disclose any such known fact to the mediation parties as soon as is practical before accepting a mediation.

(b) If a mediator learns any fact described in subsection (a)(1) after accepting a mediation, the mediator shall disclose it as soon as is practicable.

(c) At the request of a mediation party, an individual who is requested to serve as a mediator shall disclose the mediator's qualifications to mediate a dispute. . .

Note: UMA Sections 4 through 8 deal with confidentiality and impose substantive prohibitions on a mediator's disclosure of information.

Resources

If you would like to learn more about mediation, you will find the following videos, websites, books, and articles interesting.

Videotapes and DVDs (All are videotapes unless otherwise noted)

Mediation Skills

Aaron, Marjorie Corman, & Dwight Golann. (2004). "Mediators at Work: A Case of Discrimination?" *http://www.pon.org* (unscripted mediation of an age discrimination case).

CPR Institute for Dispute Resolution. (1994). "Mediation in Action," *http://www.cpradr.org* (mediation of international contract dispute).

CPR Institute for Dispute Resolution. (2003). "Resolution Through Mediation," *http:// www.cpradr.org* (mediation of international trademark case).

Golann, Dwight, & Marjorie Corman Aaron. (1999). "Mediators at Work: Breach of Warranty?" *http://www.pon.org* (unscripted mediation of commercial contract dispute).

Himmelstein, Jack, & Gary Friedman. (2001). "Saving the Last Dance: Mediation Through Understanding," *http://www.pon.org* (no-caucus mediation of a manager–organization dispute).

JAMS Foundation. (2003). (DVD) "Mediating a Sexual Harassment Case: What Would You Do?" *http://www.jamsadr.com* (vignettes of challenging situations for a mediator).

Representing Clients

Golann, Dwight. (2000). "Representing Clients in Mediation: How Advocates Can Share a Mediator's Powers," *http://www.abanet.org/cle* (unscripted examples of advocates using mediators to advance bargaining goals).

Websites

Alternative Dispute Resolution Section of the Association of American Law Schools, *http://www.law.missouri.edu/aalsadr/index.htm.*

American Bar Association Section of Dispute Resolution, *http://www. abanet.org/dispute/home* (professional association of lawyers and law students interested in mediation and other forms of ADR).

Centre for Effective Dispute Resolution, *http://www.cedr.co.uk* (information on British and European use of mediation in commercial disputes).

CPR Institute of Dispute Resolution, *http:// www.cpradr.org* (information concerning use of ADR in commercial disputes).

Information, Education, and Web Development for Mediation and Mediators, *http://www.mediate.com* (an online journal of current articles and news about mediation).

Books

Abramson, Harold I. (2004). *Mediation Representation: Advocating in a Problem-Solving Process.* Notre Dame: NITA.

American Bar Association Task Force on Improving Mediation Quality. (2008). *Final Report.* Washington, D.C.: Author.

Arrow, Kenneth J., et al., eds. (1995). *Barriers to Conflict Resolution.* New York: W. W. Norton.

Bernard, Phyllis, & Bryant Garth, eds. (2002). *Dispute Resolution Ethics: A Comprehensive Guide.* Washington, D.C.: ABA Section of Dispute Resolution.

Bowling, Daniel, & David Hoffman, eds. (2003). *Bringing Peace into the Room.* San Francisco: Jossey-Bass.

Carroll, Eileen, & Karl Mackie. (2000). *International Mediation—The Art of Business Diplomacy.* The Hague: Kluwer Law International.

Cialdini, Robert. (2001). *Influence: Science and Practice.* Boston: Allyn and Bacon.

Cloke, Kenneth. (2000). *Mediating Dangerously.* San Francisco: Jossey-Bass.

Cole, Sarah R., Craig McEwen, & Nancy H. Rogers. (2001). *Mediation: Law, Policy & Practice.* St. Paul, MN: West Publishing.

Cooley, John W. (2002). *Mediation Advocacy.* Notre Dame: NITA.

Fisher, Roger, and Daniel Shapiro. (2005). *Beyond Reason: Using Emotions As You Negotiate.* New York: Penguin.

Folberg, Jay, & Alison Taylor. (1984). *Mediation: A Comprehensive Guide to Resolving Conflicts Without Litigation.* San Francisco: Jossey-Bass.

Krivis, Jeffrey. (2006). *Improvisational Negotiation.* San Francisco: Jossey-Bass.

Kubler-Ross, Elizabeth. (1969). *On Death and Dying.* New York: Simon and Schuster.

Little, J. Anderson. (2007). *Making Money Talk.* Chicago: American Bar Association.

Mayer, Bernard. (2004). *Beyond Neutrality.* San Francisco: Jossey-Bass.

Moffit, Michael, and Robert Bordone, eds. (2005). *The Handbook of Dispute Resolution.* San Francisco: Jossey-Bass.

Picker, Bennett G. (2003). *Mediation Practice Guide: A Handbook for Resolving Business Disputes.* Washington, D.C.: ABA Section of Dispute Resolution.

Plant, David W. (2008). *We Must Talk Because We Can—Mediating International Intellectual Property Disputes.* Paris: International Chamber of Commerce.

Sandler, Joseph, and Anna Freud. (1985). *The Analysis of Defense: The Ego and the Mechanisms of Defense Revisited.* New York: International Universities Press.

Senger, Jeffrey M. (2004). *Federal Dispute Resolution: Using Alternative Dispute Resolution with the United States Government.* San Francisco: Jossey-Bass.

Articles

Aaron, Marjorie Corman. (2002). "At First Glance: Maximizing The Mediator's Initial Contact," 20 *Alternatives* 167.

———. (2005). "Finding Settlements with Numbers, Maps, and Trees," in *The Handbook of Dispute Resolution*, M. Moffit and R. Bordone, eds. (San Francisco: Jossey-Bass).

———. (2005). "Do's and Don'ts of Mediation Practice," 11 *Disp. Resol. Mag.* 19 (Winter).

Abramson, Harold I. (2004). "Problem-Solving Advocacy in Mediation," 59 *Disp. Resol. J.* 56.

Arnold, Tom. (1995). "Twenty Common Errors in Mediation Advocacy," 13 *Alternatives* 69.

———. (1999). "Client Preparation for Mediation," 15 *Corporate Counsel's Q.* 52 (April).

Bowling, Daniel, & David Hoffman. (2000). "Bringing Peace into the Room: The Personal Qualities of the Mediator and Their Impact on the Mediation," 16 *Negot. J.* 5.

Curtis, Dana, & John Toker. (December 2000). "Representing Clients in Appellate Mediation: The Last Frontier," 1 *JAMS Alert No. 3* 1.

Donahey, M. Scott. (1995). "The Asian Concept of Conciliator/Arbitrator: Is It Translatable to the Western World?" 10 *Foreign Inv. L. J.* 120.

Freshman, Clark. (2006). "After Basic Mindful Meditation: External Mindfulness, Emotional Truthfulness and Lie Detection in Dispute Resolution," 2006 *J. Disp. Resol.* 511.

Freud, Sigmund. (1917). "Mourning and Melancholia," in Strachey, J., *The Standard Edition of the Complete Psychological Works of Sigmund Freud.* London: Hogarth Press.

Golann, Dwight. (2000). "Variations in Style: How—and Why—Legal Mediators Change Style in the Course of a Case," 2000 *J. Disp. Resol.* 40.

———. (2002). "Is Legal Mediation a Process of Reconciliation—Or Separation? An Empirical Study, and Its Implications," 7 *Harv. Negot. L. Rev.* 301.

———. (2004). "Death of a Claim: The Impact of Loss Reactions on Bargaining," 20 *Negot. J.* 539.

Golann, Helaine, & Dwight Golann. (2003). "Why Is It Hard for Lawyers to Deal with Emotional Issues?" 9 *Disp. Res. Mag.* 26 (Winter).

Goldberg, Stephen B., and Margaret L. Shaw. (2007). "Secrets of Successful (and Unsuccessful) Mediators Continued: Studies Two and Three," 23 *Negot. J.* 393.

Kahneman, Daniel, et al. (1990). "Experimental Tests of the Endowment Effect and the Coase Theorem, 98 *J. Pol. Econ.* 1325, 1342–46.

Kichaven, Jeffrey G. (1999). "How Advocacy Fits in Effective Mediation," 17 *Alternatives* 60.

Lande, John. (2002). "Using Dispute Systems Design Methods to Promote Good-Faith Participation in Court-Connected Mediation Programs," 50 *UCLA Law Rev.* 69.

Moffit, Michael. (2003). "Ten Ways to Get Sued: A Guide for Mediators," 8 *Harv. Negot. L. Rev.* 81.

Nadler, Janice. (2004). "Rapport in Negotiation and Conflict Resolution," 87 *Marq. L. Rev.* 875.

Riskin, Leonard. (1996). "Understanding Mediator's Orientations, Strategies, and Techniques: A Grid for the Perplexed," 1 *Harv. Negot. L. Rev.* 7 (Spring).

———. (2003). "Retiring and Replacing the Grid of Mediator Orientations," 21 *Alternatives* 69.

Robinson, Peter. (1998). "Contending with Wolves in Sheep's Clothing: A Cautiously Cooperative Approach to Mediation Advocacy," 50 *Baylor L. Rev.* 963.

Shapiro, Daniel. (2004). "Emotion in Negotiation: Peril or Promise?" 87 *Marquette Law Review* 737.

Smith, Robert M. (2000). "Advocacy in Mediation: A Dozen Suggestions," 26 *S.F. Att'y* 14.

Stern, David M. (1998). "Mediation: An Old Dog with Some New Tricks," 24 *Litigation* 31.

Index